Six Months in 1945

FDR, STALIN, CHURCHILL, AND TRUMAN—
FROM WORLD WAR TO COLD WAR

Michael Dobbs

arrow books

Published in the United Kingdom by Arrow Books in 2013

1 3 5 7 9 10 8 6 4 2

Th... ...p
Coun... ...ation.
Our books carrying the FSC label are printed on FSC®-certified paper.
FSC is the only forest-certification scheme supported by the
leading environmental organisations, including Greenpeace.
Our paper procurement policy can be found at:
www.randomhouse.co.uk/environment

MIX
Paper from
responsible sources
FSC® C016897

ISBN 9780099574873

Printed and bound by CPI Group (UK) Ltd, Croydon, CR0 4YY

For the grandson of
Joseph
And the great-grandson of
Samuel

Contents

Maps

Chronology

Note on Names

The end of World War II produced numerous boundary changes and accompanying name changes in both Europe and Asia. The end of the Cold War and the breakup of the Soviet Union resulted in yet more name changes. Adopting the latest, politically correct (or incorrect, depending on your point of view) names for towns and villages is a recipe for confusion.

To simplify matters, I have used Anglicized names for cities and towns when they are widely familiar to English-speaking readers. Thus I write about Moscow and Warsaw, not Moskva and Warszawa. In cases where political upheavals or boundary revisions have resulted in name changes, I have used the names employed by Roosevelt, Truman, and Churchill in 1945, e.g., Breslau not Wroclaw, Stalingrad not Volgograd, Port Arthur not Lushun.

For the convenience of readers, here is a list of geographic names used in the book with modern-day alternatives.

Baerwalde	Mieszkowice
Breslau	Wrocław
Dairen	Dalian
Danzig	Gdańsk
Eastern Neisse	Glatzer Neisse (Polish: Nysa Kłodzka)
Kiev	Kyiv
Königsberg	Kaliningrad
Leningrad	St. Petersburg
Lwów	Lviv
Oppeln	Opole
Port Arthur	Lushun
Stalingrad	Volgograd
Stettin	Szczecin
Western Neisse	Lusatian Neisse
Wilno	Vilnius

Transliterating Russian personal names into English presents a different problem for authors. The academic systems of transliteration involve complicated diacritics, which can be off-putting to contemporary readers. I have therefore adopted a simplified system, avoiding diacritical marks and apostrophes. I have used the letter "y" to denote the two Russian letters ий frequently found at the end of proper names, such as Georgy and Vyshinsky.

While I have tried to be consistent, I have used the Library of Congress system of transliteration for the bibliography (excluding diacritics), to make it easier for readers to locate references. Names used in the bibliography and notes are therefore not always identical to names in the main text.

Part One

The Best
I Could Do

—Franklin D. Roosevelt

———

FEBRUARY 1945

Roosevelt

February 3

The big four-engine airplane with the gleaming white star stood on the tarmac of the little airfield in Malta, ready to take Franklin Delano Roosevelt on a final mission. The new Douglas C-54 Skymaster had been specially fitted with all the latest conveniences, including an elevator that could lift the president and his wheelchair off the ground and deposit him in the belly of the plane. FDR voiced his displeasure to the Secret Service agents who wheeled him up to the tiny elevator cage. "I never authorized that," he muttered. "It's quite unnecessary." The embarrassed agents insisted that the device was required for security reasons. The alternative was a long ramp, a signal to enemy spies that the polio-stricken president of the United States was about to arrive or depart. Roosevelt, who disliked needless fuss and expense, was unconvinced.

The departure schedule had been planned with choreographic precision. Thirty military planes were lined up next to the small control tower, waiting for permission to take off. At ten-minute intervals, the lead plane moved to the head of the darkened runway, shades drawn, exterior lights extinguished. As each plane roared into the Mediterranean sky, the next plane moved into position behind. The night was filled with the roar of

Skymaster and York transports warming their engines for takeoff and the high-pitched whine of fighter planes circling the airfield.

Few people were aware of the existence of a presidential aircraft. Code-named Project 51, its construction was such a closely guarded secret that those in the know referred to the plane as the *Sacred Cow*. Roosevelt had become the first U.S. president to travel by airplane two years earlier, in February 1943, when he took a Pan American flying boat to Casablanca for a conference with Winston Churchill. But commercial air travel was obviously impractical for a wartime president—particularly one paralyzed from the waist down. The flying White House was ready for its inaugural trip.

Roosevelt boarded the *Sacred Cow* at 11:15 on the evening of February 2, 1945. The plane was not scheduled to depart until 3:30 a.m., but his doctors had decided this was the best way for him to get a decent night's rest. He was rolled straight to his stateroom, just aft of the wing. His black valet, Arthur Prettyman, helped him off with his clothes and made sure that he was lying comfortably on the plush three-seat couch emblazoned with the presidential seal. Other amenities included a swivel chair, a conference table, several closets, a private toilet, and a panoramic bulletproof window twice the width of regular portholes that was framed by blue curtains. A console next to the window provided communication with the cockpit and other parts of the plane. The interior wall opposite contained a set of maps on rollers that could be pulled down for in-flight briefings. A painting of a nineteenth-century clipper tossing in the waves filled the wall above the couch, evoking Roosevelt's love of the sea.

The president was chronically tired. He had whiled away the twelve-day crossing of the Atlantic on a U.S. Navy cruiser with endless rounds of gin rummy, deck games, and movies in the evening. He frequently slept twelve hours a night—but however much rest he got, it never seemed enough. Much of his remaining energy had been spent on his last election campaign, riding in open limousines and braving a torrential downpour in New York in a desperate attempt to show he was fit enough to serve a fourth term. The campaign appearances were designed to remind the voters of the FDR of popular imagination—strong, indomitable, optimistic—but they concealed his rapidly deteriorating state of health. He had lost some forty pounds over the last few months and looked like a skeleton. His blood pressure was out of control, sometimes as high as 260 over 150. The man he had chosen as vice president, Harry S. Truman, was alarmed when they met for a symbolic photo-taking session at the White House.

"I had no idea he was in such a feeble condition," Truman confided to an aide. "In pouring cream in his tea, he got more cream in the saucer than he did in the cup. There doesn't seem to be any mental lapse, but physically he is going to pieces."

Roosevelt's heart specialist, Howard Bruenn, slipped into the cabin shortly before takeoff. The president was already snoozing. The young navy lieutenant commander wanted to make sure his patient did not roll off the couch as the *Sacred Cow* accelerated down the runway. Knowing that Roosevelt would not have the strength to prevent himself from falling deadweight to the floor, Bruenn turned the swivel chair so that its back was against the couch. He would sleep sitting down, alert to the noises behind him.

Bruenn was worried about FDR. When he first examined the president, at Bethesda Naval Hospital in March 1944, he knew at once there was something "terribly wrong" and gave him no more than a year to live. His patient was having trouble breathing, and was suffering from bronchitis. His heart was greatly enlarged, no longer able to pump blood efficiently. The cardiologist prescribed digitalis to control the heartbeat, an easily digestible diet, greatly increased rest, and a sharp cutback in the number of official visitors and duties. Roosevelt's chief physician, Vice Admiral Ross McIntire, had resisted Bruenn's recommendations because he did not want to disrupt the president's routine, but eventually agreed to a scaled-down version. On McIntire's insistence, nobody outside a small circle of trusted White House doctors would know the facts about the boss's medical condition. Even Roosevelt was kept in the dark. Averse to unpleasant news, he displayed little interest in finding out the truth.

The roar of the engines and the shuddering of the aircraft frame as the *Sacred Cow* rose from the ground awoke the president from his fitful sleep. His nose and throat were stuffed up. Bruenn could hear FDR toss around on the couch behind him. His clinical notes recorded that Roosevelt "slept rather poorly" on the plane because of "noise and vibration" and was frequently woken by "a paroxysmal cough which was moderately productive." Apart from that, "the patient" was doing better than expected. He had "thoroughly enjoyed" his two weeks of travel away from the United States—"via train, ship, aeroplane and motor car"—and had "rested beautifully" on the trip across the Atlantic, "sleeping late in the morning, resting in the afternoon, and retiring fairly early at night despite fairly rough seas."

After taking off from Malta, in the center of the Mediterranean, the

Sacred Cow headed due east, cruising at a speed of two hundred miles per hour. The doctors had insisted that the unpressurized plane stick to an altitude of six thousand feet to minimize the president's breathing problems. The plane danced in and out of the clouds. About an hour out of Malta, it hit bumpy weather. The head of the Secret Service contingent heard a noise in the president's bedroom and went to investigate, but it was just a door slamming back and forth. The pilots shifted course northeast to avoid Crete, parts of which were still held by the Germans.

Dawn broke as the *Sacred Cow* passed over Athens, clearly visible on the port side of the aircraft. Six P-38 fighter planes appeared out of the clouds to escort the president's plane onward across the Aegean Sea to the snow-covered plains of northern Greece and Turkey, and finally the Black Sea. Roosevelt's daughter, Anna, was already up to watch the "beautiful sunrise" and the "outlines of tiny villages" in the otherwise barren Greek islands. Everyone had been instructed to put their watches and clocks forward two hours overnight. The president was dressed and served his usual breakfast of ham and eggs an hour before landing.

The Allied planes had been instructed to execute a ninety-degree turn as they entered Soviet airspace, to identify themselves as friendly and avoid being shot down by antiaircraft defenses. The *Sacred Cow* followed the agreed routing along the railway track from the town of Eupatoria on the western edge of the Crimean Peninsula to the airfield at Saki. The landscape was flat and uninteresting, a seemingly endless expanse of snow. The president's plane, now accompanied by five fighters (one had turned back because of engine trouble), circled the airstrip once and landed on schedule at 12:10 Moscow time, "bumping the full length of the short concrete-block runway."

During twelve years as president, Franklin Roosevelt had helped rescue the United States from the depths of the Great Depression, persuaded a reluctant nation to support Great Britain in its hour of need, and assembled the mightiest military coalition in history to resist the assaults of Nazi Germany and imperial Japan. Victory in both wars was within sight. Allied troops had reached the frontiers of Germany and were rolling back Japanese gains in Asia. The dying commander in chief had decided to make a dangerous, potentially suicidal, voyage across the ocean just two days after his fourth inaugural because he was obsessed by two final goals. He wanted to make sure that victory was secured at the lowest possible cost in American lives. And he had promised Americans, exhausted by more than three years of war, "a lasting peace."

Prior to FDR's arrival in the Crimea on Saturday, February 3, 1945, no serving U.S. president had set foot in Russia, much less the Soviet Union. None would do so again for nearly three decades.

American attitudes toward Russia had veered wildly since the 1917 Bolshevik Revolution. U.S. troops had intervened on the side of the Whites in the Russian civil war, battling the Reds in the snows of northern Russia before eventually retreating in disarray from Arkhangelsk with more than two thousand casualties. Americans were shocked by Stalin's agreement with Hitler in 1939, the carving up of Poland, and the Soviet invasions of Finland and the Baltic states. But the pendulum swung back sharply when the German armies invaded the Soviet Union on June 22, 1941, reaching the gates of Leningrad and Moscow within a few months. When the United States entered the war after the Japanese attack on Pearl Harbor on December 7, Communist Russia became its most important military ally. Hollywood movies began portraying the Soviet Union as a land of brave soldiers, contented workers, and smiling commissars, a one-hundred-eighty-degree turnaround from the thuggish buffoons depicted in the 1939 smash hit *Ninotchka*. The image of a mighty, trustworthy nation, under a strong yet benevolent leader, grew with every Red Army victory, with the active encouragement of the Roosevelt administration.

There were some dissenting voices, particularly among the handful of American diplomats with firsthand experience of life in Russia. The U.S. ambassador to Moscow, Averell Harriman, complained that the Russian bear was turning into the "world bully." He feared that Stalin would use "strong-arm methods" to establish a "sphere of influence" in eastern Europe under his exclusive control. Harriman's deputy, George Kennan, agreed that a division of Europe was inevitable. America and Russia had little in common—other than a shared enemy. In a letter to his friend Charles E. Bohlen on the eve of the Yalta conference, Kennan urged the U.S. government to make the best of geopolitical realities: "Why should we not make a decent and definite compromise with [Moscow]—divide Europe frankly into spheres of influence—keep ourselves out of the Russian sphere and keep the Russians out of ours?"

Dividing Europe with Russia was not at all what FDR had in mind when he risked his life to meet with Joseph Stalin and Winston Churchill in the Crimea in the waning days of World War II. Like most Americans, he was repulsed by anything that smacked of "empires," "balance of

power," and "spheres of influence." In the grand Rooseveltian scheme, a
new world organization would assume primary responsibility for ensuring the "lasting peace" under the benign supervision of the victorious
allies. The president wanted American soldiers to come home from
Europe and Asia as quickly as possible.

Stalin was not at Saki airport to greet Roosevelt. Instead, he had sent
his foreign minister, Vyacheslav Molotov, who was pacing up and down
on the tarmac in a heavy overcoat and fur hat, surrounded by Allied
officials. Through the window of the president's cabin, FDR and Anna
could see knots of Russian women sweeping snow from the runway with
brooms made out of birch twigs. They waited inside the warm plane until
Churchill's C-54 Skymaster, a gift from the United States, landed twenty
minutes later, accompanied by its own escort of six P-38 fighters.

Originally, Roosevelt and Churchill had planned to take only modest entourages with them to Yalta, consisting of thirty to thirty-five key
aides. But the delegations grew in size as more and more officials deemed
themselves "indispensable" to either the president or the prime minister, until they reached a combined total of some seven hundred people,
support staff included. The Russians had erected large army tents, heated
with wood-fired stoves, to provide hospitality to the throng of field
marshals, ministers, generals, ambassadors, and assorted aides-de-camp.
New arrivals were invited inside for their first Russian breakfast, consisting of giant dollops of caviar, assorted garlic-heavy cold cuts, smoked
salmon, eggs, curd cake with a sour cream sauce, sweet champagne,
Georgian white wine, vodka, and Crimean brandy, all washed down by
tumblers of boiling tea.

Eventually, everybody shuffled into place for the arrival ceremony.
After lowering the president to the ground in his elevator, Secret Service agents lifted him into an open lend-lease jeep covered with rugs.
A Red Army band played "The Star-Spangled Banner," "God Save the
King," and the new Soviet national anthem ("The Great Lenin lit our
way / Stalin brought us up to serve the people"). Seated in the jeep in
his dark navy cape, Roosevelt reviewed a goose-stepping honor guard,
flanked by Churchill and Molotov on foot. FDR seemed "frail and ill"
to the prime minister. "He was a tragic figure." His face was the color of
parchment, waxlike and drained of energy. His right arm rested on the

side of the jeep, the hand hanging limply downward. Churchill's doctor, Charles Moran, described the scene:

The PM walked by the side of the President, as in her old age an Indian attendant accompanied Queen Victoria's phaeton. They were preceded by a crowd of camera-men, walking backwards as they took snapshots. The President looked old and thin and drawn; he had a cape or shawl over his shoulders and appeared shrunken; he sat looking straight ahead with his mouth open, as if he were not taking things in. Everyone was shocked by his appearance and gabbed about it afterwards.

Anna Roosevelt felt "a bit worried" about her father, knowing that he was "tired after his hard day yesterday and a short night's sleep on the plane." She decided to ride alone with him to Yalta so that "he could sleep as much as he wanted and would not have to make conversation." If they were to reach Yalta by nightfall, they had to get going immediately. Declining the offer of refreshments, they climbed into one of Stalin's Packard limousines, accompanied only by an American bodyguard and a Russian driver, and set off across "a desolate steppe." Carloads of Secret Service agents and "armed Russians" drove ahead, with the rest of the American and British delegations strung out in a long convoy.

Crossing the Atlantic, FDR had been bombarded by alarming messages on conditions in the Crimea. His aide, Harry Hopkins, reported that Churchill was predicting great discomfort. "He says that if we had spent ten years on research we could not have found a worse place in the world than Yalta, but he feels he can survive it by bringing an adequate supply of whiskey. He claims it is good for typhus and deadly on lice which thrive in those parts." Two days later, a telegram arrived from the prime minister describing the roads between Saki and Yalta as impassable because of blizzards. British and American advance men were said to have "endured most terrifying experience" negotiating a "mountainous track" en route to the summit venue.

No other traffic was permitted on the road, which was guarded by thousands of Interior Ministry troops, stationed at two-hundred-yard intervals along the entire eighty-mile route. Many of the soldiers were women dressed, like the men, in long heavy greatcoats, with leather belts and tommy guns slung across their backs and shoulder boards similar to "those worn by an American admiral." The Russian women were "immense, tough, and had the largest legs I have *ever* seen," marveled one of Churchill's female assistants in a letter home. "You at once realized why the Huns did not spare them." The soldiers presented arms as the president passed, looking him straight in the eye, repeating the procedure with all the cars that followed.

The road was lined with the debris of the thirty-month German occupation of the Crimea: gutted buildings, burnt-out tanks, overturned freight trains, abandoned villages, and wounded soldiers, particularly in the towns. Roosevelt had read reports about the aerial bombardment of Coventry and Rotterdam and the leveling of Warsaw and Lidice, but this was the first time he had seen the Nazi destruction up close. It made a profound impression. He told Anna that the gruesome sights along the road made him want "to get even" with the Germans more than ever.

A few cars behind FDR, Churchill was complaining loudly about the "endless and very boring" drive. He wanted to know "how long have we been going?"

"About an hour," replied his daughter Sarah.

"Christ! Five more hours of this!"

Sarah described her father's mood in a letter to her mother the following day. "On, on through bleak country peopled by a few grim-faced peasants. . . . On, on, bearing all with fortitude, patience and a bottle of very good brandy!" To amuse himself, Churchill recited Byron's epic poem *Don Juan* to his companions.

After passing through Simferopol, "another dingy town with wide, straight streets," the Allied convoy began to climb into the mountains. The countryside became more interesting but was still very barren. Looking out the window in between catnaps, Roosevelt noticed scrub oaks "but almost no evergreens." His thoughts turned to the three hundred thousand trees he had planted at Hyde Park, his home in the lush Hudson River valley in upstate New York. He made a mental note to tell Stalin that "this part of the country needs reforesting."

It was now past 3:00 p.m., and father and daughter were getting hungry. They stopped by the side of the road to munch on some day-old sandwiches prepared on the *Quincy*, the warship that had brought them across the Atlantic to Malta. Ambassador Harriman drove up to inform them that Molotov had invited the entire party to lunch at a rest house forty-five minutes farther on, near the seaside town of Alushta. The tables were "groaning with food and wine"; the Russians had even built a special ramp covered with decorative rugs for the president's wheelchair. The thought of two hours' eating and drinking was too much for FDR, who wanted to press on to Yalta before it got dark. Churchill ("that tough old bird" in Anna's description) fell upon the feast with his usual Rabelaisian gusto.

After Alushta, the road swung inland, along the "Romanov route" built by the last tsar to connect his summer palace at Yalta with his hunting estate and completed the year before the Great War that sealed his fate. Here the scenery became dramatic, even romantic: mountains rising to five thousand feet, sweeping views of crags and rushing streams, thick beech woods and pine forests, numerous switchbacks carved into the hillside. It was fortunate that the road was closed to all nonofficial cars: this was the narrow "mountainous track" the advance men had warned about. The president's naval aide, Vice Admiral Wilson Brown, noted that "the curves were short and sharp, without retaining walls, [along the] edge of a continuous precipice. Passengers were thrown about in the constant change of direction; one escape from the edge was quickly followed by another hairbreadth escape; the bumping and banging on an unsurfaced road was continuous."

And then suddenly, one last mountain pass, and the presidential party

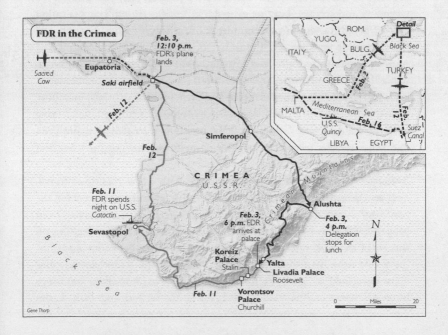

reached "another country," a land of cypresses and vineyards and houses with red tiled roofs set against a dark blue sea. The climate was balmy, almost Mediterranean, with the sweet-smelling fragrance of olive trees and orange groves. The mountains protected this short stretch of coast-line from the harsh north winds that swept down from Russia. There was no snow: winter had given way to spring. Everyone's spirits rose.

Around 6:00 p.m., as dusk was falling, FDR's limousine pulled into a driveway lined with pine, palm, and cypress trees. Banks of roses and oleander parted to reveal a large Renaissance-style villa, set on a bluff two hundred feet above the sea. He had reached the Livadia Palace, the favor-ite vacation spot of Tsar Nicholas II.

"I can't understand Winston's concern," muttered Roosevelt, as he was wheeled around the ground floor of the one-hundred-sixteen-room pal-ace in his wheelchair. "This place has all the comforts of home."

The Russians had done their best to make the president comfortable. Big log fires were burning cheerfully in most of the downstairs rooms. A maître d'hôtel greeted FDR "with many bows from the waist," address-ing him as "Your Excellency." The palace had been stripped bare by the Germans and subsequently renovated in a frantic, monthlong operation that involved the shipment of hundreds of railway wagons of supplies to the Crimea from Moscow. Thousands of NKVD secret police and Red Army soldiers were mobilized to paint walls and repair the plumbing, while Romanian prisoners of war restored the grounds to a semblance of their tsarist splendor. The furniture and principal furnishings, including plates, china, and bed linen, came from Moscow's leading hotels, along with the maids, waiters, and cooks. The Russians were still scouring Yalta and other nearby towns for accessories such as "shaving mirrors, coat hangers, and wash bowls."

Roosevelt was shown the large ballroom with white marble columns, next to the entrance hall, with a round table already prepared for the conference with Stalin and Churchill. A private suite of rooms had been prepared for him in the adjoining wing of the palace, also leading off the entrance hall, next to a Moorish garden. The bedroom and din-ing room were furnished in what a member of the American advance team described as "early Pullman car" style. "Heavy, outsize paintings hung on mahogany-paneled walls; brass lamps with orange silk shades and long fringe were scattered around on tables; and Bukhara rugs and bottle-green plush harem cushions were scattered on the floors. Here and there a handsome Russian Empire piece glowed in contrast to the stolid chests, sofas, tables, and chairs, that Moscow had scraped together for the occasion."

The hosts had spent much of the last few days moving rugs and paintings in and out of the president's bedroom, unable to decide "which oriental colors looked best." They had set and reset the dining room table, experimenting with various place settings. FDR was much more concerned about his evening martini routine, a hallowed tradition at the White House. After a long day, he loved to relax with friends at "children's hour," mixing the gin, vermouth, and olive brine in a silver cocktail shaker, with large helpings of ice. When Anna sent for the necessary ingredients, she was dismayed to learn there was no ice. Instead of martinis, the maître d' proposed "some sweet concoction" that appeared to be "a mixture of just about everything."

The presidential party quickly gave up on the cocktails and sat down to dinner in the tsar's billiard room. "Immediately our tiny glasses were filled with vodka," Anna recorded in her diary that night. "We were served delicious caviar, then some sliced fish which is uncooked but cured in some way (and which even my hardy tummy found a bit hard to take). This was followed by a game course, then some meat on a skewer with potatoes. And finally two kinds of dessert, and coffee—AND—white wine, red wine, champagne with dessert, and liquor with coffee. Every time anything was refused the maître d'hôtel looked either like a thunder cloud or mortally wounded."

FDR retired to bed after dinner, leaving the rest of the party to argue over the next day's arrangements. Harriman had been dispatched to Stalin's headquarters, twenty minutes farther down the road, to organize a meeting with the Soviet dictator. Harry Hopkins felt very strongly that the president should meet first with Churchill to discuss strategy for the plenary sessions, even though they had spent the day together in Malta before flying to the Crimea. A ghostlike figure fueled by nervous energy, Hopkins had spent much of the war shuttling back and forth between Washington and London as a semipermanent houseguest of both the president and the prime minister. Relations between Roosevelt and his "special adviser" were no longer as intimate as they once were: Hopkins had moved out of the White House at the end of 1943 after marrying for a third time. Nevertheless, the former social worker still enjoyed huge power and was one of the few aides who dared to openly criticize the president.

Anna wanted to spare her father unnecessary meetings, even with the British prime minister. She found Hopkins lying in bed in a room the size of a broom closet, two doors down from Roosevelt's suite, pale and haggard and "in a stew." In addition to stomach cancer, he was suffering from "terrible dysentery," brought on by too much rich food, too many late nights, and, above all, too much to drink. A couple of nights earlier, while they were still onboard the *Quincy*, Hopkins had made off with her last bottle of whiskey. He had "misbehaved" so often that he was beyond the help of antidiarrhea tablets. According to Harriman's daughter Kathleen, his doctors "ordered him to eat nothing but cereal & the fool had 2 huge helpings of caviar, cabbage soup with sour cream, and then his cereal."

Hopkins brushed aside Anna's argument that a preliminary British-American meeting might provoke the distrust of "our Russian brethren." It was "imperative" that the president and prime minister get together the following morning.

FDR "asked for this job," snapped Hopkins. "Whether he likes it or not, he has to do the work."

The sun was streaming through the windows of Roosevelt's east-facing bedroom when he woke up on Sunday morning. He had slept reasonably well, helped by a dose of codeine and terpin hydrate to clear his cough and stuffed-up nose. A Filipino mess boy served him breakfast. Prettyman, the valet, who had been sleeping in the study next door on an army cot, helped him get dressed, pulling his suit pants over his withered legs. The president no longer bothered with the heavy steel braces that had enabled him to defy the ravages of polio, at least in the popular imagination. "They hurt me," he explained to intimates. The last time he had worn the braces was on Inauguration Day, January 20, when he had taken a few symbolic steps to the lectern set up on the south portico of the White House, assisted by his oldest son, James. Never again would he stand up, strong and confident, on his own two feet.

Now that it was light, it was easier to understand why the last tsar and tsarina had chosen this remote spot for a summer vacation retreat. The rugged coastline was reminiscent of the French Riviera, a juxtaposition of majestic mountains and sparkling sea. This particular stretch of the Black Sea had been a recreation place for the rulers of Russia since 1860 when Alexander II built a couple of summer palaces and a little Byzantine-style church at a place called Livadia in the hills above the resort town of Yalta. Early visitors include Mark Twain, who was granted an imperial audience. The scenery reminded FDR's favorite writer of the Sierra Nevada in California, "tall, gray mountains . . . bristling with pines, cloven with ravines, here and there a hoary rock towering into view." The tsar impressed him with his ordinariness, as he recorded in his travelogue, *Innocents Abroad*:

> It seemed strange—stranger than I can tell—to think that the central figure in the cluster of men and women, chatting here under the trees like the most ordinary individual in the land, was a man who could open his lips and ships would fly through the waves, locomotives would speed over the plains, couriers would hurry from village to village, a hundred telegraphs would flash the word to the four corners of an Empire that stretches its vast proportions over a seventh part of the habitable globe, and a countless multitude of men would spring to do his bidding. I had a sort of vague desire to examine his hands and see if they were of flesh and blood, like other men's.

Convinced that her sickly son had contracted typhoid fever in the damp and gloomy wooden buildings, Tsarina Alexandra persuaded her husband to have the old palaces torn down in 1909 and replaced by a grand Florentine villa. Construction took just sixteen months, allowing the imperial family to occupy their new vacation home in September 1911. Inspired by a trip to Italy, Alexandra ordered the architect, Nicholas Krasnov, to incorporate features from various Italian palazzi, including the Villa Medici in Rome, into the design. But she insisted on including other architectural traditions as well. A Turkish salon and an Arab courtyard, with a fountain in the middle, evoked the eastern heritage of the Crimea. The nearby Italian courtyard was modeled after the cloisters of a church in Florence. Some rooms were influenced by Queen Victoria's residence on the Isle of Wight where Alexandra had spent many summers. The billiard hall, which served as FDR's dining room, was Tudor. In the end, Krasnov became so exasperated with his royal clients that he quietly included a caricature of the tsar in the armrests of the marble benches outside the main entrance. Parks and tropical gardens surrounded the creamy white villa, providing the imperial family with fifteen miles of private alleyways lined with cypresses, cedar, and bay trees.

Nicholas and Alexandra had been very happy at Livadia, perhaps their last moments of real happiness before being swept away by the tide of history. "We can't find words to express our joy and pleasure of having such a house, built exactly as we wished," the tsar wrote to his mother. The imperial family came to Livadia every summer up until the outbreak of war in August 1914. Life in the White Palace was largely free of the suffocating court ritual of St. Petersburg. "In St. Petersburg we work, but at Livadia we live," was how one of the tsar's daughters described it. Nicholas played tennis, swam off the rocky beach below the palace, and went for long horseback rides in the surrounding mountains. Alexandra liked to dress the hemophiliac tsarevitch, Alexei, in a sailor's suit and preside over an annual charity bazaar, leading the grand duchesses in their long white dresses through the streets of Yalta. In the evenings, the family listened to music in the Italian courtyard, played by a regimental orchestra. After Nicholas was forced to abdicate in February 1917, he asked the provisional government for permission to retire to Livadia. The request was refused: instead the palace was turned into a rest home for "the victims of tsarism."

Unfortunately for FDR and his entourage, the tsar had failed to anticipate modern-day sanitary requirements. When he needed to relieve himself, he simply summoned a servant with a pot. After the ruler of all Russia had accomplished his business, the pot was removed, its contents deposited somewhere in the vast garden. The White Palace had not been designed to accommodate more than one hundred conference goers. There were just three bathrooms on the ground floor of the palace, one of which was reserved for the president. The secretary of state shared a bathroom with his seven closest aides, including the Soviet spy Alger Hiss. In the top two floors of the palace, eighty-odd generals, admirals, and senior diplomats had access to a grand total of six bathrooms.

Even though a U.S. Navy medical detachment had sprayed the palace with vast amounts of DDT, bedbugs and lice were still a problem, particularly in the beds "loaned" from Russian hotels and other institutions. "There were complaints from a good many this a.m. of unwelcome bed-fellows," Anna wrote her husband that night. "I was lucky—but the delousing is still going on!"

All but the most senior officials, such as Hopkins and Admiral William Leahy, the president's chief of staff, were obliged to share a bedroom. The nation's top soldier, General George C. Marshall, shared the tsarina's apartment with the head of the U.S. Navy, Admiral Ernest King. As the senior of the two officers, Marshall was assigned Alexandra's bedroom; the crusty, humorless King settled into the boudoir. They also had access to an exterior staircase reputed to have been used by the mad monk Rasputin for secret visits to the empress. Lower down the chain of command, two dozen colonels were "billeted bed to bed in two big rooms, just like GIs in an army camp."

Then there was the language problem. Admiral Leahy was indignant about a Russian waiter "speaking no known language" who showed up in his room as he was dressing. The admiral used a loud voice and gestures to communicate his regular breakfast order, "one egg, toast, coffee." The waiter nodded vigorously and returned fifteen minutes later with a tray laden with caviar, ham, smoked fish, and a flask of vodka. He was greeted by a stream of navy curse words and a bellow of "for God's sake, send me someone who speaks English—and get this fellow and his wares out of here!"

By traveling to Yalta, a third of the way around the globe from the United States, FDR had reached the logistical limits of the wartime American presidency. The Constitution stipulated that he respond to legislation passed by Congress within a maximum period of ten days. Since it took five days for couriers to reach Yalta from Washington, and vice versa, the president had to sign legislation immediately in order to comply with constitutional requirements. An elaborate system had been established to maintain communications with Washington at all times. When the president was at sea, mail was dropped over the stern of the *Quincy* in a torpedo-shaped canister for pickup by an accompanying destroyer. Anna brought her father up on deck in his armless wheelchair to watch one of the transfer operations. Clutching "for dear life" onto the railings, Roosevelt watched as sailors made repeated efforts to retrieve the can with ropes and hooks as it bobbed about on the high waves. They eventually succeeded but only after seven or eight tries. Subsequent pouches took roundabout journeys by sea, air, and land. Shorter, more urgent messages could be delivered via a special communications ship, the USS *Catoctin*, moored in Sevastopol harbor.

The Big Three conference was scheduled to open at 5:00 p.m., the day after FDR's arrival. After attending to routine presidential business, Roosevelt summoned senior members of the delegation at 10:30 a.m. to go over his talking points with Stalin and Churchill. He chose to hold the meeting in the Sun Room, which had been constructed for the ailing tsarevitch as a light-filled bedroom overlooking the sea. A stack of black-bound briefing books lay on the table in front of the president, but he waved them away impatiently. He had little interest in reading turgid State Department position papers. What mattered was his personal relationship with the Soviet leader. He thought back to their first meeting, in Tehran in November 1943, when they had toasted each other with champagne, cracked jokes at Churchill's expense, and shared political confidences. FDR felt he had done well to secure Stalin's agreement for a new United Nations organization, even if it had meant recognizing Soviet territorial claims to eastern Poland. He viewed Stalin as a politician like himself, with whom he could strike a deal.

Of course, he had no illusions about the tyrannical nature of the Soviet regime. He had been outraged by the Hitler-Stalin Pact of August 1939 carving up Poland. A few months later, after the Soviet invasion of Finland, he had described the Soviet Union as "a dictatorship as absolute as any other dictatorship in the world." But that had not prevented him from forging an alliance with Stalin after Pearl Harbor. "I know you will not mind my being brutally frank," Roosevelt cabled Churchill in March 1942, "when I tell you that I can personally handle Stalin better than your Foreign Office or my State Department. Stalin hates the guts of all your top people. He thinks he likes me better, and I hope he will continue to do so."

Roosevelt's relationship with Stalin was based on a harsh political calculation: to defeat one dictator, FDR had to ally himself with another. His White House files included a "military-strategic estimate," dated August 1943, that Russia would occupy a "dominant position" in the anti-Hitler alliance even after the United States and Britain opened their long-awaited "second front" in France. The estimate stated bluntly that "without Russia in the war, the Axis cannot be defeated in Europe." It went on to predict that Russia would dominate postwar Europe. "With Germany crushed, there is no power in Europe to oppose her tremendous military forces." The inescapable conclusion was that Russia "must be given every assistance, and every effort must be made to obtain her friendship."

It came down to a matter of arithmetic. Throughout 1943 and 1944, Hitler had deployed between one hundred eighty and one hundred ninety divisions on the eastern front with Russia. That left between forty and fifty divisions facing the western Allies in France, and fifteen to twenty

German divisions in Italy. The balance did not change appreciably after the D-day landings in Normandy in June 1944. In February 1945, at the start of the Yalta conference, a total of sixty-eight Nazi divisions were battling U.S. and British troops on the border between Germany and France. Another twenty-seven German divisions were stationed in Italy. This compared with one hundred seventy-three German divisions deployed on the eastern front. To put it another way, "every mile of front on which the Americans and British fought, every German soldier deployed in the West, was multiplied three- or four-fold in the East."

Casualty figures showed an even more dramatic disparity. An exhaustive postwar survey would show that 2,742,909 German soldiers perished on the eastern front up until the end of 1944. This was more than five times the number of German casualties in France, Italy, and Africa combined. By the end of the war, some 8 million Soviet soldiers would be reported killed or missing in action, compared with 416,000 Americans and 383,000 Britons. Churchill was correct in concluding that it was the Russians, not the Americans or the British, who had "done the main work in tearing the guts out of the German army."

From Roosevelt's perspective, there was an inverse relationship between Russian sacrifices and American sacrifices. The political calculation was brutally cynical and realistic: more dead Russians meant fewer dead Americans. Once Nazi Germany was defeated, a similar logic would apply to Japan. As the military planners had concluded in 1943, "with Russia an ally in the war against Japan, the war can be terminated in less time and at less expense in life and resources than if the reverse were the case. Should the war in the Pacific have to be carried on with an unfriendly or a negative attitude on the part of Russia, the difficulties will be immeasurably increased." The question was the price Stalin would exact in return for committing his country against Japan.

Harriman sketched out Stalin's likely demands during the meeting in the tsarevitch's bedroom. He explained that the Bolshevik leader dreamed of regaining the territories lost by Nicholas II in the disastrous Russo-Japanese War of 1904. That meant the handover of the southern half of the island of Sakhalin and the restoration of Russian rights in Manchuria, a Chinese province now occupied by the Japanese. The Soviets sought to regain control over the old tsarist railroad leading to the ports of Dairen (Dalian) and Port Arthur (Lushun). They also wanted the Kurile Islands, off the northern tip of Japan. (See map on page 353.)

FDR did not have a detailed game plan for his meetings with Stalin. He

preferred to improvise, to try whatever seemed to work. He was the ultimate situational politician, a superb tactician responding to the pressures
and opportunities of the moment. His approach to foreign affairs was
similar to his approach to domestic policy in rescuing America from the
Great Depression: "Take a method and try it. If it fails, admit it frankly
and try another. But above all, try something." He nodded his tentative
agreement to the Soviet territorial claims, as outlined by Harriman.

Shortly before leaving for Yalta, Roosevelt had read a private six-page
memo on Kremlin politics from the war correspondent Edgar Snow. It
was based on a three-hour conversation that Snow had held in Moscow
with the former Soviet foreign minister Maksim Litvinov and was full
of confidences about Stalin that "tremendously interested" the president.
According to Litvinov, the Soviet leadership was growing increasingly
mistrustful of the West and was ready to turn its back on the alliance and
go its own way. The only way to turn things around, Snow reported, was
through direct talks between Roosevelt and "Mr. Big."

The president believed he knew how to win over the Russian dictator. He would rely on his personal charm and hard-edged political skills
that had served him well over the course of an extraordinary career. "Stalin?" he scoffed, a few weeks before the Yalta conference. "I can handle
that old buzzard." He protested when cronies commiserated with him on
the hard time he would have negotiating with the man he called Uncle
Joe. "Everybody expresses sympathy with me for having to do business
with Churchill and Stalin," he joked. "I wish someone once in a while
would extend their sympathy to Churchill and Stalin too." In the words
of Harry Hopkins, FDR had "spent his life managing men, and Stalin at
bottom could not be so very different from other people." Tired and ill,
he remained confident that he could achieve what other, more workaday,
politicians assumed was impossible. His greatest gift—demonstrated in
election after election—was getting people to like and trust him. That is
what he planned to do with Stalin.

Roosevelt's optimism at once awed and disturbed aides who were more
knowledgeable, and skeptical, about the Soviet Union. Harriman was
worried by FDR's propensity for "dreaming aloud" and his sometimes
unrealistic view of his own powers of persuasion. After lengthy
consultations at the White House in November 1944, the ambassador
noted in his private journal that the president "has no conception of the

determination of the Russians to settle matters in which they consider they have a vital interest in their own manner, on their own terms. They will never leave them to the President or anyone else to arbitrate. The President still feels that he can persuade Stalin to alter his point of view on many matters that, I am satisfied, Stalin will never agree to."

The boss spent the rest of the morning admiring the view from the porch outside the tsarevitch's bedroom. He had lunch with Anna and a few aides, but made little attempt to discuss serious business. Through Molotov and Harriman, Stalin had stated his intention of calling on the president at 4:00 p.m. for a private meeting before the conference began at five.

Around 3:30 p.m., a flurry of excitement surged through the corridors of the Livadia Palace. The motor-pool officer had received a telephone call from Stalin's headquarters announcing that "all roads are now closed." Nobody was permitted to leave or enter the palace grounds until further notice.

"Uncle Joe" was on his way.

2

Stalin

February 4

Joseph Vissarionovich Stalin had arrived in the Crimea by special train from Moscow three days earlier, on Thursday, February 1. Rail was his preferred means of transportation on the rare occasions he traveled outside Moscow. He still had unpleasant memories of his first and only experience in an airplane flying across the Caspian Sea from Baku to meet Roosevelt and Churchill in Tehran. The C-47 lend-lease American transport plane had hit a patch of severe turbulence during the flight, dropping into air pockets above the mountains, leaving Stalin clinging to the armrests. Rumors circulated in Moscow that the Great Leader had suffered from a terrible nosebleed, in addition to an earache that lingered for days. The Politburo issued an instruction prohibiting him from flying as long as the war continued.

Peeking out through the heavy brown velvet curtains of his bulletproof railway carriage, numbered FD 3878, the dictator caught glimpses of a devastated wasteland. Some of the bitterest fighting of the war had taken place in the area southwest of Moscow, around towns like Tula, Orel, and Kharkov, in the eight-hundred-mile rail corridor to the Crimea. "Stations all down the line consisted of temporary log cabins; towns and villages had been practically wiped out; whole forests seemed to have been mowed down by gunfire." But Stalin was enclosed in his own little bubble, inside the green railway car emblazoned with the hammer-and-sickle crest of the Union of Soviet Socialist Republics. His compartment was furnished with a couch, a conference table, and a heavy mahogany drinks cabinet. A gleaming samovar dispensed boiling hot tea, served with thin slices of lemon. Special high-frequency communications equipment had been installed in the train and the main stations along the route to enable the supreme commander to keep in touch with Moscow and his generals.

For his Crimean headquarters, Stalin had chosen a palace that once belonged to the transvestite prince Felix Yusupov, the murderer of Rasputin. The Yusupov summer residence was designed by the same architect who built the Livadia Palace, five miles down the road, in the heavy Moorish Revival style then favored by the Russian aristocracy. A pair of lions guarded the stone steps up to the white villa, surrounded by terraces of palms and cypresses. The General Staff had set up an operations room, or *Stavka*, on the ground floor of the palace, from which Stalin and his generals could follow the movements of Soviet armies as they penetrated deep into Germany from Poland. A communications center in the basement allowed instant telephone and telegraph links with Moscow and frontline army units. Ten planes were on standby to provide courier services between Yalta and Moscow, plus another two planes for Stalin's private use, with his own personal pilots.

No effort had been spared on the security front. The soldiers stationed along the road from Saki to Yalta were merely the visible tip of a vast operation stretching twelve miles on either side of the highway. Four regiments of NKVD Interior Ministry troops had been sent to the Crimea in the middle of January to cleanse the region of "unfriendly elements." The palaces used by Stalin, Roosevelt, and Churchill were each surrounded by three concentric security zones. The two inner zones were patrolled by NKVD troops reporting to the secret-police chief, Lavrenty Beria; the outer zone was guarded by Red Army soldiers with watchdogs. In a memorandum dated January 27, Beria assured Stalin that "100 operational workers and a special unit of 500 NKVD troops" would ensure his personal protection, in addition to his regular bodyguards. Antiaircraft defenses had been strengthened throughout the Crimea; a hundred sixty fighter planes were ready to take to the skies to shoot down enemy aircraft. Beria ordered a "first category" underground bunker to be constructed on the grounds of the Yusupov Palace, known to the Russians as Object Number 1, in case a German bomber miraculously penetrated the formidable defenses. The three-room bunker was protected by six feet of reinforced concrete, sufficient to withstand a direct hit by a five-hundred-kilo bomb. A somewhat more modest "second category" bunker had been installed beneath the Livadia Palace (Object Number 2).

Although the Crimea seemed dead as a graveyard to the visitors from abroad, from the perspective of Stalin and Beria, the Sicily-sized peninsula throbbed with unseen threats and dangers. The NKVD suspected the Germans of training a stay-behind network of spies and saboteurs prior to their retreat the previous spring. Immediately after the liberation of the Crimea, Beria had organized the deportation of the entire Tatar population on suspicion of "collaboration" with the Nazis. On the night of May 17–18, 1944, Beria's men surrounded Tatar villages and ordered everybody out of their homes. "The noise and the shouting were indescribable," remembered one eyewitness. "All you could hear throughout the village was crying. People lost their daughters, their sons, their husbands." Roughly one hundred eighty-nine thousand men, women, and children were rounded up, forced into freight cars, and transported to the deserts of Uzbekistan on the same railway system that Stalin had used to reach the Crimea. Thousands of people died of thirst in the railcars, which became known to the Tatars as "crematoria on wheels." The doors and windows on the boxcars were bolted shut, forcing the survivors to live alongside piles of rotting corpses. By the NKVD's own statistics, at least 17 percent of Crimean Tatars died within eighteen months of their deportation. After it was all over, Beria boasted to Stalin that his troops had committed "no excesses at all" and encountered practically no resistance.

The charge that the entire Tatar nation had cooperated with the Germans was wildly overblown. Some Tatars had joined the occupiers, but others served in the Red Army. But such distinctions were unimportant to Stalin and Beria, who operated on the basis of collective discipline and preemptive punishment. It mattered little to Stalin whether an accused person was actually guilty of a crime. What mattered was the potential motive. If someone had a reason to be disloyal, that was sufficient proof of his disloyalty. In Stalinist terminology, he was "objectively guilty." This was the principle on which the Great Purge had been conducted in the thirties before it degenerated into a crazed competition to fulfill arbitrary quotas of suspected traitors. It was also the principle that justified the elimination of the kulaks, or rich peasants, and the ethnic cleansing of entire nations. The Tatars, who had been living in the Crimea since the thirteenth century, were by no means the only nation to have incurred

Stalin's wrath, which also fell on Chechens, Kalmucks, Volga Germans, and others.

It is likely that at least some of the destruction that had disturbed Roosevelt during his car journey the previous day was caused not by the Nazis but by the Soviets themselves. In driving from Saki to Yalta, the president had passed through once-flourishing, now-abandoned Tatar villages. Much of the desolation was the consequence of the most brutal experiment in social engineering the world had ever seen. The collectivization of the countryside had been followed by forced industrialization, which was followed in turn by massive ethnic deportations. Villages had been left to die; fields had been neglected; churches, mosques, and graveyards had been destroyed. Soviet officials did their best to blame the entire catastrophe on the Germans, but their claims were unconvincing. When a Russian guide pointed to several ruined villas in Yalta as examples of wanton Nazi devastation, Churchill's bodyguard "could not resist pointing out that fully grown trees were flourishing in the rubble." Trees grew fast in the subtropical climate of the Crimea, but not that fast. The Englishman concluded that "most of the damage had, in fact, been caused during the Russian Revolution."

The hunt for saboteurs and traitors continued right through the Yalta conference. Beria reported to Stalin at the end of January that security checks had been "carried out on 74,000 people, of which 835 individuals have been arrested." Operatives from SMERSH, the military intelligence unit named after the slogan *Smert' Shpionam,* or "Death to Spies," kept watch for German agents and fifth columnists. In addition to the exiled Tatars, other suspect nationalities included Bulgarians, Armenians, and Greeks.

Mistrust and cynicism were the most pronounced character traits of the man Roosevelt viewed as key to his hopes for establishing a constructive long-term relationship with Russia. There was a kind of twisted Darwinian process at work in the selection of Soviet leaders. In the cutthroat world of Kremlin politics, survival of the fittest meant survival of the most paranoid. The most ruthless politicians rose naturally to the top, eliminating their rivals, thereby ensuring their own survival and the survival of the Bolshevik system. Whatever checks and balances that had once existed had been eliminated by the late thirties. Stalin had taken care to eliminate potential rivals in both the party and the army in a series of purges, culminating in the trial of Nikolai Bukharin in 1938. There was now no source of authority except for Stalin himself, a name synonymous with the dictatorship of the proletariat. The onetime Georgian seminary student saw enemies everywhere. He divided the world into friends, meaning people who were subordinate to him, and rivals, people he could not completely control. There was no intermediate category. "We are surrounded by enemies—that is clear to all," he had told a Communist Party congress in 1923. "Not a moment passes without our enemies trying to seize some little chink through which they could crawl and do harm to us."

Stalin's paranoia was combined with cold pragmatism. His daughter, Svetlana, observed that he "was neither hot-tempered, nor openhearted, nor emotional, nor sentimental; in other words, he lacked all that was characteristic of a typically Georgian temperament. Georgians are impulsive, kind, easily shedding tears when moved by compassion or happiness, or when enraptured by beauty. . . . In him, everything was the other way round, and cold calculation, dissimulation, a sober, cynical realism became stronger in him with the years." The man born Iosif Dzhugashvili spoke Russian with a thick Georgian accent but became angry when reminded of his Georgian origins. "Fools!" he would explode. "Georgians are fools!" There was no room for sentiment in his world. His very nickname, Stalin, the "Man of Steel," implied a lack of ordinary human feeling. "You have to control your emotions," he advised a visiting Yugoslav Communist shortly before the Yalta conference. "If you are guided by your emotions, you lose." In Svetlana's judgment, "human feelings in him were replaced by political considerations. He knew and sensed the political game, its shades, its nuances. He was completely absorbed by it."

Life in the Yusupov Palace was already settling into a routine by Sunday, February 4. Stalin, Molotov, and Beria lived alongside one another in the main twenty-room wing, supported by a host of generals and diplomats in the annexes. As in Moscow, Stalin worked late and got up late. He pored over memos drawn up by the Soviet foreign office on the postwar future of Europe and psychological portraits of Roosevelt and Churchill that had been prepared by the NKVD. He held two sessions a day with the General Staff in the *Stavka,* or HQ. The first meeting was usually convened at 11:00 a.m., soon after Stalin got out of bed, to review developments overnight. The second, more important meeting took place at 9:00 p.m., to issue orders for the following day. He typically sat down to dinner with a few top aides around midnight and often did not get to bed until 5:00 a.m.

The dictator was at the height of his power and prestige. The chaotic early days of the war, when he retreated to his dacha in panic, stunned by the suddenness and ferocity of the Nazi invasion, were a distant memory. It had taken the Germans just four months to reach the outskirts of Moscow, inflicting more than 2 million casualties on the enemy. At the most desperate moment, when the capital itself seemed about to fall, Stalin had restored some spine to the Soviet resistance by ordering deserters to be shot and stationing "blocking troops" in the rear of the front line. "Not one step back" became the order of the day. Russian infantrymen quickly discovered that it was more dangerous to retreat than to advance. As Stalin told Roosevelt and Churchill over dinner in Tehran, cowardice was not an option for his troops. "Even cowards become heroes in Russia. Those who do not are killed."

The Red Army had held the line at Moscow and Leningrad and Stalingrad and had then gone on the offensive, driving the Wehrmacht back into the Reich. In the last three weeks alone, starting on January 12, Soviet forces had advanced three hundred miles from the Vistula River to the Oder. They had liberated what remained of Warsaw after it was blown to smithereens by the Nazis and captured Silesia, Germany's most important coal-mining region. Fifty-three German divisions were trapped behind Russian lines in East Prussia and the Baltic states. Marshal Georgy Zhukov had reported to Stalin on January 29 that the entire western part of Poland, occupied for the last five and a half years by the Nazis, had been freed. "Your order—to shatter with a powerful blow the resistance of the enemy armies and stage a lightning advance to the German-Polish border—has been fulfilled."

During the three days he had been in the Crimea, Stalin had approved a succession of triumphant communiqués that appeared to seal the fate of the Third Reich. Red Army troops were fighting "the Hitlerites" in the streets of the Hungarian capital, Budapest. They had reached the outskirts of Danzig, the Polish port city where the first shots of the war had been fired on September 1, 1939. They held several bridgeheads on the western side of the frozen Oder River. Finally, on February 4, a Soviet communiqué reported that Zhukov's troops had reached the railway station at Baerwalde, just thirty-nine miles east of Berlin. Zhukov had made preliminary plans for the capture of the German capital by the middle of February.

Into the Reich

JANUARY – FEBRUARY 1945

SWEDEN

DENMARK

LITHUANIA

Baltic Sea

5 *Jan. 25*
Königsberg surrounded

Army Group North

Königsberg

3rd Belorussian Front

POMERANIA

Danzig

EAST PRUSSIA (GER.)

Army Group Vistula
Himmler

8 *Feb. 4*
Zhukov captures Baerwalde

Stettin

Oder R.

Baerwalde

Berlin ★

Kienitz

Vistula R.

2nd Belorussian Front
Rokossovsky

7 *Jan. 31*
Zhukov crosses Oder

Poznan

2 *Jan. 17*
Zhukov takes Warsaw

Warsaw ★

4 *Jan. 25*
Zhukov bypasses Poznan

1st Belorussian Front
Zhukov

Elbe R.

Army Group Centre

Neisse R.

GERMANY

POLAND

Lublin

Breslau

Oder R.

SILESIA

3 *Jan. 22*
Konev crosses Oder

Oppeln

Vistula R.

1 *Jan. 12*
Russians launch Vistula-Oder offensive

Kraków

Prague ★

CZECHOSLOVAKIA

Auschwitz

1st Ukrainian Front
Konev

6 *Jan. 27*
Konev liberates Auschwitz

4th Ukrainian Front

Army Group South

Danube R.

Vienna ★

AUSTRIA

2nd Ukrainian Front

Front line
— Jan. 12
···· Feb. 4

Budapest ★

HUNGARY

N

Lake Balaton

Danube R.

3rd Ukrainian Front

ITALY   YUGOSLAVIA

0   Miles   100

Gene Thorp

"What's the news from the front?" was Churchill's first question, when Stalin called on him at 3:00 p.m. that day en route to the Livadia Palace, prior to the opening of the conference.

"Not bad at all," came the satisfied reply.

Stalin explained that Germany was running out of the resources needed to make war, such as oil, coal, and bread. Hitler had turned out to be a poor strategist. Instead of pulling his most capable armies out of East Prussia, he had allowed them to be surrounded, leaving only the poorly led, poorly trained Volkssturm to defend Berlin. If he lost the Ruhr in addition to Silesia, he would be finished. The prime minister wanted to know what the Red Army would do if Hitler decided to abandon the capital and "move south," to Dresden for example.

"We shall follow him."

Churchill invited Stalin to see his Map Room, already installed in a cubbyhole on the ground floor of the Vorontsov Palace, the British residence in the Crimea. The Englishman was intensely proud of his invention, which allowed him to follow the progress of the war hour by hour, collecting information from all the major battlefronts in a single command center. The walls were covered with maps of the principal battle areas covered with clear plastic, grease-pencil marks showing the movements of Allied and enemy troops. Colored pins, of various different shapes and sizes, studded the oceans.

It was clear from the disposition of the pins and pencil marks that the outcome of the war was being decided on the eastern front. In the West, American and British forces were still mopping up after the serious reverse of the Battle of the Bulge, in the Ardennes region of eastern France. The western Allies had resumed the offensive at the beginning of February, but it was a slow, cautious advance that lacked the panache, brutality, and complete disregard for casualties of the Red Army's operations in the East. The Red Army suffered more than three hundred thousand fatalities between January 12 and February 4, close to the total number of American battlefield losses for the entire war.

Casualty figures mattered little to the man the Russian people knew as the *vozhd,* their supreme leader. "For him, only the goal mattered. He was never tormented by conscience or grief at the enormous losses," a Russian biographer, General Dmitry Volkogonov, later wrote. "He believed that both victories and defeats inevitably reaped a bitter harvest, that it was an inescapable fact of modern warfare." The essential questions were the long-term political ones: which piece of territory would fall to which army, how the frontiers of Europe would look once it was all over, who would control what. He had sharply criticized the western Allies for postponing the D-day landings in Normandy for two years for fear of excessive casualties. When Churchill talked about the huge losses the British were likely to suffer in a cross-Channel operation during a visit to Moscow in August 1942, Stalin had sarcastically observed that the Red Army was losing ten thousand soldiers every day. "You cannot wage war without taking risks."

Over the next few hours, Stalin would have to make one of the most important decisions of the war. Should he authorize Zhukov's troops to continue their all-out advance on Berlin, now that the last major natural obstacle had been cleared? Or should he proceed more deliberately, consolidating his armies for the final assault while eliminating pockets of German resistance hundreds of miles behind the front line, in Poland and East Prussia? Pushing forward promised great rewards—a rapid end of the war on Soviet terms—but also carried great risks in the event of a last-ditch enemy counterattack.

The *vozhd* was unimpressed when Churchill asked Field Marshal Harold Alexander to describe the fighting taking place in Italy. British and American forces were advancing slowly up the peninsula, but the Germans were resisting stubbornly. Italy was a sideshow, Stalin insisted. It would be better to leave a few British divisions in Italy for defensive purposes and transfer the rest across the Adriatic to Yugoslavia and Hungary where they could assist the Soviet assault on Vienna. Churchill believed it was far too late for such a switch in strategy, which he himself had advocated at an earlier stage in the war, over Russian and American objections. Now, it seemed, Stalin was taunting him with a suggestion he knew to be impractical.

"The Red Army," the prime minister replied diplomatically, "may not give us time to complete the operation."

Soviet soldiers appeared to be stationed behind "every shrub and every bush" as Stalin drove up to the Livadia Palace in his gleaming black Packard Twelve shortly before 4:00 p.m. that Sunday afternoon. Molotov sat beside him on the plushly upholstered rear seat of the limousine, which was weighed down by four tons of extra armor plating. The windows were at least three inches thick, sufficient to withstand the blast of a heavy machine gun, reflecting back the images of the soldiers standing at erect attention all around. A red Soviet flag fluttered from the hood. Occupying the front seat next to the driver was a stocky NKVD general named Nikolai Vlasik, who had served as Stalin's personal bodyguard since 1931 and was now closer to him than anyone else. The guards formed a tight circle around the Packard and kept a wary watch from the palace roof. The Americans staying in the palace had all been issued multiple passes, which were checked and rechecked whenever they ventured outside. An American colonel observing the scene felt the guards "would shoot if one even made a face" at the dictator.

As the Packard Twelve came to a halt on the driveway in front of the entrance to the palace, Vlasik leaped out to open the door for his master. Stalin emerged in a heavily worn marshal's overcoat, exchanged salutes with the honor guard, and strode inside, followed by Molotov, Vlasik, and a knot of Soviet generals. FDR was waiting for the dictator in his study, formerly the tsar's antechamber. Lined with dark mahogany panels, the room was decorated with heavy Italian furniture and thick Bukhara rugs. The two leaders greeted each other like old friends. The American interpreter, Chip Bohlen, noticed that Stalin allowed himself "one of his rare, if slight, smiles" as he responded to Roosevelt's firm handshake. Harry Hopkins's son Robert, a photographer with the U.S. Signal Corps, was allowed into the room to record the scene. The president and the "supreme leader" were seated together on a divan beneath a picture of the frozen Russian countryside. Stalin leaned forward in his crumpled military uniform, his chubby hands resting on his knees. Roosevelt looked pale and haggard in a light gray suit with a brightly colored tie.

FDR opened the conversation by congratulating the *vozhd* on his latest military triumphs. During the voyage over on the *Quincy,* he told Stalin, he had laid bets on whether the Red Army would reach Berlin before the U.S. Army reached Manila. Stalin batted back the compliment, saying Manila would certainly fall first, as there was heavy fighting going on along the Oder River. He carefully avoided dropping any hint about his thinking on the timing of an offensive against the German capital.

Roosevelt had decided that the best way of winning over Stalin was through a mixture of flattery and snide remarks about the other allies. He was determined to dispel the impression of an Anglo-American cabal against the Russians. He wanted to establish a bond with Stalin, to talk "like men and brothers." FDR reminded the dictator of an incident that had occurred in Tehran that underscored the point that they could find a common language, over Churchill's objections if necessary. Over dinner one evening, Stalin had demanded the execution of fifty thousand German officers at the end of the war, to ensure that their country never committed aggression again. It was unclear whether this was meant as a threat, a joke, or, as was often the case with Stalin's verbal sallies, a mischievous combination of the two. Knowing that Stalin was more than capable of such atrocities, Churchill was outraged. "The British Parliament and public will never tolerate mass executions," he huffed. Roosevelt preferred to take a lighthearted view of the exchange, suggesting, "as a compromise," that only forty-nine thousand German officers be taken out and shot.

FDR now told Stalin that the war damage he had witnessed the previous day had caused him to become "more bloodthirsty in regard to the Germans" than he had been at Tehran. He hoped the marshal "would again propose a toast to the execution of 50,000 officers of the German army."

"We have all become much more bloodthirsty," replied Stalin. "The Germans are savages."

The president then broached the question of direct communications between the commanders of the Allied armies, General Dwight D. Eisenhower in the West and Marshal Zhukov in the East. Coordination of the war effort would become much simpler if they could talk with each other directly rather than going through Washington, Moscow, and London, as at present. This was a touchy subject with Stalin. Soviet officers were attached to Eisenhower's staff in France, but he had no intention of allowing American and British officers to roam freely behind Red Army lines. Nor did he want to allow his own generals to deal directly with their western counterparts, without a full grasp of the political considerations. Stalin did not want to reject Roosevelt's proposal out of hand, so he gave a noncommittal reply. Let the military people "work out the details."

FDR seized the opportunity to distance the United States from its traditional European allies, Britain and France. He began by running down the "Free French" leader, General Charles de Gaulle, as a self-proclaimed Joan of Arc who acted as if he was the savior of France. Adopting a confidential tone, the president announced that he planned "to tell the Marshal something indiscreet." The British were trying to "artificially" build up France into "a strong power" with a two-hundred-thousand-man army. They wanted France to "hold the line" against Germany after the war until Britain, impoverished and exhausted by the long fight against Hitler, could regain its strength. Roosevelt added that he was having a "good deal of trouble" with the British in agreeing to zones of occupation in Germany.

"The British are a peculiar people. They want to have their cake and eat it too."

Stalin was not entirely immune to the presidential-charm offensive. On a personal level, he liked FDR, sympathized with his physical infirmities, and admired his stoic sense of duty. On the other hand, there was little room for personal considerations in Stalin's overall worldview, which was based on a cold calculation of national and class interests and the balance of power. Temporary alliances with one or another imperialist government were acceptable, indeed necessary, to consolidate the gains of socialism, according to Marxist-Leninist teaching. It was to the Soviet Union's advantage to attempt to split the enemy camp and join forces with the most reasonable people on the other side. In the end, however, an imperialist remained an imperialist. There could be no permanent accommodation between the forces of progress and the forces of reaction. Amused by Roosevelt's attempts to curry favor, Stalin did not rise to the anti-Churchill baiting. Instead he asked if France should have its own occupation zone in Germany. He was already pondering the "concessions" he could make to the western Allies in return for a free hand in eastern Europe.

"That's not a bad idea," replied Roosevelt. "But if we give them one, it will only be out of kindness."

"That would be the only reason," observed Stalin and Molotov, almost in unison.

The *vozhd* had another concession to offer. He had rejected proposals for a Big Three meeting on neutral ground, explaining that his doctors would not allow him to travel outside the country and were even opposed to "a change of climate." It had taken him a full two weeks to recover from his earache after the Tehran trip. Stalin proposed that all the plenary sessions of the conference be held at the Livadia Palace, out of consideration for FDR's precarious state of health. To accommodate his Russian counterpart, Roosevelt traveled all the way to the Crimea from Washington, a round-trip of "approximately 13,842 miles by rail, sea, air and auto." Stalin would respond by traveling twelve miles every day to meet the dying president.

It was nearly 5:00 p.m., time to move to the big white ballroom around the corner from the president's study for the opening plenary session of the conference. Roosevelt was wheeled in first, so that he could take the time he needed to settle into his seat at the round table, which was covered with white fabric. Stalin chatted with the other delegates in the entrance hall of the palace for a few minutes, holding a cigarette in his withered left arm. Churchill drew a smile from the dictator as he showed off his alligator-skin cigar case. He was wearing the uniform of a British colonel and a high fur-skin hat that swallowed his bald pate. As was his custom, he had been traveling "incognito," under the pseudonym "Colonel Kent," a disguise that fooled no one but appealed to his fascination with the cloak-and-dagger.

The conference table occupied the far end of the cavernous ballroom, which had served as the backdrop for the first formal event at the Livadia Palace in September 1911, a glittering coming-out party thrown by the tsar in honor of his oldest daughter. "It was a perfect night," recalled one of the guests. "The gowns and jewels of the women, and the brilliant uniforms of the men, made a striking spectacle under the blaze of the electric lights." The huge room now seemed cold and empty. Roosevelt had his back to the unlit fireplace, with Stalin to his right and Churchill to his left. Each leader was flanked by four top aides, two on either side. Interpreters and a few other officials pulled up chairs behind the principals. The curtains were drawn, blocking a view of the Moorish courtyard on one side and majestic mountains on the other. Padded leather armchairs had been reserved for the three leaders, uncomfortable wooden seats for everyone else. Each delegate was furnished with a legal-sized notepad and an ashtray. It had been agreed that the opening session would be devoted exclusively to military matters. Apart from FDR and the three foreign ministers, nearly everyone else was in uniform.

The president waved away several aides who attempted to gate-crash the meeting, including his chief doctor, Vice Admiral McIntire. According to his daughter, Anna, these were people with little to do other than "sit on their fannies and play gin rummy." The British air force chief was alarmed by FDR's haggard appearance. "He is very thin and his face is drawn and deeply lined, and he looks uneasy all the time and as if he might be in bad pain. Also, his brain is obviously not what it was. Altogether it looks as if Truman might be in for a job."

As he had done at Tehran, Stalin again invited the president to chair the conference, as the only head of state present. (Stalin's official positions were chairman of the Council of People's Commissars, the Soviet equivalent of prime minister, and chairman of the State Defense Committee.)

Brutal with subordinates, he was unfailingly polite to foreign leaders, asking his guests for their opinions before stating his own. He spoke in clipped, short sentences, never raising his voice. He was exceptionally well prepared, relying not on notes but his own copious memory and mastery of the subject. He enjoyed sparring with Churchill but went out of his way to be deferential to Roosevelt. The British prime minister might be a wartime ally, but he was also an ideological enemy, the very incarnation of imperialism. With FDR, Stalin was not so sure. Although he was unimpressed by the battlefield achievements of the U.S. Army, he was awed by America's military-industrial might and her ability to churn out huge quantities of military equipment for all three Allies. He privately acknowledged that the task of negotiating with the leading capitalist power was a lot easier with Roosevelt in the White House than any other conceivable president.

Churchill, Stalin told intimates, was "the kind of man who will pick your pocket of every kopeck if you don't watch him." Roosevelt was "not like that. He dips his hand only for bigger coins. But Churchill? Churchill will do it for a kopeck!"

Those who had never seen Stalin in person before were surprised how small he was. Soviet photographers had instructions to take pictures of him from a low angle, to make him seem more imposing. In reality, he was no more than five feet seven inches tall, with a compact torso, gangly legs, and a shriveled left arm. He moved his head stiffly, with his neck stretched out, to avoid drawing attention to his double chin. His sallow, pasty complexion and spiky, brushed-back hair reminded one of the British delegates of "a puzzled porcupine." Westerners were struck by the pockmarked face, the result of a childhood brush with smallpox and only partially disguised by several layers of talcum powder. A walrus mustache chopped off at the sides helped conceal his twisted, blackened teeth. His most expressive feature was his yellow eyes, which darted restlessly around the room. They provided the best clue to his mood, sparkling mischievously one moment, gazing at the ceiling during Churchill's flights of rhetoric, turning suddenly to slits when something aroused his anger.

The Soviet armed forces chief of staff, General Alexei Antonov, spread a map across the ballroom table to illustrate the positions on the eastern front. His American counterpart, George C. Marshall, provided an update on the fighting in the West, holding out the prospect of a crossing of the Rhine by early March. The proceedings were interrupted around 6:00 p.m. "by a long procession of tail-coated waiters holding silver trays high over their heads," an American remembered. The Russians were serving tea "in Hollywood's concept of the grandest English style." A couple of "stiff-collared British Foreign Office gentlemen" supervised the operation. They moved about on tiptoe, handing cups of tea to Russian servants, who dispensed them to delegates in strict order of rank, along with cake and sandwiches. A "funereal hush" settled over the rest of the Livadia Palace, "as though behind those doors lay someone desperately ill."

The quiet was soon disturbed by what Harriman called "an extreme case of conference fever—of everyone wanting to go to every meeting because it made them feel important." It involved the ambitious James F. Byrnes, a former Supreme Court justice and segregationist senator from South Carolina who viewed himself as "assistant president" for the home front. Byrnes was already bitter at being denied the vice presidency in favor of Truman. He was now furious at being excluded from the opening session of the conference, even though it was supposed to be restricted to military matters. He had received a message to be at the doors of the conference room at 6:00 p.m., when he would be invited in. As Anna Roosevelt recorded in her diary, the director of the Office of War Mobilization "had cooled his heels outside said doors for 45 minutes and nobody said boo to him, so he retired to vent his piled up spleen" on anyone who would listen. "A tantrum was putting it mildly! Fire was shooting from his eyes!"

Anna was organizing a dinner party to be hosted by her father for Stalin and Churchill later that evening. The table in the tsar's old billiard room could seat fourteen people. The American guests included Byrnes, who announced that he would boycott the dinner and "order a plane" to take him home to protest the way he had been treated. "I am asking the only favor I will ever ask you in my life," he told Anna. "Tell your father that I won't attend the dinner."

After much arguing and pleading, Anna told Byrnes that his absence would leave "13 at the dinner table, which I knew would give superstitious FDR 10 fits!" She persuaded him to back down "on the stupid basis of superstition—Jimmy saying that this was the only ground on which he would give in."

The Soviet delegation was seized by a different sort of panic at the conclusion of the formal conference session. After leaving the ballroom, Stalin disappeared from his security men who patrolled every corridor in the palace, except for a curtained-off section adjoining Roosevelt's private quarters, which was the preserve of the U.S. Secret Service. Somehow, all these bodyguards had managed to lose track of the *vozhd*. Vlasik and his minions rushed up and down the corridors, shouting "Where's Stalin? Where has he gone?" It turned out that he had wandered off in search of a toilet. Since the washroom closest to the ballroom was occupied by the prime minister, a U.S. diplomat escorted Stalin to the nearest available facility at the other end of the palace. For a moment, Kathleen Harriman wrote an English friend, there was "havoc—everyone meléeing around whispering. I think they thought the Americans had pulled a kidnapping stunt or something. A few minutes later a composed U.J. [Uncle Joe] appeared at the door & order was restored."

At dinner that night, the three leaders sat at the center of the table, Roosevelt in the middle, between Stalin and Churchill. The meal was a joint American-Russian production. It began, as usual, with large helpings of caviar from deep crystal bowls. The president's Filipino mess boys prepared a tomato sauce for the Black Sea sturgeon, which was followed by beef and macaroni, American style. The food was washed down with some of Stalin's favorite Georgian wines, including a sweet white Tsinandali, which was served as an appetizer, and a dry red Mukuzani. The Americans noticed that Stalin encouraged the others to drink but drank very little himself, pouring water into his vodka glass when he thought no one was watching.

The three leaders were soon toasting one another, celebrating a victory that seemed all but certain. As the evening wore on, discordant notes began creeping into the congratulatory speeches. Stalin declined, "as a republican," to toast the health of the king of England. He was also unable to accept the idea that small countries should have a voice in determining a postwar settlement; by winning the war, the Big Three had also won the right to dictate the peace. Roosevelt and Churchill agreed that the big powers would have the biggest say, but small nations should also be heard.

"Yugoslavia, Albania, and such small countries do not deserve to be at this table," insisted Stalin. "Do you want Albania to have the same rights as the United States?"

The Englishman replied with a quotation from Shakespeare's *Titus Andronicus:* "The eagle suffers little birds to sing / And is not careful what they mean thereby." The lines that immediately followed might have been more to Stalin's liking: "Knowing that, with the shadow of his wings, / He can at pleasure stint their melody."

The talk turned to rights of dissent and free speech. Andrei Vyshinsky, who had served as Stalin's prosecutor in the show trials of the thirties and was now deputy commissar of foreign affairs, reacted sharply to a remark by Bohlen about the importance of public opinion in the United States. The American people, said Vyshinsky, "should learn to obey their leaders."

Seeking to restore amity, Churchill raised his glass "to the proletariat masses of the world" but followed up with a lecture on the virtues of parliamentary democracy. He noted that he was often accused of being a reactionary, but the fact remained that he was the only leader present who risked being thrown out of office by the will of the electorate. Britain would hold elections for a new Parliament as soon as the war was over. He reminded Stalin and Roosevelt that Parliament had the right to dismiss a prime minister at any time through a simple vote of no confidence.

"You seem to fear these elections," Stalin teased.

Not at all, replied Churchill vigorously. "Not only do I not fear elections, I am proud of the right of the British people to change their government at any time they see fit."

By now, the sweet Soviet champagne was flowing, and Roosevelt felt confident enough to attempt a further bonding with the dictator. He revealed that he and Churchill referred to Stalin as "Uncle Joe" in their transatlantic cable traffic. Stalin seemed offended by this disclosure. The Russian term for "uncle," *dyadya,* carries the connotation of a harmless old man who can be easily fooled. He demanded to know precisely what FDR meant by the nickname.

"It's a term of endearment," the president assured him. "As if you are a member of the family."

There was a moment of embarrassed silence. Roosevelt had mentioned the "Uncle Joe" moniker to Stalin before, at Tehran, but had done so in private. Sensitive to any slights to his dignity, real or perceived, the *vozhd* did not like being insulted at the dinner table in front of his own subordinates, not to mention the waiters. Molotov insisted that Stalin was not really angry. "All of Russia knows you call him Uncle Joe," he told FDR.

Roosevelt ordered more champagne. Stalin looked at his watch and suggested it was time for him to leave. The tension was partly relieved by Byrnes, who had told Anna Roosevelt earlier that he planned to keep his mouth shut the entire meal. The fourteenth guest jocularly reminded the Russians that they had turned a symbol of American power into a caricature of western capitalism.

"You do not mind talking about Uncle Sam, so why should Uncle Joe be so bad?"

Churchill persuaded Stalin to stay another half hour, and he eventually left at 11:10. Everybody parted amicably, but it was generally felt that the opening dinner had not been a success. Before retiring to bed, the British foreign secretary, Anthony Eden, penned a gloomy diary entry:

> Dinner with Americans; a terrible party I thought. President vague and loose and ineffective. W[inston] understanding that business was flagging made desperate efforts and too long speeches to get things going again. Stalin's attitude to small countries struck me as grim, not to say sinister. We were too many and there was no steady flow and brisk exchanges as at Tehran. I was greatly relieved when whole business was over.

Roosevelt's intentions were transparent enough. He wanted to build a joshing, friendly relationship with Stalin, like the one he had with Churchill, to make him feel that he belonged to the club and could be trusted with its little secrets and rituals. But the ploy had fallen flat. Stalin's sense of humor was limited to jokes about other people. Unlike Churchill, he was unwilling to laugh at himself.

Unwittingly, FDR had discovered a chink in the dictator's psychological armor. For all his skill at dissembling, particularly in front of foreigners, Stalin sometimes gave himself away. While he was modest in his demeanor and personal habits, he was not at all modest about himself. He had an elevated view of his achievements and historic importance. His image was everywhere, in newspapers, on billboards, on pedestals, in propaganda pamphlets celebrating "the genius Stalin." Even with his children, he would often talk about himself in the third person as the symbol of the Soviet state rather than as an ordinary mortal. "You're not Stalin and I'm not Stalin," he lectured his wayward son Vasily. "Stalin is what he is in the newspapers and the portraits, not you, no, not even me!" He saw himself as both the incarnation and the guardian of the Bolshevik Revolution, the instrument of grand historical forces much larger than himself. To insult Stalin was to insult the Soviet state.

Stalin had permitted a gigantic personality cult to grow up around him that seemed to reflect not only the demands of realpolitik but a deep psychological need. The wave of officially inspired adulation had begun with the celebration of his fiftieth birthday, in 1929. He became the *vozhd*, the leader of the tribe, "the most outstanding continuator of Lenin's cause." No superlative was too excessive to bestow on him: wisest statesman, most brilliant military strategist, greatest friend of the working class, most outstanding Marxist theoretician. He came to believe his own propaganda.

FDR's assumption that Stalin was not so very different from a typical western politician was fatally flawed. The *vozhd* had more in common with Tamerlane or Ivan the Terrible than George Washington. He was unresponsive to public opinion. American notions of political pluralism and constitutional checks and balances meant nothing to him. He ruled through the traditional methods of the Russian tsars: secrecy, brute force, the concentration of power in the hands of the state. His favorite tsars were not westernizers like Peter the Great but nationalists like Ivan, whom he privately described as his teacher. Early on in the war, he had ordered Sergey Eisenstein to make a film about the fifteenth-century despot, stressing his role in defeating Russia's enemies and crushing internal dissent. Ivan was depicted as an absolute ruler who relied on his secret police, the *oprichnina*, to build a mighty state and destroy the troublesome boyars. If anything, Stalin felt Ivan was too soft. He thought Ivan should have acted "even more decisively." The tsar took too long to move against the feudal families and spent too much time praying to God and repenting of his sins. That was one mistake that Stalin would never make.

Bolshevism was the perfect ideology for Stalin: it provided him with a historical justification for the accumulation of unlimited personal power. The Bolsheviks believed that they were an elite chosen by history to implement the will of the masses. Only the politically conscious avant-garde could divine the true interests of the people as determined by Karl Marx: the people themselves were unable to see clearly because their minds were muddled by "false consciousness," including religion and nationalism. Since the revolution was historically necessary, any action that contributed to its success was not only permitted, but required. Stalin believed the ends always justified the means.

Like Roosevelt, Stalin was raised by a doting, domineering mother who lavished attention on her only child. From a very early age, both men were encouraged to believe they were destined for great things. They both overcame physical hardship. Roosevelt had suffered from debilitating illness most of his adult life; Stalin served repeated stints of political exile in Siberia. But the similarities ended there. FDR grew up in an atmosphere of loving security in a luxurious mansion surrounded by trees and parks;

Stalin lived in a wooden shack and was beaten mercilessly by his alcoholic father. The Hudson Valley landowner had a naturally optimistic, upbeat view of the world; the cobbler's son looked at life through the bleakest possible lens. The American attended Groton and Harvard; the Georgian was expelled from a seminary for political activism. The master of the White House relied on his charisma and family name to win over his rivals; the master of the Kremlin made his early reputation as a highway bandit, robbing banks and extorting money from factory owners in order to raise funds for the Bolsheviks.

Fate had brought the crippled president and the pockmarked revolutionary to the edge of the Black Sea to lay the foundations for a new world order with an English aristocrat. With its shattered towns and drafty palaces, devastated countryside and ethnically cleansed villages, the Crimea provided a fitting metaphor for the continent that lay prostrate at their feet.

3

Churchill

February 5

"G reat dissatisfaction here regarding paucity of news from home," the prime minister's private secretary had cabled London the previous night. "Pray do what you can to improve matter."

Cigar ash and sheaves of paper were scattered across the big double bed at the center of the walnut-paneled room overlooking the Black Sea. Winston Churchill was propped up against the pillows in his well-worn silk dressing gown, fuming over communications glitches. Even ordinary diplomatic traffic was going astray or arriving late. It was Monday morning, February 5, and there was still no sign of the Sunday newspapers that should have arrived by special courier flight from London. The daily report from the War Cabinet on the status of the fighting on different fronts had not yet landed. To add insult to injury, Stalin had complained that the charts in the prime minister's beloved Map Room failed to reflect the latest Soviet advances. A Russian "colonel, drenched in scent," had turned up at the Vorontsov Palace to correct the inaccuracies.

Churchill needed information like an ordinary man needs oxygen. Back in London, he got a daily intelligence briefing that included a sheaf of decrypted German and Japanese cable traffic from his spymaster, "C." On good days, he could imagine himself reading over Adolf Hitler's shoulder. He marked up the decrypts with his red ink pen, taking particular delight in comments like "I trust that this information will be confined to Your Excellency and the smallest number of other persons." For security reasons, it had been decided that he should not get copies of the ULTRA decrypts while in the Crimea. Deprived of his best source of intelligence, Churchill felt bereft.

The head of the Map Room, Captain Richard Pim, finally appeared with a battered red box. The dispatch box was organized so that the most urgent messages were always at the top, with routine material down below. In keeping with the "Argonaut" code name for the conference, incoming messages were labeled "Fleece," outgoing "Jason." Churchill focused his attention on a "Fleece" cable near the top of the box concerning the political situation in Greece, which was teetering on the brink of a civil war. He had made a dramatic personal intervention in the crisis in December, flying out to Athens on Christmas morning in an attempt to forestall a Communist insurrection. Order had been restored, but the Communists were now demanding a general amnesty and seats in a coalition government. The prime minister dictated a "Jason" telegram to Athens instructing his representatives to hold firm against the Communist demands.

Churchill observed certain rituals meticulously wherever he was in the world. At the top of his list of requirements was a big bed, not primarily for sleeping, but as a place to work. He had made this very clear during his first visit to the White House in December 1942 when he refused the offer of the Lincoln Bedroom. "Won't do," he had complained. "Bed's not right." After switching to a bedroom with a larger bed, he made sure that the White House staff understood his other needs. "One, I don't like talking outside my quarters. Two, I hate whistling in the corridors. And three, I must have a tumbler of sherry in my room before breakfast, a couple of glasses of scotch and soda before lunch, and French champagne and well-aged brandy before I go to sleep at night."

The prime minister remained in bed all morning, reading the papers in the dispatch box and scrawling notes in the margin. His advance team had experienced some difficulty persuading the Russians of the importance of a large bed. They finally succeeded on protocol grounds: the president had been allocated a double bed so it was clearly unacceptable for the leader of Great Britain to sleep in anything smaller. A bed of appropriate size was ordered from Moscow, arriving just in time to avert a diplomatic crisis. Churchill summoned his staff with the aid of a little bell next to his bed.

"Sawyers, Sawyers. Where are my glasses?"

The valet assumed a soothing, Jeeves-like expression and pointed to the pocket of his master's dressing gown.

"There, sir."

Another ring of the bell. The prime ministerial fountain pen needed filling with more red ink. Marian Holmes, one of his favorite secretaries, appeared. She had seen Churchill in various states of dress and undress and was accustomed to his rapidly changing moods. He could be infuriating, almost childish, in his demands, but was always great fun. He was given to outbursts like "Get hold of that bloody fly and wring its neck!" He treated his staff members abysmally but made them feel privileged to be part of a special, albeit crazy, family. At times, he was very considerate, expressing concern for their welfare. "What a hole I've brought you to!" he told Holmes after the long journey from London to the Crimea.

A sticky sliding door separated Churchill's bedroom from the office where the secretaries worked. Holmes could only get it open a few inches. The sight of the prim, convent-educated twenty-three-year-old squeezing through the narrow opening amused the seventy-year-old warlord. He burst out laughing.

"You look like a lizard."

To those who did not know him well, his work habits could seem disorganized, even chaotic. But there was a method to the madness. The time he spent in bed in the morning was part of his preparation for the "big show" in the afternoon. He composed memorable lines in his head and tested them on his "secret circle" prior to unleashing them on the president and the marshal. He had a unique ability to combine the sententious and the trivial in almost the same breath: back home in Britain, he would rehearse an important speech to the House of Commons while simultaneously carrying on conversations with his beloved marmalade cat. The aging thespian knew how to husband his energy so that he rose to the big occasion.

Lunch was served, in bed, at 1:30 p.m., following consultations with the foreign secretary. By the time lunch was over, Churchill was ready for his hour-long afternoon nap. He often stayed up until three in the morning, rising at eight. The siesta enabled him to "press a day and a half's work into one" and survive on five hours' regular sleep. But first he had to make sure that everything was in its proper place. Another irritated ring of the bell.

"Sawyers, where is my hot-water bottle?"

"You are sitting on it, sir. Not a very good idea."

"It's not an idea, it's a coincidence," replied the PM, amused by his riposte. Soon he was snoring soundly.

The prime minister woke from his nap like "a giant refreshed." He took a bath, drawn for him by Sawyers. The valet patted him down with a huge towel and helped him on with his regimental uniform. As a young lieutenant, Churchill had taken part in the British Army's last significant cavalry charge, at the Battle of Omdurman in 1898. Pink faced and rested, the colonel in chief of the Fourth Queen's Own Hussars was finally ready to do battle with Stalin and Roosevelt.

In addition to the bedroom and bathroom, Churchill's suite on the ground floor of the Vorontsov Palace consisted of an office for his secretaries, a small dining room, and his Map Room. Beyond the Map Room were a conservatory, billiard room, and baronial banquet hall. The palace was a mix of jarring architectural styles. The original owner, Prince Mikhail Vorontsov, had been raised on Arabian folk tales and romantic Scottish novels, and had decorated his castle with crenellated towers and battlements, Tudor chimney tops resembling minarets, Arabian-style fountains, finely sculptured lions in various states of repose, and soaring Persian arches inlaid with mosaic.

"You never saw such a place," a senior British diplomat, Alexander Cadogan, reported to his wife. "It's a big house, of indescribable ugliness— a sort of Gothic Balmoral—with all the furnishings of an almost terrifying hideosity." Sarah Churchill was a little kinder, describing the villa as "quite fantastic . . . a bit like a Scottish baronial hall inside and a Swiss chalet plus mosque outside!" Like the FDR and Stalin residences, the Vorontsov Palace at Alupka had been saved from destruction by the greed of the Nazis. Earmarked as war booty, it had served as the headquarters for the German military commander Erich von Manstein. When the Germans retreated from the Crimea in the spring of 1944, they did not have time to blow the place up.

Churchill was excited to find family portraits of some distant relatives, the Herberts, hanging on either side of the fireplace in the dining room. It turned out that Prince Vorontsov's sister had married a Herbert while their father was serving as Russian ambassador to the Court of St. James's in the early nineteenth century.

It was 3:30 p.m., time to leave for the conference, which had been moved forward from five to four, at Roosevelt's insistence. The cornice road between Alupka and Livadia ran along a stretch of mountainous coastline. From Alupka, Churchill drove three miles toward Koreiz, where Stalin was staying, and a further five miles to Livadia. Dolphins feeding on shoals of fish were visible off the coast, along with gulls and cormorants. The little town of Yalta, with its crumbling sanatoria for tuberculosis patients and memorials to its most celebrated resident, Anton Chekhov, was another four miles farther on.

The Big Three meeting should have been a moment of triumph for the already legendary British leader. After five and a half years of war, including eighteen months when his country stood virtually alone against the Nazis, victory was at last within sight. But illness, physical exhaustion, and a host of worries about what the peace would bring prevented him from fully savoring the occasion. He seemed to have recovered from a fever and high temperature the previous week, but, as his doctor noted, it was not "the flesh only that is weaker." His spirits were also down. He suffered from intermittent bouts of depression. Moran had recognized the symptoms in Malta when his patient turned his face to the wall and called for his wife, Clementine, a continent away in England.

Churchill thrived on adversity. As long as he was at the center of events, making history through the sheer force of his will, what he euphemistically called his Black Dog remained in check. His "finest hour" had come in 1940 when he inspired Britain, and the world, to resist the Nazi juggernaut. It was then that he "felt as if I were walking with Destiny." He had become leader of a country in its hour of despair, promised his people nothing but "blood, toil, tears, and sweat," and defied seemingly insurmountable odds. By comparison, everything that came after was almost mundane. As usual, Churchill coined the perfect expression to describe the new, unglamorous phase of the war: "We must just KBO." *Keep Buggering On.* Once Russia and America came into the war in 1941, history ceased to revolve around the man with the cigar. KBO became his operative mode.

Churchill understood better than most of his advisers that military power, and therefore the power of strategic decision making, had shifted to Stalin and Roosevelt. He could not help but feel that he had become the junior Allied partner. The disparity in contributions to the war effort became particularly evident after the invasion of Normandy in June 1944. Churchill had to remind his generals that Britain had only contributed a quarter of the troops involved in the D-day landings and could not expect to have a dominant voice in the shaping of military strategy. The contrast was even starker with the eastern front. To put it at its simplest, America was funding the war against Hitler, and Russia was doing most of the fighting.

The prime minister imagined himself as "a small lion . . . walking between a huge Russian bear and a great American elephant." But still, he secretly hoped, "it would prove to be the lion which knew the way."

A slightly different cast of characters was gathered around the table at the end of the Livadia ballroom for the second day of the conference. Diplomats in dark suits now sat in the chairs previously occupied by generals and admirals. The prickly Jimmy Byrnes had finally claimed his place midway between FDR and Churchill. Enamel cigarette cases and matchboxes appeared in front of each delegate, alongside the ashtrays.

Churchill was taken aback by an unexpected pronouncement from the president. The United States wanted to preserve the peace but not at the expense of maintaining a large army for an indefinite period of time three thousand miles from home. American troops could not stay in Europe "much more than two years." Congress would never agree to an openended commitment.

"Formidable questions" formed in Churchill's mind as he digested this "momentous statement." If the Americans withdrew, "Britain would have to occupy single-handed the entire western portion of Germany. Such a task would be far beyond our strength." There would be little to prevent the Red Army from pushing into western Europe from eastern Europe. He felt all the more determined to push for a bigger role for France in the postwar occupation of Germany. France was the only European power capable of building up an army of sufficient size to contain a resurgent Germany—or an expansionist Russia.

Churchill thought, correctly, that he had greater experience dealing with Stalin than Roosevelt. Prior to Yalta, FDR had met with the dictator just once, in Tehran, in November 1943. The Englishman had made two additional trips to Moscow, the first in August 1942, when he assigned himself the unenviable task of delivering the news that there would be no "second front" until mid-1944. Stalin accused the British of being "scared" of the Germans, but made amends by inviting Churchill to a dinner in his private Kremlin apartment that lasted until 3:00 a.m. The prime minister returned to Moscow in October 1944 when he negotiated his infamous "percentages" deal with Stalin. Anxious to prevent Russia gaining control over Greece, the eastern Mediterranean, and the trade routes to India, Churchill jotted down proposed spheres of influence in the Balkans on a scrap of paper, reproduced below:

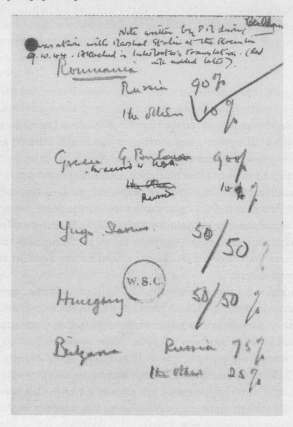

Churchill later described how he pushed the piece of paper across the table. After examining it for a few seconds, Stalin expressed his approval with a large blue check mark. There was an awkward silence as the document lay in the center of the table. The Englishman suggested burning the paper to avoid the impression that "we had disposed of these issues, so fateful to millions of people, in such an offhand manner." Stalin dismissed this concern.

"No, you keep it."

The percentages deal strengthened Churchill's view of Stalin as a pragmatic leader with whom he could do business, despite the ideological gulf. He had originally viewed Bolshevism as a "great evil," comparable to Nazism, and Russians as a "vast, dumb people . . . ruled by terror, fanaticisms and the Secret Police." When the Germans invaded Russia in June 1941, Churchill acted according to the "enemy of my enemy is my friend" principle. Now, suddenly, Mother Russia had fallen victim to the hideous "Nazi war machine, with its clanking, heel-clicking, dandified Prussian officers," commanding "brutish masses of Hun soldiery plodding on like a swarm of crawling locusts." He explained his remarkable about-face in typically lighthearted fashion: "If Hitler invaded Hell, I would at least make a favorable reference to the Devil in the House of Commons." Churchill veered between being awed by Stalin and being repelled by him. Trying to maintain good relations with a Communist, he told his aides, was "like wooing a crocodile. You do not know whether to tickle it under the chin or to beat it over the head. When it opens its mouth you cannot tell whether it is trying to smile or preparing to eat you up."

In the words of one of Stalin's earliest biographers, Isaac Deutscher, they made a strange couple, "the descendant of the Duke of Marlborough and the son of serfs, the one born in Blenheim Palace, the other in a one-room hovel." Churchill was combustible, "full of eccentric idiosyncrasies," a hangover from Victorian England "whose imperial heritage he was guarding with the full vigor of his romantic temperament." Stalin thought long and hard about his every move and "had in him all the severity of Tsarist and Bolshevik Russia, whose storms he had ridden in cool, icy self-possession." Their differences made them great sparring partners. They thrived on each other's hostility and warmed to each other's quirks. Stalin had a grudging respect for people who stood up to him, like Churchill and General de Gaulle, and became more animated in their presence. Churchill came to like, even trust, the man he knew to be a brutal dictator. "I have had very nice talks with the old Bear," he wrote Clementine in October 1944, after his Kremlin dinner with Stalin. "I like him the more I see him. Now they respect us and I am sure they wish to work with us." Churchill felt that if he could only "dine with Stalin once a week, there would be no trouble at all. We get on like a house on fire."

Churchill's main concern about Stalin was that he was surrounded by shady, sinister forces in the Kremlin who had no interest in good relations with the West. The idea that Stalin was not fully in command of his own little circle was completely erroneous but was widely shared by western diplomats. Even George Kennan, the most hardheaded Kremlinologist of all, believed that Stalin was severely constrained by "his own extreme dependence on his own friends and advisors" who fed him "misleading information" and took advantage of "his ignorance, his extreme seclusion, and his suspicious Georgian nature." The truth was that western politicians and diplomats understood very little of the inner workings of Soviet politics, which Churchill himself had described, in a speech at the beginning of the war, as "a riddle wrapped in a mystery inside an enigma."

Stalin asked his former ambassador to London, Ivan Maisky, to outline Russia's demands for postwar reparations from Germany, which were based on the doctrine of proportional compensation. Since Russia had suffered the most in the war, and had contributed the most to victory, it was only right that she should receive the largest share of the spoils. Maisky mentioned a figure of $20 billion, with $10 billion reserved for Russia. This seemed a fantastic sum to Churchill, who doubted that Germany could ever pay such a bill. Under the Maisky plan, Germany would be left with only 20 percent of its heavy industry. That meant that Germany would be forced to take out large loans from the United States, as had happened after World War I, or there would be mass starvation.

"If you want a horse to pull a wagon, you have to give it some fodder."

Stalin reluctantly conceded the point but added a characteristic twist. "That's right, but you need to take care that the horse doesn't turn around and kick you."

Churchill switched to a nonkicking analogy. "If you have a motor car, you must give it a certain amount of petrol to make it go."

The discussion went round in circles, before the session wound up at 8:00 p.m. with nothing being decided. "It's always the same with these Conferences: they take days to get on the rails," Cadogan complained in a letter back home. "The Great Men don't know what they're talking about and have to be educated, and made a bit more tidy in their methods. I think we're making some progress, but this place is still rather a madhouse."

The prime minister returned to the Vorontsov Palace to dine with Eden and his daughter Sarah. There was still a depressing lack of information from home. His private secretary, John Martin, was saddened "to hear Colonel Kent calling again and again for news and being offered only caviar."

Churchill's spirits improved after the five-course Russian meal. A terrific fire had been built for him in the dining room. He leaned back in a cushioned armchair, sipping brandy and taking occasional puffs on his cigar, surrounded by portraits of Russian and British aristocrats. Except for the mountains outside, he might have been back at Chartwell or Chequers. The food, the alcohol, and the sense of being in familiar surroundings caused him to forget all his earlier warnings about the disasters that would ensue if the Big Three met in the Crimea. "I don't know why people grumble about Yalta," he told his aides. "I find it very comfortable indeed. I think it is a very nice place."

Churchill's comment became the subject of grim amusement to his staff members, who were living on top of one another in the rest of the villa. There was a strange dichotomy between "the luxuriousness and even magnificence" of huge meals served by waitresses with starched white aprons tottering around on new high-heeled shoes and "the inconvenience and squalor" of the living accommodation. The British chiefs of staff ate "squashed up in the only other dining room" and had to make a detour "into the garden and through the mud to get to their bedrooms in order not to disturb the P.M." Many Britons had been tormented by bedbugs; even Churchill was bitten the first night prior to a thorough delousing of the premises by an American sanitation team.

The washroom situation was even direr in the Vorontsov Palace than Livadia. Inside the main house, there was one bathroom for twenty-four people. "Efforts to keep a roster were frustrated by individual enterprise as each V.I.P. tried to outdo the other by getting up earlier and earlier to catch the bath." Field marshals sent their batmen to stand in line for them. The head of the Royal Air Force, Sir Charles Portal, resorted to picking the lock of the door with a piece of wood and evicting "anti-social people who didn't realize that it is a bad show to spend half an hour in the bath." One morning, he burst in on a blushing field marshal who stumbled out, "clutching his dressing gown round him." Another morning, he surprised Churchill's valet, Sawyers. "He hopped out of the bath and put on his pajamas without drying himself, but I got my shaving water all right!"

A communal bathroom had been set up in a little hut in the garden, with "a sweet peasant girl in attendance who scrubbed your back vigorously, irrespective of your sex. . . . You ploughed down the garden in your great coat and hoped you wouldn't get pneumonia returning." The garden also served as a communal toilet. Impeccably raised Britons "lost all

shame and openly discussed the best bushes" to visit without being seen by
the ubiquitous guards. Behind a Lenin statue was a popular spot. Delegates
would later agree that the bathroom and toilet facilities were the "most
generally discussed subject" at the Yalta conference after the war itself.

Cultural differences abounded. The Russians could not understand
the reluctance of the English female secretaries to "bath and swim in the
nude together" with the men, as was the custom in the Red Army. The
British were taken aback by the universal absence of bath plugs. They
were also amazed by the extreme lengths the Russians were prepared to
go to satisfy some of their needs, such as flying in lemon trees from the
other side of the Black Sea so that Churchill could enjoy his gin and ton-
ics and FDR could add a lemon twist to his martinis. Another source of
puzzlement was the "extraordinary fashion" in which the Russians made
up beds, folding the top sheet and blankets into "a sort of envelope" that
had to be taken apart and remade before getting in.

The lavish Russian hospitality contrasted with the penury and devastation that Churchill had seen with his own eyes in the Crimea. He had also
read newspaper reports describing forty-mile-long columns of German
women and children fleeing the advance of the Russian armies. "I am
clearly convinced that they deserve it," he wrote Clementine, "but that
does not remove it from one's gaze. The misery of the whole world appalls
me and I fear increasingly that new struggles may arise out of those we
are successfully ending." That night, before going to sleep, he shared his
worries with Sarah. "I do not suppose that at any moment in history has
the agony of the world been so great or widespread. Tonight the sun goes
down on more suffering than ever before in the world."

Churchill was an indefatigable traveler and explorer. He had already
logged tens of thousands of miles during the course of the war, crossing
the Atlantic six times to meet with Roosevelt, in addition to his two trips to
Moscow to meet with Stalin. He had persuaded FDR to make the reverse
journey across the ocean for conferences in Casablanca, Cairo, and Tehran.
He had also made many solo trips across the English Channel to buck up
the French when they were on the verge of defeat in the spring of 1940, and
to flag his support for British troops as they advanced into Nazi-occupied
Europe after D-day. It was at his suggestion that the Yalta meeting was
code-named Argonaut, evoking the heroic voyagers of ancient Greece. He
was a firm believer in the value of face-to-face diplomacy, deriding the

telegraph and other modern communication technologies as "dead, blank walls compared to personal contacts."

All these journeys involved a good deal of danger—not merely from enemy fire. The risks were underlined by the loss of one of the two planes that had accompanied the prime minister from Britain to Malta. The RAF York transport plane overshot the island and crashed into the sea, killing most people onboard, including personal aides to both Churchill and Eden. Churchill blamed the accident on "the strange ways of fate." He understood he owed his own survival to luck, as much as anything else. He had been shot at many times in his life, beginning with the Cuban Revolution of 1895. "Bullets are not worth considering," he wrote his mother after coming under fire for the first time on his twenty-first birthday. "Besides I am so conceited that I do not think the Gods would create so potent a being for so prosaic an ending." Knowing he might not return from one of his wartime excursions, he wrote a letter to King George VI naming Eden as his designated successor.

As the wartime summits became larger and more grandiose, they lost much of their country-house intimacy. During his first trip to Washington, in December 1941, Churchill had simply moved into the White House, living, eating, and working alongside FDR for three straight weeks. At Tehran, Roosevelt joined Stalin in the Soviet embassy to avoid the security risks of commuting from the American embassy on the other side of town. At Yalta, the residences of the three leaders were several miles apart from one another, but other traditions were maintained. Delegates greeted one another like long-lost friends, sharing jokes and anecdotes. Even the domestic staff was part of the extended Big Three family. At breakfast the first morning in the Livadia Palace, a Russian waiter rushed up to embrace Chip Bohlen. It turned out that he had been employed in the U.S. Embassy in Moscow before the war. Living up to his nickname, *Verny Slug,* or "Faithful Servant," the old retainer made sure that Bohlen's room was well stocked with caviar and vodka.

Perhaps the quirkiest of summit rituals was the short-snorter game. Invented by Alaskan bush pilots, it had been embraced by presidents, prime ministers, ambassadors, and generals alike. The rules were simple. A group of people traveling together signed banknotes recording who was present. Anybody unable to produce the banknote upon request at a subsequent meeting was obliged to buy a drink (a "short snort") for his companions. Previous conferences had resulted in countless short snorters signed by everybody from Churchill to George C. Patton. At the second

Yalta plenary session, Harry Hopkins made it his business to get Stalin's signature on a short snorter for his photographer son, Robert. FDR and Churchill had no hesitation signing the ten-ruble note bearing the sacrosanct image of Vladimir Lenin, but Stalin balked, obviously mystified. Roosevelt explained the rules, adding that anybody who flew across the Atlantic could join the club, provided that he was invited by at least two existing members. This gave Stalin an easy way out. He pointed out that he had never flown across the Atlantic and was therefore ineligible.

"I am taking it upon myself to waive that requirement in this instance," replied the president magnanimously. The *vozhd* signed—but was not amused.

The wartime camaraderie concealed growing differences between the Americans and the British, which extended from matters of military strategy to postwar aims. At Malta, British and American commanders had clashed over plans for the invasion of Germany. The British repeatedly called for diversionary attacks on the Wehrmacht in the Mediterranean and elsewhere, which the Americans rejected as a pointless distraction from the main offensive. Senior American officials, including the president, viewed Churchill as a die-hard imperialist determined to hang on to every last colony. The prime minister suspected FDR of transferring his attention, if not his affections, to Stalin. He felt jilted. It wounded him deeply to see the Americans and Russians dealing with each other directly, without consulting him. In general, the Americans were less suspicious of the Russians than were the British, and did not regard the Red Army as an immediate threat.

Although the two leaders remained close, the familiarity, exuberance, and grandeur of the early days of the wartime alliance had faded. Nothing could ever match the emotion of their first meeting, back in August 1941, when they sat together on the deck of a British battleship, the *Prince of Wales,* singing "Onward, Christian Soldiers," united by a common religion, a common cause, and a common language. "Every word seemed to stir the heart," Churchill would recall. "It was a great hour to live." They had marked the occasion by issuing an Atlantic Charter setting out their common war aims:

- No aggrandizement, territorial or other;
- No territorial changes that do not accord with the freely expressed will of the peoples concerned;

- All peoples have the right to choose the form of government under which they will live;
- Free access to trade and raw materials for all states, great or small, victor or vanquished;
- Freedom from fear and want;
- Freedom to traverse the high seas and oceans without hindrance;
- Permanent abandonment of the use of force in international relations.

At their next meeting, in the White House the following December, the president had walked in on a "completely starkers" prime minister, dripping wet from his bath. FDR had apologized and started to retreat but was stopped by the naked Churchill. "You see, Mr. President, I have nothing to hide from you." Roosevelt laughed uproariously, cabling his friend later, "It is fun to be in the same decade with you." By the time they met in Morocco in January 1943, a misty-eyed Churchill was telling his aides, "I love that man." He would confess after the war that "no lover ever studied every whim of his mistress as I did those of President Roosevelt." It was a comment that captured the unequal relationship between the two western leaders, beneath their extrovert exteriors. An impulsive romantic, the Englishman was cast in the role of the wooer. The American was a coldhearted realist, the one being wooed. A voracious reader and chronicler of military campaigns, Churchill loved to talk about the great affairs of state even when he was off duty. Roosevelt relaxed through small talk and trivial routines that had nothing to do with his official cares and obligations. Churchill liked to make long, florid speeches, while Roosevelt preferred the informality of the fireside chat.

Churchill had to wait until the third day of the conference, Tuesday, February 6, for his own private meeting with FDR. They lunched together in the tsar's billiard room of the Livadia Palace with a small group of aides, in front of an arched Tudor fireplace. The lunch had been arranged by Harry Hopkins, who felt that more coordination was required with the British. As often happened, however, Roosevelt did not want to talk substance, preferring to stick to pleasantries that disguised his true intentions. "Quite agreeable and amusing, but not awfully useful," wrote Cadogan, the only other Englishman in attendance. "The President has certainly aged."

To avoid putting too much strain on FDR, Hopkins had agreed with

Anna to wind up the lunch by 2:45 p.m. This would allow both leaders to take a nap before the plenary, which had been scheduled for 4:00. Hopkins offered Churchill use of the tsarevitch's sitting room, overlooking the Black Sea, around the corner from the billiard room. Unfortunately, it was already occupied. General Edwin "Pa" Watson, Roosevelt's military aide, was taking his afternoon nap. The naval aide, Admiral Brown, was in an adjoining army cot. Since there were no closets, their belongings were stacked along the walls. Hopkins sent a navy lieutenant junior grade to tell the two men to make way for the prime minister. The much-loved Pa was known around the White House as the man who loaned his arm to FDR on state occasions as he shuffled to a podium in his iron braces. His main job was to keep everybody relaxed and amused: he had danced the fox-trot with Churchill in Cairo to make up for the lack of female company. But the big, jovial general with the booming voice had suffered a series of heart attacks over the last few months and was gravely ill. He had come to Yalta against the advice of his doctors and was unwilling to give up his bed for anybody.

"You tell Harry Hopkins, if he wants a place for Churchill to take a nap, to give up his own room. The admiral and I are not going to move."

The lieutenant trudged back down the corridor to convey this message to the equally ill Hopkins, who had already retired for *his* afternoon rest. He was unsympathetic. He regarded Pa as a useless hanger-on who was sick much of the time. He raised the stakes, threatening to wake the president from *his* nap if the two aides did not "get out right away." That settled the argument. Complaining vociferously, the dying general surrendered his bed to his former dance partner.

4

Poland

—

After two days of sparring, the Big Three finally reached what Churchill called "the crucial point of the Conference" during the third plenary session on Tuesday, February 6. They had to tackle the problem of Poland, sandwiched between Russia and Germany on a vast plain that had served as an invasion route in both directions for the armies of Napoleon and Hitler, Tsar Alexander and the Mongols. Stalin had been very clear about his demands. He wanted to move the troublesome country nearly two hundred miles to the west by changing its borders. He was determined to ensure that Poland would never again pose a military or political threat to Mother Russia.

For Roosevelt and Churchill, Poland was the touchstone of Stalin's intentions. The war would almost certainly leave the Red Army in control of a vast swath of central and eastern Europe, in addition to a sizable chunk of Germany. As the largest and most important of the countries falling into the Soviet orbit, Poland was key to the future of the entire region. There were now effectively two Polish governments, each with its own army, each claiming to represent 30 million Poles. One government had been based in London since the beginning of the war, when it was forced into exile following the Nazi-Soviet partition of Poland. A second government had been set up in the eastern city of Lublin by the Red Army and was in de facto control of much of the country. As far as America and Britain were concerned, the London government was the legitimate government of Poland; the Soviet Union recognized the Lublin government.

FDR opened the discussion as chairman by striking a conciliatory tone. He noted that the United States was "further away from Poland than anyone else here" and therefore in a position to offer a balanced perspective. He had effectively conceded many of the Soviet Union's territorial demands at Tehran. He agreed that Poland would give up its eastern provinces, where there was a majority Ukrainian and Belorussian population, to the Soviet Union, in return for compensation in the west, at the expense of Germany. Roosevelt urged Stalin to make an exception for the city of Lwów, where Poles were in a majority, but did not press very hard. Instead he stressed the need for a broadly based provisional government to prepare for free elections. American public opinion would not accept the Communist-dominated Lublin government, which represented "only a small section" of the Polish nation. Roosevelt favored the creation of a new government of national unity, representing all the main political parties.

Churchill spoke next. Like Roosevelt, he did not push the territorial issue. In Tehran, he had endorsed the idea of moving Poland to the west, allowing the Soviet Union to retain the territory it had occupied in 1939 under the Molotov-Ribbentrop Pact. By way of illustration, he had placed three matchsticks on the table, representing the Soviet Union, Poland, and Germany. He then rolled the matchsticks east to west "like soldiers at drill executing 'two steps left, close.'" The prime minister now said that "a strong, free, and independent Poland" was much more important than the question of its borders. He reminded Stalin that Britain had gone to war against Germany in September 1939 to protect Poland's independence. This was a point of "honor" for Great Britain that "nearly cost us our own life." He agreed that Poland must not be allowed to "intrigue" against Russia but insisted she "must be mistress in her own house and captain of her own soul."

Stalin asked for a short break. He wanted to collect his thoughts so that he could present his case calmly and forcefully. He, more than anyone else, understood what was at stake. Beneath the fancy words about freedom and independence, an underlying question of political power had to be settled: *Kto kogo? Who* would control *whom?* Moving Poland two hundred miles to the west would achieve two goals simultaneously. At a stroke, Russia would regain all the territory signed away under duress to Germany by Lenin in 1918 as the price for exiting World War I in the humiliating Treaty of Brest-Litovsk. Equally important, Poland would become dependent on Soviet security guarantees in order to succeed in swallowing large chunks of Germany.

The seminarian–turned–central committeeman was a master debater, wearing his rivals down with his remorseless if tortuous logic. He knew how to take the essential point in an opponent's argument and throw it back in his face. When the session resumed, he launched into a riff on Churchill's use of the word "honor." The future of Poland was not simply a matter of "honor" for the Soviet Union; it was also a matter of "security." Poland stood astride the traditional invasion route to Russia from the west. Russia needed a "free, independent, and powerful" Poland to shut this corridor down once and for all.

Next, Stalin ruled out any significant concessions on the territorial question. His proposed new frontier between the Soviet Union and Poland was very similar to the so-called Curzon Line endorsed by Britain and France back in 1919, at the Versailles conference. Then British foreign secretary Lord Curzon had assigned Lwów and the surrounding region to Russia. It would be "shameful" for Soviet leaders to be perceived as "less Russian than Curzon." As the dictator got into his rhetorical stride, he rose from his chair and began making sweeping gestures with his healthy right arm. To those who knew him well, this was a sure sign of his inner agitation and resolve. Ivan Maisky thought he was about to leave the conference table and walk around the ballroom, as he did in his Kremlin office, but he restrained himself. Instead, he merely pushed the chair back and spoke "with unusual fervor."

It was getting late. Hopkins was seated behind FDR, along with Alger Hiss of the State Department. He was concerned about the health of his boss, who was looking even more feeble than usual. He scribbled a note and passed it forward. "Mr. President: Why not let this wind up today when Stalin is thru—and say we will talk it over tomorrow."

Stalin was far from finished, however. People might call him "a dictator" but he had "enough democratic feeling to refuse to create a Polish government without the Poles being consulted." The problem was that the rival governments were not on speaking terms: they denounced each other as "criminals and bandits." Supporters of the London government were raiding Soviet arms depots; they had already killed 212 Russian soldiers. In Stalin's view, the Lublin government was "good" because it was establishing peace in the rear of the Red Army. The London government was "bad" because it was disrupting military operations.

"Without a secure rear there can be no more victories for the Red Army. Any military man, and even the non-military man, will understand this situation."

FDR tried to bring the session to a close, but Churchill, who had fortified himself with a "snifter" during the break, insisted on the last word. He agreed that attacks on the Red Army should be punished, but said the Lublin government lacked popular legitimacy. Some kind of compromise was necessary.

"Poland has been a source of trouble for over five hundred years," remarked a weary Roosevelt, finally ending the discussion.

Poor health had made Roosevelt less tolerant of Churchill's idiosyncrasies and particularly his excessive volubility. He had once joked that "Winston has fifty ideas a day, and three or four are good." Alone with Byrnes after the meeting on Poland, he grumbled that the lengthy session was "Winston's fault because he made too many speeches."

"Yes, he did," agreed the "assistant president," now restored to intimate status. "But they were good speeches."

FDR laughed. "Winston doesn't make any other kind."

Behind the scenes of the conference, frantic efforts were under way to conserve the president's waning strength. Anna had formed an alliance with the cardiologist Howard Bruenn, who had finally decided to confide in her, against the wishes of his superior, Vice Admiral McIntire. She was doing her best to keep "the unnecessary people" out of her father's way and "steer the necessary ones in at the best times." Roosevelt himself was contributing to the problem. "He gets all wound up, seems to thoroughly enjoy it all, but wants too many people around, and then doesn't go to bed early enough. The result is that he doesn't sleep well." Anna confided her concerns in a letter to her husband, John Boettiger:

> I have found out thru Bruenn (who won't let me tell Ross that I know) that this "ticker" situation is far more serious than I ever knew. And, the biggest difficulty in handling the situation here is that we can, of course, tell no one of the "ticker" trouble. It's truly worrisome—and

there's not a heluva lot anyone can do about it. (Better tear off and destroy this paragraph.)

The impasse over Poland imposed an extra strain on FDR. He knew that Stalin was in a position to dictate terms, as his troops occupied most of the country. The time had come to play what he imagined to be his trump card: he would make a personal appeal to the Russian dictator urging him to compromise. He dictated his thoughts to Bohlen, emphasizing the danger of an open rift on the Polish issue. Americans were asking themselves, "If we cannot get a meeting of the minds now when our armies are converging on the common enemy, how can we get an understanding on even more vital things in the future?" Roosevelt suggested summoning a representative group of Polish leaders to Yalta to hammer out an agreement on a future provisional government in the presence of the Big Three.

The president signed the letter and sent it to the Yusupov Palace before retiring to bed.

Five miles away, in Koreiz, Stalin was meeting with his military advisers in the *Stavka* on the ground floor of his gray stucco villa. He had spent the last week debating whether to authorize an all-out assault on Berlin. His frontline commanders, particularly Vasily Chuikov, the hero of Stalingrad, wanted to push ahead. Now that Soviet troops were across the Oder River, Chuikov was convinced that the enemy capital could be captured in as little as ten days, before Hitler was able to summon sufficient reinforcements. The General Staff opposed a lightning advance. They were worried about a counterattack by German forces in Poland and East Prussia, exploiting gaping holes in the Soviet line and driving a wedge between the armies of Zhukov, in the center, and his fellow marshal, Konstantin Rokossovsky, in the north.

The situation had become clearer over the last few days. A sudden thaw had melted the ice on the Oder, making it much more difficult to get Russian troops across the river and consolidate the bridgeheads on the western bank. Zhukov's forces had made stunning progress, covering three hundred miles in twenty days, but were now overstretched and undersupplied. During the most recent offensive, some units had recorded casualty rates of 35 to 45 percent and tank losses that were almost as heavy. In the meantime, the *vozhd* had learned from Roosevelt and Churchill that the western Allies would not be crossing the Rhine until the middle of March at the earliest. There was no risk of Eisenhower reaching Berlin before Zhukov. To launch an all-out attack on Berlin at this point was not only extremely risky. It was also unnecessary.

Another factor weighing on Stalin's mind was the struggle for power in Poland. As he had indicated in the afternoon plenary session, Soviet troops were facing heavy resistance from the underground Polish Home Army, which was loyal to the government-in-exile in London. The Home Army had suffered a catastrophic reverse the previous summer when it lost twenty thousand fighters during a failed two-month uprising in Warsaw but still retained significant popular support. Home Army leaders bore a lasting grudge against the Russians for waiting on the opposite bank of the Vistula River while the uprising was brutally suppressed by the Germans. They suspected Stalin of wanting the Nazis to kill as many pro-London Poles as possible prior to the liberation of Warsaw by Soviet forces. The *vozhd* had condemned the leaders of the uprising as political adventurists; he had even refused permission for Allied aircraft to land on Soviet territory after dropping supplies over Warsaw. Home Army leaders now viewed Russia—not Germany—as their principal enemy. Over the last few weeks, they had organized a series of attacks on Red Army supply lines and police stations set up by the Communist-dominated Lublin government. To counter the threat from the Home Army, Stalin had to station three NKVD divisions in Poland, troops that could otherwise be used against the Wehrmacht.

In military matters, as in politics, Stalin preferred to move cautiously rather than strike out blindly. Bukharin had once called him the *genialny dozirovshchik,* the "genius of dosage." He knew when to advance, when to retreat, and when to consolidate his gains. He liked to keep his options open for as long as possible, wearing down opponents and probing for weaknesses before striking the decisive blow. The prospect of ending the war with a lightning attack on Berlin was certainly attractive, allowing the Red Army to penetrate deep into Germany. But the risks were too great. It was better to gain full control of Poland and East Prussia before finishing off Hitler.

The *vozhd* picked up the special high-frequency phone that had been installed in the Yusupov Palace to provide a direct link with the field commanders. Zhukov came on the line. He was attending a conference with Chuikov and other frontline generals. Maps of Berlin and the Oder were laid out on the table.

"What are you doing?" Stalin demanded.

"We are planning the operation against Berlin."

"You are wasting your time." The *vozhd* ordered Zhukov to turn north, protect his right flank, and close the gap with Rokossovsky's forces. A German breakout from Pomerania and northern Poland must be prevented at all costs. Chuikov "understood that the offensive against Berlin was being postponed for an indefinite period."

The weather had improved markedly since the start of the conference, and it was now unseasonably warm for early February, with temperatures in the forties. Wednesday, February 7, was a day of bright sunshine, combined with a brisk wind from the east. As Churchill and his daughter drove past Stalin's villa on the road to Livadia, they stared ahead at the austere granite peaks. Apart from the ubiquitous Soviet guards, every hundred yards or so, there was little sign of modern civilization. The sun "shone so hard on the sea that the reflection made one blink," Sarah noted. The scene reminded the prime minister of something. Eventually he blurted it out.

"The Riviera of Hades."

When the conference reconvened at 4:00 p.m. for the fourth plenary session, Stalin complained that he had just received the president's letter of the previous night and had been unable to act on his suggestions on Poland. He had tried to reach leaders of the Lublin government by telephone, but they were traveling. He did not know the addresses of the opposition leaders. There was "not sufficient time" to bring them to Yalta.

Stalin gave the floor to Molotov to read what he presented as a compromise proposal. The Soviets were still insisting on the Curzon Line as Poland's eastern frontier but were willing to make adjustments "in some regions of five to eight kilometers in favor of Poland." Poland's western frontier would follow the line of the Oder and Western Neisse Rivers, deep inside the Third Reich. It was "considered desirable" to add "some democratic leaders from Polish émigré circles" to the Lublin government; the "enlarged government" would then be formally recognized by Washington, London, and Moscow. Elections for a new parliament should be held as soon as possible.

There were no maps at hand as the Soviet commissar for foreign affairs outlined his proposals for Poland's new frontiers. Churchill later acknowledged that he did not grasp the distinction between the Western (Lusatian) and Eastern (Glatzer) Neisse, two tributaries of the Oder. This point was also lost on FDR, who had failed to read a State Department study showing that the region between the two rivers was roughly equivalent in size to Massachusetts, with a population of 2.7 million ethnic Germans. This was in addition to the 7 million Germans, and 2 million Poles, who would be uprooted under previous plans already approved in principle by Churchill and Roosevelt. The bottom line was that Stalin was proposing the forcible relocation of some 12 million people inhabiting territories equivalent in area to Italy or Arizona. The State Department briefing paper went on to predict that such huge population transfers would turn Poland into a "full-fledged Soviet satellite" entirely dependent on Moscow for protection.

The population transfers would represent the biggest single episode of organized ethnic cleansing in history, larger than Hitler's extermination of 6 million Jews, although not as deadly. Even though he did not grasp the full scale of the proposed demographic upheaval, Churchill was taken aback. He told Stalin there was "a large school of thought in England which is shocked at the idea of transferring millions of people by force." He himself did not share such sentiments, but he doubted that Poland could absorb such huge territories in the West.

"It would be a great pity to stuff the Polish goose so full of German food that it dies of indigestion," said Churchill.

Stalin believed that the problem would solve itself. There would soon be "no more Germans" left in these territories. In general, "when our troops come in, the Germans run away."

A chill descended on the large white ballroom. Germany had committed unspeakable atrocities against Russia in the early years of the war and was now being repaid in an orgy of killing, raping, and looting. Although western leaders did not have direct sources of information from Poland and East Prussia, they could guess what was going on. The hugely popular Soviet propagandist Ilya Ehrenburg had long incited Red Army troops to kill as many Germans as possible, without making a distinction between soldiers and civilians. "The Germans are not human beings," he declared in a widely distributed 1943 pamphlet, titled simply "Kill." "If you have not killed at least one German a day, you have wasted that day. . . . If you kill one German, kill another. There is nothing more amusing for us than a pile of German corpses." Now that Soviet soldiers were fighting on

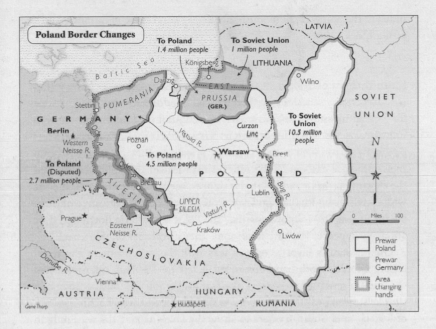

Poland Border Changes

To Poland
1.4 million people

To Soviet Union
1 million people

LATVIA

Königsberg

Baltic Sea

Danzig

LITHUANIA

Wilno

EAST
PRUSSIA
(GER.)

SOVIET

UNION

Stettin

POMERANIA

GERMANY

Berlin

*Western
Neisse R.*

Krsia R.

Curzon
Line

To Soviet
Union
10.5 million
people

N

Poznań

Warsaw

Brest

To Poland
4.5 million people

P O L A N D

To Poland
(Disputed)
2.7 million people

Breslau

SILESIA

Lublin

Bug R.

0   Miles   100

Prague

UPPER
SILESIA

Vistula R.

Kraków

Lwów

Prewar
Poland

Eastern
Neisse R.

Prewar
Germany

C Z E C H O S L O V A K I A

Danube R.

Vienna

AUSTRIA

HUNGARY

ROMANIA

Area
changing
hands

Budapest

Gene Thorp

German soil, he stepped up his demands for retribution. "German towns are burning. I am happy, Germany, you now whirl round in circles, and burn, and howl in your deathly agony; the hour of revenge has struck."

Roosevelt and Churchill were also slow to pick up on Molotov's reference to an *enlarged* Polish government as opposed to a new government. The choice of adjective was crucial. A *new* government, as proposed by Roosevelt in his letter the previous evening, would represent a real compromise between Communists and non-Communists. An *enlarged* government, as outlined by Molotov, would build on the existing Communist-dominated Lublin government, adding a few token outsiders. The basic structure of power would not be affected. It was a controversy that would consume months of diplomatic argument, but its significance was not immediately apparent.

"I think we are making definite progress," said Roosevelt.

Stalin continued to strike Cadogan as "much the most impressive" negotiator of the Big Three. "Uncle Joe is in great form," the Eton-educated diplomat wrote his wife. "The President flapped about and the P.M. boomed, but Joe just sat taking it all in and being rather amused. When he did chip in, he never used a superfluous word, and spoke very much to the point. He's obviously got a very good sense of humor—and a rather quick temper!"

Stalin thought of Poland in the manner of the tsars, as a country that was perpetually scheming against Russia. In addition to being a corridor for foreign invasions, Poland was also a conduit for undesirable western influence. In Russian operas, such as *Boris Godunov,* Polish rulers are traditionally surrounded by wily Catholic priests, looking for ways to extend their influence eastward. The refined manners of the Polish court, and the elegant mazurka and polonaise dances, seem like affectations, at odds with rough-hewn Russian honesty. Poland was an eternal source of trouble for Russia; in Molotov's words, "the Poles never calm down and they are never at peace. They are irrational. They are always on one's neck."

One of Stalin's favorite operas was *Ivan Susanin.* Prior to the revolution, Glinka's work had been titled *A Life for the Tsar,* but Stalin had the libretto rewritten to remove the tsar and emphasize the heroism of a simple Russian peasant. The opera is set in 1613, during a Polish invasion of Russia. In it, Susanin offers to show the foreign army the way, only to lead them into a dense forest from which there is no escape. When the Poles realize they have been tricked, they kill Susanin. Too late: their own fate has been sealed. Stalin liked to sit in his box in the Bolshoi Theatre, occasionally munching a hard-boiled egg, his eyes fixed grimly on the stage as the Polish soldiers froze to death in the snow. He always left the theater immediately afterward rather than remain behind for the final act of triumphant Russian celebration. He was frequently accompanied by his daughter, Svetlana, who could not understand his fascination for "this destruction of Poles in a forest." She later speculated that it reminded her father of a more recent massacre of Polish officers that took place in the woods of Katyn.

The Katyn tragedy was a prime example of Stalin's genius for turning difficult, even impossible, situations to his advantage. On March 5, 1940, the *vozhd* had signed a secret decree, drafted by Beria, to "apply the supreme penalty, shooting" to Polish POWs who refused to accept Soviet authority. A total of 21,857 Poles, mainly army officers captured during the Russian invasion of Poland, were executed as a result of this order. The bodies of many of the Poles were dumped in mass graves in the forest of Katyn, where they were discovered by the Germans three years later, in April 1943. The Nazis seized the opportunity to drive a wedge between the Soviet Union and its western Allies. They published evidence of the crime, including photographs of Polish officers shot in the back of the head and diary entries that ceased abruptly in March 1940. The German claims seemed shockingly plausible to the Polish government-in-exile, which had tried to find out what had happened to the imprisoned compatriots for more than three years, only to be fobbed off with lame excuses.

Rather than acknowledge responsibility for the missing Poles, Stalin raised the stakes, accusing the government-in-exile of siding with the Nazis. HITLER'S POLISH COLLABORATORS! ran the headline in *Pravda* on April 19, 1943. A week later, Moscow broke off diplomatic relations with the London Poles for failing "to offer a rebuff to the vile Fascist calumny." The Russians accused the Nazis of murdering the Polish prisoners and fabricating evidence against the Soviet Union. The Soviet counterclaims were riddled with contradictions, but this scarcely mattered. As far as Stalin was concerned, anyone who questioned his story was undermining the war effort against the Nazis. The Soviet government stuck with Stalin's version of events for almost half a century, right up until the collapse of communism in 1991, when the execution orders were finally made public.

Stalin had maneuvered the London Poles, and their western patrons, into a trap as cunning and complete as the one devised by Susanin. He now had the perfect excuse for refusing to do business with a government he deemed deeply anti-Russian. The Poles faced an impossible choice. They could either participate in a lie or be branded as traitors. A similar dilemma confronted the British and American governments. Unwilling to break with the country that was doing most of the actual fighting against the Germans, they were forced to maintain an uncomfortable silence. Both Roosevelt and Churchill actively discouraged efforts to tell the truth about Katyn. Stalin had converted a position of weakness into a position of strength.

The precise political complexion of a future Polish government was of less concern to the Russian leader than the issue of personal loyalty. It was important to maintain democratic appearances. Countries liberated by the Red Army would be allowed to keep their parliaments, their political systems, and even their kings and queens. Communist power would be exercised behind the scenes, through the "power ministries" that controlled the police and the army. Stalin advised the ideologically rigid Yugoslav Communists not to do anything that would unnecessarily antagonize the western Allies. "What do you want with red stars on your caps?" he angrily asked a Yugoslav delegation. "The form is not important but what is gained, and you—red stars! By God, there's no need for stars!"

Stalin was willing to allow two or three outsiders into the Polish provisional government that he had established to replace the London-based government-in-exile. But he would not budge on the core principle of political control. His position was virtually identical to the position of Tsar Alexander who informed a British foreign secretary, back in 1815, that the question of Poland "could only end in one way, as he was in possession."

Eastern Europe was not the only prize coveted by Stalin as his reward for victory in World War II. He wanted to extend his vast empire in the opposite direction by extracting territorial concessions from Japan and China that would redress the humiliating defeats of tsarist times. Although Russia had a nonaggression pact with Japan, Stalin now saw an opportunity to enter the Pacific war on the side of the victors.

The secret deal was consummated in a thirty-minute meeting between Stalin and Roosevelt on the afternoon of Thursday, February 8. The *vozhd* agreed to declare war on Japan within "two or three months" of Germany's surrender. In return, Russia would receive the southern part of the island of Sakhalin and the Kurile Islands from Japan. In addition, its interests in the Chinese province of Manchuria would be restored, including the right to lease a warm-water naval base at Port Arthur. While Sakhalin had belonged to Russia prior to the 1904 war with Japan, the Soviet claim to the Kurile Islands was much more tenuous. The southern section of the Kuriles had never been part of Russia and was regarded by the State Department as "historically and ethnically Japanese."

Stalin prepared carefully for his meeting with the president. Beria supplied him with daily transcripts of bugged conversations involving Roosevelt, Churchill, and their advisers. The NKVD had long-distance direction microphones that were able to pick up outdoor conversations, in addition to bugs in their offices and private rooms. The surveillance operation was supervised by Beria's son, Sergo, who had performed similar duties in Tehran fourteen months earlier. The Russians were constantly surprised by how little attention the Americans paid to the electronic bugs, even as they swept the Livadia Palace daily in their battles against the nonelectronic variety. "It's bizarre," Stalin had mused in Tehran, as he leafed through reports of Roosevelt's conversations. "They say everything in fullest detail." The Americans assumed that every room of the Livadia Palace was "wired for sound" and avoided conversations on the most sensitive subjects, such as the top-secret atomic bomb project. But they let down their guard on other matters, providing the eavesdroppers with a wealth of useful information.

In addition to the bugging reports, Stalin also had access to secret American briefing papers, delivered to him by his spies. After the collapse of communism, his personal files were found to contain a copy of an internal State Department memorandum prepared in December 1944 opposing the transfer of the Kurile Islands to the Soviet Union. Roosevelt could not be bothered to read the views of his own experts on such matters, but Stalin devoured every nuance.

Stalin was delighted by FDR's failure to follow the State Department's advice. Apart from a few Japanese fishermen, the Kuriles were largely uninhabited. But the eight-hundred-mile island chain between Kamchatka and Japan controlled access to the Sea of Okhotsk, a Gulf of Mexico-sized body of water that would now effectively become a Russian lake. The southernmost island, Kunashiri, was only ten miles from the Japanese home island of Hokkaido and clearly visible across the water. Discussing the American concessions later with his staff, Stalin paced up and down his study in the Koreiz villa, muttering, "Good, very good."

The *vozhd* employed a typically Rooseveltian gambit to justify his territorial demands in the Far East: public opinion. He had grown tired of endless lectures from Roosevelt and Churchill about the difficulties they faced with their legislatures, which were simply "an excuse" for avoiding negotiations. If they could resort to such a shameless "bourgeois ploy," so could he. He told FDR that it would be difficult for him to justify a war with Japan to the Russian people unless they could see a direct benefit from it. This would not be like the war against Germany, which had threatened the Soviet Union's very existence. Stalin had a point here, although he vastly exaggerated the political constraints. He even alluded to problems that might arise with the Supreme Soviet unless he got his way. This raised an eyebrow from Bohlen, an old Moscow hand serving as Roosevelt's interpreter, who knew very well that the rubber-stamp legislature had "no power whatsoever."

The president was not disposed to quibble. His overriding goal was to reduce American casualties. The "miracle weapon" that could end the war in the Far East once and for all was unfinished and untested, the dream of a few physicists out in New Mexico. The Joint Chiefs of Staff had drawn up plans for a protracted island-hopping campaign against the Japanese, which, they believed, could last eighteen months after the defeat of Germany. Two hundred thousand American lives might be saved if the Russians entered the Asian war prior to amphibious assaults on the main Japanese islands. Bohlen later conceded that the United States would not have given the Kuriles to Stalin so readily "if the president had done his homework, or if any of us had been more familiar with Far Eastern history." But such considerations seemed trivial when weighed against the benefits that would flow from Russia's entry into the war.

At Stalin's insistence, the deal was kept secret from the Chinese, even though the Soviets were demanding joint control over the Manchurian railroad and "preeminent" rights in two Chinese ports, Port Arthur and Dairen. Roosevelt agreed that "one of the difficulties in speaking to the Chinese was that anything said to them was known to the whole world in twenty-four hours." He promised to arrange things privately with the Chinese nationalist leader, Chiang Kai-shek.

It was now almost 4:00 p.m., time for the daily plenary session. When Churchill arrived at Livadia, he was taken aback to learn that Roosevelt was in private conference with Stalin. The secretary of state, tall, bluff, ineffectual Edward Stettinius, had also been excluded from the meeting. He asked an aide to let the president know that the prime minister had arrived. FDR had just confided to Stalin that the British colony of Hong Kong should be returned to China. He had also raised the possibility of an American-Soviet-Chinese trusteeship for Korea, excluding the British. Stalin joked that Churchill might "kill us" if he found out what they were discussing.

Roosevelt had no desire to include his English friend in the politically sensitive conversation. He sent a message back to Stettinius.

"Let him wait."

The fifth plenary session finally got under way at 4:15 p.m., after a fifteen-minute delay. Roosevelt seemed even more decrepit than usual as he was wheeled into the Livadia ballroom behind Stalin. An American military planner was "shocked" by his appearance. The president "was gaunt, his eyes sunken deep in his lined face; he looked very tired and ill, as though he were existing on pure iron determination to see the war to the end."

Poland remained at the top of the agenda for the third day running. There was little progress on the vital issue of the composition of a provisional government. Churchill complained about the lack of information from Poland, which was sealed off from the outside world. He warned of an outcry in Britain if the London Poles were simply pushed aside. Stalin insisted that his Polish puppets had at least as much popular legitimacy as General de Gaulle, who had never been elected to anything. Nobody was talking about a power-sharing arrangement between de Gaulle and the French Communists; it was unreasonable "to demand more of Poland than of France." An "enlarged" Lublin government would lead the country to democratic elections.

"How long will it take you to hold free elections?" Roosevelt wanted to know.

"About one month," Stalin replied reassuringly. "Unless there is some kind of catastrophe on the front and the Germans defeat us."

He smiled at his own caveat. "I do not think that will happen."

Stalin had invited Roosevelt and Churchill for a ceremonial dinner in Koreiz. He announced he would be accompanied by his closest aides, including the three top military leaders. Roosevelt wanted to make the occasion a more informal, relaxed affair. He left the generals and admirals behind at Livadia and instead brought his daughter, Anna, and Averell Harriman's daughter Kathleen. Churchill was accompanied by his daughter Sarah, as well as his senior military people.

The guests were shown into the dining room of the Yusupov Palace, decorated with two large tropical plants and a Moorish-style fireplace. There was barely enough room to move around the long table, which was set for thirty places. A "most sinister appearing gent," in Anna's description, began plying the ladies with vodka. He was short and plump, with a bald head, moon-shaped face, and dark, beady eyes magnified by a pair of rimless spectacles. The president was reminded of certain American "big businessmen" of his acquaintance. Chip Bohlen thought he "looked like a schoolmaster." It was Lavrenty Beria, head of the NKVD.

The conversation took a surrealistic turn when Sarah Churchill tried out her very limited Russian on the dreaded secret police chief. A utilitarian entry from a phrase book for English visitors to Russia had somehow stuck in her memory. "Can I have a hot-water bottle please?"

Ambassador Maisky helped translate Beria's reply. "I cannot believe you need one. Surely there is enough fire in you!" At this point, dinner was served, and Sarah went off to test her hot-water bottle line on her neighbor, "twinkle-eyed" Andrei Vyshinsky. The prosecutor at Stalin's great show trials was momentarily speechless. "Why?" he asked, full of concern. "Are you ill?" Sarah, an aspiring actress more accustomed to life in English country houses than tsarist palaces, resorted to charades "to make him see that it was a joke." After that, they got on splendidly. Sarah reported to her mother the following day that the man who had sent thousands of Stalin's supposed enemies to their deaths was "very nice and easy." Vyshinsky helped her remain sober by diluting the vodka and wine with sparkling Narzan mineral water as they "toyed delicately" with their suckling pigs.

The more seasoned conference goers found the twenty-course dinner—which included forty-five standing toasts—a terrible ordeal. The chief of the British Imperial General Staff, Alan Brooke, noted in his diary that "the standard of the speeches was remarkably low and most consisted of insincere slimy sort of slush! I became more and more bored, and more and more sleepy, and on and on it dragged." Indeed, slushy insincerity was the hallmark of the despot's court. Stalin had surrounded himself with acolytes who praised him, none more artfully than Beria, his fellow Georgian, and Vyshinsky, the clever Russian. Since foreigners had been invited to join the show, the king and his courtiers were on their best behavior, but the show itself was little changed. Long, boozy dinners had become part of the Kremlin ritual under Stalin, with a menacing undertone beneath the boorish companionship. The *vozhd* used social occasions to test the loyalty of his subordinates, set them against one another, and ensure they remained under his tight control.

For members of Stalin's inner circle, the dinners were terrifying affairs. A suspicious glance or sarcastic remark could turn a favored courtier into an "enemy of the people" in an instant. The tyrant would often humiliate his aides by plying them with drink until they made fools of themselves. "Those dinners were frightful," recalled Nikita Khrushchev, a Stalin favorite, who was forced to squat down on his haunches and perform a Ukrainian folk dance for his master, kicking out his fat little legs. "When Stalin says dance, a wise man dances." Since they never knew when they would be invited to an all-night drinking session, Soviet leaders had to adjust their schedules accordingly. Khrushchev took naps in the afternoon, just in case he received a summons to dinner in the evening. "There was always a risk that if you didn't take a nap and Stalin invited you for dinner, you might get sleepy at the table; and those who got sleepy at Stalin's table could come to a bad end."

Beria had already gained a reputation on the Moscow gossip circuit for his nocturnal adventures, which revolved around raping young girls picked up by his underlings and delivered to his villa on Kachalova Street. Piles of human bones were later found in the cellar. The prudish Stalin turned a blind eye to these escapades, storing them away for use should his secret police chief ever displease him. The sycophantic Beria knew how to make himself indispensable to the *vozhd,* feeding his paranoia, destroying his enemies, efficiently accomplishing tasks that were beyond the power of anyone else. According to Svetlana, Beria exercised a malign influence over her father, flattering him in a way that made old friends "wince with embarrassment." The organizer of the Katyn massacre was also the chief practical joker at court, slipping tomatoes onto the chairs of other dinner guests and leading the assembled company in howls of laughter when the victim sat down.

Beria might have struck Svetlana as "the embodiment of Oriental perfidy, flattery, and hypocrisy," but the dictator knew how to keep him in his place. When Roosevelt pointed to the man with a pince-nez sitting across the table and asked who he was, Stalin replied with a sneer, "Ah, that's our Himmler. That's Beria." The Soviet ambassador to Washington, Andrei Gromyko, reported that FDR was "obviously uncomfortable" with the comparison, and Beria was mortified. In the company of foreigners, at least, he craved respectability. He hated to be reminded that he was merely the latest in a long line of bureaucratic monsters that had included the "Bloody Dwarf," Nikolai Yezhov, and the colorless apparatchik Genrikh Yagoda.

Dinner began with different kinds of caviar, pressed and unpressed, small pies, and various fish courses, including Atlantic salmon, beluga sturgeon, red herring and white herring, gray mullet, whitefish in champagne, and little fish from the Black Sea. This was followed by cold piglet, broth of game, and chicken cream soup. Next came grilled fillet, shashlik of baby lamb, tenderloin of veal, and a rice dish from central Asia called *plov* that was served with quail, baby partridges, and black-tailed gazelle. Cauliflower in bread crumbs, a Russian favorite since the time of the tsars, completed the main course, before everyone moved on to various desserts and fruits. The meal was rounded out by Churchely, or "Churchills," which turned out to be a sickeningly sweet Georgian nut dish that resembled a long cigar. The ingredients of this remarkable feast were the stuff of fantasy for ordinary Russians, having long since vanished from a cuisine impoverished by war and revolution.

The toasts got under way almost immediately, with Molotov serving as *tamada,* or "toastmaster." The lengthy speeches interfered with the serving of the food, much of which was cold by the time it arrived. Stalin had offended the monarchist Churchill on the first night of the conference by refusing to drink to the king. He now explained that he had always been "against kings" as he was "on the side of the people" but would raise a glass to the king on this occasion as he felt nothing but esteem for the British people "who honor and respect their king." The toast was so circuitous and backhanded that it offended Churchill again. To make amends, Stalin hailed the prime minister as the "bravest governmental figure in the world," who had "stood alone" against "the might of Hitlerite Germany at a time when the rest of Europe was falling flat on its face before Hitler."

Upping the rhetoric stakes, Churchill toasted the marshal as the "mighty leader of a mighty country, which took the full shock of the German war machine, broke its back, and drove the tyrants from her soil." He piled adjectives on top of superlatives to laud "this great man whose fame has gone out not only over all Russia but the world."

Roosevelt was the next toastee. Stalin praised the president as the leader who had done the most to mobilize an international coalition against Hitler, even though the United States "had not been seriously threatened with invasion." In the past, the *vozhd* had been reluctant to acknowledge the assistance Russia had received from its western Allies. On this occasion, he went out of his way to express gratitude for the lend-lease program, which had helped keep the Red Army "in the field against Hitler." FDR replied with a woolly speech lauding the "family atmosphere" at the dinner. His pious talk about providing security and well-being to "every man, woman, and child on this earth" did not impress the other guests. The head of the Royal Air Force complained to his diary that Roosevelt "spoke more tripe to the minute than I have ever heard before, sentimental twaddle without a spark of real wit." The president, clearly exhausted, did little talking after that.

By this time, bugs were gnawing at the ankles of the guests. A further round of toasts was launched to include everyone in the room and anyone else who might conceivably have contributed to the coming victory. Stalin walked around the table after each toast to clink glasses personally with the toastee, a gesture of respect marred only by his refusal to look anyone in the eye "for more than ⅕ of a second." ("Never trust a man without a firm handshake who does not look you in the eye," growled Averell Harriman.) He was followed by Churchill and Molotov, Roosevelt looking on from his seat. One of Stalin's ever-present bodyguards hovered in the background, disguised as a rather shabby waiter. "Just in case, I suppose," commented a British guest.

Most guests succeeded in limiting their alcohol intake by watering down their champagne or pouring the vodka into the potted plants. The only westerner who appeared at all inebriated was the British ambassador to Moscow, Sir Archibald Clark Kerr. A stocky man nicknamed Partisan by Stalin, Clark Kerr was a true English eccentric. He did two hours of physical exercise a day to keep in shape and kept a flock of geese to ensure a steady supply of quill pens for his diplomatic dispatches. He had tripped and fallen flat on his face in front of Molotov at a Kremlin reception in honor of Revolution Day, bringing down a pile of glasses and plates. After receiving a courtesy call from the new Turkish ambassador, a man named Mustapha Kunt, he wrote a gleeful note to a foreign office colleague. "We all feel like that, Reggie, now and then, especially when spring is upon us, but few of us would put it on our cards. It takes a Turk to do that." In Yalta, he somehow managed to get into a long discussion with Beria about the sex life of fish. The ambassador now rose to propose a toast to the "man who looks after our bodies," meaning Beria as the person in charge of security arrangements for the conference.

The unusual turn of phrase amused Kathleen Harriman, who knew Clark Kerr well from Moscow, where she served as the official U.S. Embassy hostess. "Archie always seems to get an obscene touch to his toast," she wrote her sister. Churchill was less pleased. He walked around the table to the diplomat but, instead of clinking glasses, wagged his finger.

"No, Archie, none of that," the prime minister growled. "Be careful."

Stalin demanded the floor again as "a garrulous old man." He wanted to drink to the health of "our three-power alliance." It was easy to maintain unity in time of war, he noted, but much more difficult in time of peace, when the Allies pursued "diverse interests." But Stalin was confident that the alliance would "meet this test also," by refusing to deceive one another and remaining frank and intimate. Churchill was touched, never suspecting the *vozhd* could be "so expansive." He might have been less emotional had he known that Stalin had used similar language to toast his nonaggression pact with the Nazis in the Kremlin in August 1939. "I know how much the German nation loves its führer," he had told German foreign minister Joachim von Ribbentrop on that occasion, attempting to stave off a war he secretly regarded as inevitable. As far as Stalin was concerned, there was no such thing as a permanent alliance, either with states or with other politicians. There were merely tactical marriages of convenience.

Waiters served an Armenian brandy specially selected by Stalin for the occasion. There were still more toasts to be proposed and drunk. Churchill rambled on about the view from "the crest of the hill" and "the broad sunlight of victorious peace." Stalin applauded the military leaders, adding ominously that their prestige would "go down" after the war when "the ladies turn their backs on them." This inspired Molotov to raise a glass to the ladies in the room. Kathleen Harriman replied in Russian on behalf of the "Little Three," praising the conference accommodations. Jimmy Byrnes drank to the "common man." Finally, when it was all over, Stalin proposed a toast to the three interpreters "who have no time to eat or drink," prompting Churchill to offer a parody of Karl Marx's Communist slogan. "Interpreters of the world, unite!" he joked. "You have nothing to lose but your audience." The dictator could hardly stop laughing. His guests left soon afterward, at 12:45 a.m.

Churchill was still in an excellent mood when he got back home to the Vorontsov Palace, three miles up the road. He wrote a minute to the War Cabinet back in London, describing the "extraordinary efforts" of the Russians to make everybody comfortable, combined with a "prodigality" that "excels belief." Marian Holmes heard him singing a popular evangelical hymn, "The Glory Song," through the sliding wooden door.

Back at the Livadia Palace, Roosevelt was attended by his doctors, like a boxer returning to his corner between rounds in a championship fight. The sparring with Stalin and Churchill was taking a steadily greater physical toll. "Color very poor," wrote Bruenn in his medical notes. "Tonight, after an especially arduous day and emotionally disturbing conference (patient was worried and upset about the trend of the discussions at the Conference) he was obviously greatly fatigued." The cardiologist was alarmed to discover the first signs of an alternating pulse pattern—weak beats following strong beats—that could be a symptom of congestive heart failure.

There was not much that Bruenn could do other than urge the president to take it easy. Worried that FDR was working too hard and missing out on his afternoon naps, he jotted down his prescription. "Hours to be rigidly controlled so that he obtains adequate rest, i.e., no visitors until noon, and is to have at least an hour's rest in the afternoon."

5

Grand Design

February 10

The president received one last visitor before going to sleep in the early morning hours of Friday, February 9. He was already in bed when Ed Stettinius entered the oppressively decorated room with the dark wooden paneling. The secretary of state had proposed various sites for the founding United Nations conference—New York, Philadelphia, Chicago, Miami—but Roosevelt was not satisfied with any of them. "Go back to work, Ed," he instructed. "We haven't hit it yet."

The establishment of a new world body to replace the discredited League of Nations was FDR's most important objective at Yalta after winning the war. At his fourth inaugural, fewer than three weeks before, he had stood on the South Portico of the White House and promised "a durable peace." A politician to the core, he understood he had to deliver on that pledge or tarnish his historical legacy. The defeat of America's enemies was not enough. He had to convince his fellow citizens that the sacrifices had all been worthwhile. Roosevelt remembered how another president had lacked the authority and political skill to persuade Congress, and ultimately the country, to accept his internationalist vision at the end of the last world war. The results had been disastrous. America had turned inward, Germany had taken its revenge, and "the war to end all wars" was fought all over again.

FDR was determined not to repeat the mistakes of Woodrow Wilson. As a young assistant secretary of the navy, he had finagled a trip to Paris during the 1919 peace conference. While he played no role in the formal diplomatic negotiations, he stayed at the Ritz along with the other delegates and witnessed the backstage maneuvering. He felt that Wilson had made a fatal error in failing to win over centrist Republican senators who had the power to block ratification of the Versailles treaty. Without the United States in the League of Nations, the project was doomed. Roosevelt shared the Wilsonian belief in collective security, but he was not an ideologue. The creation of a new world body was not a supreme end in itself, as it had been for Wilson. It was the means to an end, a way to justify the war to the American people, a symbol of the "durable peace" Roosevelt had promised. The details were unimportant. What mattered was the hope it would inspire in millions of people.

Roosevelt was haunted by the image of physical and mental decrepitude that surrounded the former president toward the end of his life. A few months earlier, he had watched a private screening of the movie *Wilson,* which depicted an embattled, self-righteous leader brought down by a near-fatal stroke in October 1919. "By God, that's not going to happen to me," FDR muttered to himself as he watched the Hollywood version of the final, tragic months of Wilson's presidency. The battle with the Senate over the Versailles treaty destroyed Wilson both physically and mentally. He was so paralyzed by his stroke that he was unable to attend cabinet meetings and had to leave key decisions to his wife and aides.

FDR's own physical decline was obvious to everyone. He had become a part-time president, working only four to five hours a day. His vision was often blurred, forcing him to rely on oral briefings for most of his information. He had neither the stamina, nor the inclination, for historical analyses or detailed discussions of policy. The problem was compounded by inadequate staff work. His closest aide, Harry Hopkins, was almost as sick as the president and missed many important meetings. "Harry is a complete d-fool about his health," Anna Roosevelt complained to her husband in a February 9 letter. "Doesn't think straight when he is not well, and so can't be counted on." Stettinius was what the English called a lightweight, a former salesman for the U.S. Steel Corporation known to his State Department subordinates as Brother Ed. He was genial and eager to please but hardly a serious foreign policy thinker. According to

Anna, "The only practical guy here, on our side, who is smart is Jimmy B[yrnes]. But he is not 100% loyal to the boss."

Although Roosevelt's body was giving out on him, his mind was still sharp. The master politician operated on many different levels, disguising his true purposes from enemies and friends alike, and even occasionally from himself. "I am a juggler," he told his Hyde Park neighbor, Henry Morgenthau Jr. "I never let my right hand know what my left hand does." He juggled many balls in the air at once: domestic policy, foreign policy, the waging of war, his hopes for the postwar world, Stalin's demands, Churchill's moods, casualty figures, public opinion. Through it all, he remained what he had always been, an extraordinary amalgam of idealism and cynicism, self-confidence and cunning. His labor secretary, Frances Perkins, was correct when she called FDR "the most complicated human being I have ever known." It was difficult to distinguish between what he truly believed and what he affected to believe for tactical reasons. He was sometimes accused of naïveté toward Stalin, but his naïveté served a larger political purpose. The alliance with the Soviet Union, and the millions of Soviet casualties, were key to winning the war at a tolerable cost in American lives; to preserve the alliance, he had to emphasize the trustworthiness of America's most important ally. Had he told the truth—that Russia was ruled by a dictator as bloody and as ruthless as Hitler—the Grand Alliance would have been fatally undermined. But that did not bother the president, who acknowledged to Morgenthau that he was "perfectly willing to mislead and tell untruths if it will help win the war."

Some of Roosevelt's aides were exasperated by what they called his "globaloney," a preoccupation with abstract ideas and woolly "One World" philosophy at the expense of hard geopolitical realities. The White House chief of staff, Admiral Leahy, opposed his desire to give the future United Nations organization sovereignty over various Pacific islands captured from the Japanese. But the president understood that abstract ideas were necessary to sustain the American will to fight. Americans could not be asked to die for a few specks of land in the Pacific. They needed a righteous cause, an overarching vision. FDR had responded to this need, promising to create "a world in which tyranny and aggression cannot exist, a world based on freedom equality and justice." It might be a pipe dream, but Roosevelt was adept at putting America's deepest aspirations into words.

Selling the peace was as important to Roosevelt as selling the war. The essence of his Grand Design consisted in the creation of a system of collective security to replace the traditional European reliance on balance of power politics. He boasted that the United Nations would evolve into "the best method ever devised for stopping war." Unlike Wilson, FDR paid great attention to congressional opinion. He had formed an informal alliance with the leading Republican on the Senate Foreign Relations Committee, Arthur Vandenberg, who had just announced his conversion from isolationism to internationalism. The senator was "a big, loud, vain, and self-important man, who could strut sitting down," in the phrase of *New York Times* columnist James Reston, but he was enormously influential among mainstream Republicans. With Vandenberg's support, the president believed that he could keep the isolationists at bay, as long as he returned from Yalta with an agreed blueprint for a new world organization. He planned to recruit the Republican leader to the U.S. delegation for the founding conference of the United Nations.

Roosevelt focused his waning energy on the issues that were most important to him, paying scant attention to everything else. He had achieved most of his goals in coming to the Crimea. Stalin had agreed to join the war against Japan within six months of the defeat of Nazi Germany. The Soviet leader had also endorsed the American plan for the United Nations with only minimal changes. His most irksome demand had been for two extra seats for the Soviet Union in the General Assembly, to be allocated to Ukraine and Belorussia, the two Soviet republics that had suffered most as a result of the Nazi invasion. FDR was prepared to satisfy that requirement, even though it violated the principle of equal representation of big and small states. That part of his agreement with Uncle Joe would be kept secret for the time being, to be revealed at an opportune moment, like the understanding on Japan. The president had taken the precaution of extracting a promise from Stalin of two extra seats for the United States in case he needed to make the concession more palatable back home.

Stalin, it was true, had shown no such flexibility over Poland. For FDR, however, that unfortunate country was already lost. It belonged to the category of things he could not affect, however desirable it was to try. Short of going to war with Russia, there was little he could do to change the realities of political power in a country that was now occupied by the Red Army. Roosevelt's view of Poland was very different from Churchill's. For the British prime minister, Polish freedom and independence were matters of "honor," a word that resonated deep within his Victorian soul. Poland conjured up images of cavalry officers charging across the plains at German tanks, of Chopin and Piłsudski, of Polish soldiers under British command dying at Monte Cassino, of a brave, romantic nation on whose behalf England had gone to war. For Roosevelt, Poland's plight was primarily a matter of practical politics. When he thought of Poland, he thought first of 6 million Americans of Polish descent. He wanted to resolve the Polish problem in a way that would not turn these voters permanently against the Democrats or give ammunition to the isolationists.

A good night's sleep worked wonders for the president's spirits. He woke refreshed on Friday morning, ready to return to the ring with Stalin and Churchill. He summoned his secretary of state, who had spent the night thinking about a suitable venue for the first United Nations conference. The solution—San Francisco—had finally come to "Brother Ed" at three in the morning. His mind "raced with enthusiasm and freshness" as he imagined Nob Hill, the opera house, the Veterans Building, the Pacific-Union Club, the Fairmont, "each filling its purpose." Lying in bed on the shores of the Black Sea, the former salesman could see the "golden sunshine" and "almost feel the fresh and invigorating air from the Pacific." Holding the opening conference of the United Nations on the West Coast would remind the world that the war was shifting from the Atlantic to the Pacific.

The parsimonious president was not immediately convinced. His first reaction was that the selection of San Francisco would result in unnecessary inconvenience and expense. "We have called off all unnecessary movements of people, conventions, and so forth," he reminded Stettinius. But he promised to think about it.

At 4:00 p.m., the Big Three gathered for their formal group photo in the Italian courtyard of the Livadia Palace, covered for the occasion with Oriental rugs. Soviet guards armed with tommy guns slung across their chests watched warily from the second-floor balcony as Stalin entered in his soft leather boots and sat down beside Roosevelt. A skeletal figure in his dark blue navy cape, the president seemed more alert than on previous days as he chatted amiably with the marshal. Churchill was the last to arrive, in colonel's uniform and extravagant fur hat, which drew a chuckle from the other two leaders. Generals and diplomats jockeyed for position to be photographed behind the principals. Guests at Stalin's banquet the previous night were amused to see one of the "waiters" now resplendent in the uniform of an NKVD general.

The sixth plenary session began immediately afterward in the white ballroom. A droning speech from Stettinius on the United Nations was soon enlivened by an emotional outburst from Churchill. Angry about being excluded from the private Roosevelt-Stalin meeting on Thursday, the prime minister had worked himself up into a high dudgeon. He suspected the Americans of plotting with the Russians to take away chunks of the British Empire under the guise of creating United Nations trusteeships, a kind of halfway stage between a colony and an independent country. He announced that he had not been consulted about the American plan on trusteeships and "under no circumstances" would ever consent to "forty or fifty nations thrusting interfering fingers into the life's existence of the British empire."

"As long as I am prime minister, I will not yield one scrap of our heritage," he growled.

Stettinius tried to calm the prime minister, insisting that the American plan referred to Japan, not Britain. Unwittingly, he had touched a raw nerve in the Englishman, who had been raised on the stories of Rudyard Kipling and tales of gallantry on the North-West Frontier. Churchill had a particular blind spot about India, which he regarded as the jewel in the British Crown, to be passed down to future generations. He was horrified by the prospect of Indian independence, denouncing Hindus as a "beastly people with a beastly religion." The idea that Britain, weakened by its sacrifices during the war, would be forced to surrender some of its colonies was more than the descendant of the Duke of Marlborough could abide.

"Never, never, never," he insisted.

Churchill's explosion delighted Stalin, who "got up from his chair, walked up and down, beamed, and at intervals broke into applause." The *vozhd* was amused by the hypocrisy of his allies who behaved as if the principles of independence and self-determination should apply to everyone but themselves. Under the Atlantic Charter of August 1941, they had guaranteed "the right of all peoples to choose the form of Government under which they will live." But the Americans made exceptions for the Western Hemisphere when they talked about the Monroe Doctrine. The British excluded their colonies. Whenever Churchill or Roosevelt tried to carve out a sphere of influence for themselves, they strengthened Stalin's case for a Russian sphere of influence in eastern Europe.

Stalin was not much interested in sweeping declarations and grandiose visions for the postwar world. He described them as "algebra," in contrast to the "arithmetic" of practical agreements. As he told Anthony Eden back in 1941, "I do not wish to decry algebra, but I prefer arithmetic." Under the heading "arithmetic," he included such matters as territories under his control, the number of divisions in his armies, the number of opposing divisions, quantities of tanks, airplanes, and other military equipment, statistics on industrial production, demographic breakdowns, and so on. These factors added up to what Marxist-Leninists referred to as "the correlation of forces," the relative strength of the Communist world compared to its real and potential enemies. Everything else was rhetoric, or "algebra," in Stalin's formulation. He confessed that he had not studied the American plan for a United Nations organization, even though it had been submitted for his approval two months earlier. His attitude toward the new world body was primarily defensive. He was ready to go along with Roosevelt's wishes as long as the Soviet Union retained the right to veto any decisions it did not like.

Typical of what Stalin considered "algebra" was a Declaration on Liberated Europe that had been tabled by FDR with an eye to western public opinion. Modeled on the Atlantic Charter, it included a promise to establish "representative" transitional governments, hold "free elections," and "enable liberated peoples to destroy the last vestiges of Nazism and Fascism and to create democratic institutions of their own choice." The declaration was worded vaguely enough to be acceptable to Stalin. The phrase "free elections" might cause problems in the future but was open to different interpretations. In any case, he had long taken the view that elections were decided not by "the people who cast the votes" but by "the people who count the votes." The passage about destroying the "last vestiges of Nazism" was welcome because it could be used to justify the banning of any political party that the Kremlin decided to call pro-Nazi or Fascist.

Stalin surprised everyone by announcing that he was willing to accept the American draft of the declaration with only minimal changes. Encouraged by the dictator's unexpected flexibility, Roosevelt mentioned the future election in Poland, insisting that its purity should be "beyond question."

"It should be like Caesar's wife. I did not know her, but they said that she was pure."

Stalin gave a cynical laugh. "They said that about her, but in fact she had her sins."

The president said that the declaration would of course apply to "any areas or countries where needed," in addition to Poland. This caused

Churchill's imperialist antennae to quiver anew. He was still angry about the trusteeships issue. He wanted it clearly understood that the Atlantic Charter "did not apply to the British Empire." He had stated this clearly in the House of Commons. Furthermore, he had given a copy of his statement to presidential envoy Wendell Willkie.

FDR could not resist the opportunity to make a joke at the expense of both Churchill, for his spirited defense of the empire, and Willkie, a former Republican presidential candidate, who had died of a heart attack a few months previously.

"Was that what killed him?"

The president's sarcastic response was a sign that he was recovering from his exertions of the previous day. That evening, he dined with a small group of American military leaders, impressing them with his martini concoction. He told the group that he had had "a great deal of trouble with Winston" during the plenary. He then recounted how the prime minister had "drifted off into a sound sleep from which he would awaken very suddenly making speeches about the Monroe Doctrine" that were irrelevant to the debate. Amid much laughter, FDR blamed the prime minister's ill humor on the interruption of his midday nap.

Commander Bruenn was relieved by the clear signs of improvement in his patient's health. "Spirits are much better," the cardiologist wrote in his diary for Saturday, February 10. "Is eating well—delights in Russian food and cooking. *Pulsus alternans* has disappeared. No cough. Appetite continues to be good."

The Big Three assembled around the table in the ballroom of the Livadia Palace shortly before 5:00 p.m. for their seventh plenary session. An agreement, or at least a form of words that everybody could endorse, was finally within sight on the contentious issue of Poland. The foreign ministers had hammered out a formula that called for the Lublin government to "be reorganized on a broader democratic basis with the inclusion of democratic leaders from Poland itself and from Poles abroad." Molotov would meet with the American and British ambassadors in Moscow to nail down the details. Once a new "Polish Provisional Government of National Unity" was formed, it would be recognized by the three big powers. The new government would be "pledged to the holding of free and unfettered elections as soon as possible on the basis of universal suffrage and secret ballot." All "democratic and anti-Nazi parties" would have the right to take part in the elections.

The proposed compromise was closer to the Soviet draft than the American. The phrase "reorganized on a broader democratic basis" implied that the existing Lublin government would form the core of the new government as Stalin had demanded. Everything would likely depend on the negotiations in Moscow among Molotov, Harriman, and Clark Kerr. In practice, the Russians could still veto unacceptable Polish leaders. The only recourse for the Americans and the British was to refuse to recognize the government.

Admiral Leahy was quick to spot the potential loopholes. "Mr. President," the chief of staff objected, after looking over the document. "This is so elastic that the Russians can stretch it all the way from Yalta to Washington without ever technically breaking it."

"I know, Bill," FDR replied wearily. "But it's the best I can do for Poland at this time."

The question of Poland's future frontiers was only partly settled. The three leaders agreed to a statement endorsing the Curzon Line as the eastern border of the country with minor modifications. This meant that a region the size of Missouri, stretching from Wilno to Lwów, would be ceded to the Soviet Union. In return, Poland would receive "substantial accessions of territory in the north and west." The "final delimitation" of Poland's western frontier would be decided by a peace conference. Stalin wanted to include a mention in the final communiqué of "the return to Poland of her ancient frontiers in East Prussia and on the Oder," but this was too much for Roosevelt and Churchill. The president wanted to know when the territory in question last belonged to Poland.

"Very long ago," conceded Molotov, knowing the Poles would have to go back to at least the thirteenth century to claim the city they called Wrocław, better known by its German name, Breslau.

Roosevelt joked that this might encourage Great Britain to reclaim the United States. He turned to the prime minister. "Perhaps you want us back?" Stalin did not press the point. He had got what he wanted in the East. The question of Poland's western frontier could wait a little. He noted, humorlessly, that the existence of an ocean prevented Britain from reclaiming its American colonies.

By agreeing to move Poland two hundred miles to the west, the Big Three had turned the Wilsonian principle of self-determination on its head. After the First World War, statesmen attempted to draw up frontiers that reflected demographic realities, creating more or less homogeneous nation-states. Stalin's approach was the opposite. He moved the people around to accommodate the lines he had drawn on a map for his own political purposes. The former commissar of nationalities had used this technique in the Soviet Union, particularly in the Caucasus, to reward "loyal" ethnic groups at the expense of "disloyal" ones like the Chechens and the Tatars. The time had come to employ a similar demographic technique on a larger scale, with the tacit consent of the western Allies. Eastern European countries that bowed to the wishes of the master of the Kremlin, such as Poland or Romania, would be awarded extra territory. Nations that displeased him would be punished.

Another issue that remained to be settled was the amount of compensation Russia would receive for war damage inflicted by the Germans. Stalin stuck to his demand for $10 billion in reparations, to be paid in kind, in the form of dismantled factories and industrial equipment, goods, and labor. Roosevelt was prepared to negotiate on the basis of this figure, but Churchill was adamantly opposed. Harry Hopkins, who had dragged himself from his sickbed to attend the meeting, wanted to reward Stalin for his cooperation on the United Nations. He scribbled a note to the president. "The Russians have given us so much at this conference that I don't think we should let them down." Roosevelt accepted his special assistant's suggestion that the divisive issue should be referred to the Reparations Commission meeting in Moscow.

As far as FDR was concerned, there was not much point in further discussion. The façade of Allied unity had been preserved on the most important topics: Poland, the United Nations, Germany, Japan. The differences between the allies had been reduced to "a question of etymology—finding the right words." It was all "a matter of drafting," a job for diplomats, not for presidents. The remaining divisions between the three big powers would be concealed in an artfully written final communiqué. This seemed the right moment to inform everybody that he would be leaving Yalta at 3:00 p.m. the following afternoon. "Three kings"—the rulers of Saudi Arabia, Egypt, and Ethiopia—were awaiting him in the Orient.

The president's announcement took Stalin and Churchill by surprise. They were dubious that the conference could wrap up by Sunday, as Roosevelt desired. Much work remained to be done in nailing down the details of the agreements. Anthony Eden felt that the president was "deluding himself" with his trust in the magical powers of linguistics.

Words like "elections," "democracy," "independence," "fascism," and "freedom" meant very different things to the men gathered around the round table in the ballroom. In the Soviet lexicon, anybody who was anti-Communist could be termed a "Fascist," a word that had been stretched at times to include democratic politicians like Churchill. According to the Marxist-Leninist understanding of history, a "democratic government" was a government that ruled on behalf of the people, as defined by the Communist Party. These were "rubber words," in the phrase of the rising State Department star Alger Hiss.

A heavy price would be paid for papering over the most difficult problems at Yalta in communiqués full of what Anna Roosevelt called "glittering generalities." The misunderstandings would grow and fester, with each side accusing the other of bad faith and breaking solemn agreements. The words that temporarily united the World War II victors would return to divide them.

Concern about the emerging agreement at Yalta was not limited to the western side. Some of Stalin's aides felt that the *vozhd* had given away too much under pressure from Roosevelt and Churchill. Molotov was worried about the wording of the Declaration on Liberated Europe, which committed Russia to guaranteeing "the right of all peoples to choose the form of government under which they will live," as enshrined in the Atlantic Charter. The foreign affairs commissar complained that the declaration "amounted to interference in the affairs of liberated Europe," but was overruled by his boss. "Don't worry," Stalin instructed him. "Work it out. We can deal with it in our own way later. The point is the correlation of forces."

The Russians resented the hectoring, morally superior tone of the Anglo-Saxons. Ivan Maisky remarked that "England and the USA fancied themselves as Almighty God, with a mission to judge the remainder of the sinful world, including my own country." Kremlin leaders believed that the American rhetoric about making the world "safe for democracy" was merely a pretext for meddling in other people's business. Americans suspected Russians of wanting to convert everyone to communism, but from Stalin's perspective, the reality was quite the reverse: America was intent on exporting its ideology to the rest of the world. What the Americans saw as benign internationalism was viewed by Russians as an insidious form of imperialism. "Roosevelt believed in dollars," Molotov later recalled. "He considered America to be so rich, and we so poor and worn out, that we would surely come begging."

Stalin did not know quite what to make of FDR. On the one hand, he seemed much more reasonable than other capitalist leaders and had gone out of his way to be friendly to Russia. On the other, he remained a representative of his class, a staunch believer in the universality of American ideas. The president had done his best to persuade Stalin of his good intentions, but he also rejected the whole idea of closed spheres of influence. He had pointedly reminded the *vozhd* that "in this global war there is literally no question, political or military, in which the United States is not interested." The Americans refused to abide by the rules that Europeans had lived by for centuries. They rejected the notion, formalized at the Congress of Westphalia in 1648, that every ruler is sovereign in the territories he controls and is therefore free to determine the religion of his subjects. There was a Latin phrase for this centuries-old concept, *cuius regio, eius religio.* "Whose realm, his religion." The logical implication of the Atlantic Charter was that the Americans wanted to export their ideas, their religion, to areas like eastern Europe that were under the control of someone else's army. This Stalin could not accept.

The Americans attached at least as much importance to ideology as any Marxist, in the Soviet view. The publisher of *Time* magazine, Henry Luce, had coined a new expression, "the American century," to describe the inevitable triumph of free market economics and liberal democracy throughout the world. Stalin's own ambitions were more modest. He was willing to give the Americans and the British a free hand in the countries they occupied, such as Italy and Greece. In return, he wanted a free hand in his chunk of the globe. This was, after all, the ancient right of sovereigns.

The *vozhd* was willing to play along with the Americans by signing their meaningless, algebralike declarations. The Soviet Union was exhausted by four years of war and occupation and in no condition to fight another war in the near future. Rebuilding the devastated country would require a massive infusion of resources. Potential sources of funding included war reparations from Germany, loans and credits from the United States, and squeezing consumer consumption at home, or some combination of all three. If there was any possibility of raising at least some of the funds needed for Russia's recovery from Germany or from the West, that was obviously preferable to a total reliance on the country's depleted domestic resources. Standard Marxist-Leninist theory taught that war with the imperialists was unavoidable in the long run. "The war will soon be over," Stalin told the Yugoslav Communist Milovan Djilas. "We shall recover in fifteen or twenty years, and then we'll have another go at it." In the short term, however, there was much to be gained from maintaining good relations with the leading imperialist power. Russia needed a breathing space, a *peredyshka*, to build up its strength.

Stalin had accepted an invitation to dine with Churchill and Roosevelt at the Vorontsov Palace. A magnificent ceremonial staircase led up to the southern Moorish façade of the prime minister's residence from the gardens, flanked on either side by marble lion sculptures. The lions at the bottom of the staircase were sleeping, those in the middle were in various stages of repose, while the ones at the top were on their paws and fully awake, guarding the gates of the palace. Soviet security men spent the day examining the lion statues, along with every corner of the house and garden. "They locked the doors on either side of the reception rooms which were to be used for dinner," Churchill recalled. "Guards were posted and no one was allowed to enter. They then searched everywhere—under the tables and behind the walls."

Saturday night's dinner was the most intimate of the Yalta get-togethers, attended only by the Big Three and their foreign ministers, plus interpreters. Churchill waited for his guests in the baronial hall, surrounded by portraits of Russian and English aristocrats, "eyeing the Russian soldiery." The massive oak doors finally opened shortly after nine, and Roosevelt was wheeled in, apologizing for arriving late. "I couldn't get something done up." Churchill's female secretaries stood in the entrance, along with an honor guard of Royal Marines, ogling the visitors. "Stalin's entrance was ruined as he came hard on the heels of the president," recorded Marian Holmes. Churchill disentangled himself from Roosevelt to escort Stalin and Molotov into the banquet room.

Standing in front of a blazing fireplace, nibbling caviar appetizers, Molotov asked Stettinius about the location for the inaugural United Nations conference. The secretary of state crossed the room and leaned down to Roosevelt, still in his portable wheelchair. "Are you ready to say San Francisco?" The president nodded his assent, and the Big Three drank to "the success of the San Francisco Conference, to open on April 25, just eleven weeks later."

The Russian kitchen staff had prepared a twenty-five-course dinner, ranging from the ubiquitous suckling pig to wild goat from the steppes. The toasts began immediately. After much thought, Churchill had devised a strategy for avoiding unwelcome caveats from Stalin in drinking to the health of His Majesty the King. Instead of individual toasts, he proposed a collective toast to all three heads of state. All went smoothly. As the only head of state present, Roosevelt exercised the right of reply. He recalled an incident that took place in 1933, prior to the opening of diplomatic relations with the Soviet Union. "My wife visited a school in our country. In one of the classrooms, she saw a map with a large blank space on it. She asked what was the blank space, and was told they were not allowed to mention the place. It was the Soviet Union." It was as if the world's largest country, covering one-sixth of the earth's landmass, did not exist.

Stalin was still focused on business and particularly the failure to reach agreement on war reparations. He said he was afraid to tell the Soviet people that they were "not going to get any reparations because the British were opposed." Churchill protested that he was in favor of reparations in principle but remembered what happened after the First World War when Germany was unable to meet its debts. Pressed by the marshal, the two western leaders agreed to include a section in the final communiqué stipulating that Germany make compensation "in kind" for damage inflicted on the Allies. An accompanying secret protocol would make clear that the Americans, but not the British, accepted Stalin's $10 billion figure as "a basis for discussion."

As the Big Three moved on to the wild-game courses, talk turned to domestic politics. The prime minister reminded his guests that he would soon be facing a "difficult election." Stalin could not imagine that he would have any trouble getting reelected. "The people will understand that they need a leader, and who could be a better leader than the person who had won the victory." Churchill explained that there were two political parties in Britain, and he was leader of only one of them.

"One party is much better," Stalin insisted.

After dinner, Churchill invited his guests to his Map Room down the corridor. Charts on the wall showed the Russians within thirty-eight miles of Berlin, the Americans entering Manila, and the British and Canadians advancing toward the Rhine. Fortified by cigars and brandy, the ebullient Englishman struck up a few bars of a popular song from World War I, "When We Wind Up the Watch on the Rhine." He looked hurt when Stalin suggested that the British might consider an armistice with the

Germans. Retreating to a corner of the Map Room in mock dismay, he launched into another old favorite, "Keep Right on to the End of the Road."

"Stalin looked extremely puzzled," recorded the head of the Map Room, Captain Pim. FDR cracked a broad grin, explaining to Stalin that Churchill's singing was "Britain's secret weapon." The prime minister finally bade good night to his guests around 12:30 a.m., leading the assembled British officials in a lusty "three cheers for Marshal Stalin."

The diplomats stayed up all night drafting the communiqué and secret protocols. Roosevelt remained determined to wrap everything up the following morning, even though he had told Stalin that he would stay until Monday if absolutely necessary. He planned to spend a final night aboard the American communications ship *Catoctin* in the port of Sevastopol before flying to Egypt for his meeting with the "three kings." He wanted to make the eighty-mile drive to Sevastopol, via a treacherous coastal road, in daylight.

The Big Three gathered for their last plenary session at noon on Sunday, February 11, in the ballroom of the Livadia Palace. A pile of documents lay on the round table, in front of each delegate. The leaders leafed through them, section by section, checking the wording. Churchill, who prided himself on his literary style, objected to a number of Americanisms in the final communiqué. "Too many joints," he complained, pointing to a sentence about "our joint military plans." He preferred "our combined military plans." To an Englishman, the word "joint" evoked thoughts of "the Sunday family roast of mutton." A compromise was eventually reached on "the military plans of the three Allied powers."

Roosevelt and Stalin were in no mood to quibble. They switched into each other's language to approve great chunks of text. "OK," laughed Stalin, in heavily accented pidgin English. "*Khorosho,*" agreed FDR, in Americanized Russian.

The leaders moved on to a section titled "The Occupation and Control of Germany." The prime minister gazed disapprovingly at a sentence beginning "It is our joint purpose to destroy German militarism and Nazism . . ." The offending word was deleted. "Our joint purpose" became "our inflexible purpose." Churchill's vigilance flagged as the session wore on, either through fatigue or the sheer magnitude of the task he had set for himself. He ended up agreeing to "jointly declare" the willingness of

the Big Three to undertake "joint action" to discharge their "joint responsibilities" to "jointly assist" the liberated peoples of Europe.

Churchill expressed reservations about the agreement on Poland—
"the cause for which Britain drew the sword"—even as he signed off on
it. He feared that he would be "strongly criticized" for yielding to Russian
political and territorial demands. "The London Poles will raise a dreadful outcry," he predicted gloomily. "They will say that I have completely
swept away the only constitutional government of Poland."

There was good-humored debate over who should sign the communiqué first. Churchill staked his claim on the grounds of alphabetical order
and age. This was fine with Stalin, who preferred to sign last. "If Stalin's
signature is first, people will say that he led the discussion." Roosevelt
let the other two leaders have their wish and agreed to go second. They
adjourned for lunch in the tsar's billiard room while the documents were
prepared for signature. Since this process was so protracted, the three
leaders ended up signing "blank sheets of paper" for many of the agreements, to be filled in later.

A photograph, taken by Robert Hopkins and splashed across the pages
of *Life* magazine, captured the scene at lunch. "Last meeting of the Big
Three" read the caption, beneath the picture of Stalin, Roosevelt, and
Churchill seated alongside one another at the dinner table. "Together
they represent a large part of the earth's population. One is a cobbler's
son, another an aristocrat, the third a descendant of thrifty Dutch set-
tlers. In character and temperament one could hardly find three more
different men. Their debates are now over—and the hopes are high for a
peaceful world. Look at them! Churchill is taking a large spoonful of the
caviar and is out for more; Stalin's helping is a moderate one; FDR passes
it up. Does it have any significance?"

Roosevelt did not achieve his wish of leaving Yalta by 3:00 p.m., but
he was gone by four. The Russians presented him with a huge basket of
vodka, champagne, Georgian wine, caviar, butter, and tangerines, with
smaller baskets for other members of the delegation. The three leaders
said good-bye to one another on the steps of the Livadia Palace.

Churchill returned to the Vorontsov Palace, despondent at being left
to himself. He had planned to leave on Monday but suddenly realized
there was no reason to stay. He resembled the old retainer Firs in Chekhov's play *The Cherry Orchard*, stumbling about alone in the huge
house, abandoned by his masters, as the world changes forever around
him. His secretary Marian Holmes detected his melancholy mood. She

felt that the prime minister understood that he was overshadowed by the "two giants," the Soviet Union and the United States, and "was not going to have much influence over affairs in the future."

"Why do we stay here?" Churchill demanded. "I see no reason to stay a minute longer. We're off!"

After a "stunned silence," the staff sprang into action. Sarah Churchill attended to her father, who could not decide whether to fly to the Middle East in pursuit of the president or repair to a British ship and read the newspapers. "Trunks and large mysterious paper parcels given to us by the Russians—caviar we hope—filled the hall. Laundry arrived back clean but damp." The prime minister's valet, Sawyers, had "tears in his eyes" as he labored over half-packed suitcases, murmuring, "They can't do this to me." Sarah described the mayhem in a letter to her mother the following day:

Papa, genial and sprightly like a boy out of school, his homework done, walked from room to room, saying: "Come on, come on." Believe it or not, 1 hour and 20 minutes later, about 5.30, saw a cavalcade of cars groaning with bulging suitcases winding its way to Sevastopol! And quick though we had been, we were last! The President left an hour before us—but on an orderly plan laid days ago. Stalin, like some genie, just disappeared. Three hours after the last handshake, Yalta was deserted, except for those who always have to tidy up after a party.

6

Euphoria

February 13

The first press comments on the Yalta conference reached Churchill while he was still onboard the luxurious Cunard ocean liner *Franconia* in Sevastopol harbor. The early reaction was "almost hysterically enthusiastic," a British diplomat noted in his diary. The London *Times* applauded the "remarkable harmony of policy" among the three wartime Allies on a series of "controversial" subjects. The tone of the commentary was so flattering, British propaganda chief Brendan Bracken cabled the prime minister, "I might have written the article myself." Clementine Churchill described her "happiness and pride" in a handwritten letter dated Tuesday, February 13. "What a wonderful result equal to a major military victory or a whole victorious campaign."

Sevastopol was even more severely damaged than the rest of the Crimea. "A pretty horrific sight," recorded John Martin, Churchill's private secretary. "It must have been a large place, with great solid stone buildings, but it is almost completely wrecked—square miles of ruins with scarcely a house left. It is absurd to think of any little inconveniences the war has brought us compared with what these people have gone through." The Germans had mined the great port city at the end of their twenty-month occupation, reducing its squares and courtyards to a stone wilderness. "This is only one of many Russian cities that have suffered such a fate," Martin noted. "No wonder if they talk about Reparations." Sarah Churchill was amazed by the sight of lights twinkling at night "from basements, from piles of stone," a sign that life was returning to the ruins.

Churchill spent the day with his generals traipsing over the nearby battlefield of Balaclava where the Light Brigade had charged in an exploit immortalized by Lord Tennyson. The past merged with the present as a Russian admiral, oblivious to the British fascination with the events of 1854, described the monthlong siege of Sevastopol by the Nazis. "The German tanks came at us from over there," the admiral exclaimed as the Englishmen gazed at the place where the "noble six hundred" rode into "the valley of Death." Stirred by the ghosts of imperial grandeur, Churchill decided to follow Roosevelt to the eastern Mediterranean and organize his own meeting with the "three kings" of the Orient. He had been "flabbergasted" by the signs of American meddling in a part of the world that had long been a British preserve. Harry Hopkins had tried to persuade him that the president was indulging in a "lot of horseplay" and that his primary goal was to "enjoy the colorful panoply of the sovereigns of this part of the world." None of this comforted Churchill, who was deeply suspicious of American calls for decolonization and self-determination. According to Hopkins, he remained convinced that "we had some deep laid plot to undermine the British empire in these areas."

American reaction to the news from Yalta began filtering through to FDR as he prepared to receive the Middle Eastern potentates aboard the *Quincy* on the placid waters of the Great Bitter Lake, in the center of the Suez Canal. It was almost uniformly enthusiastic. The *New York Times* said the agreements "justify and surpass most of the hopes placed on this fateful meeting." The *Washington Post* congratulated the president for his "all-encompassing achievement." On the CBS radio network, William Shirer called Yalta "a landmark in human history." For Raymond Gram Swing of Mutual Broadcasting, the conference answered "the greatest question of all—the allies can work together." Former president Herbert Hoover predicted that the agreements would "open a great hope to the world." Most important of all for FDR's hopes of securing bipartisan support for his Russia policy, Senator Vandenberg blessed the communiqué as "by far the best issued from any major conference."

"We really believed in our hearts that this was the dawn of the new day we had all been praying for and talking about for so many years," Hopkins later recalled. "We were absolutely certain that we had won the first great victory of the peace—and, by 'we,' I mean all of us, the whole civilized human race. The Russians had proved that they could be reasonable and farseeing and there wasn't any doubt in the minds of the President or any of us that we could live with them and get along with them peacefully for as far into the future as any of us could imagine." The only uncertainty was what might happen to Stalin. "We felt sure that we could count on him to be reasonable and sensible and understanding—but we never could be sure who or what might be in back of him there in the Kremlin."

A rare note of dissent came from the brooding George Kennan in Moscow. Harriman's number two felt that the occupation arrangements for Germany were a "meaningless platitude" and was dismayed by the promise of huge reparations for Russia. He predicted a grim future, both for Germany and for Europe. "Since we ourselves have no constructive ideas for the future of Germany, our influence can only be negative. And without our support the British can do nothing. The result is that the Russians will do as they please, first within their own zone and then, in increasing measure, in ours." This would lead first to "spreading economic chaos" and "declining living standards," then to "general confusion and hopelessness," and finally to "violent hatred and unrest" stoked and exploited by the totalitarian power to the east. "In this gulf of human despair, which will cover the heart of Central Europe, the Russians and their helpers will fish for opportunities to improve their own fortunes and apply pressure on neighboring countries."

One of Roosevelt's last acts prior to leaving Yalta had been to present Stalin with a specially bound coffee-table book entitled *Target Germany,* featuring aerial photographs of the bomb damage inflicted on the Third Reich by U.S. warplanes. The western Allies were anxious to demonstrate the efficacy of airpower, given the fact that the Russians were doing most of the fighting on the ground and their own offensive had stalled in the Ardennes. Disrupting German troop movements from the western front to the eastern front was high on the list of Russian requests at Yalta. Soviet generals specifically mentioned the need "to paralyze the junctions of Berlin and Leipzig," just to the northwest of the Saxon capital Dresden. After surveying various possible targets, Allied planners settled on Dresden itself. Germany's seventh-largest city was an important communications hub and had previously been spared large-scale bombing raids. Fewer than seventy miles from the Russian front line, Dresden was crammed with refugees fleeing the advance of the Red Army. British briefing notes informed pilots that the goal was to "hit the enemy where he will feel it most, behind an already partially collapsed front . . . and incidentally to show the Russians when they arrive what Bomber Command can do." The need to impress the Russians determined the fate of the ancient Saxon capital as much as purely military considerations.

The attack on Dresden was launched on the evening of February 13, two days after the Yalta conference. The Royal Air Force struck first at 10:14 p.m., blanketing the city center with 500 tons of high explosives and 375 tons of incendiaries. Fires spread rapidly through the heart of the baroque city, known as the Florence of the Elbe, consuming railway yards and cathedrals and palaces and private homes alike. The Lancaster heavy bombers attacked again three hours later in the early morning hours of Ash Wednesday as the emergency services were fighting the blaze, dropping another 1,800 tons of bombs. The U.S. Eighth Air Force returned to finish the job on February 14 and 15, with "precision" daylight attacks against the marshaling yards that involved 527 heavy bombers dropping 1,247 tons of explosives. Fierce winds fueled the resulting firestorm.

"Dresden?" scoffed Air Chief Marshal Arthur Harris, the head of Bomber Command, when it was all over. "There is no such place as Dresden."

Roosevelt got "a great kick" out of meeting the Oriental kings behind Churchill's back, according to Anna. "Whole party was a scream!" FDR reported to his cousin, Margaret Suckley. "We got away safely from the Crimea, flew to the Canal & saw King Farouk, then emperor Haile Selassie, & the next day, King Ibn Saud of Arabia with his whole court, slaves (black), taster, astrologer & 8 live sheep." The Saudi monarch refused the offer of a cabin on the American destroyer dispatched to bring him from Jeddah, preferring to pitch his tent on the main deck, surrounded by scimitar-bearing warriors and servants, who included a fortune-teller and a coffee preparer. The sheep grazed on food scattered on the stern of the destroyer until they were ceremonially slaughtered. The president received Saud on the deck of the *Quincy*, covered for the occasion in Oriental rugs. Decked in gold robes and red-and-white-checked head scarves, the king struck Roosevelt as "a great whale of a man sitting there in a Quinze chair." The two leaders bonded at once. FDR won Ibn Saud's lasting gratitude by presenting him with one of his wheelchairs and a

DC-3 passenger airplane, complete with rotating throne that allowed the king to always face Mecca.

More than five years of war and geopolitical upheaval had upended the international order in ways that statesmen were groping to comprehend. Everything was in flux. The future of the Middle East had barely been mentioned in Yalta because it seemed a peripheral issue, albeit one that was steadily pushing its way to the fore. Nevertheless, the dying president chose to travel a thousand miles out of his way to pay court to an Oriental potentate whose oil would be crucial to the peacetime American economy. Roosevelt understood that it was vital to establish a strong relationship with Saudi Arabia but was taken aback by the vehemence of Ibn Saud's opposition to the idea of a Jewish state in Palestine. In a clumsy attempt to establish the friendly rapport he had sought with Stalin, he jokingly offered the king "six million Jews" from the United States, in addition to Jews displaced from Europe. Ibn Saud was horrified: he predicted "a holy war" and "no end of trouble." Arabs and Jews "could never cooperate, neither in Palestine, nor in any other country.... Arabs would choose to die rather than yield their lands to the Jews." FDR responded by assuring the king that the United States would "do nothing to assist the Jews against the Arabs" and would not agree to the partition of Palestine "without full and prior consultation with both Jews and Arabs."

Churchill met with FDR on board the *Quincy* the next day, February 15, following a flying visit to Athens. In addition to finding out about American plans in the Middle East, the prime minister wanted to discuss a topic he had been reluctant to raise at Yalta because it was so sensitive. For nearly three years, American and British scientists had been working on a top-secret project to build an atomic bomb, an entirely new kind of weapon thousands, perhaps millions, of times more powerful than conventional explosives. Nobody knew if the uranium device would work, as it had never been tested. Code-named the Manhattan Project, the vast research-and-development effort was under the control of the U.S. War Department, which supervised a network of nuclear sites from New Mexico to Tennessee to Washington State. The British had been relegated to a supporting role. If the new weapon functioned as the scientists predicted, the president of the United States would control the destiny of mankind. The prime minister wanted to ensure that Britain had access to nuclear technology in the future "on a scale commensurate with our resources."

Roosevelt seemed amenable, although his attention was obviously elsewhere. He told Churchill that the prospects for exploiting atomic energy commercially seemed less promising than originally believed. According to his information, the "first important trials" of the atomic bomb would probably come in September. The serious part of the discussion over, he invited his English friend to "a small family luncheon" in his cabin, attended by Sarah and Anna, as well as Hopkins. The president "seemed placid and frail," Churchill recorded later. "I felt that he had a slender contact with life. I was not to see him again. We bade affectionate farewells." The prime minister was onboard the *Quincy* for a total of two hours and thirty-one minutes.

One by one, FDR was losing touch with the people who had been closest to him during the most trying years of the war. His loyal military aide "Pa" Watson suffered a heart attack as the presidential party was leaving the Crimea, a week after being forced to surrender his bed to Churchill. No one, including Anna, had the courage to tell the president how ill he was. He died at sea on February 20, just as the doctors thought he might be recovering. Roosevelt hid his grief behind a veil of fortitude, but his friend's death left him "deeply depressed" and reluctant to work. "He said very little about Pa at lunch or dinner that day or later," recorded his speechwriter, Sam Rosenman, but "it was plain to all of us how deeply affected he was." In the meantime, Hopkins was also getting worse. He left the *Quincy* in Algiers after three days confined to his cabin as the presidential party headed back to the United States. Roosevelt was relying on Hopkins to work on his report to Congress, but the desperately ill special assistant could not face the prospect of another week at sea. The president was "disappointed and even displeased," according to Hopkins's authorized biographer, Robert Sherwood. Their farewell was "not a very amiable one—a circumstance which it is sad to record, for Hopkins never saw his great friend again."

The prime minister returned to a gray and gloomy England on February 19. His plane was diverted to a different airport at the last minute because of fog, and there was nobody on hand to greet him. His optimism in the immediate aftermath of Yalta was giving way to foreboding. When his aides finally caught up with him, he grumbled that "the Americans had been very weak. The President looked old and ill, had lost his powers of concentration and had been a hopelessly incompetent chairman." Churchill was also troubled by complaints that the Yalta agreements amounted to a betrayal of Poland, the country whose honor and freedom Britain had gone to war to defend.

The Pole whose opinion mattered most to Churchill was General Władysław Anders, commander of the exiled Polish army. For the past three years, his men had fought alongside the British and the Americans, first in North Africa and then in Italy. His army had grown to some fifty thousand men and had been involved in some of the heaviest fighting of the Italian campaign, including the battle for the heights of Monte Cassino. After the failure of three successive attempts by their allies to capture the strategic position, the Poles had planted their red-and-white flag in the ruins of the bombed-out monastery on May 18, 1944. More than thirty-five hundred men of Polish II Corps were killed and wounded in the battle. Many of them were from the eastern region of Poland around Lwów that was to be transferred to the Soviet Union under the agreement signed by Roosevelt, Churchill, and Stalin.

A lean man with a muscular, bald head and trim mustache, Anders had good reason to be suspicious of the Russians. Together with many of the soldiers serving under him, he had been captured by the Red Army during the September 1939 carve-up of Poland. As a senior Polish officer, he was taken to the Lubyanka Prison in Moscow and tortured. After the German attack on Russia in June 1941, Stalin ordered his release from prison and permitted him to form an exile Polish army. The Anders army made its way out of the Soviet Union through Iran and Iraq and hooked up with the British in Egypt. Prior to leaving Russia, Anders was summoned to the Kremlin for an interview with Stalin during which he attempted to find out what had happened to his brother officers who had been sent to Katyn. Stalin insisted that they had all "escaped" to Manchuria. The idea that twenty thousand Poles could have vanished in China after being released from prison in Russia strained the bounds of credibility. Anders pushed Stalin for more information.

"They have certainly been released, but have not yet arrived," replied the man who had signed the execution orders for the missing Poles.

Anders learned about the Yalta deal over the radio. He was so disturbed that he could not sleep for several days. His men had sworn an oath of allegiance to the government-in-exile in London, which had been abandoned overnight by the western Allies. Up until that moment, it had been easy to persuade them that they were fighting for Poland's freedom and independence after the war. Now, as Anders saw it, the Allies had "sold"

Poland to the Soviets, torn up her constitution, and replaced her government with a slightly modified version of the Communist-dominated Lublin administration. To make matters worse, Polish representatives had not even been invited to the conference that had sealed their fate. The Yalta decisions represented a "death warrant" for Poland, which was doomed to become a "Soviet republic."

American and British generals argued that Roosevelt and Churchill were honorable men who had attempted to get the best deal possible. The exact composition of the future Polish government would be decided by negotiations in Moscow between the Soviet foreign minister and the American and British ambassadors. This failed to reassure Anders, who pointed out that Russian armies were "on the spot." The Russians would have the decisive say in shaping the new government and stage-managing the elections. "To imagine anything else is a delusion." The former Lubyanka prisoner felt he was "in a better position to judge Russian intentions than the president or the PM." Anders preferred to pull his army out of the front line in northern Italy rather than fight on for a lost cause but agreed to discuss the matter with Churchill in a meeting in London on February 21.

The prime minister received the Polish general in the annex of his official residence at 10 Downing Street, above the underground bunker that served as his wartime headquarters. His personal respect for Anders—"a gallant man [who] has long fought with us"—was outweighed by his frustration with the Polish government-in-exile. The London Poles had denounced the Yalta agreements as "a fifth partition of Poland, now accomplished by her allies," a reference to three successive partitions of the country in the eighteenth and nineteenth centuries and the Molotov-Ribbentrop Pact of 1939. Such harsh criticism wounded Churchill deeply. While he sympathized with the Poles, he was also exasperated by their stubbornness and intransigence. They refused to draw the logical, sensible conclusions from their unenviable geographic location, sandwiched between Russia and Germany. Instead of negotiating with Stalin while it was still possible, the London Poles had rejected any territorial concessions. They were their own worst enemies.

Churchill was unable to hide his impatience as Anders bemoaned the "great calamity" that had befallen his country. "Our soldiers fought for Poland, fought for the freedom of their country. What can we, their commanders, tell them now? Soviet Russia, until 1941 in close alliance with

Germany, now takes half our territory, and in the rest of it she wants to establish her power."

"It is your own fault," snapped the prime minister. He was unmoved by threats to withdraw Polish units from Allied command. "We have enough troops today. We do not need your help. You can take away your divisions. We do not need them."

Churchill's angry comments concealed a troubled conscience. He was haunted by the image of his predecessor, Neville Chamberlain, returning from his meeting with Hitler in Munich in September 1938, waving a little piece of paper and proclaiming "peace in our time" in a reedy voice. The man with the rolled-up umbrella had been greeted as savior, but he was now a figure of derision, a symbol of the discredited appeasement policy. In public at least, Churchill rejected any comparison between Czechoslovakia in 1938 and Poland in 1945, Munich and Yalta, Hitler and Stalin. But the parallels were unsettling, which is why he felt it necessary to go out of his way to refute them. "Poor Neville Chamberlain believed he could trust Hitler," he told cabinet ministers on the morning of February 23. "He was wrong. But I don't think that I am wrong about Stalin."

The Chamberlain analogy was on the prime minister's mind as he drove to Chequers, the official country house, for the weekend. He spent the one-hour drive to Buckinghamshire working on the first draft of a report on the Yalta negotiations that he planned to deliver to Parliament the following Tuesday. He was dictating "the most difficult and agitating part" of his speech—the section on Poland—as he stepped out of his Austin sedan onto the gravel driveway in front of the residence. He defended the country's new eastern frontier as "the fairest division of territory that can in all circumstances be made between the two countries whose history has been so . . ." At this point, he paused on the steps of the Tudor-style mansion and looked around him, searching for inspiration. "Chequered and intermingled." The draft speech included a line about Soviet Russia seeking "not only peace, but peace with honor." Churchill's private secretary, Jock Colville, was horrified. "? Omit," he scrawled in the margin. "Echo of Munich." The passage was swiftly deleted.

At dinner that evening, the prime minister seemed "rather depressed," according to Colville. He worried about the possibility of "Russia one day turning against us, saying that Chamberlain had trusted Hitler as he was now trusting Stalin (though he thought in different circumstances)." As he had many times during the war, Churchill comforted himself with a German proverb, "God takes care that trees don't grow up to the sky." By this he meant that there is a self-correcting mechanism in politics and international affairs: if Stalin grew too tall and betrayed the trust of western leaders, he would inevitably be toppled like a tree that had grown too big for its roots. Churchill's morose mood carried over after dinner, when he sat in the Great Hall of Chequers, listening to *The Mikado* "played much too slowly" on the gramophone, with Colville and "Bomber" Harris, the destroyer of Dresden. In 1940, the prime minister mused, everything had been clear: Britain was fighting for its very survival. Now everything was confused: "shadows of victory" had fallen over the land. He wondered "what will lie between the white snows of Russia and the white cliffs of Dover" once Harris had completed the destruction of Germany. The optimistic scenario was that something unexpected would happen to stop the Russians from sweeping on to the Atlantic, just as the death of Genghis Khan had stopped the advance of the Mongols in the thirteenth century. The Mongols, Churchill reminded his aides, had simply "retired and never came back."

"You mean now they will come back?" asked Harris, trying to figure out the connection between the Mongols and the Russians.

The prime minister did not have the answer to that question. "Who can say? They may not want to. But there is an unspoken fear in many people's hearts." He was sure of one thing. "After this war, we will be weak. We will have no money and no strength and we will lie between the two great powers of the USA and the USSR."

Churchill's ambivalence about Stalin and Russia reflected his emotional ups and downs, his knowledge of history, and the political demands of the moment. He and Roosevelt had traveled to Yalta hoping to recruit the Soviet dictator to their club. But the bonding worked in both directions. They bonded with Stalin at least as much as he bonded with them. In order to win over Stalin, western leaders were obliged to practice "make-believe diplomacy," in the damning phrase of a senior Foreign Office official, also known as the doctrine of therapeutic trust. As Churchill put it in his memoir, "I felt bound to proclaim my confidence in Soviet good faith in the hope of procuring it." Having placed such a large wager on Stalin, Churchill and Roosevelt had to persuade their own people of the wisdom of the bet. They had to reassure themselves, and everyone else, that their political instincts were correct.

It was a trap of their own making, but it was also a product of the historical circumstances in which they found themselves. Churchill could not imagine quarreling with the Russians at a time when the Germans were ready to unleash "three or four hundred divisions" against Great Britain. "Our hopeful assumptions were soon to be falsified. Still, they were the only ones possible at the time."

Churchill was encouraged by Stalin's restraint on Greece. The Russian leader had "scrupulously" abided by the spheres-of-influence understanding reached during the prime minister's visit to Moscow in November 1944. He had refrained from doing anything to encourage the Greek Communists in their rebellion against the British-backed government. It seemed that the *vozhd* could be relied upon to keep his side of a bargain. Churchill was also struck by the way in which Stalin had talked about Poland, condemning the "sins" of the tsars and promising to make amends for the past.

The prime minister's doubts about Stalin were similar to those expressed by Harry Hopkins. No one knew how long he would live or who would succeed him. It was possible to do business with the genial dictator, but what of the shadowy "committee of commissars" lurking behind his back in the recesses of the Kremlin? Like Hopkins and FDR, Churchill drew a distinction between "(a) Stalin himself, personally cordial to me" and "(b) Stalin in council, a grim thing behind him, which we and he both have to reckon with." His hopes lay with "a single man." This was the foreign equivalent of the old "good tsar" myth that attributed all the cruelty and injustice of Russia to evil advisers acting behind the back of a reasonable, well-intentioned ruler.

The Yalta agreements were put to a vote in the House of Commons on February 28. A group of Conservative members of Parliament vociferously opposed the deal on Poland. One dissident accused Churchill of negotiating an arrangement that would cause Poland to "lose nearly half her territory, a third of her population," and much of her natural resources. Another quoted the disillusioned comment of a young British officer: "It is perfectly obvious that we have fought the war in vain; every principle for which we started the war has been sacrificed." The prime minister brushed aside the criticism, arguing that the Soviet leaders wished "to live in honorable friendship and equality with the Western democracies. I feel also that their word is their bond." When the House divided at the end of the two-day debate, the government had a majority of three hundred seventy-one, with twenty-seven members voting for a motion of censure and eleven junior ministers abstaining. The rebellion had been quashed, but it would not be long before Churchill reconsidered his vote of confidence in Stalin.

It was almost twelve years to the day—three presidential terms—since FDR stood on a rain-swept platform and charted a way out of the Great Depression with his celebrated line "The only thing we have to fear is fear itself." He had come back to the U.S. Capitol to promote his vision of "a lasting peace" to the American people and persuade Congress to support the Yalta accords. Shortly before entering the chamber of the House of Representatives, the ever-competitive Roosevelt told congressmen that he planned to "do in an hour what it took Winston three hours to do" in his report to Parliament earlier in the week.

An audible gasp greeted the president as he was pushed down the aisle in his armless wheelchair at 12:31 p.m. on Wednesday, March 1. There was a shocked hush followed by a burst of loud applause from the packed chamber. Fewer than two months before, the same audience had seen him walk into the chamber on the arm of "Pa" Watson, now dead. "He had then begun to show the ravages of age and mountainous duty, but he was still on his feet, still indomitable against his infirmity," recorded *Time* magazine reporter Frank McNaughton, gazing down from the press gallery. "Everyone knew that Roosevelt couldn't walk without steel braces; it was something else to see him wheeled in a chair, admitting his physical difficulties." Never before had the president "uncloaked his infirmity so openly, so frankly, before so many people." As Roosevelt swung himself into a chair in front of a bank of microphones, reporters scribbled notes about his haggard appearance. His blue suit "hung slackly on his shoulders"; his slender wrists "seemed to have lost their beefy, rugged marks of strength"; the skin of his neck drooped in folds around the collar; his bony hands were leaner than ever and trembled as he reached for a glass of water.

He began by apologizing "for this unusual posture of sitting down during the presentation of what I want to say," explaining that it was a "lot easier" not to carry "about ten pounds of steel around on the bottom of my legs." Another burst of supportive applause enveloped the invalid seated in front of the small mahogany table. The public confession of his disability "grabbed the throats of those who heard him," according to an eyewitness. "It was so quietly and naturally spoken, so obviously sincere and human, that it hit with a wallop." Members leaned forward, straining to hear the president's words over a public-address system that had been turned down to prevent an echo from the network microphones. His voice lacked the rich timbre so familiar to the American people as he addressed the subject that was on everyone's minds, his own health. "It was not the old operatic voice; it was something strained and worn even as the body behind it was strained and worn and tired," wrote McNaughton. Sympathetic laughter greeted his remark that "I was not ill for a second until I arrived back in Washington," but the worries were not dispelled.

FDR had once told Orson Welles that the two of them together were the finest actors in America. Even in his parlous state, he remained a showman. He used his acting abilities to conceal the fact that he was having trouble focusing on the words in front of him because his vision was blurred. His tone of voice became even more conversational than usual to allow for extensive ad-libbing as he struggled to find his place in the written text. The departures from the prepared speech were rambling and sometimes nonsensical, horrifying Sam Rosenman, who had labored for days over the draft. His difficulties increased the more he talked as phlegm clogged up his throat. By the time he got to the section on Poland, he was coughing frequently. "His voice weakened, faded, almost seemed to go out. He cleared his throat uneasily, then hacked vigorously several times, and from there on the process was repeated agonizingly at intervals." He took off his reading glasses and started to follow the lines of outsize type with a lean right index finger. At times, it seemed as if he would not have the strength to continue. "Congress and the galleries suffered for and with the man in the big red chair."

FDR had sent emissaries on ahead to reassure the American people that he had achieved what he set out to achieve at Yalta. Jimmy Byrnes, the "assistant president," told the press that the outmoded concept of "spheres of influence" had been eliminated at the conference. The three great powers would assume joint responsibility for ensuring order in Poland and other liberated territories until free elections were held. Such claims were misleading, at the very least, but they were an essential part of the post-Yalta sales pitch. To persuade Congress to support the agreements, the president had to present them as an important step toward the fulfillment of FDR's Grand Design for a new world order. Roosevelt had explicitly acknowledged Russia's right to expect "friendly" governments on its western borders and had agreed to an "enlarged" version of the

Kremlin-imposed provisional government in Poland. All this was at odds with his promise to Congress that Yalta spelled "the end of the system of unilateral action, the exclusive alliances, the spheres of influence, the balances of power, and all the other expedients that have been tried for centuries—and have always failed." It took all of the president's skills as a communicator to conceal the gap between reality and make-believe.

Public opinion surveys suggested that the salesmanship was effective. Pollsters reported that 51 percent of Americans believed that the Yalta conference had been "successful," compared with just 11 percent who felt it was "unsuccessful." Satisfaction with Big Three cooperation rose from 46 percent in January to 71 percent at the end of February, an all-time high. A similar proportion of Americans were confident that a "fifty-year peace" could be established after the war. At the same time, a government study reported, "public ignorance concerning the actual decisions of the Crimea declaration is colossal." Only two in eight Americans were able to respond to detailed questions about the contents of the Yalta commu-niqué. Americans formed their opinions on the basis of general impres-sions, which FDR was adept at manipulating.

It was at this precise moment—the moment when public confidence in Roosevelt's ability to pull off a "lasting peace" was at its peak—that the great juggling act began to fall apart. As FDR was addressing Congress, troubling reports were arriving from eastern Europe suggesting that the spheres-of-influence way of thinking supposedly confined to the ash heap of history was very much alive. On February 27, the day Churchill defended the Yalta agreements in front of the House of Commons, Andrei Vyshinsky arrived in the Romanian capital Bucharest with an ultima-tum. The deputy commissar for foreign affairs had been a familiar face at Yalta, proposing toasts to the two western leaders. His mission now was to compel the young King Michael to replace his American-backed gov-ernment with a Communist-dominated coalition.

The Russian ultimatum to the pro-western monarch jolted both Roosevelt and Churchill, upsetting the confident assumptions that had held sway in the two weeks immediately after Yalta. In a series of telegrams to FDR, Churchill fretted that Stalin was pursuing policies in Romania that were "absolutely contrary to all democratic ideals." He also drew attention to reports of "deportations" and "liquidations in Poland," noting growing uneasiness in Britain that "we are letting the Poles down." An ominous commentary appeared in *Pravda* refuting the American interpretation of the Yalta declaration on eastern Europe. The official Communist Party newspaper pointed out that the three Allies attached different meanings to words like "democracy." Liberated peoples should be free to create democratic institutions "according to their own choice." The message was clear: Anglo-Saxon ideas of political freedom were by no means universal.

The new, more downbeat assessments of Yalta seeped through to the White House, the fortress of positive spin. On March 5, the president received a visit from an old friend, Adolf Berle, the U.S. ambassador to Mexico. Berle worried that FDR had made too many concessions to Stalin. Roosevelt explained that he needed Russian cooperation in the war against Japan. Unable to convince Berle of the soundness of the Yalta deal, he threw up his arms in a gesture of surrender.

"Adolf, I didn't say the result was good. I said it was the best I could do."

Part Two

An Iron Curtain
Is Drawn Down

—Winston S. Churchill

———

FEBRUARY–JUNE 1945

7

Comrade Vyshinsky

February 27

There were few more attractive postings for an American intelligence officer at the end of the war than Bucharest. The city that called itself the Paris of the Balkans offered everything an ambitious young man fresh out of Yale or Harvard could want: beautiful women; high-class socializing; luxurious, easily affordable accommodations; international intrigue in exotic surroundings; intelligence galore. For a few giddy months, it was possible to flit between the royal palace, Communist Party rallies, aristocratic salons, foreign legations, and lavish parties thrown by millionaire industrialists while laying the foundations of a high-flying career. The Athénée Palace, one of Europe's grand hotels, still hosted "the world's premier concourse of spies, blondes, beards, and monocles," in the phrase of *Life* magazine. Romania was occupied by the Red Army, but America was the focus of the hopes and expectations of the Romanian elite, exercising an influence way beyond her token military presence. Everyone, even the Russians, wanted to be friends with the Americans. And then, as suddenly as it had appeared, the good life vanished.

The first American to make an impression on the Romanian capital was Frank Wisner, a Wall Street lawyer turned professional spy. The former Rhodes Scholar hitched an airplane ride to Bucharest in September

1944, days after Romania switched sides from the Axis to the Allies, trapping twenty-one German divisions. His ostensible mission for the Office of Strategic Services was to repatriate nearly two thousand American pilots shot down over the Ploieşti oil fields, but he soon focused on intelligence gathering. As the senior American in Bucharest, the thirty-five-year-old navy lieutenant commander had easy entrée to the young king, Michael, who had engineered the August 23 coup that evicted Marshal Ion Antonescu, Romania's mini-führer. The Hohenzollern monarch had relied on support from the Communist underground, the best organized opposition force in the country, to rid himself of Antonescu's Nazi-backed clique. After the Red Army moved into Romania unopposed, Wisner sought to shore up the position of pro-western politicians wary of a Soviet takeover.

Energetic and gregarious, Wisner sent a stream of reports back to Washington on the political maneuvering in the capital and attempts by Moscow "to subvert the position of the government and the King." By the end of September, he and his staff had moved out of the Ambassador Hotel into the thirty-room mansion of the country's largest brewer, Mita Bragadiru, on the exclusive Aleea Modrogan. Wisner was adopted by the beer magnate's wife, Tanda Caradja, a Romanian princess who had inherited the dark flashing eyes and high cheekbones of her distant ancestor, Vlad Dracula.

The twenty-four-year-old Tanda set about organizing the social life of Wisner and the other Americans, lubricated with generous supplies from her husband's alcohol business. "I became his hostess," she said later. "He wanted to meet everyone right away in court society," a simple matter to arrange for someone who was both rich and beautiful. Princess Tanda threw elaborate dinner parties for Wisner, complete with maids in starched aprons, glistening white tablecloths groaning with food, and fine French wine served from crystal glasses. "There were parties every night," recalled one participant, "parties which lasted until dawn, some of them dignified, some of them wild." Suspicious of the Russians, upper-class Romanians rushed to find American patrons. They rented their apartments for practically nothing in return for placards emblazoned with the Stars and Stripes asserting American diplomatic protection. They also loaned their automobiles indefinitely to U.S. diplomats rather than let them fall into the hands of the Russians. The garden of the Bragadiru house soon became a "crowded motor pool," jammed with Ford and

Mercedes limousines. Even the lowliest members of Wisner's staff had personal cars at their disposal.

Life in the Bragadiru mansion was later satirized in a roman à clef written by one of the Americans, Beverly Bowie, titled *Operation Bughouse*. This was a reference to Wisner's habit of naming sources and subsources after virulent illnesses. His own code name was Typhoid; other agents included Influenza, Bronchitis, Jaundice, and the highly prized Tonsillitis, a Romanian General Staff liaison officer with the Red Army. In the fictional version, the Wisner character becomes Commander Drowne, a prototype for later Cold War warriors, who establishes his headquarters in "the mansion of Madame Nitti, a large white building which resembled a rather expensive funeral home." The bellicose commander dispatches telegrams to Washington reporting "startling rise in number rapes" by Russian soldiers and warning of takeovers by "coalition worst elements including Communists, other riff-raff" prior to calling for "dispatch twenty American divisions and immediate declaration of war on USSR." In real life, Wisner took care to play down his anti-Soviet views, knowing that his superiors back home remained committed to the preservation of the wartime alliance. After two months in the Bragadiru mansion, the Americans commandeered a large villa on Strada Batiștei in the old residential district, a mile and a half away. "Eating, working, sleeping, drinking and loving other men's wives under one roof while husbands and enlisted men were around was just a bit too much for some of us," recorded Wisner's deputy for counterintelligence, Robert Bishop. Nevertheless, the saturnine Tanda continued to fulfill her role as den mother–hostess–lover for the Americans.

Information flowed freely in the hothouse atmosphere of Bucharest. American, Russian, and British intelligence operatives shared one another's sources and mistresses, many of them inherited from the recently departed Germans. Well-connected Romanians switched patrons freely, depending on which big power appeared to be coming out on top. Despite her obvious preference for Americans, Princess Tanda took care to keep in touch with the Russians and was later investigated by the FBI for her Communist connections. Bishop's lover, Zsokie Cristea, was notorious in Bucharest for "gathering information from aristocratic and democratic circles" on behalf of the German intelligence service under the code name Mona Lisa. An OSS report later noted that Cristea "is a beautiful woman, has plenty of money, knows several foreign languages but has a very bad reputation in Rumanian society." Prior to hooking up with Bishop, she had numerous affairs with German and Hungarian diplomats. Bishop's colleagues later concluded that many of his intelligence coups, including a supposed "three-year plan" for the communization of Romania, were "pure drivel." His prized Romanian sources fabricated intelligence reports to suit their own political goals and his extreme anti-Soviet views.

The first threats to this sybaritic lifestyle appeared in January 1945 when the Russians began signaling their impatience with the pro-western government led by Nicolae Rădescu. A right-wing army general, Rădescu had been imprisoned under the Antonescu dictatorship after criticizing the German ambassador for interfering in Romanian affairs. His status as a former political prisoner had given him credibility with the Russians— until he began exhibiting an independent streak. The Soviets now accused him of failing to purge the bureaucracy of former Fascists and of ignoring the agreement on war reparations. On January 6, the Soviet military command issued orders for the deportation of all ethnic German men between the ages of seventeen and forty-five and women aged eighteen to thirty. The ancestors of many of these *Volksdeutsche* had settled in the Carpathian Mountains of Transylvania in the twelfth and thirteenth centuries, but Stalin needed them as slave labor in Russia. NKVD units armed with census lists sealed off German neighborhoods in Bucharest and other towns, just as they had sealed off Tatar villages in the Crimea the previous year. Nearly seventy thousand people were loaded into boxcars behind hastily erected barbed-wire barricades and shipped to towns in the Ural Mountains. Some of the more affluent deportees had frequented Princess Tanda's salon, but the Americans were powerless to help. Wisner drove around the city in his jeep rousing his German-Romanian acquaintances from their beds but was unable to stop the deportations. The OSS operative was "brutally shocked" by the spectacle of raw Soviet power at the same time that Russians were toasting a new era of Allied cooperation. He left Bucharest soon afterward, determined to alert Washington to the threat of a Soviet takeover of eastern Europe.

In the meantime, the Bucharest rumor mill was working overtime. The OSS picked up hints of an anti-Rădescu coup. A Communist source reported on January 22 that the party's two most prominent leaders, Gheorghe Gheorghiu-Dej and Ana Pauker, had returned from Moscow with a promise of Soviet support. The time was "ripe" for the Communists, or one of their front organizations, to "seize the government." Once Romania was under firm Soviet control, she would be treated as a full ally and co-belligerent in the war against Nazi Germany. As a reward for her compliance, she would receive the disputed region of northern Transylvania from her neighbor, Hungary. Some OSS analysts felt the reports were "alarmist," but the pace of events soon began to accelerate. Peasants took over large landed estates and began dividing up the land. Bloody clashes broke out in Bucharest's largest metallurgical factory, the Malaxa plant, between Communists and non-Communists. Newspapers supporting the mainstream prewar political parties were closed on the grounds that they had violated military censorship. The Communist-controlled press stepped up the propaganda campaign against Rădescu, accusing him of plotting a "Fascist counterrevolution" in league with the Germans.

It was now obvious that the Russians and the Romanian Communists had a radically different interpretation of the Yalta agreements from the western Allies. Roosevelt and Churchill believed they had secured a commitment from Stalin for "free elections" in eastern Europe. Soviet commentators seized on the passage in the Declaration on Liberated Europe that talked about the need to eliminate "the last vestiges of Nazism and Fascism" and create "democratic" institutions. In the Communist lexicon, Rădescu was a "reactionary," not a "democrat." It was therefore necessary to replace his administration with "a government broadly representative of all the democratic elements in the population," in accordance with the Yalta decisions. Prominent prewar politicians, such as Iuliu Maniu, founder of the National Peasants' Party, were excluded on grounds that they too were "reactionaries" and "Fascists," even though they had opposed the Antonescu dictatorship. A new government could only be based on the Communist-led coalition of left-wing parties known as the National Democratic Front, the sole legitimate representative of "all the country's democratic forces." Like Lewis Carroll's character Humpty Dumpty, Stalin used words to mean what he chose them to mean, "neither more nor less."

The anti-Rădescu propaganda barrage reached a crescendo on February 23 when Romanian newspapers reprinted an editorial from *Pravda* accusing the prime minister of "opposing the forces of democracy." Statements by Rădescu promising to suppress anarchy and prevent rule by "foreigners" only added fuel to the flames. The Communist-controlled press claimed that Rădescu and his "reactionary clique" were plotting a civil war and urged "the Romanian people and its army" to defend democracy. As a precaution, two newly formed divisions of Soviet NKVD troops moved into positions around the capital. By nightfall, the city was awash with handbills summoning "all democratic forces" to a rally in the center of Bucharest at 2:00 p.m. on Saturday, February 24. "Death to the Fascists!" screamed one pamphlet. "Officers, non-commissioned officers, soldiers!" read another. "Do not carry out the orders of the Fascists, the enemies of the people." "Long live the gallant Red Army!" proclaimed a third. "Long live its great Commander, the liberating Marshal, Josef Vissarionovich Stalin!" Information reached the U.S. military mission that the Communists had mobilized "3,500 armed men" who would "organize a general demonstration in front of prominent buildings" and "make a definite effort to incite the government forces to open fire." The countdown to the coup had begun.

"Citizens of the Capital!" announced the Communist Party newspaper *Scânteia* (Spark) in its February 24 edition. "Your rights and your freedom are in danger. The remnants of Fascism, grouped around Maniu and supported by General Rădescu, have become aggressive and are trying to stifle your struggle for a better life. The dark shadow of dictatorship is again hovering over us. . . . The reactionaries under Maniu and Rădescu have awakened distrust in the allies of the sincerity of Romania's policy. The international position of the country is in danger. This situation cannot last. . . . Come, all of you, to the mass meeting summoned for today at two o'clock in Nation Square."

A hundred thousand people gathered around the fountains in the square on high ground overlooking downtown Bucharest. Most came from factories around the city, but some had been bused in from provincial towns. They carried banners with slogans such as "Death to Fascism!" "Down with Rădescu!" "Long Live the King!" and "Down with Saboteurs in the Government." The prime minister had withdrawn many of his police units from the center of the city on the insistence of Soviet military commanders, and the mood was relaxed. People carried pictures of Stalin, King Michael, Churchill, and Roosevelt, along with Romanian, Russian, American, and British flags. At 4:00 p.m., the rally began to disband. Led by the Communist leader Ana Pauker, some twenty-five thousand demonstrators marched northward along the grand boulevards of the French-accented city, toward the government buildings clustered around the Athénée Palace Hotel.

The mood became much more tense after the crowd reached the Royal Palace. Fighting broke out between Communists and anti-Communists beneath the King Carol I statue, a grandiose monument featuring the former monarch on a prancing bronze stallion high above the crowd. Order was quickly restored as more people crammed into the square from Victory Avenue. The demonstrators massed in front of the Ministry of the Interior, a half-completed neoclassical palazzo on the southeastern corner of the square, where the prime minister had his office. Suddenly, automatic pistol shots rang out from a bank building opposite the ministry. People scattered in panic but returned after the shooting died down. Some of the armed demonstrators fired pistol shots at the ministry, narrowly missing Rădescu, who was standing at the window of his office observing the protests. A thousand or so demonstrators forced their way through locked gates into the courtyard, causing panicky soldiers to fire several volleys of warning shots from the upper floors of the building, perhaps one hundred and fifty rounds in all. They were ordered to fire into the air, above the heads of the demonstrators. Russian and British officers helped the guards persuade the demonstrators to leave the courtyard and close the gates.

A dozen or so people lay wounded in the square. A railway worker and one of the protesters who had arrived from out of town were dead. There was so much confusion that it was unclear whether the fatal shots had been fired by soldiers defending the Interior Ministry, unknown snipers in nearby buildings, or armed men accompanying the demonstration. The protest leaders blamed "the executioner" Rădescu.

"They have shot without shame at the masses of the people," yelled Lucrețlu Pătrășcanu, a Communist who had helped organize the August 1944 coup against Antonescu. "Those who ordered this, those who carried out the order, and those who are really responsible will pay with their heads." For Pătrășcanu and his fellow Communists, everything was clear. The Rădescu government had blood on its hands and must be replaced by a National Democratic government. "It alone will be capable of weeding out the Fascists."

The Soviet military command issued an ultimatum to Rădescu at 5:40 p.m., within half an hour of the shooting incidents around the Interior Ministry. The Red Army would be "compelled to intervene" unless the firing ceased immediately. Later that evening, several thousand government supporters gathered in front of his office, shouting patriotic slogans. Around 9:00 p.m., a car with its headlights off rounded the corner of Palace Square into the street next to the Interior Ministry. Someone from inside the car fired a volley from a machine gun into the pro-Rădescu crowd, killing two and wounding eleven others. Ignoring Soviet censorship regulations, the beleaguered prime minister went on Bucharest radio at 10:00 p.m. to address his "brother Romanians" in defiant, nationalistic tones. He blamed the Communists for what had happened, describing them as "the nationless and the godless," a tactless reference to Pauker's Jewish origins. Romanians, he insisted, would not allow "these frightful hyenas" to take control of the country. The Communist-controlled press promptly labeled Rădescu's speech "criminal," saying it "finally unmasks him as the most dangerous Fascist agent and an enemy of the people."

It was never conclusively established who fired the shots that wounded and killed the demonstrators in Palace Square. *Scânteia* claimed that the shots came from government buildings and "above all from the Royal Palace." Rădescu supporters cited autopsies showing that the bullets that caused the injuries came from Russian weapons not used by the Romanian army. A leading Communist journalist who was present in the square later conceded that many more people would have been killed had the soldiers in the Interior Ministry building fired directly into the crowd, rather than over their heads. In the end, it hardly mattered. The Communists were able to point to "the murder of peaceful citizens" as evidence that the prime minister had lost control. In the words of a National Democratic Front communiqué on February 25, "the blood of the people has flowed under the very walls of the Royal Palace." The Communists had their martyrs—and the Russians their pretext to intervene.

Andrei Vyshinsky arrived in Bucharest on the afternoon of Tuesday, February 27, three days after Bloody Saturday, on a "special mission." He headed straight for the Soviet embassy, where Russian diplomats and military commanders had formed a crisis center to follow the latest developments. Rădescu was still in office, but his power was hanging by a thread. Sensing the winds blowing from Moscow, the Communists and their left-wing allies had stepped up their threats to "mercilessly annihilate the Fascist beasts." The news media were under Communist control, with Soviet censors refusing to publish the government's version of the shootings around the Interior Ministry. "Death to the Fascists!" demanded a National Democratic Front communiqué on Tuesday morning. The prime minister told western diplomats he expected to be arrested at any moment. The king, who had returned to the capital the previous day, began a round of consultations with political leaders on the formation of a new government. Vyshinsky requested an audience "between nine and ten this evening." Constitutional appearances had to be preserved.

The deputy commissar was well known to the Americans and the British. His round glasses, florid face, trim mustache, and white hair gave him a grandfatherly, Dickensian appearance. Harold Macmillan, Churchill's envoy to North Africa and Italy, thought he looked "exactly like Mr. Pickwick." The two men got to know each other well during negotiations for the formation of a new Italian government following the collapse of the Mussolini regime. After their first meeting, in Algiers in November 1943, the Englishman felt that Vyshinsky could be mistaken for a "Conservative mayor or constituency chairman." It was difficult to square this genial image with his reputation as "the cruel persecutor of the Russian terror—the scourge of prisoners, the torturer of witnesses, the gloating, merciless, bloody figure of which we read six or seven years ago." Only his eyes gave him away. Humorous and sparkling in casual conversation, they turned hard and menacing as he subjected Allied officials to a tough cross-examination. The prosecutor-turned-diplomat enjoyed debating political opponents. His benevolent veneer would disappear as he sought to get the best of both sides of the argument. Macmillan noted a couple of "gems" that revealed his true colors:

> Democracy is like wine. It is all right if taken in moderation.
> Free speech is all right, so long as it does not interfere with the policy of the Government.

Vyshinsky was one of a handful of senior Soviet officials who had managed to win Stalin's confidence through a combination of intellectual sophistication and blind obedience. He was more personable, more calculating, and quicker witted than his boss, Molotov. He spoke several foreign languages, including Polish (his father was a successful Polish chemist), French, and decent English and German. As a former Menshevik who only joined the Bolshevik Party in 1920, he was vulnerable to political blackmail. Among the black marks in his dossier was an attempt to implement an order for Lenin's arrest from the provisional government, shortly before the 1917 Bolshevik Revolution; many other Mensheviks had been sent to their deaths as "class enemies" for lesser crimes. The bourgeois, highly educated Vyshinsky understood that his survival depended on repeated displays of loyalty to Stalin, his "deeply respected teacher and beloved leader." He could never be too obsequious, too extreme in his denunciations of the ideological foe. He put his legal and rhetorical talents completely at the service of the tyrant. This helps explain his vitriolic diatribes during the Stalinist purges, which were bloodthirsty even by Soviet standards. "Shoot these rabid dogs!" he demanded at the first of the great Moscow show trials, in August 1936. "Down with these abject animals! Let's put an end once and for all to these miserable hybrids of foxes and pigs, these stinking corpses! Let's exterminate the mad dogs of capitalism, who want to tear to pieces the flower of our new Soviet nation!"

The deputy commissar had a delicate mission in Bucharest. A year earlier, as the Red Army approached the frontiers of Romania after storming across Ukraine, Stalin had denied any interest in annexing Romanian territory or changing the political and economic structure of the country. Soviet troops were ordered to respect "all existing Romanian organs of power" and avoid introducing a Soviet-type regime. During an earlier visit to Bucharest, in December 1944, Vyshinsky had expressed confidence in the new bourgeois government headed by Rădescu, who was known for his anti-Communist views. It mattered little to Stalin if a conservative politician was in charge of a country like Romania, as long as he respected Soviet wishes and carried out the terms of the armistice. Loyalty and reliability were more important than ideological correctness. But Rădescu had shown that he could not be trusted. His government was attempting to wriggle out of its obligations under the armistice agreement, refusing to turn over its Black Sea fleet in compensation for war damage inflicted on Russia by Romanian troops serving under the Germans.

Russian rulers had long had a jaundiced view of their exuberant Latin neighbor, which corrupted everyone who set foot in it, easterners and westerners alike. "Romania, bah!" snorted Tsar Nicholas II, in 1914. "It is neither a state, nor a nation, but a profession!" Thousands of Red Army soldiers had simply deserted, seduced by the relatively good life in Romania. Reports were reaching Moscow of attempts by Romanian Fascists, in collusion with the Germans, to stir up trouble behind Soviet lines and organize uprisings against the Russians. Incidents of sabotage and murder against Red Army installations increased sharply in early 1945. German parachutists had landed in Romanian military airfields and made contact with Romanian officers. Left to itself, Romania would drift into the western camp, perhaps even back into the German camp. This was unacceptable. The Romanian Communists lacked popular support—but, from the Soviet point of view, they were the only political force that could be counted on.

King Michael received Vyshinsky at his family home in a residential district of the capital, the white stucco Elizabeth Palace, off the Kiseleff Chausée, not far from the Soviet embassy. The scion of the Hohenzollerns had been forced to move out of the Royal Palace after it was bombed by the Germans in revenge for the August 1944 coup. The Soviet envoy told the king that the only way out of the crisis was the formation of a new government based on "the truly democratic forces of the country," a euphemism for the Communist-dominated National Democratic Front. The twenty-three-year-old monarch played for time, saying he had to consult all the political parties. He did not tell Vyshinsky that he had earlier signed a decree, prepared by the General Staff, dismissing a group of ten left-wing army officers who had written an open letter calling for Rădescu's replacement. When the Russian found out about the decree the following morning, he demanded another audience with the king, on Wednesday, February 28. This time he was much more direct, even brutal. The Soviet Union would tolerate no further delay. Vyshinsky looked at his wristwatch.

"You have just two hours and five minutes to make it known to the public that General Rădescu has been dismissed," he told the king. "By eight o'clock you must inform the public of his successor."

When the Romanian foreign minister objected that the king had to proceed "in a constitutional manner," the Russian told him brusquely to shut up. He then described the royal decree dismissing the anti-Rădescu officers as "an unfriendly act." It must be annulled immediately. Even more red faced than usual, Vyshinsky got up and left, followed by a royal aide. He grabbed the heavy door with both hands and "thrust it from him in a violent explosion of rage," causing "a resounding crash." King Michael sat dazed at his desk for a few moments until his aide returned from escorting Vyshinsky to his car. The aide asked him to come out into the hallway. There, next to the door frame, was a long crack in the plaster that quickly became the symbol of a decisive turning point in modern Romanian history.

It was an unequal contest with a predictable outcome. The earnest, inexperienced king had teamed up with underground Communist activists and prewar politicians to arrest Antonescu in August 1944. The Germans, in full retreat across Europe, had lacked the strength to respond aggressively and restore the marshal to power. King Michael's gamble had succeeded—but the situation was radically different now. The Red Army had occupied Romania in force and could dictate its will. The king and the prime minister made a fatal error in imagining they were independent actors who could preserve some freedom of maneuver by balancing the Soviet Union against the western Allies. The royal court, known as the kindergarten in Bucharest because of the youth of the king and his principal advisers, was no match for the Kremlin. Tolerated by the Russians as long as he did their bidding, the Anglophile Michael was a lonely, isolated figure, shuttling between his palaces. He enjoyed the company of western diplomats but felt constrained by royal protocol to decline their social invitations. Neither the Americans nor the British could help him. The U.S. political representative, Burton Berry, refused to discuss candidates for the prime minister's post for fear it might be interpreted as "putting our finger into the Romanian political broth." This perplexed the king, who asked sadly, "Why should you hesitate to put your finger in the broth when you know that your ally has put his hand down my throat?"

While Vyshinsky was delivering his ultimatum to the king, Soviet commanders ordered Romanian military units in Bucharest to surrender their weapons. Simultaneously, Soviet tanks appeared on the broad, tree-lined boulevards of the capital. Statements from the royal court were screened by Russian military censors—and modified if they failed to reflect the current line from Moscow. King Michael had become a political fig leaf, unable to influence events or even to express his personal opinion. Having dealt with the Nazis, and then with the Communists, he had learned the hard way "not to say what I feel and to smile at those I most hate."

The crisis ended in the manner demanded by Vyshinsky—with the appointment of a leftist coalition government dominated by the Communists. The new prime minister was Petru Groza, head of an agrarian party known as the Ploughman's Front. But Communists occupied key posts in the government, including the Interior and Justice Ministries. The new government committed itself to fulfilling the armistice terms, weeding out Fascists from the army and the police, and breaking up the old landed estates. Its makeup reflected the Stalinist notion of a People's Democracy, an intermediate stage between capitalism and communism that stopped short of the establishment of full Soviet power. Countries occupied by the Red Army would be permitted to retain their national institutions—in Romania's case, the king, the Orthodox Church, and the parliament—as long as they were "friendly" to the Soviet Union. The precise definition of "friendly" was left fluid, but it included a ban on any public criticism of

Russia, a tilt toward Moscow in economic relations, and an unrelenting focus on maintaining law and order behind the front lines.

The payoff followed swiftly. On March 9, three days after the formation of the new government, Vyshinsky announced that northern Transylvania would be returned to Romania. A huge ceremony was organized in Cluj, which had a large majority of ethnic Hungarians; Nazi Germany had awarded the city, and surrounding region, to Hungary at the beginning of the war in an attempt to curry favor with Hungarians. British and American representatives declined to attend the celebration, not wanting to legitimize the new Communist-dominated government. Vyshinsky brushed the western protests aside with his own twist on Churchill's remark at Yalta about "the eagle" permitting "the little birds to sing." He described opponents of the new political order in Romania as "chirping sparrows."

At first, the changes seemed imperceptible. The king still lived in his palace, millionaire industrialists continued to throw extravagant parties, foreign spies still congregated in the bar of the Athénée Palace. "Everything in town is very quiet," the U.S. military representative in Bucharest, General Cortlandt Schuyler, wrote in his diary on March 9. "Have talked to a number of upper class Romanians, and their general feeling seems to be that things are not as bad as they had expected. They think they are in for a period of gradual changeover to leftist ideas and that they will be able to adapt themselves to the new situation without too much trouble." The people in question had thrived under parliamentary democracy in the years before and after World War I and the Ruritanian-style royal dictatorship of Carol II, known for his scandalous love affairs and extravagant military uniforms. They had adapted to rule by the Fascist Iron Guard during World War II and the arrival in force of the Red Army in the fall of 1944. They felt they could deal with one more change of government.

The shift in the balance of political power soon became apparent in subtle ways. Large numbers of Russian advisers arrived in town, commandeering the villas of departing American and British officials. Flights of U.S. military aircraft were held up at the airport for mysterious reasons. Meetings of the Allied Control Commission, the joint Russian-American-British military committee that was meant to be supervising the Romanian government, became a formality. Russian soldiers insisted that they were now responsible for the fleets of luxurious Romanian automobiles that had been placed under American "protection." They also detained a pair of American intelligence officers who observed a National Democratic Front rally from a rooftop overlooking Palace Square, to the shock of Romanian bystanders who regarded all foreigners as untouchable. The secret police, the Siguranța, trailed western diplomats and prevented them from moving freely around the country.

Politically active Romanians had to decide whether to go into exile, risk imprisonment or perhaps even death, or seek an accommodation with the new regime. Torn between foreboding about the future and his sense of royal duty, King Michael agonized over whether to abdicate. He eventually chose to stay, telling Burton Berry that he might still be able to do something for his people if he "ate some humble pie." Rădescu sought refuge in the British embassy after learning that he was being hunted by "Communist armed bands." The head of the British military mission, Air Vice-Marshal Donald Stevenson, ordered his men to use firearms if necessary to protect the ousted prime minister. His action alarmed Foreign Office officials in London, who wanted at all costs to avoid "a direct clash between us and the Russians." They also had doubts about the capabilities of the embassy guards, describing them as "a very scratch lot," certainly no match for the Red Army or even the Romanian army. Churchill overruled the objections of his officials and authorized Stevenson "to open fire" in Rădescu's defense "in the last resort."

"Whatever you deem necessary to do in defense of British honour we shall support," he cabled.

This display of Churchillian grit heartened Stevenson, a large, ruddy-faced man fond of fox-hunting metaphors. The Russians, he cabled London on March 10, had taken "their crooked fences in grand style and left us nowhere at the kill. Nevertheless I hope after next draw we will have a straighter line of country and our second horses will be more evenly matched. The hunt is by no means over."

But it was over, at least in Romania. Despite his personal support for Rădescu, Churchill did not want to get into a heated argument with Stalin over a country that had been allied with Nazi Germany for much of the war. He recognized that the February 27 demonstrations, followed by the Vyshinsky visit, amounted to a coup d'état against a pro-western government. On the other hand, he also sympathized with Russian security concerns. Intelligence intercepts showed that German commandos were attempting to organize stay-behind sabotage operations in northern Romania, in cooperation with Fascist elements in the Romanian army. In some cases, Red Army deserters had joined the German-led partisan bands. The fledgling insurgency helped explain the Soviet decision to deport tens of thousands of Romanian *Volksdeutsche* back in January. Stalin had made clear at Yalta that he would not tolerate any kind of rebellion behind his front lines.

An even more important factor, from Churchill's point of view, was his spheres-of-influence agreement with the *vozhd,* reached in Moscow in September 1944. Stalin had kept his side of the bargain on Greece, where Churchill claimed a 90 percent stake. According to a British Foreign Office minute, "There is no getting away from the fact that we have agreed to a 10 per cent interest in Romanian affairs, which entitles us to do little more than protect British interests." British officials worried that any attempt to invoke the Yalta agreements on Romania would only encourage Stalin to claim the same rights "in respect of Greece, Italy, and eventually Western European affairs." At Yalta, Stalin had pointedly emphasized that he had "every confidence" in the way the British were handling the Communist rebellion in Greece and had no intention of interfering with Churchill's decisions. His unspoken expectation was that the western Allies would give him a free hand in the rest of the Balkans.

The prime minister set out his thinking in a March 8 cable to Roosevelt. He was "distressed" by the turn of events in Romania, which ran "absolutely contrary" to all "the principles of Yalta." He predicted "an indiscriminate purge of anti-Communist Romanians" on the pretext of weeding out "Fascists." At the same time, he wanted to avoid giving Stalin the opportunity to say, "I did not interfere with your action in Greece, why do you not give me the same latitude in Romania?" This would only serve as a distraction from "the much more important issue of Poland," which had consumed so much time in Yalta.

Replying to Churchill on March 11, FDR acknowledged that "the Russians have installed a minority government of their own choosing" in Bucharest. On the other hand, he did not feel that Romania was "a good place for a test case" of the Crimean agreements. "The Russians have been in undisputed control from the beginning." In addition, "with Rumania lying athwart the Russian lines of communications," it was "difficult to contest the plea of military necessity and security which they are using to justify their action." Neither Roosevelt nor Churchill had the stomach for a showdown with Stalin over Romania. Instead they were bracing themselves for a test of wills at the other end of eastern Europe, in Poland. The attention of the two leaders quickly switched to Moscow, where negotiations had already begun for the formation of a new Polish government.

8

"An Impenetrable Veil"

March 7

On March 7, 1945, the U.S. 9th Armored Division captured a bridge over the Rhine River at Remagen, eliminating the last significant natural obstacle on the road to the heart of Germany. The seizure of the strategic bridge heartened the small band of Americans in Moscow after a series of Red Army triumphs drawing attention to the disparity in fighting on the western and eastern fronts. "The war is going wonderfully well again now," Kathleen Harriman enthused in a letter to her sister Mary the following day. "Gosh, it's exciting. But the news is slightly dampened here by our gallant allies who at the moment are being most bastard-like. Averell is very busy—what with Poland, PWs, and I guess the Balkans. The house is full of running feet, voices, and phones ringing all night long—up until dawn."

As Kathleen noted in another letter, to her English friend (and future stepmother) Pamela Churchill, "The honeymoon after Yalta was short-lived, shorter than even the more pessimistic guessed." The optimism felt by many westerners in the wake of the Big Three meeting had been punctured by a series of disputes with the Russians over implementation of the Yalta decisions. American commentators initially blamed the difficulties on Kremlin hard-liners unhappy with Soviet concessions at Yalta.

Time magazine speculated that the unsettling events in Romania showed that "Stalin needed time to bring his bureaucracy into line with the Yalta doctrine." But the "good tsar, bad advisers" explanation became increasingly difficult to sustain as the quarrels multiplied to include everything from Vyshinsky's activities in Romania to the formation of a new Polish government to the repatriation of American prisoners of war liberated by the Red Army. It was beginning to look as if Stalin had a fundamentally different interpretation of the Yalta agreements from Roosevelt and Churchill—and that little of substance had been agreed at all.

A sense of gloom and foreboding enveloped Spaso House, the poorly heated, war-battered residence of the U.S. ambassador to Moscow. Built by a Russian textile baron in 1914, the once-luxurious neoclassical mansion was now dank and drafty, many of its windows blown out by German bombs and replaced with sheets of leaky plywood. The garden was filled with mounds of dirt from excavating a bomb shelter. The housing shortage had obliged Harriman and his daughter to share their home with members of the embassy staff and visiting Americans. In the evening, they huddled together around the fireplace in his upstairs bedroom, playing bezique and trying to keep warm. It was hard to imagine now the spectacular receptions that had taken place here just a few years before, including a grand ball immortalized in Mikhail Bulgakov's novel *Master and Margherita.* Bulgakov's wife, Elena, described the scene in her journal for April 23, 1935. "Dancing in the hall with columns, colored lights from above. Behind a net, masses of birds flying. An orchestra imported from Stockholm. . . . Dinner in a dining room specially attached to the mansion for the ball, with separate tables. In the corners, small pens with kid goats, lambs, baby bears. Along the walls—cages with roosters. At around 3:00 a.m. accordions played and the roosters started singing. *Style Russe.* Masses of tulips, roses—from Holland. On the upper floor a barbecue. Red roses, red French wine. Downstairs—everywhere champagne, cigarettes." Another party featured three sea lions from the Moscow circus who balanced bottles of champagne on their noses before running amok when their trainer fainted from too much alcohol. The great ballroom now served as an overflow embassy chancellery and the setting for war games pitting the Russians against the Japanese.

The handsome, polo-playing heir to a railroad fortune, Averell Harriman had arrived in Moscow as ambassador in October 1943 with high hopes. As Roosevelt's special envoy to Britain for the lend-lease program, he had enjoyed easy access to Churchill and was frequently invited to spend weekends at Chequers. The Russians had rolled out the red carpet for him when he visited the country on a special mission in September 1941, promising vast quantities of tanks, trucks, and airplanes, to help throw back the Nazis from the approaches to Moscow and Leningrad. Like many American politicians and diplomats before him, he tried to bond with Kremlin leaders. "I know it will be difficult," he told his predecessor, Admiral William Standley, "but they're only human, those Russians. Stalin can be handled." He believed that he "could get on an intimate basis with several of the commissars, all of whom have been extremely friendly." Initially, at least, he was inclined to take a benign view of Stalin's postwar intentions toward eastern Europe. "In spite of the conjectures to the contrary, there is no evidence that he is unwilling to allow an independent Poland to emerge," he wrote in a March 1944 dispatch. He saw no reason to dispute Soviet claims of German responsibility for the massacre of Polish officers murdered by the NKVD at Katyn. At his suggestion, Kathleen was included in a group of diplomats and journalists invited by the Soviet foreign ministry to tour the execution site. While she expressed some reservations about the evidence presented by the Russians, she was persuaded that "the Poles were murdered by the Germans." The ambassador endorsed his daughter's report.

Harriman's views about the Soviet Union hardened under the pressure of events. He was dismayed by the Russian refusal to grant landing rights to American and British planes seeking to drop supplies to Polish underground fighters during the Warsaw Uprising. Stalin was motivated primarily by "ruthless political considerations," Harriman felt. He suspected that the Soviets felt they had nothing to gain, and a lot to lose, from the victory of insurgents loyal to the anti-Communist Polish government in London. The ambassador was also upset by the Russian refusal to express gratitude for the huge quantities of war matériel they were receiving under lend-lease. By the summer of 1944, he had come to advocate a much tougher line toward Moscow, based on the idea of hard bargaining and "a firm but friendly *quid pro quo* attitude." He demanded an end to the policy of giving the Russians whatever they requested, simply because they were fighting the Germans. "This is not the way to get along," he told lend-lease officials. "They are tough and they expect us to be tough."

The ambassador's change of heart also reflected his growing irritation at working and living conditions in Moscow. Although he saw Stalin once or twice a month, more frequently than any other foreign ambassador, their sessions were formal and usually unproductive. Conducting

The Livadia Palace was built as a summer residence for Russia's last tsar, Nicholas II, and his family. During the Yalta conference, FDR held meetings with his aides in the Sun Room overlooking the Black Sea, originally designed as a bedroom for the sickly tsarevitch, Alexei.

FDR had a private meeting with Stalin on the first day of the Yalta conference in his study, formerly the tsar's antechamber. They are accompanied by their interpreters, Charles Bohlen (partially obscured), and Vladimir Pavlov (back to camera). Photograph by Robert Hopkins, U.S. Signal Corps.

Plenary sessions of the Yalta conference were held in the white ballroom of the Livadia Palace, the scene of glittering parties thrown by Russia's last tsar. In this photo, visible from Stalin's left are Vladimir Pavlov (Russian interpreter, seated behind), Ivan Maisky, Andrei Gromyko, Admiral Leahy, Secretary Stettinius, FDR, Charles Bohlen (with papers), Vyacheslav Molotov (standing), Arthur Birse (British interpreter, back to camera), Winston Churchill, Edward Bridges, Archibald Clark Kerr, Fyodor Gusev, and Andrei Vyshinsky. Alger Hiss is seated in the second row, between Stettinius and Roosevelt.

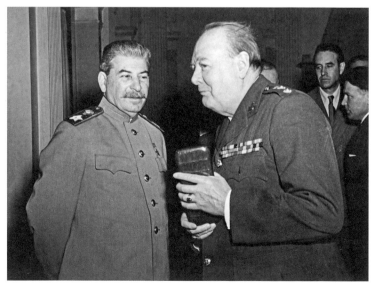

Stalin and Churchill, with his favorite cigar case, during a break in the conference. The prime minister is dressed in the uniform of a Royal Air Force colonel. Averell Harriman is visible in the background.

The bedroom used by FDR during the Yalta conference. The Soviet maids came from the National Hotel in Moscow. Roosevelt was the only member of the U.S. delegation to have a private bathroom.

Harry Hopkins (left) was FDR's closest adviser at Yalta, but he was almost as ill as the president. He was already suffering from stomach cancer, in addition to dysentery brought on by too much rich food and alcohol. With British foreign secretary Anthony Eden.

Iconic photograph of the Big Three at Yalta. Officials standing from left are British admiral Sir John Cunningham, Admiral Ernest King (chief of naval operations), Sir Charles Portal (marshal of the Royal Air Force), Admiral William Leahy (immediately behind FDR), General Alexei Antonov (Red Army deputy chief of staff), Sergei Khudyakov (marshal of aviation), and Lieutenant General Anatoly Gryzlov (Antonov's assistant).

ABOVE The "Little Three."
Accompanying their fathers to Yalta
were (from left) Sarah Churchill,
Anna Roosevelt, and Kathleen
Harriman.

RIGHT Secretary Stettinius and
his aide, Alger Hiss, who was
subsequently unmasked as a Soviet
spy. Hiss advised FDR on United
Nations matters at Yalta and served
as secretary general of the founding
United Nations conference in San
Francisco in April 1945.

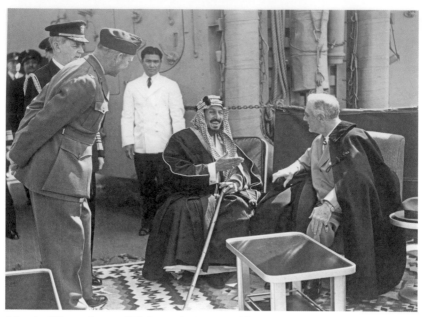

After the Yalta conference, FDR flew to the Suez Canal for a meeting with Saudi king Ibn Saud on the deck of the USS *Quincy*. The king was accompanied by his personal coffee taster, his astrologer, and eight live sheep.

Winston Churchill arrives for the opening session of the Yalta conference at the Livadia Palace with a Russian fur hat and his trademark cigar.

German refugees in Torgau fleeing the Red Army advance. Some are carrying looted possessions.

A soldier from the 69th Infantry Division demonstrates the functioning of the American M-1 rifle to his curious Red Army comrades, shortly after crossing the Elbe River on April 25.

Soviet soldiers share *Yank* magazine with U.S. airmen in Poltava, Ukraine.

A U.S. Army tank meets a Red Army supply train on the road to Berlin.

business with lower-level officials was even more frustrating. Weeks or months could go by without a reply to a diplomatic démarche. Harriman complained about being given a "complete runaround" by Molotov, despite the superficial cordiality of their relations. He soon discovered that there was a vast difference between the Russian treatment of visiting special envoys and diplomats permanently stationed in Moscow. The visitors were typically wined and dined by Kremlin leaders determined to leave a good impression; resident ambassadors were often simply ignored. Unable to get appointments with Soviet officials, Harriman often stayed in bed until late morning, writing cables to Washington and waiting for instructions. There were many days when he never left Spaso House. When he did venture outside, to attend the ballet or go skiing on the hills above the Moscow River, he was automatically followed by four NKVD agents, ostensibly for his personal protection. His contacts with ordinary Russians were closely regulated. The Russian criminal code stated that it was a crime, punishable by three years' imprisonment to death, to provide any kind of unauthorized "assistance" to "the representatives of the international bourgeoisie." A virtual prisoner in his huge house, Harriman felt physically isolated and worn out from the endless battles with the Soviet bureaucracy.

Life in Spaso House would have been even more burdensome without the company of his vivacious twenty-seven-year-old daughter. Harriman had left his wife, Marie, in America because of her poor health and relied on Kathleen as his hostess and confidante. In London, she had worked as a journalist and representative of the Office of War Information, the U.S. propaganda agency. When they moved to Moscow, she took over responsibility for the management of Spaso House. She was gregarious and fun and had a lively sense of humor that contrasted with his dour, self-important personality. Her "loosening up program" at Spaso included inventing new types of vodka cocktail (vodka with sherry, vodka with wine, vodka with synthetic fruit juice), playing bottle billiards, and swapping stories about the Mexican ambassador's sex life. But even Kathleen acknowledged that there were times when the oppressive, hothouse atmosphere of Moscow became difficult to bear. "Living here is like being surrounded by four big high menacing walls," she told Pamela Churchill on March 20, 1945. She had spent the evening "sitting and knitting," listening to the liberal Czechoslovak foreign minister, Jan Masaryk, ruminate about his fears for the postwar world. It depressed her to think that the matters that preoccupied Masaryk and her father—"common garden decency and freedom"—were "the kind of things I took for granted before I came to this country."

Contrary to the hopes of foreign residents, life in Moscow was not getting any more relaxed with the approach of final victory. Quite the reverse, in fact. The NKVD was now enforcing security regulations that had been eased during the height of the war, when everyone was united by a common purpose. A Volga German who worked as a gardener for the British embassy was arrested and banished to Siberia for failing to turn over his radio to the authorities. British diplomats were convinced that a few months earlier, prior to the adoption of "a new and more rigid party line," they would have been permitted to retain their "criminal gardener." The secret police also stepped up their harassment of Russian women who had fallen in love with Americans and other westerners, even if they were legally married. Personal pleas to Molotov to help resolve these cases were greeted with a stony silence.

Despite the Soviet restrictions on contacts with foreigners, Kathleen managed to assemble an eclectic collection of "tame Russians," people who were willing to associate with American diplomats for one reason or another. Her latest recruit was a Russian actor who assumed the role of a visiting American millionaire in a play and therefore had an excuse for observing real-life capitalists in action. Another "tame Russian" was Aleksei Tolstoy, a distant relative of the great writer and leading member of the Soviet literary establishment. The count—he was permitted to keep his aristocratic title by the Communists—invited the Harrimans to his dacha outside Moscow, where they had long discussions about "his favorite subject, the Russian soul." Spaso House parties often included the journalist Ilya Ehrenburg, who affected the look of a French intellectual, complete with black beret. The bloodthirsty *Red Army* commentator gathered a circle of diplomats and military men around him as he dispensed such Ehrenburgisms as "Yonder balustrade would be an excellent place from which to hang Germans." Ehrenburg had spent two decades in Paris as a correspondent for *Pravda*. "As a result of his experiences abroad he has formed some very erroneous but nonetheless deeply rooted ideas of the rest of the world," observed a Harriman aide. "They are fundamentally the common misconceptions of the Russian Communist concerning the world beyond the frontiers, modified and strangely distorted by a veneer of Western culture and exposure to the traditionally provincial outlook of La Rive Gauche."

The boldest members of the Spaso House set were the former Soviet foreign minister Maksim Litvinov and his English wife, Ivy. A short, rotund man with round metal-rimmed glasses, Litvinov occupied a unique position in the Soviet bureaucracy. As an Old Bolshevik living in London prior to the revolution, he had befriended Lenin and rescued Stalin from being beaten up in a pub by East End dockers. He was the Soviet diplomat most identified with the policy of collective security in the thirties, seeking an alliance with the western democracies as a bulwark against the growing power of fascism and Nazism. His replacement as commissar for foreign affairs by Molotov in May 1939 was a sign of a fundamental shift in Soviet foreign policy and a harbinger of the nonaggression pact with Hitler. Litvinov was brought back from diplomatic obscurity after the German attack on Russia in June 1941 and sent as Soviet ambassador to Washington. His intellectual sophistication, combined with a deep knowledge of the West, made him an ideal envoy at a time when Stalin was once again trying to woo America. But he never regained the dictator's trust. Molotov regarded him as a dangerous rival and kept him away from real decision making. Summoned back to Moscow as an assistant foreign minister in August 1943, Litvinov made little attempt to conceal his dislike of his boss. On the diplomatic cocktail circuit, both he and Ivy made snide remarks about the gray bureaucrats now in charge of the Foreign Affairs Commissariat.

In a gesture toward wartime patriotism, Molotov insisted that his subordinates wear a military-style diplomatic uniform that he had designed himself. Litvinov looked "less like a general than anybody I have ever seen," Cyrus Sulzberger of the *New York Times* recorded in his diary. "His grey uniform was rumpled and unpressed and there were food stains on the lapels." The vice commissar struck Sulzberger as "a regular Jeremiah, full of gloom" about the prospects for East-West relations. "First the Western powers make a mistake and rub us the wrong way, and then we make a mistake and rub you the wrong way," he fretted. Litvinov grumbled that nobody in the Kremlin paid attention any longer to what he had to say.

Ivy was even more outspoken, saying things that her husband felt privately but was cautious about expressing aloud. "Mrs. Litvinov is getting very pally with me," Kathleen Harriman noted in her March 8 letter to her sister. "She's sort of a bitch but rather an amusing one and certainly worth cultivating." Soon after this conversation, Ivy reminded Kathleen's father of a piece of advice she had first given him the previous year. Attempts to ingratiate yourself with the Soviet authorities will be interpreted in Moscow as weakness. If you want to get on well with Kremlin leaders, be firm in all your dealings. She complained that the Americans had failed to follow the advice, and relations were now deteriorating. Harriman filed her comments away to report to FDR. They coincided very much with his emerging hard-line views.

Even in the best of times, Harriman had a dejected, hangdog expression that made him seem perpetually gloomy. "How can a man with $100 million look so sad?" Litvinov once asked an American diplomat. The ambassador's mood darkened even further in the month following the Yalta conference. Visitors noticed that he was looking increasingly haggard and had developed a nervous tic in his right eye. He now spent much of his time shuttling back and forth between Spaso House and the Kremlin negotiating with Molotov on the shape of a new provisional government in Poland. It was a frustrating, time-consuming ordeal.

The Big Three had delegated responsibility for implementing the Polish agreement to a commission consisting of Molotov, Harriman, and Archibald Clark Kerr, the British ambassador to Moscow. The three men were supposed to summon representatives of different Polish factions to Moscow for consultations on the formation of a "reorganized" government that would include "democratic leaders from Poland itself and from Poles abroad." The wording of the Yalta declaration was maddeningly imprecise. The three commissioners were soon engaged in heated arguments about the meaning of words like "democratic" and "enlarged." Harriman and other American diplomats complained that negotiating with the Russians always involved "buying the same horse twice." You agreed to the sale—and then you spent endless hours haggling about the condition of the horse you had just bought, counting its teeth, examining its pedigree, and so on. Every detail had to be nailed down separately.

Molotov immediately questioned the credentials of the "democratic leaders" whom Harriman and Clark Kerr wanted to invite to Moscow. As far as he was concerned, any Polish politician who had expressed reservations about the Yalta agreement on Poland could not participate in the consultative process. No one was permitted to challenge the new Polish-Soviet frontier endorsed by the Big Three. Molotov's formula excluded Stanisław Mikołajczyk, a former Polish prime minister viewed by the Americans and the British as a moderate open to dialogue with Moscow. Mikołajczyk had issued a statement calling for the city of Lwów to remain part of Poland on demographic grounds. He was also opposed to the creation of any new government based on "the broadening and reorganization of the so-called Provisional Government in Lublin." Molotov insisted that the political consultations be restricted to "the *real* democratic leaders" of Poland, a euphemism for the Communists and their allies. The western ambassadors were willing to sacrifice most members of the Polish government-in-exile in London, who were vehemently anti-Soviet, but they drew the line at excluding Mikołajczyk. They had reached an impasse.

Another obstacle soon arose. The English-language version of the Yalta agreement specified that the three-man commission would "consult in the first instance in Moscow with members of the present Provisional Government and with other Polish democratic leaders from within Poland and from abroad." The Americans and the British understood this to mean that representatives of various rival political factions would be invited to Moscow to discuss the creation of a new government. Molotov pointed out that the order of words was reversed in the Russian text. "To consult in the first instance in Moscow" became "to consult in Moscow in the first instance with members of the present Provisional Government." In Molotov's interpretation, this wording granted a privileged position to the Communist-dominated provisional government. The Lublin Poles would appear before the Moscow commission "in the first instance"—and would help screen the "democratic" credentials of other Polish groups, including their rivals in London. There could be no parity between the different groups of Poles. The Lublin government had to serve as "the basis" for a "reorganized" government of Poland.

News of the tough new Soviet line soon reached Washington and London. FDR expressed concern but was reluctant to intervene personally with Stalin. He wanted the ambassadors to keep pushing Molotov. Churchill felt that time was running in favor of the Soviets and their Polish puppets. He agreed with Harriman that "every day the Lublin Government is becoming more and more the Warsaw Government and the Rulers of Poland." He feared charges of a sellout of Poland by members of the British Parliament already uneasy with the territorial concessions made to Stalin at Yalta. "Poland has lost her frontier," he cabled Roosevelt on March 13. "Is she now to lose her freedom?" He was also worried by the lack of reliable information from inside Poland. In another telegram, three days later, he noted that "all entry into Poland is barred to our representatives. An impenetrable veil has been drawn across the scene."

Harriman was so disheartened by his experience negotiating with

Molotov that he drafted a personal letter to the president and secretary of state. It was dated March 21, the day after his fireside chat with Jan Masaryk. The Russians, he warned, were "attempting to wear us down step by step" in order to impose their views about the shape of postwar Europe. The time had come "for us to reorient our whole attitude and our methods of dealing with the Soviet Government . . . unless we wish to accept the 20th century Barbarian invasion of Europe." For the record, Harriman insisted that he was not advocating a division of the continent into "spheres of influence," a concept that remained anathema to Roosevelt. He nevertheless favored "a forceful policy of supporting those people that have the same general outlook . . . and concept of life that we do." The United States should use its economic power to strengthen pro-American governments in western Europe. Lend-lease, and postwar reconstruction credits, could be "a weapon" to encourage Soviet cooperation with the West. If the Russians failed to live up to their Yalta commitments, America should indicate its displeasure "in a manner costly to their interests." It was also necessary to be "very much more precise in the wording of our agreements with the Soviet Union and spell out with greater care the meaning that we have in mind." Ambiguity made it easier for the Russians to renegotiate agreements after they had been reached.

After dictating a draft of the cable, Harriman agonized over whether to send it. The proposed policy he outlined ran counter to many of FDR's deeply held views on how to deal with the Russians. The president believed that it was possible to win Stalin's trust by forging a personal relationship with him. He had paid little attention to the detailed drafting of the Yalta agreements on the assumption that everything would eventually work out, given goodwill on both sides. The ambassador's cable echoed the skepticism of his deputy, George Kennan, who poured scorn on the notion that Soviet officials could be influenced "by games of golf or invitations to dinner."

Closely attuned to the prevailing political winds back home, Harriman stuffed his cable into the "unsent file." He decided it would be better to present his arguments in person in Washington, where he could observe the reaction of his interlocutors.

There was no single issue about which Harriman felt more strongly than the fate of American servicemen captured by the Germans. Nearly thirty thousand Americans had been held in German prison camps in Poland

and other territories liberated by the Red Army. Soviet officials insisted that the men had everything they needed and would be repatriated to the United States through the Black Sea port of Odessa. Harriman believed that Stalin was failing to implement an agreement negotiated at Yalta allowing free access to POW transit camps. He had no idea how many Americans were wandering behind Red Army lines without food or shelter.

The first concrete information on the fate of the released prisoners came from a trio of haggard Americans who walked into the U.S. Embassy in Moscow on Mokhovaya Street, directly opposite the Kremlin. The men had no passports and no possessions, apart from the tattered rags they were wearing. It turned out they were U.S. Army officers, captured by the Germans in western Europe and North Africa in 1943 and 1944 and held in a prison camp at Szubin in northwestern Poland. During the chaos of the Red Army's advance, they had managed to escape from the prison camp and hook up with a Russian frontline unit. Their only way of getting back to America was to head eastward, hitchhiking across Poland and western Russia. During the night, they sought shelter in barns and farmhouses. By day, they got rides on Russian supply vehicles returning to the rear, eventually reaching Moscow after a three-week odyssey. "I don't think that any officers ever had a more sincere welcome than those first three bedraggled ex-prisoners did when they came into our headquarters," recorded General John Deane, the head of the American military mission. A supply of "hot baths, clean clothes, insignia of rank, American food, and whisky" transformed the three men back into officers of the U.S. Army.

Captain Ernest M. Gruenberg and his two companions regaled Harriman with stories of Allied soldiers being robbed of watches and other valuables at gunpoint by drunken Russian soldiers. They described conditions in a makeshift camp that the Russians had established outside Warsaw to accommodate freed Allied prisoners. Water was scarce; sanitation was poor; everybody, including the Russian guards, slept on the floor. Food consisted of a thick barley soup called kasha, which was tasteless but filling. Information about repatriation arrangements was nonexistent. The three officers preferred to fend for themselves, relying on the hospitality of Polish civilians, who invited them into their homes and shared their meager supplies of food. The Red Army had been too busy fighting the Germans and hunting down Polish insurgents to pay much attention to the escapees.

On March 13, Harriman finally managed to obtain an interview with Molotov on the subject of the released prisoners of war. He pointed out that Soviet officers accredited to General Eisenhower's headquarters were permitted to travel freely around France and inspect former German prison camps. Allied contact officers should enjoy the same privileges in Poland. The foreign affairs commissar brushed aside the comparison. He noted that the Soviet Union had diplomatic relations with France while the United States had yet to recognize the Polish provisional government. The Polish authorities, he claimed, were raising objections. It was clear to Harriman that the problem lay not with the Poles but with the Soviets. They did not want Americans to witness what was going on behind Red Army lines in Poland.

Most Americans freed by the Red Army waited in camps in Poland and Germany until they could be repatriated across the front lines following the linkup of the Allied armies. But several thousand made it to Odessa, where the American military mission was permitted to establish a "collection point." The former prisoners were loaded into unheated box-cars and transported two thousand miles across Poland and Ukraine to the Black Sea. Their reports provided American intelligence officers with the first detailed insights into the military ethos of the Red Army. The Americans marveled at the way Soviet soldiers lived off the land, foraging for food and other supplies as they advanced into Germany. This enabled them to avoid many of the logistical problems that hampered the movement of western armies. When Russian troops occupied a town, they would take over the bakeries, which would then become responsible for supplying frontline units with bread. Paperwork seemed practically nonexistent. Individual Russian soldiers were friendly toward Americans, except when drunk. Then they became boastful, demanding to know why progress was so slow on the western front. Many Americans commented on the lack of discipline among Soviet soldiers. "The Russians dearly love to murder German civilians," reported a lieutenant. "It is relatively common practice to rape, then murder." He foresaw "a great deal of trouble" when Russians and Americans finally got together in the heart of Europe, listing several areas of concern:

- The Russians are justifiably cocky about their accomplishments in driving the German army out of Russia. They are outspokenly critical, in some instances even contemptuous, of the Allied armed forces in the West.

- Zones of occupation of Germany must be so drawn up that lines run around towns. Under no circumstances should a Russian and American garrison occupy the same town.
- If there is to be any post-war amity between the USA and the USSR, every effort will have to be made to foster it. Allowing Russian and American troops to mingle promiscuously is the surest way to engender ill feeling.

A single American repatriation team succeeded in piercing the "impenetrable veil" drawn around Poland by Stalin. Accompanied by a doctor and an interpreter, Lieutenant Colonel James Wilmeth had been permitted to travel to the eastern Polish city of Lublin, one of four official gathering points for former American prisoners of war prior to being shipped to Odessa by the Soviets. By the time Harriman finally obtained his interview with Molotov in mid-March, Wilmeth had become disillusioned and worn down by his battles with the Soviet military authorities in Poland. He complained to Deane that he had been prevented from accomplishing his mission by a supposed ally of the United States.

Wilmeth reported that American ex-POWs were "forced to eat, sleep, and march" with captured German prisoners in violation of the Yalta agreements. They were stripped of watches, rings, clothes, food, and documents by Russian guards. Many had gone into hiding in private homes around Poland until they received assurances that they would be safely evacuated from the country. "The Soviet attitude toward liberated American prisoners is the same as the Soviet attitude toward the countries they have liberated," he wrote in disgust. "They may be robbed, starved, and abused—and no one has the right to question such treatment."

When the former American prisoners first arrived in Lublin, after wandering around Poland for several weeks, they were directed to the former Nazi death camp at Majdanek on the outskirts of town. They were then transferred to a ramshackle building near the university with "no hot water, no bath facilities, no clothing, no toilet articles and no medicines." Most of the men were lice ridden. They slept on the floor or on wooden benches covered with straw. For food they received two servings of black bread and kasha a day. They had to dig their own latrines and collect wood for heating fuel. Wilmeth supplied them with medicine, soap, toothbrushes, light bulbs, books, and shovels for the latrines. He tried to get permission to evacuate the ex-POWs in American planes, but his request was rejected. Instead, they were sent to Odessa by rail.

Relations between Wilmeth and his Red Army minders deteriorated rapidly. The colonel was forbidden to travel to other Polish towns where ex-POWs were gathering. He was assigned Russian bodyguards who insisted he needed protection from "German spies"; his Russian driver removed a wire from the distributor cap of his jeep to prevent his team from driving around the city without permission. The colonel eventually drew up a report listing twenty-seven separate causes of friction with the Russians, ranging from purchasing gasoline and medical supplies on the black market to unauthorized communications. He accused his Soviet escorts of withholding information on former American prisoners and lying to him about conditions in other Polish cities. For their part, the Russians complained that the Americans violated rules established for foreigners and went out after curfew. They were alarmed by the number of Poles who visited Wilmeth in his hotel to claim U.S. citizenship or complain about the Soviet occupation. Red Army officers repeatedly ordered Wilmeth to return to Moscow, but he refused to go without written orders from Deane.

The Russian treatment of former POWs was not as uniformly bad as Wilmeth maintained. According to a Pentagon survey of repatriated Americans, 56 percent of those interviewed reported good or adequate treatment by the Red Army, taking into account "the tactical situation, the Russian standard of living, and the facilities available." One in three said he was treated indifferently. Only 7 percent complained of harassment or serious physical hardship. Officers were much more likely to report mistreatment than ordinary soldiers, presumably because they had higher expectations. A majority of liberated prisoners felt that their living conditions were no worse than those endured by the average Russian soldier, an admittedly low standard. Had Wilmeth been permitted to travel freely around Poland, he would probably have come away with a rather more positive picture than he got in Lublin, where his movements were severely restricted. As often happened, the Russians exacerbated their image problem through clumsy public relations.

The Red Army minders who made Wilmeth's life so difficult were not acting out of spite. They were following instructions from above. The NKVD was fighting a largely secret war with the underground army loyal to the government-in-exile in London and did not want westerners snooping around. The lone American was getting in the way of a high-stakes political struggle for the future of Poland. The Russians asked him to leave on eight separate occasions, threatening a *bolshoi skandal*—"big scandal"—every time. It was not until March 28, after an American military plane arrived in Lublin to collect him, that the obstreperous colonel finally agreed to leave. From the Soviet point of view, his departure came just in time.

Secrecy was essential to Stalin's plans for Poland. To control the country, he first had to control the dissemination of information both within Poland and between Poland and the outside world. At Yalta, he had resisted demands by both FDR and Churchill for access to Soviet-occupied territories in eastern Europe. He would not repeat the mistake he had made in Romania, where western diplomats, spies, and military personnel had been allowed to establish offices and cultivate anti-Soviet politicians. The Allies would not be permitted into Poland until they recognized the government set up by the Red Army. Stalin's "impenetrable veil" served a double purpose. The Americans and the British would find it much more difficult to complain about what was going on in Poland if they were deprived of news. Control over information was also key to the Stalinist political tactic of divide and rule. Opponents of the Communist-dominated provisional government depended on independent information networks for their very survival. If they were unable to contact one another or their supporters abroad, they could be picked off one by one. The information curtain was the necessary precursor to what later became known as the iron curtain.

Responsibility for establishing order in Poland rested primarily with Beria's secret police. As the Red Army battled the Wehrmacht, the NKVD conducted a series of "cleansing operations" on the "internal front." According to data presented to Stalin by Beria, the NKVD interned 38,660 Poles between January and mid-April. The "enemy elements" included not only confirmed "terrorists" and "saboteurs" but anyone suspected of supporting the government-in-exile in London. Reports to Beria indicated no relaxation in the war between the Communists and the underground Home Army, or Armia Krajowa, which was loyal to the London government. In a typical incident, Home Army fighters stormed a prison in Lublin on February 19, killing two guards and freeing prisoners awaiting execution for "political crimes." Home Army sympathizers succeeded in infiltrating Polish military formations serving with the Red Army, persuading entire units to desert. The NKVD hunted down the deserters and issued an order confiscating the personal radio sets of Polish soldiers to prevent them from listening to broadcasts by the London government. The ban on radio sets was soon extended to Polish civilians.

Home Army commanders rethought their policy of unbending opposition to the Soviet authorities in the weeks after Yalta. The Americans and the British encouraged the government-in-exile to reach a compromise with Moscow and form a national unity government. There were signs that the Red Army was ready for a dialogue. A March 6 letter addressed to the underground by a Soviet officer named Colonel Pimonov suggested a meeting "to solve very important problems and prevent their worsening." Some underground leaders suspected the offer was a trap, but a majority voted to open talks with Red Army representatives. Senior underground leaders were invited to "a luncheon" at Soviet army headquarters in the Warsaw suburb of Pruszów on March 28, the day Colonel Wilmeth was finally persuaded to leave Poland. In preliminary talks, Pimonov told the Poles they would meet Marshal Zhukov, who was responsible for all Soviet forces in Poland. Their safety was guaranteed.

The morning of March 28 was warm and sunny, the first day of real spring. Anticipating a historic meeting that could determine Poland's future, they put on their best clothes but left their heavy overcoats at home. One underground activist persuaded his neighborhood tailor to loan him the jacket of an unfinished suit as he had nothing else that was suitable. There were thirteen delegates in all, representing all the major prewar political parties. Another three Poles, including General Leopold Okulicki, the leader of the Warsaw Uprising and commander in chief of the Home Army, had been invited to attend a preliminary meeting the previous day. The plan was for everyone to meet at lunch and then hold negotiations with the representatives of the Red Army. The London government had forwarded the names of at least six of the Poles to Moscow for consideration by the Molotov commission.

Their Soviet hosts were polite and affable, praising the beauty of Polish women and the delights of Polish food. But the promised luncheon never took place. Instead the Poles were driven to another building, nine miles away, which was surrounded by barbed wire. They suspected they were under arrest but could not be sure. Their hosts were still friendly, offering them vodka and food from the officers' mess. The Russians explained that Zhukov had been detained by important business at the front but had placed his personal airplane at their disposal. They would be taken to meet the marshal the following morning.

A plane was waiting for them at Warsaw airport. Instead of flying west, toward the front, it headed east. This further alarmed the Poles, but their Soviet escort told them not to worry. The marshal had been summoned unexpectedly to Moscow. They would meet not only with Zhukov but "important personalities" of the Russian government. A violent storm caused the pilot to get lost in the clouds. He crash-landed into a snow-covered field just as the plane was about to run out of fuel. The passengers felt a sharp jolt but were uninjured. "All around was a virgin whiteness, becoming bluish on the horizon," remembered Zbigniew Stypułkowski, a leader of the right-wing National Party. They had overshot the capital and ended up near the town of Ivanovo, a hundred and fifty miles to the east. The pilot stumbled off in search of a rescue party while the passengers huddled together for warmth in the leaking fuselage. They completed their journey to Moscow by overnight train. There was nobody to greet them at the station. They waited for half an hour on the freezing platform, shivering in the light clothes that they had worn for the luncheon in Warsaw. Eventually, a convoy of cars arrived to take them to their "hotel."

The "hotel" turned out to be a massive neo-baroque building with an inlaid-marble entrance that led to an interior courtyard surrounded by high walls. The Poles noticed that all the windows were covered with iron shutters. As each man stepped out of the car, he was grabbed firmly by the arm and pushed into a long, dark passageway. Soon they found themselves in a line of small cells, the walls of which were covered with felt. Stypułkowski instinctively reached for a few sheets of paper in his pocket that contained some notes and instructions. He tore the papers up and swallowed the shreds. After a few moments, a powerfully built young woman with hair hanging down over her shoulders entered the cell. She was wearing an NKVD uniform and looked very grim. "Undress," she ordered. Stypułkowski understood that he had arrived at the infamous Lubyanka Prison.

9

Death of a President

April 12

Although he controlled a vast empire, stretching across eleven time zones, Stalin's own world was very small. He spent most of the war shuttling back and forth between the Kremlin and what his aides called "the nearby dacha," his country retreat on the western outskirts of Moscow. He rarely ventured outside the capital. His trips to Tehran and Yalta to meet with Roosevelt and Churchill were highly unusual breaks from a routine that consisted of long nights in his Kremlin office, continuous meetings with military and political leaders, and an occasional movie or dinner for relaxation. The supreme commander of the Red Army visited the front on just one occasion, in August 1943, largely for propaganda purposes, to show that he was directing the battle. A memorial plaque was attached to the little peasant hut where he stayed the night, transforming it into a national shrine.

The "nearby dacha" had been built especially for Stalin in 1931 on a princely estate known as Volinskoe, near the village of Kuntsevo. Like many of his personal retreats, the wooden building was painted green for camouflage purposes. A twenty-acre thicket of firs and two tall fences, the outer one fifteen feet high, ensured complete privacy. The seven rooms on the ground floor were large and utilitarian, suitable for hosting banquets and Politburo meetings but devoid of personal touches. A second floor was added during the war. Shortly after completing the renovations, the architect Miron Merzhanov disappeared into the Gulag. The nature of his infraction was never explained to his family: Merzhanov's son was reminded of Ivan the Terrible, who ordered the blinding of his favorite architect so that he could never build anything as beautiful as St. Basil's Cathedral. The *vozhd* was forced to abandon his dacha during the most dangerous months of the German siege of Moscow in 1941 when mines were laid around the estate. When Churchill visited Moscow the following year, he was put up at Volinskoe without being told that it was Stalin's personal home. He was impressed by the "spotless cleanliness" and the "blazing almost dazzling electric lights." An aide described the place as "vulgarly furnished and possessed of every convenience a Soviet commissar's heart could desire," including a spacious bomb shelter ninety feet below the garden.

With other traffic banned from the road, it took Stalin fewer than twenty minutes to make the six-mile drive from Kuntsevo to the Kremlin in a convoy of black American Packards. Awestruck pedestrians watched the cars go past as they trudged through the sludge of the late Moscow winter along dim-lit streets lined with empty stores. The poet Boris Slutsky captured the scene in a few lines of verse:

> *Once I was walking along the Arbat*
> *When God drove by in five cars,*
> *Trembling bodyguards stood around*
> *Almost hunchbacked from fear*
> *In their mouse-like coats.*
> *It was late, and it was early.*

From the Arbat, Moscow's main shopping street, the slow-moving cortege turned into Afanasev Lane. Stalin entered the Kremlin by the Borovitskaya Gate, driving past the Grand Kremlin Palace and the gold-domed cathedrals overlooking the Moscow River. The convoy then turned left, toward a three-story, neoclassical building with a green roof that was built in the form of a triangle around three inner courtyards. This was the Senate building, the seat of Soviet power. A red flag fluttered from the domed roof overlooking Red Square and Lenin's mausoleum, on the big, right-angled corner of the triangle. Farther along the Kremlin wall, next to the Nikolskaya Tower, was the entrance known as the Little Corner. A summons to the Little Corner held many terrors. One of Stalin's generals, Nikolai Bulganin, recalled that the dictator could extend a friendly greeting and then ask menacingly, "Why are your eyes so shifty today?" An official invited to meet with Stalin never knew where he would go next: "home or to jail."

Encircled by massive red walls, one and a half miles in perimeter, the Kremlin was Muscovy's inner citadel, a fortress within a fortress. It had been the residence of Russian tsars until the early eighteenth century, when Peter the Great built a new capital on the Baltic Sea that served as his "window to the West." The Bolsheviks moved the capital back to Moscow in 1918, and Lenin took up residence in the Kremlin on the third floor of the Senate building. Commissars competed with one another for the best apartments. Stalin lived in the Poteshny Palace on the other side of the Kremlin until his wife, Nadezhda Alliluyeva, shot herself through the chest in November 1932. In despair over Nadezhda's suicide, he persuaded his friend and later victim Nikolai Bukharin to swap apartments. He then moved to the Little Corner, and it was here that he played host to Churchill in August 1942, introducing the prime minister to his sixteen-year-old daughter, Svetlana. The freckly redhead helped lay the table but was dismissed as soon as the conversation turned to "the usual guns, howitzers and airplanes." Svetlana later came to believe that her mother's death deprived Stalin of "the last vestiges of human warmth. He was now free of her moderating and, by the same token, impeding presence. His skeptical, harsh judgment of men only hardened."

The modest ground-floor flat, four rooms with vaulted ceilings, was located directly beneath Stalin's office on the second floor of the Senate building. A permanent hush reigned in the so-called Special Sector where the top Bolshevik leaders had their offices. A green carpet trimmed with red ran down the center of the long corridor. Access to the *vozhd* was controlled by his secretary, Alexander Poskrebyshev, who sat in front of a high window in the anteroom framed by a pair of drapes that filtered out the meager sunshine. The bald-headed major general kept a detailed log of everybody who entered Stalin's study, remaining at his post until three or four in the morning. He was doggedly loyal to his master, despite a series of humiliations culminating with the arrest of his young wife on charges of Trotskyism at the height of the purges in 1937. "Don't worry," Stalin had told his assistant when he attempted to intercede on his wife's behalf. "We'll find you another wife." A pair of massive oak doors to the left of Poskrebyshev's immaculately tidy desk led directly to Stalin's office.

Stalin's desk was at the far-right-hand corner of the long, oak-paneled room, piled high with maps, documents, and special Kremlin telephones. A portrait of Lenin sitting at his desk hung just above the general secretary's head, gazing down with benign approval on his successor. An ornate porcelain stove stood in the far-left corner. Next to the stove, taking up most of the left-hand side of the room, opposite the windows, was a long conference table covered with heavy green felt. Breaking with Leninist tradition, Stalin ordered portraits of the tsarist generals Aleksandr Suvorov and Mikhail Kutuzov to be installed above the conference table after the Nazi invasion. The Marxist commissar saw no contradiction in the clashing images. He identified with the tsars who had built the Kremlin, studied their military campaigns, and pursued a similar policy of territorial expansion to ensure the security of Mother Russia. In his mind, there was a direct connection between his own achievements and the feats of his imperial predecessors. It was impossible to escape the ghosts of the past. Shortly before incorporating the Baltic States into the Soviet Union in June 1940, he escorted the foreign minister of Lithuania through the darkened alleyways of the Kremlin. "Ivan the Terrible used to walk through here," he reminded his guest.

As he pored over maps of Europe in his Kremlin office toward the end of March, Stalin worried that he might win the war but lose the peace. After being delayed for weeks in the Ardennes, the western Allies were suddenly making suspiciously rapid progress. Churchill was boasting about his surprise visit to the western front on March 25 when he strolled "unmolested" on the German-occupied side of the sandbagged Rhine River. The city of Frankfurt had fallen to George Patton's Third Army on March 29. In the East, by contrast, the Soviet offensive had slowed dramatically. Zhukov's forces were no closer to Berlin at the end of March than they had been during the Yalta conference at the beginning of February. Stronger-than-expected German resistance in Hungary had obliged the Red Army to delay its drive against Vienna. Even more alarming, from the Russian point of view, was the disparity in casualty figures between the two fronts. On a typical day, nearly eight hundred Germans were killed by the Red Army, compared with just sixty German combat deaths on the western front. Conversely, roughly twenty-five hundred German soldiers were reported "missing" on the eastern front each day, compared with ten times that number in the West. The Germans were surrendering "with fanatical persistence" to the Americans, in Ilya Ehrenburg's contemptuous phrase, while conducting a desperate last-ditch stand against the Russians.

Stalin used the same type of reasoning to analyze the behavior of Roosevelt and Churchill that he applied to his own subordinates. Did they have an objective reason to betray him? The answer was obviously yes. Evidence of motivation was evidence of guilt, just as it had been with the victims of the Moscow show trials. The spectacle of German soldiers surrendering en masse to Patton and Bernard Montgomery suggested some kind of deal. In return for treating the Nazis more leniently, the western armies would meet the Red Army much farther east than originally envisaged. If they made an alliance with Nazi generals opposed to Hitler, they might even turn against the Soviet Union. The fact that Stalin himself had concluded a nonaggression pact with Hitler's Germany back in 1939 only added weight to his suspicions. He assumed that other politicians were no less cynical than himself.

Several recent incidents contributed to Stalin's paranoia. A Reuters dispatch from Montgomery's headquarters on March 27 reported that British and American troops were encountering no resistance as they raced toward the heart of Germany. Stalin was also alarmed by rumors of negotiations for a mass surrender of German troops in northern Italy. It turned out that the top American spy in Switzerland, Allen Dulles, had held a secret meeting in Berne with the commander of SS forces in northern Italy, Karl Wolff. More contacts were planned. When Molotov inquired about the meeting, he was told the talks were at a very preliminary stage. There was no need for Russian participation. This explanation did not satisfy Stalin, who wrote an angry letter to Roosevelt on March 29 accusing him of violating the Yalta agreements. He claimed that the Germans had already "succeeded in shifting three divisions from Northern Italy to the Soviet front." To signal his displeasure, Stalin announced that Molotov would not attend the inaugural conference of the United Nations in San Francisco on April 25, a project dear to FDR's heart. The official reason for the cancellation of Molotov's trip merely added insult to injury: his presence was required in Moscow for a session of the rubber-stamp Supreme Soviet.

Stalin also suspected that the U.S. military had fed the Red Army false information about German troop movements. On February 20, General Marshall had relayed the contents of an intelligence intercept suggesting that the Sixth SS Panzer Army was being transferred from the Ardennes region toward Vienna for a planned thrust into southern Poland. The information turned out to be wrong. The elite tank unit had ended up in the Lake Balaton area of Hungary, from which it launched a damaging offensive against Soviet troops around Budapest. The most likely explanation for the misinformation—a change in orders from Hitler—did not occur to the morbidly mistrustful Soviet leader. He voiced concerns about a western sellout during a meeting with Czechoslovak leaders at the end of March. "We are fighting the Germans and will do so until the end," he told them. "But we must bear in mind that our allies will try to save the Germans and come to an arrangement with them. We will be merciless towards the Germans but our allies will treat them with kid gloves."

The more power Stalin accumulated, the more he felt threatened. Newly acquired territories in eastern Europe provided Russia with security in depth but were also a source of instability. The *vozhd* could not forget that the Soviet Union had lost half its European territory in fewer than six months in the summer and fall of 1941. Millions of Balts, Ukrainians, and Poles had greeted the Nazi invaders as liberators. Entire units had surrendered to the enemy and were now waging war against the Red Army under traitors like General Andrei Vlasov. Stalin had serious concerns about the reliability of the Communist-led Polish First Army, formed on Soviet soil from Polish soldiers captured during the Soviet invasion of eastern Poland in September 1939. Reports from the NKVD suggested that many First Army troops were eager to join the anti-Communist army of General Anders. "When the Polish troops meet up, the majority of our soldiers and officers will pass over to the Anders army," a First Army commander was reported to have confided to an informer. "We've suffered enough from the Soviets in Siberia." Hoping to forestall a future rebellion, the NKVD carried out mass arrests of First Army soldiers with relatives serving under Anders.

Stalin was obsessed by the fear that the western Allies might make a dash for Berlin and reach the city before the Red Army. He was determined not to be robbed of his grand prize. On March 29, he ordered his two top field commanders, Marshals Georgy Zhukov and Ivan Konev, to fly to Moscow to outline their plans for capturing the capital of the Third Reich.

The *vozhd* was in a cold and suspicious mood on the evening of March 31 when the American and British ambassadors arrived for an appointment at the Little Corner accompanied by their top military advisers. Harriman and Clark Kerr wanted to present a letter from the supreme Allied commander, General Eisenhower, outlining his plan for the final defeat of Nazi Germany. Poskrebyshev had to choreograph the schedule carefully so that the envoys would not run into Zhukov, who was due to present his own report to Stalin later that night. The boss did not like his underlings sharing information with westerners.

Harriman handed Stalin a Russian translation of Eisenhower's message explaining that his top priority was the encirclement and destruction of German forces in the industrial Ruhr region. His military experts spread their maps out on the long table to explain the next phase of the plan. Instead of aiming for Berlin, American and British forces would mount their "main effort" through central Germany, meeting the Red Army a hundred miles south of the capital, in the Leipzig-Dresden area. A secondary line of attack would come through southern Germany and Austria to prevent Hitler from falling back on his Alpine Fortress, known to western military planners as the National Redoubt. As he listened to Harriman and Deane describe Eisenhower's intentions, the suspicious dictator "seemed to open up." He praised the plan, saying it would accomplish the goal of cutting Germany in half. The following day, April 1, he sent a message back to Eisenhower formally approving his strategy.

"Berlin has lost its former strategic importance," Stalin wrote. "The Soviet High Command therefore plans to allot secondary forces in the direction of Berlin." A future chronicler of the fall of Berlin, Antony Beevor, would describe this missive as "the greatest April fool in modern history."

Far from considering Berlin of minor importance, the *vozhd* was convinced that it would be the scene of the climactic battle of the war. The Reichstag and Reich Chancellery were the symbols of Nazi power, just as the Kremlin was the symbol of Soviet power. Unlike Eisenhower, who thought almost exclusively in military terms, Stalin thought in political-strategic terms. He would never have allowed his generals to take the kind of decisions that FDR routinely delegated to his supreme commander. The very fact that Eisenhower was authorized to communicate directly with Stalin on such an important matter, without consulting his British Allies, or even the president, illustrated the gulf between the Soviet and American systems and strategies for waging war.

Eisenhower's principal goal—fully endorsed by Roosevelt—was to win the war at the lowest possible cost in American and Allied lives. The postwar arrangements were not his concern. Stalin, by contrast, never gave much thought to the human cost of his decisions but was obsessed by the political consequences. The capture of the enemy capital would seal his reputation as the conqueror of Nazi Germany, leaving him in virtually unchallenged control of a huge swath of eastern Europe. He was ready to pay a heavy price in Soviet and German lives to achieve his goal.

The American and British visitors filed out of the Little Corner office at 8:50 p.m., after a fifty-minute session with Stalin. Zhukov was admitted to the inner sanctum twenty minutes later, according to Poskrebyshev's meticulous log. The commander of the First Belorussian Front had been delayed reaching Moscow by the same violent storm that forced the crash landing of the plane carrying the Polish Home Army leaders. After his plane came down in Minsk, he continued his journey by train and had to rush to the Kremlin for his appointment with the *vozhd*.

The squat, powerfully built marshal was one of the very few Red Army officers who did not quake at the knees when talking to Stalin. His competence and energy had made him indispensable to the Soviet warlord, particularly during the panic that followed the German invasion in June 1941. A former cavalryman, Zhukov had managed to survive the terror that wiped out half of the Red Army leadership in 1937. He had been at Stalin's side in good times and bad, serving as army chief of staff in the early weeks of the Nazi invasion before being sent to the front. In his own way, he was as ruthless as his master, although not as suspicious and devious. He delivered his orders in brusque staccatolike phrases: "Obey or die!" or "If the division is not in place by 9 a.m., I'll have you shot." He stopped the advance of the German armies in front of Moscow by forming "interceptor battalions" to shoot cowards and deserters. He was the master of the grand envelopment, involving the movement of million-strong armies, meticulous planning, and brutal execution. At both Stalingrad and Kursk, he drew overextended German forces deep into a trap that ended with their encirclement and destruction. He was both feared and loved by his men, who viewed him as a harsh taskmaster but a fierce professional. He treated them the same way Stalin treated him, like a coachman driving on his horses. "They love and pity the animals but the whip is always ready," explained a Stalin crony, Lev Mekhlis. "The horse sees it and draws its own conclusions." The *vozhd* regarded him both as an ally and as a threat. He ordered the NKVD to bug his Moscow apartment and keep a close watch on his aides.

After working with Stalin for so long, Zhukov had come to recognize his moods and tics, studying the way he stroked his mustache or played with his pipe. According to a biographer, the pipe was both "a prop and a weather vane." If it was unlit, "it was a bad omen. If Stalin put it down, an explosion was imminent. Yet if he stroked his moustache with the mouthpiece of the pipe, this meant he was pleased." Zhukov paid great attention to the dictator's eyes. "He used to pace the room slowly, stopping now and then, coming up close to the person he was talking with and looking him straight in the face." His eyes were "clear, tenacious, and seemed to envelop and pierce through the visitor." In normal conversation, Stalin was "calm and sober-minded," but this could change in a flash. When he lost his temper, he "grew pale, a bitter expression came to his eyes, and his gaze became heavy and spiteful."

Moments after bidding farewell to the western envoys, Stalin was complaining to Zhukov that the German front in the West had "collapsed completely." The "Hitlerites" were barely resisting the Americans and the British while vigorously reinforcing their positions in the East. To prove his point, the *vozhd* walked over to his desk and dug out a letter from "a foreign well-wisher," subsequently identified as a Russian spy in the British Foreign Office.

"Read this."

The letter claimed the Germans were trying to persuade the western Allies to agree to "a separate peace." The Allies had allegedly rejected the overture, but Stalin was unconvinced. "I don't think Roosevelt will violate the Yalta agreements, but as for Churchill, he's capable of anything."

Two days later, on April 2, Stalin gathered his military commanders to discuss the final assault on Berlin. This time, he included Zhukov's archrival, Ivan Konev, who commanded the adjoining First Ukrainian Front. He ordered an aide to read a report describing a joint Anglo-American operation to seize Berlin before its capture by the Red Army. The document listed a series of preparatory measures being taken by Allied commanders to ensure the success of the operation.

"Well, who is going to take Berlin, us or the Allies?" Stalin asked his marshals, after his aide had finished reading the telegram. Konev rushed to reply.

"We will capture Berlin. And we will take it before the Allies."

Stalin gave a half grin, indicating this was the right answer. "So that's the kind of man you are." He had succeeded in setting up a competition not just between the Russians and the Allies but among his own generals. He knew that Zhukov desperately wanted to crown his glittering military career by becoming the conqueror of Berlin and was already thinking of ways to cut the strutting little marshal down to size. He would allow Zhukov to stick to his plan of attacking the German capital from the east and the north but would encourage Konev to strike simultaneously from the south. To make this offensive possible, Stalin agreed to transfer an extra two reserve armies to Konev.

Maps were spread out on the table showing the disposition of the various forces and the proposed line of attack. As the two rivals looked on, Stalin traced a dotted line with a pencil to represent the demarcation line between their two army groups. He stopped drawing when he reached the town of Lübben, about fifty miles southeast of Berlin, which was supposed to be captured by the third day of the joint operation. He did not say a word, but the message was clear. The ultimate prize would go to the commander who displayed the most initiative, energy, and ruthlessness. The *vozhd* had assigned a total of 2.5 million men, 7,500 aircraft, 6,250 tanks, and 41,600 artillery pieces for what he confidently expected would be the final offensive of the Great Patriotic War. It would begin no later than April 16.

"Whoever breaks through first, let him take Berlin," said Stalin, puffing his English Dunhill pipe, a gift from Churchill.

On March 30, as Stalin was planning the capture of Berlin, Roosevelt began a much-needed holiday in Georgia. He had taken a special overnight train from Washington, passing through Atlanta around noon. He reached the spa resort of Warm Springs after lunch. It was Good Friday, and the weather was perfect, "warm and sunny." The usual crowd of well-wishers had gathered to greet him at the tiny railway station. He had been coming to Warm Springs since 1924, soon after contracting polio, and was viewed as an old friend by the five hundred or so inhabitants. He loved to swim in the fresh spring water that gushed out of nearby Pine Mountain at a constant temperature of eighty-eight degrees. The highly mineralized water relaxed his polio-wasted muscles and left him refreshed and invigorated. He built his own little white clapboard cottage on the southern edge of town and returned year after year.

A murmur ran through the crowd as the Secret Service men struggled to lift FDR out of his wheelchair and place him in the driver's seat of his 1938 two-door Ford convertible. Normally, the president assisted the agents, using his muscular arms to swivel gracefully from one seat to the other. He was now deadweight, drained of energy. FDR still insisted on driving the hand-controlled Ford up to the "Little White House," but he tired very easily, told fewer stories, and had no appetite. His administrative aide, Bill Hassett, sensed that the Boss was losing his zest for life. Hassett noticed small telltale signs, like the "feeble signature," which now simply faded away, "the old boldness of stroke and liberal use of ink gone." That evening, he blurted out his concerns to Howard Bruenn, the cardiologist who had accompanied the president to Yalta. "He is slipping away from us and no earthly power can keep him here."

The spartan bungalow in the shadow of Pine Mountain was a place of refuge for FDR, the perfect place to unwind. Surrounded by tall Georgia pines, it consisted of three bedrooms and a kitchen clustered around a large living-dining room with a stone fireplace. The house was modestly furnished, with models of nineteenth-century schooners, a painting of John Paul Jones, and a few rustic chairs on the deck. There were no steps or doorsills, so the president was able to wheel himself around with a minimum of fuss. The simple, familiar surroundings provided emotional reassurance to Roosevelt at a time of increasing personal stress and isolation. He felt more estranged from his wife, Eleanor, than ever, feeling nagged by her constant stream of advice. They had ceased to be husband and wife in the romantic sense back in 1918 when Eleanor discovered a stack of love letters from his former secretary Lucy Mercer, but they had always been political partners. Now, Eleanor acknowledged, "He could no longer bear to have a real discussion, such as we had always had." When Franklin announced his intention of traveling to Georgia to recuperate, Eleanor remained behind in Washington.

FDR was accompanied to Warm Springs by a few close aides; his Scottish terrier, Fala; and the usual coterie of adoring females. His cousins, Margaret Suckley and Laura Delano, occupied the two other bedrooms in the Little White House. His secretary, Grace Tully, was also on hand. These were the people with whom he was able to relax. They never pestered him with politics, the war, or foreign policy. Instead they attended to his physical needs, laughed at his jokes, and listened uncritically to whatever was on his mind. Unbeknownst to Eleanor, he had also made arrangements to receive a visit from Lucy, who had come back into his life more than two decades after their affair. She was now Lucy Rutherfurd, the widow of a rich New York socialite. She would be accompanied by an artist friend, Elizabeth Shoumatoff, whom she had commissioned to paint FDR's portrait. The role of trusted intermediary between Lucy and

Franklin was played by Anna Roosevelt, who felt that her father deserved "a few hours of much needed relaxation" from the burdens of international crises. Anna would later remember the statuesque Lucy as "a handsome, intelligent, quiet, and unobtrusive lady" with an "innate dignity and poise" who was a source of gay, lighthearted conversation for FDR. Unlike Eleanor, Lucy was "a wonderful listener, an intelligent listener in that she knew the right questions, while Mother would get in there and say 'I think you are wrong, Franklin.'"

Even in Warm Springs, Roosevelt was still not entirely free of Eleanor. Soon after he arrived, his wife telephoned him to lobby for increased military assistance to the Yugoslav Partisans. She kept him on the phone for forty-five minutes, even after FDR explained that her requests were impractical. Bruenn was with the president at the time and took his blood pressure at the end of the phone conversation. He noticed that it had risen sharply, up fifty points from earlier readings. The "veins stood out on his forehead."

Worries about Russia, and the postwar order in Europe, were also crowding in on FDR. Soon after arriving in Warm Springs, he was shocked to receive an insulting telegram from Stalin on April 3 accusing the western Allies of striking a secret deal with the Germans. The Soviet leader flatly rejected Roosevelt's claim that the meeting in Switzerland between Dulles and Wolff amounted to no more than a tentative feeler. According to his information, the "Anglo-Americans" had promised the Germans an easing of the peace terms in return for an agreement "to open the front and permit the Anglo-American troops to advance to the east." FDR was furious at Stalin for impugning his integrity. He took care to stifle any public criticism of Russia by his aides for fear of causing "irreparable harm" to the war effort. But the squabbling over Poland and the differences over Germany were making him question his entire approach to the Soviet Union. He was now more receptive to the arguments of advisers like Harriman who wanted to get tough with the Kremlin. "Averell is right," he had told a friend on March 24, thumping his fists against his wheelchair. "We can't do business with Stalin. He has broken every one of the promises he made at Yalta."

The president sent a telegram to Washington instructing Admiral Leahy, his chief of staff, to draft "an immediate reply" to Stalin, which was dispatched late at night on April 4. The exchange of messages marked a low point in relations between the leaders of the anti-Hitler alliance. FDR expressed "astonishment" at the claim that Eisenhower would accept anything less than the "unconditional surrender of enemy troops" on the western front. The recent advances on the western front were due to "military action," and the "terrific impact of our air power," not to any kind of secret deal. It would be "one of the great tragedies of history" if "distrust" and "lack of faith" were permitted to undermine the final victory over Nazi Germany. Roosevelt approved a final stinging sentence drafted by Leahy. "Frankly I cannot avoid a feeling of bitter resentment toward your informers, whoever they are, for such vile misrepresentations of my actions or those of my trusted subordinates."

Stalin replied on April 7 with a more diplomatically worded message insisting that he had never doubted FDR's "honesty and dependability." At the same time, he did not back down from his main point, which was that the Germans had ceased to put up much resistance on the western front. "They continue to fight savagely with the Russians for some unknown junction, Zemlienitsa in Czechoslovakia, which they need as much as a dead man needs poultices, but surrender without any resistance such important towns in central Germany as Osnabrück, Mannheim, Kassel. Don't you agree that such behavior of the Germans is more than strange and incomprehensible?"

While angry with Stalin, Roosevelt wanted to avoid a showdown. Unlike Churchill, he had no intention of using German territory to bargain with the Russians. The prime minister had been dismayed by Eisenhower's message to Stalin ceding Berlin to the Red Army. In an April 1 cable to FDR, he stressed that the German capital remained of "high strategic importance" and predicted that the Russians would become even more quarrelsome if allowed to take Berlin in addition to Vienna. "From a political standpoint we should march as far east into Germany as possible," he told FDR. "Should Berlin be in our grasp we should certainly take it." Churchill was also upset by Eisenhower's failure to discuss his military plans with the British prior to revealing them to Stalin. "There is only one thing that is worse than fighting with allies," he grumbled to his top general, Alan Brooke, "and that is fighting without them."

The prime minister's arguments failed to convince Roosevelt, who agreed with Eisenhower that there was little point sacrificing hundreds of thousands of American lives to seize territory that had already been designated part of the Soviet occupation zone. Given the fact that American troops advancing into Germany outnumbered the British by two to one, Churchill had little choice but to back down. "I regard the matter as closed and to prove my sincerity I will use one of my very few Latin quotations," he cabled on April 6, "*Amantium irae amoris integratio est.*" The White House Map Room provided a translation: "Lovers' quarrels always go with true love."

Dealing with all the conflicting political and military pressures was becoming increasingly burdensome for FDR. The great juggler could no longer keep all the balls in the air at once. Indeed, he could barely keep up with the minimum paperwork required of a president under the Constitution. His correspondence with Churchill and Stalin was conducted largely through ghostwriters in Washington like Leahy or Marshall. He slept late in the morning and took another long nap in the afternoon prior to a drive in the country in the early evening. His working day was squeezed into a couple of hours in the morning, during which he would glance at the newspapers, browse through the overnight telegrams from Washington, and sign a few bills and decrees. It required a huge effort to get to his books and beloved stamp collection, which were packed away in a long wooden crate that he now called "the coffin," a touch of black humor that alarmed Grace Tully. Above all else, he looked forward to the arrival of Lucy Rutherfurd.

Monday, April 9, was the tenth day of the president's vacation in Warm Springs, another beautiful, sunny day. His cousins had been preparing for Lucy's arrival, filling the guest cottage with freshly cut flowers. When FDR woke up from his afternoon nap, he invited Daisy Suckley to join him and Fala for an excursion in the open presidential limousine. They headed east, toward Macon, Georgia. Lucy was driving in the opposite direction, west from South Carolina, with her artist friend and a photographer. They had agreed to meet somewhere along the road.

The president impatiently scanned every approaching car "imagining that it was slowing up." After an eighty-five-mile drive, there was still no sign of Lucy, who was going through similar mental agony in her car, joking to Shoumatoff that "nobody loves us." The sun was setting, and it was getting chilly. FDR put on his navy cape to serve as a windbreaker and reluctantly agreed to turn around. They stopped in front of a country drugstore for refreshments five miles from Warm Springs when Lucy appeared in her Cadillac. A beaming Roosevelt insisted that she join him for the ride back to the Little White House. The president looked "awfully tired" all evening but was in high spirits at dinner, which was served in the living room of the cottage. He mixed drinks for his guests and entertained them with stories about life in the tsar's palace in Yalta. He had found the Russians to be "quite a nice crowd," except for "a few sinister faces appearing here and there."

"Did you like Stalin?" asked Shoumatoff, who was of White Russian descent.

FDR's talent for combining the lighthearted with the macabre had not deserted him. "Yes, he was quite a jolly fellow," he replied. "But I am convinced he poisoned his wife!"

The artist got down to work on Tuesday morning. She had the president pose for photographs in front of the bookcase in the living room. His cape helped conceal his gaunt frame, but his eyes stared off into the distance. The photographer snapped some shots of Lucy as well, an inscrutable smile on her lips. In the afternoon, Franklin and Lucy went off with Fala to visit one of his favorite places, Dowdell's Knob, at the end of the Pine Mountain trail. FDR loved to come up to the rocky overhang, 1,395 feet above sea level, to have a picnic or simply stare out over the lush green valley. He once recommended the view from the knob as a certain cure for despair to a fellow polio sufferer. The president and his former lover talked and watched the setting sun for more than an hour as Fala romped around the car. "He came back with a good tan," Suckley noted approvingly.

On Wednesday morning, the president turned his attention back to international affairs as he reviewed the overnight batch of messages from Washington. Eisenhower's forces were mopping up the last pockets of German resistance in the Ruhr. The Russians had finally captured Königsberg, capital of East Prussia, soon to be renamed Kaliningrad. FDR finalized plans to address the inaugural conference of the United Nations in San Francisco, "come hell or high water," as Hassett reported in his diary. He approved a conciliatory message to Stalin declaring an end to the quarrel over the Berne meeting, "which now appears to have faded into the past without having accomplished any useful purpose." Such "minor misunderstandings," the president told Stalin, should not be permitted to arise in the future. Pretending that an intractable problem did not exist was a classic FDR gambit that he used in his private life as well as his public life. "If something was unpleasant and he didn't want to know about it, he just ignored it and never talked about it," his wife later remarked. "He always thought that if you ignored a thing long enough it would settle itself."

The message to Stalin was drafted by Leahy. But FDR dictated a companion message to Churchill, also dated April 11, that reflected his philosophy for dealing with the Russians. "I would minimize the general Soviet problem as much as possible because these problems, in one form or another, seem to arise every day and most of them straighten out. . . . We must be firm, however, and our course thus far is correct. Roosevelt." It was the one of the very few cables that he is known to have written personally from Warm Springs.

The guests at supper that evening included the president's old Hyde Park neighbor, Secretary of the Treasury Henry Morgenthau, who dropped by for a visit. FDR produced a large bowl of caviar given to him at Yalta two months earlier by Stalin as a farewell present. He insisted on mixing the cocktails himself, even though his hands shook uncontrollably, almost knocking over the glasses. He spent most of the dinner talking to Lucy, who was seated to his right. Morgenthau tried to get him to endorse his plan for the punitive economic treatment of Germany after the war, but FDR was evasive. After Morgenthau's departure, the four women joined the president around the fireplace, swapping lighthearted stories. Shoumatoff had just finished a ghost story about Catherine the Great when Bruenn appeared, reminding FDR that it was time for bed. As the artist later recalled, "The president, like a little boy, asked to stay up longer, but finally consented to retire."

Roosevelt woke up "with a slight headache and a stiff neck" on Thursday, April 12. He joined Lucy and the women in the living room, sitting on his favorite leather chair in front of the fireplace. The spring sunlight streamed through the open terrace doors behind him, along with the scent of roses and azaleas from the garden. He had set aside a couple of hours for a portrait-painting session with Shoumatoff, much to the disgust of Hassett, who found the artist "altogether too aggressive." The appointments secretary wanted FDR to sign some papers, but Shoumatoff had other ideas. She "measured the President's nose; made other facial measurements; asked the Boss to turn this way and that. Through it all, the President looked so fatigued and weary." A stack of official documents lay on a card table in front of him. The most urgent matter demanding his attention was a telegram from Harriman in Moscow objecting to the wording of his April 11 message to Stalin. The ambassador felt that the misunderstanding over the surrender negotiations in Switzerland was hardly a "minor" matter, but "of a major character." He "respectfully" suggested delaying delivery of the cable until the president could consult with the prime minister.

Harriman's telegram reached Warm Springs through the White House Map Room, along with a draft reply from Leahy, dispatched at 10:50 a.m. The admiral favored a tougher line with Moscow but knew that FDR preferred a conciliatory approach. His draft response instructed Harriman to deliver the president's message to Stalin immediately. "I do not wish to delete the word 'minor' as it is my desire to consider the [Swiss] misunderstanding a minor matter," the suggested reply stated. The Map Room received Roosevelt's response to Leahy's cable at 1:06 p.m. "Approved," it stated simply. It was FDR's last official communication.

Nine minutes later, at 1:15 p.m., the president slumped forward in his chair. He raised his left hand shakily to his temple, staring straight ahead at Lucy and Daisy, seated together on a couch. "I have a terrific pain in the back of my head," he said softly.

Spring had come early in Moscow. By the middle of April, the snow had all disappeared, and the pussy willows lining the driveway to Spaso House were in full bloom. On the night of April 12, Averell Harriman invited foreign diplomats and a few "tame Russians" to his residence for a farewell party for an embassy staffer. People were swaying happily to a windup gramophone in the ballroom when Kathleen dragged her father off into the adjoining Blue Room. Soon afterward, the ambassador's secretary abruptly turned off the Victrola and announced it was time for everyone to go home. The guests were escorted to the door without explanation.

As soon as the guests had left, a somber Harriman gathered his aides in his upstairs room to inform them that FDR had died from a cerebral hemorrhage at the age of sixty-three. The news had been broadcast over the radio at 1:00 a.m. but the ambassador was "so used to being secretive about everything important" that he hesitated to make a public announcement. Instead he placed a phone call to the Foreign Affairs Commissariat asking for an appointment with Molotov. The commissar was still awake, after attending a late-night session at the Kremlin with Stalin and Yugoslavia's new Communist leader, Marshal Tito. At 3:05 a.m., an aide called to say that Molotov was on his way over to express his condolences. He arrived soon afterward and was shown into the Blue Room. "He seemed greatly moved and disturbed," Harriman reported later that day. "I have never heard Molotov talk so earnestly." The ambassador assured the commissar that the new president, Harry Truman, would pursue the same policies as his predecessor.

Harriman had been lobbying the State Department for weeks to be permitted to return home for consultations. He wanted to alert Washington to what he saw as the dangerous, unhealthy turn in U.S.-Russian relations since the Yalta conference. In his latest dispatch to Stettinius, drafted on April 10 but not sent, he warned that Americans were allowing themselves to be pushed around by the Kremlin. "We have accepted slights and even insults from the Soviet Government without concretely showing our displeasure," he complained. Soviet officials had "come to believe that they can force their will on us." He ticked off the "almost daily insults," ranging from the impasse on Poland to the friction over the American prisoners of war to a grounding of U.S. planes operating from Soviet-controlled territory. Harriman wanted to be given "some concrete means"—perhaps a suspension of certain kinds of lend-lease assistance—to show "Russian officials that their outrageous actions against us are affecting their vital interests." He was convinced that "roughness" was the only language Stalin understood. "The longer we wait the more difficult it will be and the more drastic the action on our part will have to be."

After his meeting with Molotov early on the morning on Friday, April 13, Harriman cabled Stettinius to say he planned to leave Moscow on Monday morning "to talk to you and the President unless you instruct me otherwise." The secretary of state overruled him yet again. "Now of all times it is essential that we have you in Moscow," he cabled. But the ambassador had another trick up his sleeve. He would use Roosevelt's death to persuade Stalin to drop his refusal to send Molotov to the opening session of the United Nations in San Francisco. If Stalin agreed, it would be hard for Stettinius to continue to block Harriman's repeated requests to return home. His presence back in the United States would become obligatory.

Harriman was shown into Stalin's office at the Little Corner at 8:00 p.m. that evening. He noted that the Soviet leader seemed "deeply distressed at the news of the death of President Roosevelt. He greeted me in silence and stood holding my hand for about 30 seconds before asking me to sit down." Like most foreign leaders, Stalin knew practically nothing about Truman and had lots of questions. The new president had focused almost entirely on domestic affairs as a senator from Missouri; his foreign experience was limited to seven months' service in France as an artillery officer during World War I. Harriman described Truman diplomatically as the kind of "man Marshal Stalin would like—a man of action and not of words."

"President Roosevelt has died, but his cause must live on," Stalin intoned gravely. "We shall support President Truman with all our forces and all our will."

This provided Harriman with the opening he sought. The most effective way to help the new president and signal the continuity of Soviet foreign policy, he told Stalin, would be to dispatch his closest aide to the United States. Molotov could stop off in Washington to meet with Truman and proceed from there to San Francisco. Harriman would be pleased to put a plane at his disposal, similar to the plane used by Roosevelt to travel to the Crimea. It could make the trip from Moscow to Washington in just thirty-six hours.

"We could paint a red star on the plane and man it with a mixed Soviet-American crew," offered Harriman, only half joking.

The thought of plastering an American military plane with the Communist insignia did not appeal to the *vozhd*. He suggested "a green star."

"We will paint the whole aircraft green, if that's what you prefer," the ambassador promised. Like a salesman determined to clinch the deal, he described the comforts and speed of the C-54 plane. He could not "find words to express too strongly" how much a visit by the foreign policy commissar would mean to the American people and to Truman personally. The entire world would view the event as a "great stabilizing influence."

"Time, time, time," Molotov protested in the background. He was evidently thinking of the Supreme Soviet session.

Pressed by the American, Stalin quickly relented. Molotov added one stipulation. Instead of taking the most direct route, westward across the Atlantic, he preferred to travel eastward across the length of the Soviet Union, via Siberia and Alaska. This arrangement suited Harriman perfectly. He planned to return to the United States by the faster route, in his own plane. He would arrive in Washington two days ahead of Molotov, which would give him time to begin the foreign policy education of the former haberdasher from Independence, Missouri.

10

The Neophyte and the Commissar

April 23

The day after being sworn in as thirty-third president of the United States, Harry Truman returned to Capitol Hill. He had lunch with congressional leaders, men he had come to know intimately during his ten years in the U.S. Senate. A gang of reporters accosted him as he left the office of the secretary of the Senate. Many of them knew him as their poker-playing friend Harry. He shook hands with every one of them, his eyes filling with tears. "Boys," he told them, "if you ever pray, pray for me now. I don't know whether you fellows ever had a load of hay fall on you, but when they told me yesterday what had happened, I felt like the moon, the stars and all the planets had fallen on me."

"Good luck, Mr. President," said one of the reporters.

"I wish you didn't have to call me that."

Overnight, Truman had become the leader of an emerging superpower at the climax of a global cataclysm. He was now commander in chief of an army of 12 million men in Europe and Asia. He was bewildered and a little frightened. He knew nothing about foreign affairs, as he himself acknowledged. His predecessor had failed to prepare him for the challenge of negotiating with giants like Stalin and Churchill, whom he knew only by reputation. During his eighty-two days as vice president, he had met with FDR privately on just two occasions. Roosevelt had never talked to him "about the war, about foreign affairs, or what he had in mind for peace after the war." He had been left almost completely in the dark on the Yalta negotiations, the dispute over Poland, and the atomic bomb project. Prior to becoming president, he had no access to the secret Map Room war files that were essential to understanding the decisions made by his predecessor. He was not a member of the White House inner circle. He had never met Harriman or any of the other Russian experts in the administration. Chip Bohlen considered Truman "an obscure vice-president, who got to see Roosevelt much less than I did and who knew less than I did about United States foreign relations."

Truman's strengths—and his weaknesses—were those of the Common Man. He exuded the solid values of the Midwest frontier: honesty, hard work, decency, modesty, simplicity. He married his childhood sweetheart and viewed life through the prism of the small town where he grew up. Decisive and plainspoken, he made his mind up quickly on the basis of his commonsense instincts, rarely second-guessing himself or expressing regrets. He was a good listener, although on occasion he could be "the contrariest man in the State of Missouri," in the words of his political patron Thomas J. Pendergast. He was deeply suspicious of "ass-kissers," a term he used to describe the clique of private advisers that surrounds any president. Despite his ignorance of current international affairs, he was a keen student of history, boasting that he had read every book in the Independence Public Library. He immersed himself in the lives of great men, from Hannibal to Robert E. Lee. If he was unusual, it was in the scope of his single-minded energy and thirst for self-improvement. After Bess Wallace accepted his marriage proposal in the fall of 1913, he described himself in a letter to her as "a clodhopper who has ambitions to be Governor of Mont[ana] and Chief Executive of the U.S." Failing that, he promised to "keep peggin' away and I suppose I'll arrive at something. You'll never be sorry if you take me for better or for worse because I'll always try to make it better."

Precisely why Roosevelt chose Truman to be his vice president in 1944—over better-known politicians like Henry Wallace and Jimmy Byrnes—remained a mystery. The most plausible explanation was that he wanted someone who could unite the rival wings of the Democratic Party. Representing a border state, Truman was neither a northern progressive nor a southern conservative. He revered FDR as the leader who had rescued America from the Great Depression and triumphed over Nazi Germany and Japan but was also aware of his faults. "He was the coldest man I ever met," Truman recalled later. "He didn't give a damn personally for me or for anyone else in the world as far as I could see. But he was a great president. He brought this country into the twentieth century."

The personalities of the two leaders were very different. Roosevelt was a patrician politician who exuded self-assurance; Truman was proud of his country-boy origins. Roosevelt got his way through stealth and calculation, rarely revealing what was on his mind; Truman was direct and down to earth. Roosevelt was an idealist, with a Grand Design for the postwar world. Truman was a realist, "a shrewd poker player," according to one of his reporter pals, who "believes in getting the best deal possible for the U.S., and doesn't bluff easily." Roosevelt's preferred method for dealing with Stalin was to procrastinate, to hope that difficulties would eventually go away. Truman believed in getting problems out into the open. FDR was a master fudger. The new president demanded clarity.

To the extent that Truman had thought about Russia at all, his views reflected mainstream American opinion. After Hitler attacked the Soviet Union in 1941, the senator from Missouri declared a pox on both their houses. He did not want "to see Hitler victorious under any circumstances," but he also mistrusted Stalin. "If we see that Germany is winning we ought to help Russia and if Russia is winning we ought to help Germany and that way let them kill as many as possible." More recently, he had developed a "tremendous respect" for Russia because of its huge wartime sacrifices. He told reporters that it was both possible and necessary to cooperate with Russia without getting tangled up in Europe's quarrels. He wanted to continue FDR's policies. But he was not a man to be pushed around.

Averell Harriman made the trip home in record time. He left Moscow at dawn on Tuesday, April 17, in the converted Liberator bomber he had christened *Becky,* traveling via Italy, North Africa, and Nova Scotia. The entire journey took forty-nine hours and twenty minutes, shaving nearly six hours off the previous record, via Tehran. Thanks to the time difference, the ambassador arrived in Washington shortly before midnight on Wednesday, April 18. At noon on Friday, he was ushered into the Oval Office of the White House to meet Truman.

During his first week in office, the new president had stayed up late studying the minutes of the Yalta negotiations in the Map Room. His eyes stung from the strain of so much reading. The low-ceilinged command center on the ground floor of the White House was modeled on Churchill's setup in Downing Street, with maps covering all the available walls and colored pins marking the movements of ships and armies. Messages flowed into the Map Room from all over the world, providing instant updates on the latest developments on the battlefront. Sitting in the center of the room, Truman could "see at a glance the whole military situation." The ever-changing map displays recorded the start of the Red Army's mighty offensive against Berlin, launched at dawn on April 16 with an earthshaking bombardment of rockets and shells across the Oder River. By April 20, Hitler's fifty-sixth birthday, Zhukov's forces had reached the outskirts of the city. A hundred miles south of Berlin, the U.S. 69th Infantry Division was closing in on the river Elbe for what promised to be a historic linkup with Konev's First Ukrainian Front.

Harriman was pleased to see that Truman had done his homework and had read through the entire Stalin-Roosevelt correspondence. The new president asked for a rundown on the most urgent problems in U.S.-Russian relations. Secretary Stettinius, Under Secretary Joseph C. Grew, and Bohlen were also in the room, but the ambassador did most of the talking. He now had the opportunity, denied to him during the long winter months in Spaso House, to pour out his frustrations in person to the commander in chief. His presentation drew on all the letters and memoranda that he had drafted in his upstairs office but never sent, fearing that it would be difficult to bridge the gulf in perception between Moscow and Washington. The ambassador wanted the president to understand some "unpleasant facts."

"We are faced with a Barbarian invasion of Europe," he blurted out, using a phrase that Truman would long remember.

The problem, Harriman explained, was that Stalin was pursuing two contradictory policies. On the one hand, he wanted good relations with the United States and Britain and was in favor of a "policy of cooperation." He needed western assistance in order to rebuild his devastated country. On the other hand, he was attempting to extend Soviet political control over neighboring states through unilateral action. The Russian concept of "friendly relations" with countries like Poland went beyond merely exerting a strong influence over their foreign policy. It involved "the extension of the Soviet system," with its reliance on an all-powerful secret police, extinction of freedom of the press, and so on. In Harriman's view, there was a very simple reason that Stalin was backing away from the promises he had made just two months earlier at Yalta to allow free elections in Poland. He understood that the Moscow-imposed provisional government represented a small minority of Poles. In a free election, a democratic leader such as Mikołajczyk could expect to get 80 to 90 percent of the vote as a rallying point against the Communists.

Harriman felt that it was not too late to reach a workable compromise with Stalin provided that the U.S. government abandoned its illusions. It was foolish to think that Russians and Americans were motivated by the same ideals and principles. "Certain elements around Stalin" were misinterpreting American generosity and the desire to cooperate as a signal that they could do anything they wished without serious repercussions. The United States should adopt a quid pro quo policy in dealing with the Soviet Union. The Russians had grounded American planes operating out of Ukraine; the Americans should respond by grounding Russian planes in Alaska. Truman had "nothing to lose by standing firm" on the issues of most importance to the United States.

The president insisted that he was not afraid of the Russians. "They need us more than we need them." He intended to be "firm but fair." He fully understood that it was "impossible to get 100 percent of what we want," but "we should be able to get 85 percent." He planned to use "words of one syllable" to let Molotov know the importance he attached to resolving the Polish dispute. Harriman told the president that he was relieved they saw "eye to eye" on the most important issues.

It took Molotov an extra two days to reach Washington, flying via Siberia and Alaska. His plane was delayed by the lack of navigational aids over much of Russia, which made it impossible to fly at night. The giant C-54 finally touched down at 5:46 p.m. on Sunday, April 22. The foreign policy commissar was invited to stay at Blair House, the official presidential guesthouse opposite the White House. The Trumans were also in residence, in a separate wing. Bess had insisted on a complete renovation of the private quarters of the White House, which were shabby and neglected: Eleanor Roosevelt had been too preoccupied with saving the world to pay attention to mildewed carpets and tattered drapes. Two carloads of Soviet security men pulled up at Blair House a few minutes before Molotov's arrival. They immediately "cased the joint," testing the windows, pulling the drawers out, and rushing up and down the stairs. "Looks like colleagues," a U.S. Secret Serviceman commented sardonically.

Truman greeted Molotov after dinner, at 8:30 p.m. The atmosphere was amicable but wary, as each man probed the other on his understanding of the Yalta agreements. It was Truman's first meeting with a senior Russian leader. He was immediately struck by Molotov's "very good looking blue eyes," "square face," and large "Cro-Magnon head, like an apple." The commissar signaled that he was unlikely to concede very much in Poland, which "was far from the United States but bordered on the Soviet Union." He wanted to know whether the new president supported the deal on Japan, granting Russia various territorial concessions in return for entering the war. Truman said that he did.

The bickering began as soon as the talks moved across the street to the State, War, and Navy Building next to the White House. The British foreign minister, Anthony Eden, joined Stettinius in trying to persuade Molotov to display some flexibility on Poland, but the commissar dug in his heels. When Truman met with his advisers on Monday, April 23, at 2:00 p.m., the secretary of state reported "a complete deadlock." The president became impatient. He complained that the Yalta accords had turned into "a one-way street." This could not continue: it was "now or never." If the Russians did not want to cooperate in the new world organization, they "could go to hell." He then went around the table asking the diplomats and generals for their opinion on how to proceed.

The president turned first to the acknowledged Wise Man of the FDR cabinet, Henry Stimson. An austere figure with gold watch chain and trim mustache, the seventy-seven-year-old secretary of war had a reputation for unbending rectitude. He lived by a few simple rules, such as "the only way to make a man trustworthy is to trust him." He liked to be addressed as "Colonel Stimson," a reminder of his service with the field artillery in France in World War I, the proudest moment in a long career in public service. As secretary of state under Herbert Hoover, he had shut down the department's code-breaking operation, insisting "Gentlemen don't read other people's mail," a position he had come to revise in the case of Japan and Germany. A lifelong Republican, he now felt like the odd man out in the cabinet, an older statesman surrounded by younger yes-men anxious to please the president. He believed that the administration, and particularly the State Department, had "got itself into a mess" with Russia. In accordance with FDR's desire to demonstrate the achievement of a "durable peace," it had convened a grandiose conference of the United Nations in San Francisco before the war was even over rather than settle differences behind the scenes. American public opinion was "all churned up" over the abstract, unenforceable promises in the Yalta declaration for a new world order. Having raised so many hopes, the administration had to deliver on them or risk public humiliation. Stimson faulted Roosevelt for focusing too much on "altruism and idealism instead of stark realities on which Russia is strong."

The secretary of war was taken aback by Truman's pugnacity, which came "like a shot out of a Gatling gun." He felt at a disadvantage compared with the other men in the room, as he had not been at Yalta. He agreed with Harriman and Deane that the Russians had caused a good deal of trouble on "minor military matters." They needed to be taught some manners. On the other hand, they had kept their word on "the big military matters." In fact, they had often done more than they had promised, mounting big offensives in the East in order to relieve German pressure on the western front. Stimson cautioned against a "headlong collision with Russia" over Poland. He pointed out that "virtually all of Poland had been Russian" prior to World War I. Having spent a lot of time in Latin America, particularly Nicaragua, Stimson was skeptical about talk of "free elections." In his opinion, the only countries in the world that permitted an independent ballot were the United States and Britain.

Next to speak was the navy secretary, James Forrestal. To Stimson's dismay, his subordinate joined Harriman in the hard-line camp. Forrestal argued that the dispute over Poland was hardly an "isolated incident": there was clear evidence of a Soviet desire to dominate other neighboring countries. A showdown with the Russians was inevitable at some point. He preferred to have it sooner rather than later. A more moderate position was taken by Admiral Leahy, who felt that the Yalta agreements were "susceptible to two interpretations." He believed that Stalin never had any intention of permitting a free government to operate in Poland. The White House chief of staff wanted to avoid a break with the Russians but felt the president should make clear to Molotov that "we stand for a free and independent Poland."

The State Department representatives in the meeting, including Stettinius and Bohlen, lined up behind Harriman and Forrestal. Stimson was clearly in the minority. He complained to his diary that night that he received support only from General Marshall, "a brave man and a wise man." The army chief of staff reminded Truman that the Red Army was expected to play a major role in defeating the Japanese. The Russians could "delay their entry into the Far Eastern war until we have done all the dirty work." Like Stimson, Marshall believed that a break with Russia over Poland would be "very serious." After the meeting ended, the president told Bohlen that he intended to follow "the advice of the majority."

Truman's second meeting with Molotov, which took place later that afternoon, would become part of Cold War mythology. Soviet historians, supported by revisionist scholars in the United States, would seize on the brief interview as evidence of a sharp turn in U.S. foreign policy after Roosevelt's death, away from compromise with Russia toward confrontation. Truman himself contributed to the mythmaking with an exaggerated account of his dressing-down of Molotov in his ghostwritten memoir, which was published in 1955, at a time when he was eager to stress his toughness with the Soviets. The real story was somewhat less dramatic.

Molotov arrived at the White House at 5:31 p.m., having made the fifty-yard journey across Pennsylvania Avenue from Blair House in a convoy of two large limousines escorted by a dozen police motorcycles. The president received him in his office, flanked by Harriman and Stettinius. He got down to business immediately, saying he was sorry to learn that "no progress" had been made on the Polish question. The commissar said he was sorry, too. Bohlen served as the interpreter on the American side, with Vladimir Pavlov as his Russian opposite number, as at Yalta. The conversation quickly became circuitous, with both sides restating existing positions. Each man stubbornly insisted that his government was meticulously implementing the Yalta agreements. They were evenly matched. Molotov had earned the sobriquet Stone Ass because of his ability to sit in his chair for hours without yielding an inch. As a Senate committee chairman and son of a Missouri mule owner, Truman had considerable experience in handling intractable partners. He eventually cut the unproductive dialogue short by producing a letter appealing to Stalin to permit three or four non-Communist Poles, including the peasant leader Mikołajczyk, to join the Moscow discussions on forming a new government. He noted sharply that an agreement had been reached on Poland "and it only remained for Marshal Stalin to carry it out in accordance with his word."

Molotov interrupted to say that some of the Poles on the American list were working against the Red Army. His face "turned a little ashy" as he tried to shift the discussion back to the war in the Far East, where both sides were in agreement. Truman cut him off, saying he wanted friendship with the Soviet Union but not on the basis of "a one-way street." He rose to say good-bye, signaling that the meeting was over. It had lasted just twenty-four minutes.

"That will be all, Mr. Molotov. I would appreciate it if you would transmit my views to Marshal Stalin."

The squat commissar collected his homburg hat and a beige raincoat that was several sizes too large for him, reaching well below both his wrists and his knees. He was escorted to the front door by the dapper, white-maned Stettinius to be greeted by a barrage of exploding flashbulbs. Reporters yelled out questions about Poland and the United Nations, but Molotov had no comment. His face betrayed no emotion.

BIG THREE DEADLOCK ON POLAND PERSISTS ran the headline in the *New York Times* the following day.

The meeting marked a change of tone toward Russia on the part of the president of the United States. "He began talking to me in such an imperious tone," Molotov later complained. Bohlen, by contrast, thoroughly "enjoyed" translating the president's remarks, "probably the first sharp words uttered during the war by an American President to a high Soviet official." As a matter of substance, however, Bohlen felt that Truman was only saying what Roosevelt would have said had he still been alive. FDR's manner would probably have been "more diplomatic and somewhat smoother," but he had also been complaining about Soviet violations of the Yalta agreements in the final weeks of his life.

"I gave it to him straight," Truman boasted a few days later. "I let him have it. It was a straight one-two to the jaw."

The story of the president's confrontation with Stone Ass would become more dramatic with each retelling. A few lines of extra dialogue made their way into Truman's memoir, which came out at the height of the Cold War. As he was getting up to leave, Molotov supposedly told Truman, "I have never been talked to like that in my life." The president allegedly snapped back, "Carry out your agreements and you won't get talked to like that."

An examination of Truman's personal records shows that these words were almost certainly never uttered. Truman himself had a different recollection of the encounter. In a May 1951 memorandum, he recalled telling a "rather truculent" Molotov that he expected Russia to live up to its agreements. Referring to a later conversation at which he was not present, he then added: "Molly [Molotov] told Bohlen that he'd never been talked to like that by any foreign power." The ghostwriters used this memorandum to spice up their account of the Truman-Molotov confrontation. There is no mention of the incident in Truman's own tape-recorded reminiscences, which were the primary source for writing the memoir. Bohlen, who took contemporaneous notes of the meeting, denied that the final angry exchange ever took place. By the time Truman's book *Year of Decisions* was published, he had already been through several teams of writers and was tired of the project. He failed to keep track of the various drafts of his own memoir. The words attributed to Molotov by Truman's ghostwriters became part of the historical record by virtue of endless repetition.

Henry Stimson had a secret he desperately needed to share with the president. For the last three years, he had been the government official primarily responsible for supervising a project that could change the course of history. Within the administration, it was cryptically known as S-1, which stood for "Section 1" of the Office of Scientific and Defense Research. Another name was the Manhattan Project, as it had been assigned to the newly created Manhattan Engineer District of the Army Corps of Engineers. By April 1945, work on the project was far enough advanced for scientists to feel "99% assured" of success. The president of the United States would soon have the power to order the destruction of entire cities with a single bomb. Nearly $2 billion had been spent on a network of secret facilities stretching across the continent, employing more than a hundred thousand people.

In common with virtually everyone else in Washington, Truman knew next to nothing about S-1 when he became president. The previous year, while still a senator, he had picked up rumors of mysterious plants in Tennessee and Washington State where costly scientific experiments were under way. He chaired a watchdog committee on wasteful military expenditures and thought of sending aides to investigate. Stimson became alarmed, referring to Truman in his diary as "a nuisance and a pretty untrustworthy man." Truman had backed down when the secretary of war assumed personal responsibility for all spending on the project, which he described as "top secret" and vital to national defense. He accepted Stimson's assurances and asked no further questions. He received no briefings on the atomic bomb project as vice president. On April 12, the day of his swearing-in as president, Stimson had whispered a few cryptic words into his ear about "the development of a new explosive of almost unbelievable destructive power." The time had come to fill in the details.

They met at noon on April 25 in the West Wing Oval Office where Truman had received Molotov two days earlier. The president was mulling over a "disturbing" cable that had arrived from Stalin overnight reiterating his refusal to budge on Poland. The Russian leader drew a comparison with Belgium and Greece. No one had consulted with him on the formation of governments in those countries, so why should he allow outsiders to determine the outcome in Poland? From the western point of view, the circumstances were quite different: the United States and Britain were fully prepared to respect the will of the electorate in liberated countries. Nevertheless, Stalin had a point about the lack of consultation. He had a talent for exposing any contradictions in the hypocrisy of the western position.

"You demand too much of me," he told Truman and Churchill. "I cannot turn against my own country."

The president was still digesting this missive when Stimson presented him with a three-page memorandum summarizing work on S-1, which he insisted on reading out loud. It began with a series of dramatic predictions:

1. Within four months we shall in all probability have completed the most terrible weapon ever known in human history, one bomb of which could destroy a whole city.

2. Although we have shared its development with the UK, physically the US is at present in the position of controlling the resources with which to construct and use it and no other nation could reach this position for some years.

3. Nevertheless it is practically certain that we could not remain in this position indefinitely.

Truman listened "with absorbed interest" as his secretary of war described the frightening possibilities ahead. The only other nation capable of producing nuclear weapons "within the next few years" was Soviet Russia. Eventually, however, it was "extremely probable" that nuclear technology could fall into the hands of "smaller nations or even groups." Atomic weapons could be constructed in secret, a development that might permit a powerful and unsuspecting nation to be "conquered within a few days by a much smaller one." Plans for a "world peace organization" were unrealistic unless they included some system for controlling the spread of atomic weapons. Such controls would be extremely difficult to put in place as they would involve draconian "rights of inspection and internal controls as we have never heretofore contemplated." The question of sharing, or not sharing, atomic weapons with other governments would soon become "a primary question of our foreign relations."

Stimson felt it was important to put the larger issues on the table before providing the president with a technical description of the atom bomb itself. For that, he called in the commander of the Manhattan Project, Leslie Groves. The general had been smuggled into the White House by an underground passageway to avoid reporters. He now appeared in the Oval Office through a back door, armed with a twenty-four-page report on the S-1 project that he wanted the president to read immediately. Stimson and Groves read along with Truman as he grappled with the complexities of the uranium-enrichment program in Oak Ridge, Tennessee, and the bomb assembly efforts at Los Alamos, New Mexico. The report described efforts by the United States to lock down supplies of uranium from Europe to the Belgian Congo. Truman would have preferred to read the document at his leisure, but this was considered a security risk.

"I don't like to read papers," he grumbled, trying to make sense of the avalanche of new information.

"We can't tell you this in any more concise language," his visitors insisted. "This is a big project."

The meeting lasted three-quarters of an hour. Truman formally approved the atomic bomb project and the establishment of a committee to determine how the terrifying new weapon should be used. His duty done, Stimson went off for his afternoon nap, only to be woken at two by an aide with the news that the president was "wandering at large" around the Pentagon. He had gone there to take a transatlantic telephone call from Churchill in London. By the time the elderly secretary of war arrived on the scene, the two leaders were deep in their first telephone conversation. The prime minister had just received word that the Gestapo chief, Heinrich Himmler, wanted to organize a separate surrender to the western Allies. Hitler was reported to be either dead or mortally ill. There was so much static on the line that it was sometimes difficult to understand what the other man was saying, but the sense was clear.

TRUMAN: I don't think we ought to even consider a piecemeal surrender.
CHURCHILL: No, no, no. Not a piecemeal surrender.

TRUMAN: That's right. That's the way I feel exactly. . . . If he is speaking
for the German government as a whole, that ought to include the
surrender of everything, and it ought to be to all three governments.

Truman had been in office for fewer than two weeks—but already felt
as if he had lived several lifetimes. It was impossible to absorb, much less
understand, everything that he had learned over the last few hours and
days. The world was changing before his eyes. Europe was in ruins, Germany was on the verge of total defeat; the Japanese were preparing for a
last-ditch stand on their home islands; a new superpower was rising in
the East. Victory was at hand, but the chances of a lasting postwar settlement seemed more remote than ever. On top of all this, a weapon had
been invented that promised to upend the assumptions of generations
of statesmen, but there was no consensus among the president's closest
advisers on what it all meant. Jimmy Byrnes assured Truman that the
bomb "might well put us in a position to dictate our own terms at the
end of the war." Admiral Leahy, by contrast, believed that the Manhattan
Project was "the biggest fool thing that we have ever done. The bomb will
never go off, and I speak as an expert in explosives."

If the bomb worked, the consequences were far-reaching and unpre-
dictable. America would become the most powerful country in the world
virtually overnight but would be exposed to unimaginable new dangers if
other nations acquired nuclear technology. The new weapon might push
Stalin to become more reasonable—but could also cause him to become
more obdurate. The bomb made war too horrifying to contemplate but
might one day destroy civilization itself.

Vyacheslav Molotov was the perfect number two—the apparatchik per-
sonified, an executor, not creator, of policy. Modest and self-effacing, he
stuck doggedly to his instructions. He was a natural subordinate, first of
Lenin, then of Stalin. Politburo records show that the only issue on which
Molotov displayed any independence to the founder of the Soviet state was
his opposition to Lenin's proposal to close down the Bolshoi Theatre as an
economy measure during the civil war. Later, when Stalin was appointed
general secretary of the Bolshevik Party in 1922, Molotov became his
deputy. The most prominent of a tiny handful of Old Bolsheviks to survive the Great Terror, he owed his life to two factors: loyalty and indis-
pensability. Appointed chairman of the Council of People's Commissars,

or prime minister, in 1930, he faithfully implemented the *vozhd*'s policies on the collectivization of agriculture, supervising the elimination of
the kulak class of small independent farmers. The subsequent man-made
famine led to the deaths of some 7 million Ukrainians, Russians, and
Kazakhs. Molotov displayed no remorse about sending people to their
deaths. His signature, along with Stalin's, featured prominently on documents ordering the execution of tens of thousands of alleged "saboteurs,"
"Trotskyists," and "oppositionists." "All 3,167 persons to be shot" was the
handwritten inscription on one such order signed by the two leaders on
December 12, 1938. Later that evening, the two men adjourned to the
Kremlin cinema to relax.

"Molotov" was an alias, derived from the Russian word *molot*, or "hammer," adopted during his years as an underground activist. It captured
the essence of his relationship with Stalin: the "Hammer" for the "Man
of Steel." He was born in 1890 as Vyacheslav Mikhailovich Skryabin, the
ninth of ten children of a store clerk. As a political exile before the revolution, he earned a ruble an hour by playing the mandolin in restaurants and
movie theaters. By Bolshevik standards, he was reasonably well educated,
having studied economics at the St. Petersburg Polytechnic Institute. The
self-taught Khrushchev described him as university educated, which was
a stretch, as his studies served mainly as a cover for his clandestine activity. "He knew how to dance the way students did," the Ukrainian party
boss recalled. "He loved music and could even play the violin." Molotov
struck Khrushchev as "a strong-willed, independent man who thought
for himself." Others were not so impressed. Aleksandra Kollontay, the
feminist free spirit exiled as Soviet ambassador to Sweden, described him
as the incarnation of "greyness, dullness, and servility."

It was true that the commissar could be a bit of a pedant. When other
party members teasingly called him Stone Ass, Molotov insisted that
the nickname used by Lenin was actually Iron Ass. But he had a softer
private side, albeit one that he kept well concealed in public. When the
Soviet archives were opened after the collapse of communism, researchers found a stack of love letters from Molotov to his wife, Polina, written
during his travels in the United States. "Polinka, darling, my love!" one
letter began. "I'm overcome with impatience and desire for your closeness
and caresses. I kiss you, my beloved, desired." It was signed "Your loving
Vecha." Another, addressed to "my pleasure honey," declared, "I wait to
kiss you impatiently and kiss you everywhere, adored sweetie, my love."
Molotov understood very well that his wife was a hostage to fortune. Stalin

had already arrested the wives of other close associates, such as Poskrebyshev and Mikhail Kalinin, in a crude demonstration of his power. The Jewish-born Polina, an accomplished woman who supervised the fishing and cosmetics industries, was in particular danger. Stalin was suspicious of her foreign connections: her brother was a successful businessman in the United States. Knowing that his wife could be deported or executed at any time made Molotov even more determined to hew unwaveringly to the party line, as laid down by Stalin.

In addition to an exceptional memory and extraordinary capacity for hard work, Molotov was known for his iron self-control. Andrei Gromyko, the Soviet ambassador to Washington, remembered a typical occasion when his chief decided to take a break after working on a document for many hours. "I'm going next door to rest for thirteen minutes," Molotov announced. He returned to his work, "on the dot," looking much refreshed. In many ways, he was the opposite of his predecessor as commissar for foreign affairs, Maksim Litvinov. He lacked intellectual sophistication and knowledge of the outside world, having spent his entire life in Russia, but he knew Kremlin politics inside out. He had a nose for power, which served him well in his dealings with foreign leaders as varied as Hitler and Churchill, Göring and Eden, Roosevelt and de Gaulle.

"A man of outstanding ability and cold-blooded ruthlessness" was how Churchill described him. "His cannonball head, black moustache, and comprehending eyes, his slab face, his verbal adroitness and imperturbable demeanor, were appropriate manifestations of his qualities and skill. . . . I have never seen a human being who more perfectly represented the modern conception of a robot. And yet with all this there was an apparently reasonable and keenly polished diplomatist." Like many other westerners, the prime minister concluded that a negotiation with Molotov on disputed matters was almost always "useless," but he developed a grudging respect for his Russian sparring partner. "In the conduct of foreign affairs, Sully, Talleyrand, Metternich, would welcome him to their company, if there be another world to which Bolsheviks allow themselves to go."

Prior to April 1945, Molotov had been to the United States only once before, in June 1942, at a time when the Nazis were pounding at the gates of Leningrad and Stalingrad. He had stayed in the White House as the president's personal guest under the pseudonym "Mr. Brown." ("Why not Mr. Red?" a reporter asked, when the secret finally got out.) He packed a revolver along with his dark gray diplomatic suit. His main accomplishment was to sign a lend-lease agreement with the United States, opening the way for massive American supplies of war matériel to the beleaguered Red Army. He also persuaded Roosevelt to endorse a statement that talked about "a second front in Europe in 1942," a promise the United States was not in a position to keep. "A great victory for us!" he commented later. "We knew they couldn't dare mount a second front, but we made them agree to it in writing. . . . That disgraced him [FDR] in the eyes of his own people."

Despite serving as the Kremlin's foreign spokesman for nearly six years, Molotov had little experience of a free press. He had virtually no contact with reporters during his trips to the United States and Britain in 1942 or Germany in November 1940 to cement the Molotov-Ribbentrop deal carving up eastern Europe. Like other senior Communists, he was contemptuous of the way in which western leaders constantly invoked public opinion as justification for their actions. He regarded this as a diplomatic ruse, designed to secure negotiating advantage. In the Soviet Union, public opinion played no significant role. The Communist Party spoke in the name of the working class, the leading force in society. As far as Molotov was concerned, bourgeois governments represented the interests of the capitalists, not the workers. Apart from that, their methods were the same. He could not accept the argument that immensely powerful politicians like Truman or Roosevelt or Churchill were constrained in their actions by the need to placate such a nebulous notion as "public opinion." He was therefore quite unprepared for the mob scene that greeted him in San Francisco, where more than two thousand reporters had gathered for the inaugural session of the United Nations.

The charter conference opened on the afternoon of April 25. The flags of forty-six nations bedecked the modernistic stage of the San Francisco opera house. Interspersed between the flags were four golden pillars representing the "four freedoms" promised by President Roosevelt—freedom of expression, freedom of religion, freedom from want, and freedom from fear. Batteries of floodlights roamed the velvet and stainless-steel auditorium, picking out the gold braid of generals and admirals, the striped suits of diplomats, and the occasional flowing robe and turban of an Oriental prince. The reporters and spectators seated in the rafters vastly outnumbered the delegates in the plush red seats down below. At 4:30 p.m.— 7:30 p.m. in Washington—Stettinius walked onstage accompanied by

Alger Hiss, the acting secretary-general of the new United Nations organization. The secretary of state gaveled the conference to order with a request for a "moment of meditation." He then invited Truman to address the delegates by radio from the White House. It had been a particularly intense, event-filled day. The president had already received his first briefing on the atomic bomb and spoken at length to Churchill by transatlantic telephone on the imminent surrender of Germany. His voice was "tinged with hoarseness" as he warned the delegates that the ever-increasing brutality of modern warfare might ultimately "crush all civilization itself."

"In your hands rests our future," he told them. "We must build a new world—a far better world—one in which the eternal dignity of man is respected."

Molotov kept away from the ravenous press hordes for the first two days of the conference, protected everywhere he went by a phalanx of bodyguards. The ever-popping flashbulbs made him nervous, but he derived a vicarious thrill from his celebrity status. "Polinka, my love," he wrote his wife. "Here among the bourgeois public, I was the focus of attention, with barely any interest in the other ministers!"

On the third day, he finally agreed to meet the newsmen at his hotel. Some four hundred reporters crowded into the St. Francis ballroom, shouting questions about the formation of a new Polish government. He treated them to an icy smile and retreated behind the ambiguity of the "excellent" Yalta decisions.

"We shall carry them out. Is that clear?"

"No," yelled the reporters.

Everything went reasonably well until a society columnist asked Stalin's top aide for an authoritative ruling on whether Russia's favorite drink should be spelled "v-o-d-k-a" or "w-o-d-k-a." Her question was greeted by laughter from the assembled journalists, but the people's commissar was not amused. "Permit me to excuse myself," he responded stiffly, bringing the session to a close.

In the first few days of the conference, Molotov established himself in the eyes of American public opinion as the original "Mr. Nyet." He objected to American plans to have Stettinius chair the conference as host, arguing that chairmanship duties should be split equally with Russia, Britain, and China. He opposed a proposal to seat Argentina as a member of the United Nations unless Poland was also seated. His objection to Fascist-ruled Argentina had a certain logic. The Yalta conference had set a March 1 deadline for countries to declare war on Nazi Germany if they wanted to become founding members of the United Nations. Argentina, which was ruled by a junta of generals sympathetic to Hitler, had waited until March 27 to join the bandwagon. Even though they had missed the deadline, Stettinius wanted to seat the Argentines as a sop to Latin American opinion. Molotov did not see why the Fascist government of Argentina should be represented in San Francisco when the Communist-dominated government of Poland was excluded.

He got his way on the chairmanship issue but was overruled on the question of Poland and Argentina. Only Czechoslovakia and Yugoslavia joined the Soviet Union in demanding the seating of the Polish Communists. The Czech foreign minister, Jan Masaryk, received a note from Molotov saying that he must vote for the Soviet proposal "or forfeit the friendship of the Soviet government." He complied but complained bitterly in private to his American friends about Soviet diplomatic techniques. "You can be on your knees and that is not enough for the Russians."

The rift between Russia and her western Allies, which had been papered over at Yalta, was finally on public display for all to see. The charter conference in San Francisco was getting more press attention than the war itself—and the headlines dramatized the deadlock. "Conference hopes dimmed as Red blocks Stettinius," proclaimed the *Washington Post.* "Big Three wrestle again over Poland," declared the *New York Times.* "What do Russians want?" asked the *Atlanta Constitution.*

Behind the scenes, Averell Harriman was doing his best to alert his journalist friends to the hardball tactics of Molotov and Stalin. He convened a series of off-the-record briefings in his penthouse suite at the Fairmont Hotel, the headquarters of the American delegation. His message to the reporters echoed his earlier message to Truman: the Russians were seeking full political control over eastern Europe, either through "Communist dictatorships or coalition governments in which the Communists held the whip hand through terror or intimidation." Some reporters were receptive to Harriman's warnings, which they repeated in analyses published under their own bylines. Others were upset by the change of tone toward Moscow. For the previous four years, they had been fed a stream of official propaganda about "our gallant Soviet ally." The Red Army had been depicted in speeches, books, magazine articles, and Hollywood movies as a bulwark against the Nazis. It was now being described as an instrument of Communist domination over half a continent. Two members of Harriman's audience, Walter Lippmann and Raymond Gram Swing, were so shaken by what they heard that they left the room in protest. *PM* magazine accused the ambassador by name of inspiring a lot of the "get tough with Russia" talk at the conference.

In between conference sessions, Molotov did his best to acquaint himself with the powerful country that was changing before his eyes from ally to rival to putative enemy. One day, he was taken to visit the Kaiser Shipyard in San Francisco, which produced many of the Liberty ships and aircraft carriers used for the war effort. He was deeply impressed. "So these are the American working classes," he remarked in amazement as his eyes feasted on the hive of activity. "What power this represents!" It made him wonder what the Communists could do if they had the opportunity of organizing and running such a mighty, economically thriving country. He was also struck by the obvious prosperity surrounding him, the "tidy houses, carefully tended lawns and automobiles in every driveway, all of them owned by ordinary working-class Americans." He told intimates later that the United States was "the country most suitable for socialism. Communism will come there sooner than in other countries."

Russia had exhausted and practically ruined itself in order to win the war against Nazi Germany. America, as far as Molotov could see, had achieved its victory almost effortlessly, by dint of its extraordinary wealth and industrial capacity. American sacrifices, in both human and economic terms, had been a fraction of those borne by Russia. Fewer than half a million Americans had been killed in the war, compared with more than 20 million Russians. Real wages had dropped in Russia by a crippling 60 percent during the five years of fighting. Production of steel was down 33 percent, pig iron by 41 percent, tractors by 76 percent. By contrast, the average American was actually better off as a result of the war, with a 40 percent higher disposable income. In 1945, the United States was producing twelve times as much oil as the Soviet Union and six times as much steel and electricity.

Wherever he went in America, Molotov was pursued by questions about the fate of the sixteen Polish underground activists who had disappeared mysteriously in the middle of March while on their way to a meeting with Red Army commanders. A full report on the Poles had reached his desk on March 29, the day after they were arrested and flown to Moscow. Both he and Stalin had been kept fully informed by Beria about the preparations for the arrests and the subsequent interrogations in the Lubyanka Prison. For six weeks, Molotov lied about what had happened to the Poles, claiming he had "no information" and would have to look into the matter. On the evening of May 4, on instructions from Moscow, he finally acknowledged what he had known all along. He dropped the bombshell on Stettinius at a reception at the Soviet consulate in San Francisco as they were shaking hands at the entrance. "By the way, Mr. Stettinius, about those sixteen Poles, they have all been arrested by the Red Army." The secretary of state was left standing in the doorway with "a fixed smile on his face" as Molotov turned away to greet the British foreign secretary.

Molotov's confession shocked the western Allies. Talks in San Francisco among the three foreign ministers on the formation of a new Polish government were suspended. The British were particularly outraged. Anthony Eden had previously noted in his diary that the United Nations would not be worth much unless "the Russians can be persuaded or compelled to treat Poland with some decency." Churchill agreed. On May 11, he sent his foreign secretary a cable expressing skepticism about the entire United Nations project. "In a very short time our armies will have melted, but the Russians may remain with hundreds of divisions in possession of Europe from Lübeck to Trieste, and to the Greek frontier on the Adriatic. All these things are far more vital than the amendments to a world constitution that may never come into being till it is superseded after a period of appeasement by a Third World War." The demarcation lines for the division of Europe were already being drawn.

11

Linkup

April 25

First Lieutenant Albert Kotzebue had decided to disobey orders. His company commander had selected him to lead a patrol east of the Mulde River "to make contact with the Russians" but to remain within five miles of the river. When he reached the small town of Kühren, he was meant to turn back. He chose instead to venture beyond the outer limits of his patrol zone.

A scrawny twenty one year old with a toothy grin from Houston, Texas, Kotzebue came from a military family: both his father and his stepfather were colonels in the regular army. He had volunteered for the army in November 1942, immediately after Pearl Harbor, and had earned a reputation as an outstanding platoon leader, fighting his way from Normandy to the heart of Germany. He knew the Russians were very close, and this was his opportunity to make history. Leading his platoon across the flat farmlands between the Mulde and Elbe Rivers, with their picturebook villages awash in the colors of spring, he felt an irresistible temptation to push ahead, whatever his formal orders.

The date was April 25, 1945, the day the United Nations conference opened in San Francisco and Truman learned about the atom bomb. Apple trees and cherry trees were already in bloom; fields were carpeted with yellow winter cress; tulips and lilac bushes filled neat, well-kept gardens. The villages along the road were crowded with downcast people, most of them on the move, propelled by an elemental survival instinct. Refugees pushed bicycles and carts lashed with bedding, food and clothing, pots and pans, and the occasional Oriental rug. White flags hung from the houses. An Associated Press reporter who traveled the same route a couple of days later described "an army of misery"—made up of "old and young, ill and crippled, with personal belongings hurriedly packed as the Russians drew near"—marching with grim purpose along the road. "Mothers hauled their children in carts. Women stumbled along with huge bundles on their backs in the choking dust, just as the frightened people of Belgium and France fled before the Nazis five years ago. Fear and fatigue lined their faces and there was a frantic urgency in their attitudes."

Mixed in with the refugees were columns of German soldiers, drained of the will to fight, and Allied prisoners of war, dazed by their sudden liberation. "Christ, Yanks! It's good to see you," yelled a British prisoner, who had escaped his German captors the day before. "Foive fuckin' years we've been waitin' for you blokes."

Kotzebue had been instructed to withdraw without a fight if he met any organized resistance. Instead he encountered the opposite problem. He was repeatedly held back by crowds of enemy soldiers desperate to surrender to Americans—any American—to avoid capture by the Russians. In Kühren alone, Kotzebue's thirty-six-man platoon had rounded up and disarmed three hundred fifty-five dispirited German soldiers. The Germans were herded into the courtyard of a farmhouse and put under the guard of freed British prisoners. The *bürgermeister* proceeded to round up another hundred wounded German soldiers who had been hiding around the town, terrified that the Russians would arrive before the Americans. Kotzebue ordered a German officer to assign three of his men to smash a large pile of surrendered rifles. The situation seemed "fantastic to this little knot of Americans in the heart of German no-man's land," a unit history subsequently reported. "The townspeople were in terror and many of the women were in tears, as everyone asked: 'Are the Russians coming?'"

Former POWs were reporting that the Russians had reached the east bank of the Elbe, opposite a village called Strehla, some fifteen miles down the road. Kotzebue figured that another patrol would make the long-awaited first contact if he did not—so the honor might as well go to his platoon. Besides, he had always been curious about Russians as people. One of his ancestors, the German playwright August von Kotzebue, was reputed to have been a favorite of Catherine the Great. Another distant relative, the navigator Otto von Kotzebue, had explored the coast of Alaska in a Russian sailing sloop, discovering Kotzebue Sound. American, Russian, and German blood stirred in the Kotzebue family veins. The lieutenant's men let out a tremendous cheer when he announced his decision to disregard the five-mile limit.

The patrol drove five miles east to the village of Dahlem, where they captured another thirty-one Germans, "all of them very young and scared to death." Villagers scattered in fear at the mere mention of Russians in the vicinity. A couple of middle-aged men, anxious to curry favor with the Americans, offered to show them the back way to Strehla. Eight miles farther on, the convoy of seven U.S. Army jeeps entered the hamlet of Leckwicz. Driving down the single main street, Kotzebue spotted a lone horseman, who turned into a courtyard before he could be identified. "He looked strange," the unit history recorded. "Everyone's heart beat faster. Was this it?"

Kotzebue followed the horseman into the courtyard, where they were soon surrounded by a crowd of refugees. The mysterious horseman turned out to be a Red Army cavalryman on a scouting mission. His name was Aitkalia Alibekov, and he was from Kazakhstan. He was extremely reticent, not exactly hostile, but "reserved, aloof, suspicious, not enthusiastic." It was 11:30 a.m. in Germany, 5:30 a.m. in Washington, 12:30 p.m. in Moscow. The 69th United States Infantry Division had linked up with the 58th Guards Rifle Division of the Red Army. The first encounter between the American and Russian armies was "not one of wild joy, but rather of cautious fencing. Or, perhaps, the Russian soldier was just plain stupefied and couldn't realize what had happened."

When Kotzebue asked the cavalryman for directions to his command post, he waved his arm toward the east. A freed Polish partisan offered to show the Americans the way. They raced across the flat countryside toward Strehla and the Elbe, fewer than two miles away. The river was about one hundred and fifty yards wide at this point. Through his field glasses, Kotzebue could see some brown-shirted figures moving around on the opposite bank. He had heard that Russian soldiers wore their medals into battle: sure enough, sun glinted off their uniforms. He shot off a green flare, an agreed recognition signal between the two armies. There was no response. The partisan hollered "Amerikanski," which triggered beckoning waves from the other side.

The next problem was how to get across. Kotzebue used a hand grenade to unchain a sailboat tied to a jetty on the western bank. He jumped in, followed by five of his men. The fast currents threatened to sweep the little boat downstream, but they managed to cling on to the remnants of a destroyed pontoon bridge, jutting out from the eastern bank of the river. The wrecked bridge was covered with the charred corpses of German civilians, including a little girl clutching a doll with one hand and her mother with the other. The refugees had evidently been killed while trying to cross the bridge when it was blown up either by British or American planes or by Russian artillery fire. The Americans had to "wade knee-deep through the bodies" of the Germans in order to reach the Russians.

The Russians greeted the Americans warily at first. There were formal handshakes and exchanges of salutes. Kotzebue explained that he wanted to arrange a meeting between Russian and American commanders. He was taken to meet a succession of more senior officers, culminating in a general who was "quite reserved" and unsure of the protocol for addressing an American lieutenant. The atmosphere thawed out when Kotzebue and his men were left to chat with ordinary Russian soldiers. Soon they were slapping one another on the back, drinking to the end of the war, and toasting "our great leaders—Stalin and Roosevelt." (The Russians did not seem to be aware that FDR had died and been replaced by Truman.)

Similar encounters took place later in the afternoon near the town of Torgau, fifteen miles downstream from Strehla. The platoon leader, Lieutenant William Robertson, had fashioned an American flag out of an old bedsheet with some crudely painted stars and stripes. When he waved the makeshift flag at the Russians on the other side of the river, he came under a barrage of antitank and small arms fire. After much yelling of "Amerikanski," "Tovarisch," and "Russia, America," the Russians finally ceased fire. Robertson crawled along the twisted girders of a blasted bridge to shake hands with a Russian soldier high above the Elbe River. Since he "couldn't think of anything fancy to say," and spoke no Russian anyway, he just grinned and slapped Sergeant Nikolai Andreyev on the knees. The Russians later explained that they mistook the Americans for Germans, a group of whom had waved the Stars and Stripes at them two days previously.

The 69th Division commander, Major General Edwin Reinhardt, was furious when he found out that his soldiers had failed to remain inside their designated patrol zones. He threatened to have everyone involved locked up. These threats were forgotten as soon as reporters got hold of the story and began promoting "the meeting on the Elbe" as one of the great symbolic moments of the war. Instead of being court-martialed, Kotzebue and Robertson were awarded Silver Stars. Reinhardt bathed in their reflected glory when he crossed the Elbe in a canoe the following day, April 26, for a much-photographed meeting with his Red Army counterpart, Major General Vladimir Rusakov. Nazi Germany had finally been split in two. In Washington, Truman issued a statement hailing the imminent end of "Hitler and his gangster government." In Moscow, Stalin ordered a 324-gun salute to be fired in honor of the historic linkup.

For a few glorious days, American and Russian soldiers got drunk with one another, traded cigarettes and watches, inspected one another's weapons, sang and danced to the music of accordions, and laughed at one another's jokes. A reporter for the U.S. Army newspaper *Stars and Stripes*, Andy Rooney, summed up the euphoria by describing his new Russian friends as "the most carefree bunch of screwballs that ever came together in an army. They would be best described as exactly like Americans only twice as much."

Kotzebue's platoon spent two nights on the Russian-held side of the Elbe, in the town of Kreinitz. Much of this time was devoted to drinking and celebrating, but it was enough to demonstrate that Russians were not "exactly like Americans." The Americans were surprised by the primitiveness of the Red Army. It was hardly an accident that the first Soviet soldier spotted by an American patrol was a cavalryman. The Russians relied on horse-drawn wagons for many of their logistical needs and scouting operations. Horses dragged artillery pieces into position; infantrymen slogged ahead on foot. Tanks and heavy artillery were reserved for major set-piece assaults, such as the attack on Berlin. Jeeps, many of them delivered through lend-lease, were reserved for senior officers. Kotzebue's men found it difficult to imagine how the Russians "could have advanced so well against the might of the Germans with such primitive weaponry."

They were also taken aback by the Russian practice of entering a German house and throwing the furniture and chinaware into the street. The streets of Kreinitz "looked like a disaster zone," recalled Alfred Aronson, a sergeant in Kotzebue's platoon. "It was a big departure from the way we were used to soldiering." The Americans liked to sleep in proper beds when they commandeered a place to stay. Their new Russian friends preferred to sleep on the floor, leaving the furniture to be hauled away by specially formed "trophy brigades." When it came time to eat, the Russians simply slaughtered a pig or a cow from the nearest farm, bewildering the Americans who were accustomed to a constant supply of K rations.

Senior officers recorded similar impressions. "They appear to be the lineal descendants of GENGHIS KHAN—both in looks and action," the commander of the 272nd Infantry Regiment wrote a friend back in Washington. "They are wild barbarians, make no mistake about that." While not doubting the Russians' ability to fight, Colonel Walter Buie was convinced they were no match for the U.S. Army. "We can 'take them' any day. A motley crew if I ever saw one—about 10% were in civilian clothes but armed with everything that will shoot. . . . I feel certain that they recognize only FORCE."

An American officer who crossed the Elbe two weeks later to rescue Allied prisoners of war was struck by "the Mongoloid appearance" of the Russian troops. "The men were filthy dirty," noted Major Mark Terrel. "Most were in ragged uniforms, some in only half uniforms mixed with civilian clothes. None wore steel helmets. All appeared to be absolutely fatigued. Many were asleep in the straw filled carts upon which they were riding, and some were asleep while riding horses." Russian supply trains consisted mainly of "crude carts filled with live pigs and chickens." Terrel saw Russian soldiers rounding up herds of cattle and drinking directly from running streams. On a subsequent trip, he came away with a "considerably more favorable" impression. The troops were clean and well disciplined, saluting smartly as the Americans drove past. Their horses were "very well groomed" and "excellently handled." On the other hand, his view of Russian drivers remained unchanged. "Every Russian driver drives with one hand on the horn, the other on the wheel, and both feet on the gas pedal. They use the straight line system and quick destruction comes to anything getting between the two points of the line."

If the Americans were curious about the Russians, the Russians were just as curious about the Americans. They were torn between a prickly, if justifiable, pride in their military accomplishments and a childlike desire to please their allies. They shared their meager belongings, boasted about their victories over the Germans and the sacrifices of the Red Army, and gazed with wonder at American military hardware. A U.S. Army historian, Forrest Pogue, who took part in the meeting on the Elbe, was reminded of the way "Americans of other eras" strove to impress Europeans. He reported that the Russians were "losing their provincialism," like "the Americans at the turn of the century." The soldiers he met on the Elbe represented "an infant state, conscious of its new power, aware of its awkwardness, desirous of the good will of the states which had fought beside it. . . . These Russians are wide-eyed observers of the scene about them, and they are avid to see what makes the world about them tick."

Unlike their American counterparts, the soldiers of the 58th Guards Rifle Division had fought ferocious battles right up to the Elbe. The closer they got to the river, the fiercer the resistance became. The Germans were fighting "with the stubbornness of those condemned to death." They threw everything into the battle—SS, Gestapo, Hitlerjugend—and the Russians suffered heavy casualties. A company of cavalrymen had crossed the river under cover of fog on a makeshift ferry on the morning of April 25. Encountering no resistance, they advanced to the outskirts of Strehla. The town looked deserted, but the Russians held back from entering it, fearing the Germans would spring an ambush. They found it strange, and a little galling, to watch Kotzebue's platoon drive unopposed into Strehla to be greeted as saviors by the inhabitants. The Russian commander, Lieutenant Grigori Goloborodko, would remember April 25 as "the first day our men could walk around without crouching." They had spent so much time lying in trenches and crawling through mud that their uniforms were falling apart, particularly at the knees and elbows.

"The Americans were amazed that we wore no helmets," recalled Sergeant Alexander Olshansky. In the U.S. Army, helmets were a mandatory safety precaution. Red Army soldiers regarded them as a useless encumbrance, particularly in offensive warfare. They reasoned that an infantryman was more likely to be injured by shrapnel than by bullets. Heavy metal helmets obscured the view and made it more difficult to fight. The Russians were more impressed by the bayonets on American rifles, only to be disappointed when their allies confessed that they never used their bayonets in combat—only as can openers.

The Red Army's achievements in battle rested on a complete disregard for human life. The American 69th Infantry Division had spent just sixty-five days in combat during their seven-hundred-mile advance from Normandy to the Elbe: deaths from all causes numbered three hundred nine, about 2 percent of total operating strength. By contrast, many soldiers of the 58th Guards Rifle Division had seen almost continuous combat since the Nazi invasion of Russia in June 1941. They had fought their way

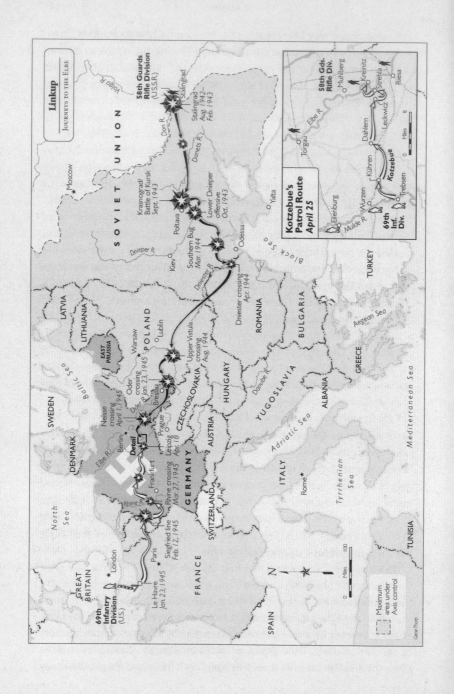

Linkup
JOURNEYS TO THE ELBE

58th Guards Rifle Division (U.S.S.R.)

69th Infantry Division (US.)

Stalingrad
Aug. 1942–
Feb. 1943

Krasnograd/Battle of Kursk
Sept. 1943

Lower Dnieper offensive
Oct. 1943

Southern Bug
Mar. 1944

Dniester crossing
Apr. 1944

Upper Vistula crossing
Aug. 1944

Oder R. Jan 23, 1945

Oder crossing
Jan. 23, 1945

Neisse crossing
April 1, 1945

Leipzig
Apr. 18

Rhine crossing
Mar. 27, 1945

Siegfried line
Feb. 12, 1945

Le Havre
Jan. 23, 1945

Moscow

Volga R.

Don R.

Donets R.

Dnieper R.

Kiev

Dniester R.

Odessa

Yalta

Black Sea

SOVIET UNION

LATVIA

LITHUANIA

EAST PRUSSIA

POLAND

Warsaw

Lublin

CZECHOSLOVAKIA

HUNGARY

ROMANIA

BULGARIA

YUGOSLAVIA

ALBANIA

GREECE

Aegean Sea

TURKEY

AUSTRIA

SWITZERLAND

GERMANY

Frankfurt

Prague

Breslau

Berlin

Detail

Elbe R.

DENMARK

SWEDEN

Baltic Sea

North Sea

GREAT BRITAIN

London

Paris

FRANCE

SPAIN

ITALY

Rome

Tyrrhenian Sea

Adriatic Sea

Mediterranean Sea

TUNISIA

Rhine R.

Danube R.

Maximum area under Axis control

Miles
0   100

N

Gene Thorp

Kotzebue's Patrol Route
April 25

58th Gds. Rifle Div.

Torgau

Kreinitz

Strehla

Riesa

Muhlberg

Elbe R.

Dahlem

Leckwitz

Kuhren

Kotzebue

Trebsen

Wurzen

Eilenburg

Mulde R.

69th Inf. Div.

Miles
0   8

fourteen hundred miles across the continent, from Stalingrad and Kursk, through Ukraine and Poland, until the final bitter battles in Germany itself. The division had been formed and re-formed after being decimated with casualties that had become too large to count.

Overall, between D-day and VE-day, Soviet losses exceeded American losses by a margin of at least five to one. The U.S. Army suffered eleven thousand fatalities during its final offensive through Germany in April 1945. By contrast, the Russians reported more than seventy-eight thousand men killed in action in the battle of Berlin alone. Marshal Zhukov later described the Russian system for advancing across a minefield to an incredulous General Eisenhower. He explained that his men simply ignored the existence of the mines, pushing forward as if they did not exist. The Soviet assumption was that losses from antipersonnel mines were no greater than casualties inflicted in the normal course of battle, by enemy artillery and machine guns. War and death went hand in hand. Once the infantrymen had crossed a mined area and established a bridge-head, combat engineers would clear the pathway for mines that could blow up vehicles.

Soviet commanders from Zhukov down resented the condescending attitude of Allied generals with a fraction of their combat experience. They listened skeptically to their tales of battlefield glory and laughed at them behind their backs. A particular target of Russian ridicule was Montgomery, the British general who had wanted to race Zhukov to Berlin only to be overruled by Eisenhower. Russian officers were unimpressed by the field marshal's boasts about his great victory over Rommel at El Alamein, which the British saw as a turning point equivalent to Stalingrad. El Alamein involved some four hundred thousand soldiers on both sides, fifteen hundred tanks, forty-five thousand casualties— a formidable encounter certainly but hardly on the scale of Stalingrad (2.1 million men, two thousand tanks, 1.9 million casualties) or Kursk, (1.5 million men, sixty-five hundred tanks, 1 million casualties). Red Army generals jokingly asked themselves how many knighthoods would be appropriate for commanders like Zhukov and Konev "who had won a whole series of brilliant victories that were several times as important as El Alamein, in both their results and their scope."

After slogging all the way to Berlin and the Elbe from Kursk and Stalingrad, Soviet soldiers believed they deserved some tangible reward. Their homes and villages had been destroyed by the Nazi invader: it was only reasonable that they should exact retribution in kind. Compared with Russia, Germany seemed a fantastically wealthy country, even after five years of war. Prior to April 1945, most Russian soldiers had never worn a watch, ridden a bicycle, or owned a decent pair of shoes. To a peasant boy from the Caucasus or central Asia, an ordinary village house in Kreinitz or Strehla took on the appearance of a palace; a country road was like a highway; well-fed German cows bore no resemblance to the scrawny animals on a Soviet collective farm. The opulence begged an obvious question: If Germans were so well off, why had they invaded impoverished, downtrodden Russia?

"How well these parasites lived!" a Russian lieutenant, Boris Itenberg, wrote his wife from Germany. "I saw ruined houses, abandoned furniture, sidewalks neatly planted with trees, libraries with new unread books, and dozens of other little signs of an incredibly good life. In the houses that are still intact, you would be amazed by what you see: chairs, couches, wardrobes. They lived so well. Why did they need any more? They wanted a war—and they got one." Dmitri Shchegolev, an officer serving under Zhukov, saw things similarly. Billeted in an apartment on the outskirts of Berlin previously occupied by a German railway clerk, he noted in his diary for April 28 that the larder was well stocked with "home-cured meat, preserved fruit, strawberry jam. The more we penetrate into Germany the more we are disgusted by the plenty we find everywhere. . . . I'd just love to smash my fist into all those neat rows of tins and bottles."

To move from envy to rage to crimes against the civilian population was a logical progression for many Red Army soldiers. They remembered the words of Ilya Ehrenburg: "Don't count days, don't count versts, count only the number of Germans you have killed." The popular propagandist had urged them not to display "any kind of mercy" toward the defeated German enemy, advice they took literally. A female Red Army doctor reported that she frequently heard soldiers remarking "how pleasant it is to see a pretty Frau crying in one's arms." When she asked if they "rewarded" the German women for their company, a typical reply was, "Does she really need another gram of ham?" The poet Boris Slutsky, who served as the political officer of an infantry platoon, believed there was "no need to justify" cruelty toward Germans. "This is not the time to speak of Law and Truth. The Germans were the first to take the road beyond good and evil. Let them be paid back in kind, a hundred fold."

The thirst for war booty trumped all moral considerations. "First let's send Germany up in smoke, then we'll go back to writing good, theoretically correct books on humanism and internationalism," a Soviet commander told his officers in East Prussia. "But now we must see to it that the soldier will want to go on fighting. That's the main thing." A decree signed by Stalin in December 1944 was widely interpreted as an invitation to loot. It permitted soldiers to send monthly packages to their families weighing up to five kilos. Officers were granted a ten-kilo allowance, generals sixteen kilos. "Our people, like a horde of Huns, threw themselves on the houses," a Red Army captain wrote his family the month following the capture of Gumbinnen in East Prussia. "In a matter of hours, wonderfully furnished apartments, the richest homes, were destroyed and now look like a dump, where torn pictures are mixed up with the contents of broken jars of jam."

A few officers were dismayed by what they saw. As Russian troops closed on Berlin, a Red Army propaganda worker named Georgi Solyus recorded a series of staccato impressions in his private diary. "Looting everywhere. Cars, Studebakers, loaded to the roof with loot. This is wild plundering in the real sense of the term. Women being raped. It is terrible to write this. Primal violence shattering all the restraining bonds of discipline. Almost all the buildings are burning. It is dark from smoke and soot. Walls are collapsing, crushing people, but that does not stop the soldiers. They enter the houses like they did before, going into the cellars, dragging everything away, dragging, dragging. These are not primarily front-line soldiers but auxiliaries, drivers, those with a means to cart the stuff away. If the front-line soldier takes anything, he takes watches, rings, vodka."

It did not take long for reports of looting and raping to reach the Americans on the west bank of the Elbe. The terrified reaction of German civilians at the approach of the Red Army was an early sign of the terrible events unfolding on the other side of the river. As fresh American units moved in force up to the new demarcation line, they were swamped by a "great mass of distraught and unorganized refugees . . . on foot, on bicycles, carts, wagons, and any other means obtainable." The movement of refugees was overwhelmingly in one direction: from east to west.

While American and Russian soldiers were slapping one another on the back on the banks of the Elbe in late April, a thousand miles away in central Ukraine, a grand experiment in U.S.-Soviet military cooperation was coming to a bitter, unmourned end. Relations between the wartime Allies had sunk to a new low at the U.S. air base in Poltava, opened with great fanfare less than a year earlier. Hailed by the press as goodwill ambassadors to Stalin's Russia, several hundred American airmen found themselves under the constant watch of the NKVD security police. Their planes had been grounded for weeks due to infractions of the rules for operating out of Soviet territory. Russian liaison officers behaved as if they expected fighting to break out at any moment—not with the Germans, who were already beaten, but with their American allies. No longer contributing anything to the war effort, ostracized by their Soviet hosts, the Americans of Poltava joked that they had become "the forgotten bastards of the Ukraine."

Like the linkup on the Elbe, Operation Frantic had begun on an upbeat note. Building an American air base on Soviet territory seemed like a brilliant idea when first mooted in early 1944. The new airstrip would permit heavy B-17 bombers stationed in England and Italy to attack German targets that had previously been out of reach. Instead of being forced to turn back over Germany, the Flying Fortresses could simply continue on to Ukraine, dropping their bombs on the way. The shuttle-bombing operation promised a political payoff as well. American and Russian ground crews would gain experience working together that would provide the foundation for joint air operations against Japan. Their collaboration would symbolize the unity and vitality of the anti-Axis alliance, disproving claims by the Nazi propaganda chief, Joseph Goebbels, of an inevitable Soviet-American rift.

The first shuttle force of one hundred twenty-nine B-17s arrived on June 2, 1944, following a successful raid against a railway-marshaling yard in Hungary. Triumph turned to tragedy three weeks later when a German reconnaissance plane shadowed a force of Flying Fortresses to Poltava following a bombing run against an oil refinery near Berlin. That night, a large force of Heinkel 111s appeared over the air base. A party of reporters from Moscow, on hand to witness a shining example of Soviet-American cooperation, cowered in trenches as fifty B-17s exploded around them on the steel-covered runway, together with a quarter of a million gallons of aircraft fuel. Wishing to restrict the number of U.S. military personnel in Poltava, Stalin had refused permission for Spitfire fighters to be stationed at the air base. Soviet antiaircraft crews, mainly women, suffered heavy casualties as they fired their guns bravely but ineffectually at the intruders. "Christ, if we only had some Spits," complained an angry American pilot as his plane went up in flames. "They'd clean out all that crap up there in ten minutes, and chase the rest of them back to

Germany." The Americans acknowledged that the Soviet defenders had performed heroically but resented the political system that had left them exposed to a devastating German attack.

More disappointments followed. After repeated refusals, Stalin finally consented to a single supply run to help the Warsaw Uprising in September 1944, but the gesture came too late to assist the rebels. Most of the drops missed their targets; operations were then suspended for the winter. Relations between Americans and Russians deteriorated sharply over the next few months. The American airmen chafed at the restrictions imposed on them by the Soviets and started flying unauthorized missions; the Russians complained that some of the Americans were anti-Soviet; Russian service personnel broke into American warehouses; Americans got into trouble for reckless driving around Poltava. An operation designed to showcase Allied cooperation became a case study in clashing cultures and ideologies.

The very presence of several hundred foreign airmen on Soviet territory was a threat to a regime that aspired to total social and political control. Nowhere was this more apparent than in attempts by the NKVD security police to regulate the dating practices of libidinous young Americans. While there was no official prohibition on Americans dating local girls, such relationships aroused intense suspicion. If a Ukrainian girl went out with an American, she was invariably summoned to NKVD headquarters for a lengthy interrogation.

"Why are you going out with an American?"
"Aren't Russian men good enough for you?"
"Does he give you presents?"
"Are you in love with him?"
"Don't you realize he only wants to sleep with you?"
"What do you talk about?"

The police interrogators told the girls they would never be allowed to marry their Americans, much less leave the country with them. If they wanted to continue the relationship, they would be required to spy on the American for the NKVD. Prior to their release, the girls were obliged to sign a sworn statement promising not to divulge any information about their interrogation.

The Soviet authorities were particularly sensitive about anyone who had experienced the two-year Nazi occupation of Poltava, between September 1941 and September 1943. Initially, many Ukrainians had welcomed the Germans as liberators, presenting them with traditional gifts of bread and salt. The Germans permitted private enterprise and dismantled the hated collective farms, earning goodwill that they subsequently squandered through excessive harshness and cruelty. When the Red Army reoccupied Ukraine, hundreds of thousands of suspected traitors were either shot or sent into exile. People who had done nothing disloyal were suspect simply because they had lived under foreign rule; they had to be indoctrinated all over again. A Ukrainian girl whispered to her American airman friend that the NKVD was determined to prevent anybody from "witnessing the superior culture of a second foreign country." The NKVD feared that the people of Poltava would notice that "Germans and Americans had more luxuries and more freedom than Russians."

The Americans shrugged off secret police lectures about the risks of consorting with local "prostitutes" and joked that the initials "NKVD" stood for "No Ketch Venereal Disease." Their Ukrainian and Russian girl-friends lived in fear of the secret police but were often willing to risk a lengthy sentence in the Gulag for the sake of a few hours of pleasure and comfort. "I will take my five or ten years of punishment later, right now all I want is to be alone with my American" was a widely expressed opinion.

The black market was another cause of friction with the Soviet authorities. The Americans were legally obliged to convert their dollars into rubles at the highly unfavorable official rate of one to five. By trading on the black market, they could get between one hundred and two hundred fifty rubles to the dollar. The temptation to increase their purchasing power by 2,000 percent was too great for many airmen. The parks and streets of Poltava soon became the scene of a thriving black-market business, involving the exchange of American cigarettes and clothing for Russian cameras and jewelry. An American study showed that more than half of the base personnel had purchased Russian cameras that they would not have been able to afford at the official dollar–ruble exchange rate. Red Army officers complained that many Poltava residents were walking around town in American flight jackets and GI shirts "which they hadn't even bothered to remodel."

Strained relations between Americans and Russians at Poltava turned into a full-blown crisis at the end of March 1945 due to events that had little to do with the air base. The Russians accused an American pilot forced to make a crash landing in Poland of attempting to smuggle a Polish dissident out of the country. In another incident, a disgruntled Russian sergeant was flown to Italy onboard an American plane that had been forced down in Hungary. Both incidents were the result of poor military discipline rather than a high-level breach of agreements with the Russians. The stowaways were promptly surrendered to the Soviet authorities, but this did not appease the Russians, who demanded court-martials for those responsible. To Stalin's suspicious mind, it was clear that American military aircraft were being used "for ulterior purposes": they were obviously "dropping supplies, wireless sets and [London government] agents to the Polish underground." To signal his displeasure, he ordered a grounding of all American flights over Soviet-controlled territory. Even wounded prisoners of war were prevented from leaving Poltava.

The Soviet commander at Poltava, Major General S. K. Kovalev, prepared for "an armed clash with the Americans." At a meeting with his subordinates on March 31, he ordered a series of "precautionary measures" in case fighting broke out:

- In the event of a combat alert, the technical battalion should surround the American camp and sever communications.
- The engineering battalion should guard planes and bombs to avoid a diversion on the part of the Americans.
- SMERSH [Red Army counterintelligence] must seize the American radio station, preventing them from broadcasting information about incidents.
- Any Americans who are in the city at the time of the alert should not be permitted to return to their garrison. A special place should be prepared for their detention.

Friends were turning into enemies in the blink of an eye.

The standoff at Poltava continued for four weeks until April 26, the day after American and Russian soldiers embraced on the Elbe. Stalin finally consented to lift the flight ban after the U.S. military mission in Moscow took disciplinary action against the offending pilots. The Poltava airmen were now free to depart, except for a couple of drivers who had been involved in fatal traffic accidents.

Unlike some of his underlings, Stalin understood that he could not treat his allies the same way that he treated his own people. He was counting on an extended period of peace with the "forces of imperialism"—or at least an absence of war—to rebuild his shattered country. He wanted to secure American loans and credits for reconstruction purposes but not at the expense of undermining his own political power. This meant maintaining correct relations with the Americans while simultaneously keeping them at arm's length. It was a delicate balancing act, reflected in his order to Red Army units in Germany on how to behave toward the western Allies. He instructed Soviet soldiers to "politely" accept requests for meetings by American and British units but not to "take the initiative" in organizing such encounters. Field commanders were expected to liaise with their western counterparts on the establishment of an agreed demarcation line but refrain from providing "any information about our plans or the combat tasks of our armies."

Above all, Stalin was determined to maintain tight personal control over all contacts between Russians and foreigners. His files show that this was almost an obsession with him. Reports on incidents involving westerners were routinely routed to the *vozhd* for his information. Unauthorized meetings were forbidden; even trivial encounters had to be explained and justified. When a Red Army commander such as Zhukov or Konev met a senior American general, he was almost always accompanied by a political commissar who reported directly to Stalin. In some cases, the dictator wanted to make sure that his subordinates were not overstepping their authority. "Calm Comrade Kovalev down," he ordered, when he learned about the military alert in Poltava from SMERSH. "Prevent him from taking independent actions." But Stalin had another reason to be suspicious of army officers who had spent too much time outside Russia: tsarist history. He was haunted by the precedent of the 1825 Decembrist uprising, hatched by disgruntled Russian officers contaminated by the liberal ideas they had absorbed in western Europe during the Napoleonic Wars.

The political risks in sending Russian troops to conquer foreign lands were summed up by a joke that became popular in eastern Europe in the summer of 1945. "Stalin made two mistakes: He showed Russians to Europe, and Europe to the Russians." Stories of Russian brutality poisoned the minds of millions of Poles, Germans, and Hungarians. The evidence of western prosperity—at least compared with conditions back home—caused Russians to ask awkward questions about their own political system.

Closeted in his wood-paneled Kremlin office, Stalin brooded over the question of how to deal with a defeated Germany. He defended the behavior of Soviet troops who raped and pillaged their way across Europe. "You have, of course, read Dostoevsky?" he lectured Milovan Djilas when the puritan Yugoslav Communist dared to criticize the actions of Red Army soldiers on territory liberated from the Nazis. "Do you see what a complicated thing is man's soul, his psyche? Well then, imagine a man who has fought from Stalingrad to Belgrade—over thousands of kilometers of his own devastated land, across the bodies of his comrades and dearest ones! How can such a man react normally? And what is so awful in his amusing himself with a woman, after such horrors? You have imagined the Red Army to be ideal. And it is not ideal, nor can it be. . . . The important thing is that it fights Germans—and it is fighting them well; the rest doesn't matter."

It took Stalin a long time to understand that cruelty toward a conquered population could be politically and militarily counterproductive, as evidenced by the continued bitter fighting on the eastern front. The first public sign of a change of policy came on April 14 when *Pravda* published an editorial criticizing Ilya Ehrenburg for his overheated rhetoric. Headlined "Comrade Ehrenburg Oversimplifies," the commentary drew a distinction between Nazis and ordinary German civilians and insisted that the Red Army had never set out to "destroy the German people." Ostensibly it was a response to an Ehrenburg article that had appeared three days earlier claiming that "Germany does not exist; there is only a colossal gang." In fact, it signaled a major reversal of policy, ordered by Stalin himself. Accustomed to the adulation of Red Army soldiers thirsty for revenge, Ehrenburg was devastated to find himself cast in the role of sacrificial victim. His attempts to explain himself to the *vozhd* went unanswered.

A week later, on April 20, Stalin issued an order of the day spelling out the new policy:

- The armies must change their attitude toward German prisoners and the civilian population, and treat Germans better.
- The harsh treatment of Germans is causing them to react with terror and encouraging them to resist stubbornly, refusing to surrender.
- The German population, fearing revenge, is organizing itself in bands. Such a development is not helpful to us.

Promulgating a new party line was a lot simpler than changing the behavior of ordinary soldiers. Ehrenburg remained hugely popular among the frontline troops who showered him with fan mail and asked why his articles were no longer being published. As Red Army troops battled their way into "the lair of the Fascist beast," attacks on the civilian population spiraled out of control, fueled by plentiful supplies of alcohol left behind by the SS and the Wehrmacht. Western historians would later estimate that at least 2 million German women were raped by Soviet soldiers, many of them repeatedly. Tens of thousands committed suicide. The phrase *"Frau, komm"* held a terrifying meaning for every Berlin woman. Soviet officers who wanted to preserve order and discipline were powerless to stop the orgy of violence. A Soviet commander reported to Beria on May 11 that "Comrade Stalin's order on the necessity for the softer treatment of Germans" had made little difference. "Up until now, unfortunately, there have been no reductions in plundering the local population or in the rape of German women." Hatred could not be turned on and off, like a tap.

As the day of victory approached, Stalin was forced to grapple with an unsettling political and military conundrum. His armies had borne the brunt of the fighting in the war against the Nazi enemy: they had "torn the guts out of the Germany army," in Churchill's phrase. German combat losses on the eastern front outnumbered losses on the western front by more than three to one. The Red Army killed at least eight hundred thousand of the 1.2 million German soldiers who perished in the final climactic battles for Germany itself between January and May 1945. By purely pugilistic standards, the typical Soviet soldier was superior to the average American or British soldier. But wars are not won only on the battlefield. They are a struggle between competing ideologies, economic systems, ways of life, and overall military-industrial potential. The society that is stronger—in all dimensions combined—will eventually emerge victorious. The American army was no match for the Soviet army when it came to killing large numbers of Germans, but it was infinitely better at securing their trust. There was no moral equivalence between the two armies. The fact that the western Allies ended up with 5 million German prisoners of war, compared with just 3 million captured by the Red Army, provided a telling indicator of the direction in which events were moving.

While Stalin had demonstrated that his armies could conquer vast swaths of territory, he had yet to show that he could win the allegiance of the "liberated" peoples. There was so far little evidence that Germans, Poles, Hungarians, and Romanians would willingly submit to domination from Moscow. But without some degree of popular consent, or at least acquiescence, the only way to maintain the Soviet hold over these territories was through coercion and terror. Walls and fences would be needed to control the movement of population: otherwise eastern Europeans would simply vote with their feet and flee to the West. One way or the other, the dictator was determined to hang on to his gains.

A willingness to resort to extreme brutality had been key to the Red Army's success; it was now becoming a fatal weakness. The military struggle would soon be overshadowed by an ideological struggle. As Stalin himself noted in his instructions to Soviet commanders preparing to occupy Berlin, "Germany has been conquered militarily, but we still have to conquer the souls of the Germans." He was describing a new kind of contest—for the hearts and minds of ordinary Europeans—that would dominate international politics for nearly half a century, pitting the traditional Russian reliance on brute force and centralized authority against the American belief in personal liberty.

12

Victory

May 8

"The war is not yet over," Stalin insisted angrily, after receiving news of the unconditional surrender of Nazi Germany on both the eastern and western fronts. The *vozhd* was in his office in the Kremlin, surrounded by his military commanders. Everyone in the room agreed that the Germans should be required to sign the documents of surrender in Berlin, the capital of the Third Reich, to the country that had "contributed most to victory." The Great Patriotic War was not going to end with a modest ceremony in a redbrick schoolhouse in a French provincial town.

Suspicious as always, Stalin was furious with the Allies for presenting him with a fait accompli by accepting the German instruments of surrender in Reims in the early hours of May 7. He was even more furious when he found out that a Red Army general named Ivan Susloparov had signed the document on behalf of the Soviet Union. "Who the hell is this famous Russian general?" he fumed. "He will be punished harshly." The unfortunate Susloparov turned out to be a Soviet liaison officer accredited to Eisenhower's headquarters. He had cabled Moscow for instructions when German generals arrived in Reims on May 6 with an offer to capitulate but received no reply by the time of the surrender ceremony. Since the surrender was unconditional, he decided to sign the document on his own initiative. Fortunately for him, he added a caveat, insisting that any of the Allies had the right to insist on a separate ceremony. Shortly afterward, he received a message from Moscow instructing him to sign nothing.

Pacing back and forth along the green carpet in his office, Stalin accused western governments of concocting a "shady deal" behind his back. He would not repudiate the Reims surrender, but he would not recognize it either. Germany's capitulation must be treated as "a most important historical fact" to be ratified in "the place where the Fascist aggression sprang from." In a telephone call to Berlin, Stalin ordered Zhukov to make the necessary arrangements. Truman and Churchill did not see the need for another surrender ceremony but were in no mood to argue with their victorious ally.

Unable to find an undamaged building in the center of the Nazi capital, Zhukov had to settle for the canteen of a military-engineering school in the eastern suburb of Karlshorst. He led the Allied representatives into the dining hall at the stroke of midnight on May 9. Eisenhower was represented by his British deputy, Air Chief Marshal Arthur Tedder. Stalin had dispatched his all-purpose troubleshooter Andrei Vyshinsky from Moscow to keep an eye on Zhukov. The victors sat down together at a long table covered with green felt. A few minutes later, the German delegates were shown into the room. The faces of the Russians registered indignation, satisfaction, and extreme curiosity as the men who had inflicted so much destruction on their country took their seats at a smaller table to the side like errant schoolboys. They were led by Hitler's chief of staff, Wilhelm Keitel, who had accepted the surrender of France four years earlier. Complete with monocle and swagger stick, the red-faced field marshal seemed perfect for the role of arrogant Prussian officer, except that his hand shook as he signed the instruments of surrender. Zhukov noted his "beaten look."

The celebratory banquet went on all night, with endless toasts to Soviet-American-British friendship. The food had been flown in from Moscow, the china and silverware looted from nearby German homes. The Americans noticed that the tablecloth was "made up of overlapping unbleached linen bedsheets and the napkins were small squares of material torn from the sheets." Everybody present felt "overcome with emotion, vodka, or both." Zhukov danced a boisterous Russian dance with Vyshinsky as his female partner, recording later that the Soviet generals were "the best dancers by far." Even Keitel and his fellow Germans were treated to the feast, albeit in a separate room reserved for the losers. At six in the morning, the Allied generals and diplomats staggered to their cars for a tour of the devastated city, beginning at the bombed-out opera house at the head of Unter den Linden, past the once-glittering Adlon Hotel, to the ruins of the Reich Chancellery, where Hitler had committed suicide eight days before.

The streets of the city had been taken over by drunken Red Army soldiers jubilantly firing their weapons. "Everyone is dancing, laughing, singing," recorded Vasily Grossman, a reporter for the military newspaper *Red Star*. "Hundreds of colored rockets are shot into the air, everyone is saluting with bursts from sub-machine guns, rifle and pistol shots." Many of these soldiers were what the Russians called living corpses. Desperate for alcohol, they had broken into barrels in the Tiergarten containing a poisonous industrial chemical that turned fatal the third day after consumption. The breakdown in discipline marred what would otherwise have been a uniquely happy occasion. "One of the greatest victories in the world," observed Grigory Pomerants, an intellectual serving in the Soviet infantry. "Everything rejoices and sings in one's breast. And sharply breaking through the rejoicing is shame. A world capital. Groups of foreign workers bunched up on corners, returning to France, Belgium, and before their eyes—what shame! Soldiers are drunk, officers are drunk. Sappers with mine detectors search in garden beds for buried wine."

Hungry civilians in tattered clothing, mainly women and old men, waited patiently in line to get a bucketful of water from a pump. Many wore white armbands as a symbol of surrender or red ones to show their support for the Red Army. Red Soviet flags hung from the buildings. Wolfgang Leonhard, a German Communist flown to Berlin by the Russians to establish a municipal administration, noticed that many of the flags had been "recently converted from swastika flags."

The first day of peace brought both joy and worries about the future. "Before, I thought, will I live?" Red Army corporal David Samoilov wrote in his diary. "Now, I think, how will I live?"

News of Germany's surrender reached ordinary Soviet citizens at 2:00 a.m. Moscow time, 1:00 a.m. Berlin time, on May 9. The triumphant announcement was made over Radio Moscow by Yuri Levitan, who had delivered the news of the Nazi invasion in June 1941 and many subsequent defeats and victories. As Levitan's sonorous voice died away, Muscovites poured out into the streets to stage the biggest spontaneous demonstration ever witnessed in the Soviet capital. By morning, several million people were surging through the center of a city draped with red flags and banners, up Gorky Street toward Red Square, along the Moscow River, and around the Kremlin's formidable redbrick walls. That night, Moscow was lit up by a splendid firework display. Searchlights picked out the golden domes of Orthodox cathedrals and the red stars atop the Kremlin towers; a thousand-gun salute rang out across the city as planes swooped low overhead, dipping their wings in a victory salute; the survivors of the Great Patriotic War danced in the streets and squares. "They were so happy they did not even have to get drunk," reported a British eyewitness. "Nothing like this had ever happened in Moscow before. For once, Moscow had thrown all reserve and restraint to the winds."

Loudspeakers attached to lampposts blared out the Soviet national anthem, along with "The Star Spangled Banner" and "God Save the King." The U.S. Embassy on Manezh Square opposite the Kremlin quickly became a focus of the popular enthusiasm, particularly after members of the military mission appeared on the balcony in uniform to wave to the throng. "Long live the great Americans!" roared the crowd, as a Soviet flag appeared next to the Stars and Stripes. "Long live Truman! Hoorah for Roosevelt!" Americans venturing into the street were tossed unceremoniously into the air. Inside the building, U.S. diplomats did not quite know what to make of the explosion of friendly feeling toward "a bourgeois power," albeit a wartime ally. The Soviet authorities made halfhearted attempts to move people away from the embassy, erecting a bandstand at the other end of the vast square, to no avail. Harriman was still in the United States, leaving his deputy, George Kennan, as acting ambassador. The dignified forty-six-year-old diplomat was "a little embarrassed" by the outpouring of popular adulation but felt obliged to acknowledge the cheers of the crowd. He finally hoisted himself up on one of the giant neoclassical pedestals that adorned the front of the building and addressed the crowd in Russian:

"Congratulations on the day of victory! All honor to the Soviet allies!"

A uniformed U.S. Army sergeant who accompanied Kennan was pulled off the pedestal and carried away to join the celebrations after "bobbing helplessly over a sea of hands." He did not return until the next day. Kennan himself escaped back to the safety of the embassy, exhilarated, but also sad. Later that evening, he told a British journalist why it was difficult for him to share the unadulterated joy of the people down below. Russia was a devastated country; the task of reconstruction would be long and arduous; peace could never match the inflated expectations of the jubilant crowds. Looking out across the packed square beneath him, he murmured, "They think the war has ended, but it is really only beginning."

The ambivalent reaction was typical of America's leading expert on Soviet Russia. A tortured, introspective man capable of flashes of brilliant insight, George Frost Kennan had always been an outsider. Descended from a Presbyterian farming family that had settled in the American Midwest, he felt more at home in the eighteenth century than the twentieth century. At Princeton, he had refused to join any clubs, partly out of shyness, partly out of disdain for the offspring of the eastern elite. Awkward and aloof, he was "an oddball on campus, not eccentric, not ridiculed or disliked, just imperfectly visible to the naked eye." Much to his surprise, after leaving Princeton in 1925, he was accepted into the Foreign Service. He chose to specialize in the Soviet Union, a country with which the United States did not even have diplomatic relations at that point. He was inspired by the example of a distant cousin, also named George Kennan, who had explored Siberia under the tsars and penned a seminal work on the Russian penal system. Unable to travel to Moscow, the younger Kennan studied Russia from a listening post in the Latvian capital, Riga. When FDR recognized Soviet Russia in 1933, the new ambassador to Moscow, William Bullitt, selected Kennan as his first interpreter and resident Russia specialist.

Both by temperament and by virtue of his own experience, Kennan was a pessimist, inclined to a gloomy view of U.S.-Russian relations, at least in the short to medium term. Nothing he witnessed during two long stints in Moscow had altered his early opinion that the Soviet Union was not "a fit ally or associate, actual or potential," for the United States. Like Tocqueville before him, Kennan based his views not so much on current events but on an in-depth analysis of the history, culture, political and economic systems, geography, and even climates of the two emerging superpowers. Russia's drive for expansion reflected "the age-old sense of insecurity of a sedentary people reared on an exposed plain in the neighborhood of fierce nomadic peoples." The need to dominate the vast Eurasian landmass determined the need for a strong, highly centralized state. That in turn presupposed a powerful army, capable of warding off external threats, and an omnipresent police force to suppress internal dissent and any signs of foreign influence. Russian rulers from Ivan the Terrible to Stalin preferred "to keep their people in darkness rather than risk illumination by contact with foreign culture and foreign ideas." Even westernizers like Peter the Great sought to limit and control the nation's contacts with the rest of Europe: their fascination was with western technology rather than western political ideas.

Although his sympathies in the great battle of ideas with Soviet Russia were obviously with his own country, Kennan was critical of many aspects of the American system of government. He felt American leaders paid far too much attention to domestic public opinion, which interfered with the conduct of a sensible foreign policy. The most important question for an American politician was often not "Is my policy effective?" but "Do I look shrewd, determined, defiantly patriotic?" Kennan disliked the moralistic strain in American foreign policy, the tendency to lecture foreign governments on their perceived shortcomings. He was wary of the grand slogans underpinning the Atlantic Charter and FDR's ideas for the creation of a new world order built around the United Nations. He believed America should remain true to its ideals but should not try to foist them on other peoples with entirely different national traditions. He detected in American statesmanship "a certain histrionic futility, causing it to be ineffective in the pursuit of real objectives in the national interest, allowing it to degenerate into a mere striking of attitudes before the mirror of domestic opinion." In the case of Russia, he was distressed by the American propensity to pursue agreements for their own sake, to demonstrate Allied unity. The United States had cast itself in the role of the "ever-hopeful suitor." Much better, Kennan thought, to agree to disagree than "to perform one act of ingratiation after another."

It was clear to Kennan that the Soviet Union was determined to carve out an exclusive zone of political control in eastern Europe. The United States should refuse to endorse a Communist-run government in Poland, even if it included a few token non-Communist ministers, and create its own sphere of influence in western Europe. A similar logic applied to Germany. "The idea of a Germany run jointly with the Russians is a chimera," he wrote in the summer of 1945. "We have no choice but to lead our section of Germany—the section of which we and the British have accepted responsibility—to a form of independence so prosperous, so secure, so superior, that the East cannot threaten it. . . . Better a dismembered Germany in which the West, at least, can act as a buffer to the forces of totalitarianism than a united Germany which again brings these forces to the North Sea."

Kennan's fatalism was the cause of endless arguments with his State Department colleagues, particularly his close friend Chip Bohlen.

Although they shared similar views on the nature of Stalin's Russia, having served in the Moscow embassy together in the thirties, their approaches were entirely different. Assigned to the White House as an adviser to FDR on Soviet matters, Bohlen was the practical diplomat, responding to the wishes and expectations of his political masters. He regarded Kennan's proposals for the partition of Germany and the division of Europe into opposing ideological blocs as "utterly impractical" from a political, public relations point of view. "Foreign policy of that kind cannot be made in a democracy," he lectured Kennan. "Only totalitarian states can make and carry out such policies." Unlike the gregarious Bohlen, the introverted Kennan was not the least concerned with public opinion. He viewed Soviet-American relations from a ruthlessly analytical perspective, as an intellectual exercise unencumbered by the messy vagaries of practical politics.

Returning to Moscow in 1944 as Harriman's number two, Kennan felt isolated and unappreciated. Restrictions on foreigners had become even more onerous since his first tour of duty, which coincided with the Stalinist purges. Despite the wartime alliance, American diplomats were treated by the Soviet secret police as if they were "bearers of some species of the plague," to be kept at arm's length from ordinary Soviet citizens. It was even difficult to get his official foreign ministry contacts to respond to routine requests for information. Consumed with curiosity about the "real Russia," Kennan mingled with the masses in parks, theaters, and crowded suburban trains. The tall foreigner in the three-piece suit cut an incongruous figure as he was jostled by rough street urchins, war widows, and peasant girls. He tried to imagine the world that was closed to him by fitting snatches of overheard conversations into his encyclopedic knowledge of Russian history. On such occasions, he felt like a "thirsting man" who throws himself into "a stream of clear water." His yearning for contact with the *narod,* the mythical Russian "people," could never be satiated.

Equally frustrating to Kennan was the lack of demand for his expertise on the part of his own government. His opinions scarcely seemed to matter. He rarely received any feedback on the long reports he sent to Washington. Nobody consulted him about the future of Russian-American relations. Even Harriman, whom Kennan regarded as an ally, spoke disparagingly about his elaborate literary efforts. He felt his deputy was wasting his time "batting out flies." The ambassador left Kennan to run the embassy while he focused on the big political questions as the president's personal intermediary with Stalin. Harriman saw his minister-counselor as "a man who understood Russia but didn't understand the United States."

Ignored in Washington, shunned in Moscow, Kennan had decided to resign from the Foreign Service. In the meantime, he had a series of dispatches to pen, for posterity if not the ungrateful bureaucracy. Soon after VE-day, he sat down to analyze "Russia's International Position at the Close of the War with Germany." He was struck by a startling paradox. For the first time in her thousand-year history, Russia found herself "without a single great power rival on the Eurasian landmass." Victory had left her "in physical control of vast new areas of this landmass, some of them areas to which Russian power had never before been extended." These new conquests were a symbol of Russia's newfound strength, but they were also a potential source of weakness and instability. Kennan noted the principal vulnerabilities:

- *Imperial overstretch.* The newly acquired western provinces had already proved "indigestible to Tsardom," and were likely to be equally indigestible to the Communists. Kennan saw little difference between the "heavy-handed generals and commissars who now command the capitals of Central Europe" and "the Tsarist satraps" of a hundred years ago. Successful revolts by Poles, Balts, or Ukrainians could "shake the entire structure of Soviet power."
- *Economic incompetence.* Soviet insistence on subordinating the economy to the needs of the military sector would depress popular living standards and ruin entire branches of industry and agriculture. Such methods worked, up to a point, in Russia, where social expectations were modest. Non-Russians were unlikely to "accept a standard of living as low as that of the Soviet peoples."
- *Ideological contamination.* In order to control its new territories, the Soviet government would need a corps of colonial administrators who risked becoming "corrupted by the amenities and temptations of a more comfortable existence and more tolerant atmosphere." Contacts with foreign countries and cultures undermined one of the cornerstones of the Soviet state.

In sum, Russia would "probably not be able to maintain its hold successfully for any length of time over all the territory over which it has today staked out a claim." At some point, she would be forced to retrench.

The western world, led by the United States, was almost certain to prevail over the long term—as long as it remained united and firm in the face of Kremlin blustering.

The cheers of the crowds massed outside 10 Downing Street and along Whitehall were ringing in his ears, but Winston Churchill found it difficult to share the popular elation. The man acclaimed as Britain's greatest wartime leader was exhausted and listless. Papers piled up in his red dispatch boxes. When it came time for his afternoon nap, a couple of marines often had to carry him upstairs to his bedroom in a chair. He told aides that he "doubted if he had the strength to carry on."

Some Downing Street insiders viewed the prime minister's lethargy as a function of his personality. Adversity brought out the best in Churchill; victory deprived him of the source of his energy. His generals quipped that "the P.M. can be counted on to score a hundred in a Test Match, but is no good at village cricket." After five years of spitting defiance at Adolf Hitler, the tough old warrior was temperamentally unsuited for politics as usual. While there was much truth to this diagnosis, his inner turmoil was also a reflection of an increasingly grim international situation. As Churchill saw it, the Nazi menace had been replaced by the Soviet menace. Calamity went hand in hand with victory: *Triumph and Tragedy* would become the title of the final volume of his war memoir. His private secretary, John Colville, used a Latin phrase as the motto for the era that was just beginning. *Bellum in Pace.* "War in Peace."

The prime minister revealed his worries about the postwar world in a telegram he sent to Truman on Saturday, May 12, four days after the final collapse of Nazi Germany. "I am profoundly concerned about the European situation," he began. The British and American armies were already "melting away," leaving a military vacuum that could be exploited by the totalitarian power to the east. "An iron curtain is drawn down upon their front," Churchill complained. "We do not know what is going on behind. There seems little doubt that the whole of the regions east of the line Lübeck-Trieste-Corfu will soon be completely in their hands." Another huge swath of German territory presently occupied by the western Allies west of the Elbe River, had been promised to the Russians in return for a share of Berlin. The way would soon be open to the Russians "to advance if they chose to the waters of the North Sea and the Atlantic."

When Churchill talked about an "iron curtain" descending across

"An Iron Curtain
Is Drawn Down"
MAY 1945

NORWAY

FINLAND

Oslo

Lake
Ladoga

Helsinki

Leningrad

Tallinn

Stockholm

ESTONIA

SWEDEN

North
Sea

Riga

LATVIA

SOVIET
UNION

Copenhagen

Bornholm Is.
(Den.)

LITHUANIA

Kaunas

DENMARK

Vilnius

Lübeck

Soviet
EAST
PRUSSIA

Minsk

Soviet

Berlin

Polish

Vistula R.

Dnieper R.

British

Warsaw

Cologne

American

"Iron Curtain"
May 1945

Frankfurt

Prague

POLAND

Kiev

French

Munich

Vienna

Prague

CZECHOSLOVAKIA

Kraków

Lwow

Dniester R.

FRANCE

AUSTRIA

Danube R.

Budapest

Bern

HUNGARY

ROMANIA

Trieste

Milan

ITALY

Belgrade

Bucharest

YUGOSLAVIA

Danube R.

Black Sea

Adriatic Sea

BULGARIA

Sofia

Germany before
1939

Soviet Union before
1939

Tirana

N

Territories annexed
by the USSR during
war

ALBANIA

Territories controlled
by Red Army or Allies

Corfu Is.

GREECE

Territories
transferred from
U.S. to Soviet control
June – July 1945

Athens

0   Miles   100

Gene Thorp

Europe, he was thinking more about an information barrier, the essential precursor to totalitarian rule, than a physical barrier. To prevent news from circulating freely, the Soviets were making it almost impossible for Allied journalists and diplomats to travel to areas they controlled. Churchill had already accused the Russians of cloaking their military operations in Poland in "an impenetrable veil" in the March 16 telegram to Roosevelt; two weeks later, on April 1, he complained to Stalin about "a veil of secrecy . . . drawn over the Polish scene." Stalin rejected his complaint, claiming that the Poles would regard the dispatch of foreign observers as "an insult to their national dignity."

The prime minister spent the first weekend after VE-day at Chequers working on a victory broadcast to the nation. He was joined by his wife, Clementine, just back from a tour of Russia, and his son, Randolph. He had been working on the speech for days, becoming emotional when he talked about the challenges facing Britain "in years I shall not see." He resumed his dictation on Saturday evening following the customary after-dinner movie. At one point, he became so distracted by his own oratory that he put the lighted end of his cigar in his mouth. "Followed an uproar of spitting and spluttering but he assured us he hadn't burned his mouth," his loyal secretary, Marian Holmes, recorded in her diary. The speech writing complete, he unwound by reciting Tennyson's "Ode to the Death of Lord Wellington" (*Great in council and great in war / Foremost captain of his time*). Tears rolled down his face as he acted out the part of the dying conqueror of Napoleon.

The prime minister struck a somber tone in his victory speech. He agreed that a period of rejoicing was necessary to the "national spirit," but worried that "the simple and honorable purposes for which we entered the war" were at risk of being "brushed aside." Words like "freedom," "democracy," and "liberation" were being stripped of their true meaning. He warned "there would be little use in punishing the Hitlerites for their crimes if law and justice did not rule, and if totalitarian or police Governments were to take the place of the German invaders." While he refrained from mentioning Stalin or Russia by name, his meaning was clear. Fresh conflicts lay ahead. Further sacrifices would be required in order for Britain to avoid falling into "the rut of inertia, the confusion of aim, and the craven fear of being great."

Unbeknownst to the public, and even to his American allies, the prime minister was preparing for a possible military confrontation with the Soviet Union. Shortly after his victory speech, he received Field Marshal

Montgomery at 10 Downing Street. The commander of British forces in Germany recorded that the prime minister was "very steamed about the Russians." He issued a verbal order to Montgomery not to destroy the weapons of 2 million German soldiers who had surrendered to the British at the end of the war, telling him that "all must be kept, we might have to fight the Russians with German help." He took similar precautions to prevent the rapid demobilization of the Royal Air Force and the destruction of captured German warplanes. "All reduction of Bomber Command is to be stopped," he ordered on May 17. "No German aircraft in British control which has a serviceable war value, including spares, is to be destroyed by the Germans or by us without Cabinet sanction." The following day, he told Soviet ambassador Fyodor Gusev that Britain "refused to be pushed about" and had postponed the demobilization of the air force in order to strengthen its negotiating hand in "discussions about the future of Europe."

Fresh geopolitical problems were crowding in from all sides. Churchill was determined to keep as much territory as possible on the western side of his imaginary iron curtain. Much more attuned than Truman to the Soviet military threat, he urged the United States to demand a high price for the "enormous area" on the west bank of the Elbe that it was to hand over to Soviet control in return for half of Berlin. The prime minister was worried that the Russians, and their allies, were grabbing land wherever they could. Red Army paratroopers had captured the Danish island of Bornholm in the Baltic Sea in a lightning raid on May 9 amid the VE-day celebrations. A dangerous face-off was developing in Trieste between Tito's Communist partisans and British troops under Field Marshal Harold Alexander. It was unclear whether the Yugoslav leader was acting on his own initiative or with backing from Stalin in trying to seize the Italian port city, but Churchill felt he had to assume the worst.

He also felt he had to prepare for the worst. A few days later, he instructed his military chiefs to plan Operation UNTHINKABLE, a preemptive strike against the Red Army. The target date for "the opening of hostilities" was July 1, 1945. The objective would be "to impose on Russia the will of the United States and the British Empire" in order to get "a square deal for Poland." Startled by the prime minister's demand, the generals responded with a paper entitled "Russia: Threat to Western Civilization." They pointed out that the Red Army had two and a half times the number of divisions of the western Allies combined. On the central front, around Dresden, the British and Americans would be "facing odds

of the order of two to one in armor and four to one in infantry." Even if
the western armies achieved some limited initial success, the Russians
still had the option of waging "total war" over a protracted period of time,
as they had done against the Germans. The odds of success would become
"fanciful" if the Americans grew weary of the project. In short, Operation UNTHINKABLE was completely unworkable. "The idea is of course
fantastic and the chances of success quite impossible!" the chief of the
Imperial General Staff, Alan Brooke, commented in his diary. "There is
no doubt that from now onwards Russia is all powerful in Europe."

Churchill felt lost and bereft in his moment of triumph. He understood
that he no longer had the power to shape events through the sheer force
of his will. The Americans seemed to want nothing more from Europe
than to pack up and go home. While he was impressed by the vigor of
President Truman and his capacity for decision making, he was disturbed
by his lack of knowledge of European affairs. The U.S. military machine
lacked "indispensable political direction." The last few months had constituted "a deadly hiatus . . . a melancholy void" in which "one president
could not act and the other could not know." Churchill understood that
he could do nothing without the support of the United States. He moved
among the cheering crowds "with an aching heart and a mind oppressed
by forebodings."

While Churchill was dictating his victory speech at Chequers, Harry Truman was settling into the White House. He had spent the first four weeks
of his presidency at Blair House while the dilapidated old mansion on the
other side of Pennsylvania Avenue was repainted and refurbished. He felt
overwhelmed by work and the responsibilities of his new office. "Things
have moved at a terrific rate here since April 12," he wrote his mother on
VE-day. "Never a day has gone by that some momentous decision didn't
have to be made."

Like Churchill, Truman was worried about deteriorating relations
with Russia, but he placed at least some of the blame on the Englishman.
Viewed through the eyes of the man from Missouri, Churchill was a dyed-
in-the-wool imperialist who became as "mad as a wet hen" when he failed
to get his way. The White House staff regaled Truman with stories of the
prime minister's drinking habits: gin and bitters first thing in the morning, champagne for breakfast, meals washed down with multiple double
brandies. The new president had already rejected Churchill's pleas in the

closing days of the war to make a dash for Berlin and Prague to improve his bargaining position with the Russians. He was not going to be pushed around by "the fat old Prime Minister of Great Britain."

On Sunday, May 13, five days after VE-day, Truman received a telephone call from an FDR crony named Joseph Davies, who had served as ambassador to Moscow in the thirties. A big Democratic Party donor, Davies was known as the most pro-Russian of Roosevelt's advisers. His determination to understand "the Russian point of view" bordered on sycophancy and willful blindness to the crimes of Stalinism. Attending the Soviet show trials in 1937, at the height of the Terror, he concluded that the defendants were guilty as charged. While the former Washington trial attorney had some reservations about the legal procedures, he was impressed by the "consistent vein of truth" in the statements of high Kremlin officials who confessed to everything from wrecking the economy to spying for Germany and Japan. As Davies saw it, the purges were "well justified." He was even more enthusiastic about meeting Stalin, noting his "sincerely modest" demeanor and "deprecatingly simple" manner. "He gives the impression of a strong mind which is composed and wise," he wrote to his daughter Emlen. "His brown eye is exceedingly kindly and gentle. A child would like to sit in his lap and a dog would sidle up to him." Ever since his return from Moscow in 1938, the former ambassador had worked assiduously to promote the cause of Soviet-American friendship.

Fearing a rift in the wartime alliance, Davies sought a personal meeting with Truman to suggest ways "to keep the situation sweet." The president told him to come right over. They met in the Oval study on the second floor of the residence. Truman was in his shirtsleeves, fuming about the way the press was handling the crisis. He was particularly upset about a *Chicago Tribune* story revealing the contents of secret diplomatic messages from Stalin to Churchill and Truman.

STALIN NOTES JAR ALLIES!
Diplomats Amazed

WASHINGTON D.C. MAY 11—Dictator Stalin startled his western allies today with an astoundingly outspoken note to Prime Minister Churchill in which he frankly declared there is no possibility of co-operation between Russia and Britain. . . . The vigor of Stalin's language in his 1,000 word message to Churchill amazed career diplomats in [London and Washington]. It was reported on high authority that

Stalin labeled Churchill a perverter of the truth and a welcher on the Yalta agreement. It was regarded as one of the most astounding documents in diplomatic history.

"These damn sheets are stirring things up," the president grumbled. "They are making everything more difficult."

The *Tribune* report was sensationalist and overwrought but contained a kernel of truth. Stalin had written to Churchill on May 4 ruling out an agreement on Poland unless the Communist-dominated provisional government formed the "basis" for the future "government of national unity." He had sent a shorter telegram along similar lines to Truman on May 10. The twin messages amounted to an outright rejection of the western interpretation of the Yalta accords. Far from backing down in response to the "straight one-two to the jaw" that Truman thought he had administered to Molotov, Stalin had come back with a stronger counterpunch. His position on Poland was now nonnegotiable. If the Allies wanted a deal, they would have to meet his basic terms.

In addition to the arguments over eastern Europe, Truman had also got himself into an embarrassing position over lend-lease. Acting on the advice of the State Department, he had signed an order canceling all lend-lease shipments to Europe on the reasonable assumption that the war was now over. Shipments of food, clothing, arms, oil, and Studebaker trucks to Russia and other European nations from ports on the East Coast ceased abruptly; some ships were turned back in the middle of the ocean. Shipments continued across the Pacific to ports in the Soviet Far East in anticipation of Russia's entry in the war against Japan. The British were affected more than the Russians as they depended entirely on shipments across the Atlantic. Russian leaders nevertheless interpreted the lend-lease decision as aimed exclusively at them. Understanding that he had "given Stalin a point of contention which he would undoubtedly bring up every chance he had," Truman revised his order. Assistance would be phased out in stages, rather than overnight. But the diplomatic damage had been done.

For all his vaunted decisiveness, Truman could not decide how to handle the Russians. He was beginning to wonder if he had made a mistake with his rebukes to Molotov. If there was a guiding principle to his actions, it was a desire to fulfill FDR's legacy, but interpreting that legacy was not always easy. The Yalta agreements were considerably more ambiguous than he had originally believed. He was torn between conflicting sets of advice. Harriman and the State Department favored a get-tough policy; Stimson and the Pentagon stressed the need for continued cooperation, if only to ensure Soviet participation in the war against Japan. The neophyte president wavered between the rival camps, uncertain whom to trust. Without sufficient knowledge and experience to form his own independent judgment, he was influenced by whoever walked in the door.

Mistrusting the "striped pants brigade" in the State Department, Truman reached out to Roosevelt's former advisers. He considered Davies one of "our three ablest foreign relations men," along with Harry Hopkins and former secretary of state Cordell Hull. Davies had written a best-selling book titled *Mission to Moscow* that had been turned into a Hollywood movie featuring John Huston as the ambassador. Shot in 1943 at a time when the American media were celebrating Soviet military triumphs, the movie depicted a workers paradise with well-stocked stores, factories churning out vast amounts of weapons, and tables groaning with food, amid the ambience of an alpine resort. State Department experts on Russia considered the movie "one of the most blatantly propagandistic pictures ever seen." It was so adulatory about Russia that it was almost embarrassing to Soviet leaders when Davies treated them to a private showing in the Kremlin. The commissar for the Soviet film industry, Ivan Bolshakov, thought the saccharine depictions of "enormous samovars, bearded men, dancing Cossacks, sledges decorated with flowers and the like," were "naïve" and laughable. But Stalin recognized the former ambassador's usefulness and awarded him the Order of Lenin in May 1945 for his contribution to "friendly Soviet-American relations."

A self-made millionaire from Wisconsin, Davies seemed an unlikely recipient of the Soviet Union's highest honor. He was married to one of the richest women in America, Marjorie Merriweather Post, heiress to the General Foods empire. He sported a gold-headed cane and was always immaculately dressed, usually in an old-fashioned three-piece suit. His teeth "gleamed like piano keys well polished"; his "flashing, probing" eyes darted about impatiently. He would have preferred an ambassadorial post in London or Paris but was persuaded to accept the Moscow embassy by FDR, who felt that he could "win the confidence of Stalin." Davies ordered a complete refurbishing of Spaso House prior to his arrival in January 1937, including new electricity circuits to operate the twenty-five deep freezers used to store regular food shipments from the United States. Inevitably, the power system failed, spoiling a hundred gallons of cream. Aides scurried to dispose of the rotten cream but were unable to keep the

story out of the American press, to the embarrassment of the ambassador and his wife. Susceptible to flattery, Davies was lavishly entertained
by senior Kremlin officials during his fifteen-month stay in Moscow.
Marjorie amassed a huge collection of valuable Russian art and china,
much of it purchased from state museums at rock-bottom prices.

The Moscow experience convinced Davies that the key to good relations with Russia was face-to-face meetings between Soviet and American
leaders or their trusted emissaries. He dismissed foreign policy profes-
sionals and State Department bureaucrats as "little fellows." The contempt
was returned in spades. Chip Bohlen depicted him as "sublimely ignorant
of even the most elementary realities of the Soviet system." George Kennan wrote witheringly of being sent "to fetch the ambassador his sandwiches" during the Moscow show trials "while he exchanged sententious
judgments with the gentlemen of the press concerning the guilt of the
victims."

Davies now told Truman that it was vital to eradicate Stalin's impression of a "hostile, capitalistic world . . . ganging up" against Russia. The
"tough approach" would never work with the Soviets: they were ready to
"out-tough" anyone they considered hostile. Russian leaders had reached
a crossroads: an understanding attitude on the part of the United States
would draw a cooperative response from the Kremlin while a confrontational stance could produce "a Soviet Napoleon." Only Truman could
"save the situation."

The president was ready for a personal meeting with Stalin but did not
want to travel all the way to Moscow. He asked Davies if he would serve as
his personal emissary to the Soviet leader, as he had done for FDR. Davies
was flattered but declined, citing serious intestinal problems and "doctor's orders" to take it easy. But he promised to write a personal note to
Stalin suggesting a U.S.-Soviet meeting in Alaska or Siberia. He proposed
sending the message through the Soviet embassy in Washington, using
Soviet diplomatic code, bypassing Harriman and the State Department.

By the end of their talk, Davies felt he was getting through to Truman.
The president invited him to stay for an informal "family supper" with his
wife, Bess; daughter, Margaret; and ninety-three-year-old mother, newly
arrived from Missouri. "We had a jolly time," Davies recorded. "They are
a fine and typical American family."

Six weeks after assuming the presidency, Truman was still unsure of
himself. He worried that Stalin might decline his invitation to a meeting. Impossible, retorted Davies, determined to strike an upbeat note.

Truman then talked about the "enormous responsibility" he had inherited and how he was the "last person fitted to handle it." Resigned to his fate, he blurted out a few lines of doggerel that summed up the gloomy thoughts rushing through his mind.

Here lies Joe Williams,
He did his best.
Man can do no more.
But he was too slow on the draw.

13

"The Salvation of the World"

May 26

The steady drizzle did not seem to bother the elderly man with a bow tie and bowler hat. Dressed in a worn gray overcoat with a burn patch on the front where it had been singed by a cigar, he gathered a few middle-aged women and small children around him in the rain. He praised their courage for braving German bombs and deflected questions about food shortages. "I have not come to promise beer and skittles." A red double-decker bus trundled past. The conductor leaned out over the stair rail and shouted, "Good old Winnie." The Edwardian gentleman lifted his hat and waved it solemnly in the direction of the bus. When he was finished speaking, the crowd yelled "Hip, hip, hooray" and sang "For He's a Jolly Good Fellow."

It was Saturday, May 26, less than three weeks after VE-day. Winston Churchill had decided to call an election. He had told Roosevelt and Stalin at Yalta that he was the only member of the Big Three in imminent risk of losing his job. That moment had finally arrived. Now that the war in Europe was over, the Labour Party had withdrawn its support from the grand coalition formed by Churchill in the dark days of 1940. In keeping with British tradition, the prime minister was kicking off the election

campaign in his parliamentary constituency on the northeastern outskirts of London. For electoral purposes, he was just one of six hundred
forty members of the House of Commons. The otherwise unremarkable
suburb of Woodford, clustered around a village green and a working-
man's club, was where Britain's wartime leader would submit his record
to the judgment of the voters. It was a quintessentially English scene.
"There were no flags, no parades as in Nazi Germany, no special presidential train as in America," an American reporter noted, "only a stoutish
gentleman holding in his hand a high-crowned hat . . . addressing a few
halting words, in a gentle shower of rain, to an audience of housewives
out on a morning of shopping."

From Woodford, Churchill motored across London to his official
country retreat at Chequers to greet an unwelcome houseguest. After
declining Truman's request to travel to Moscow to smooth things over
with Stalin on the grounds of ill health, Joe Davies had volunteered for a
mission to London. He had persuaded the president that he could make
Churchill "see the light," a euphemism for adopting a less confrontational
approach toward the Soviet Union. The British regarded Davies as a "vain
amateur" in Anthony Eden's phrase. "He is the born appeaser. . . . All
the errors and illusions of Neville C., substituting Russia for Germany."
The novice president had no qualms about selecting the recent recipient
of the Order of Lenin as his emissary to the Court of St. James's. He had
decided to send the former FDR aide Harry Hopkins to Moscow in place
of Davies. If he could dispatch Churchill's friend to meet with Stalin, why
not send Stalin's friend to meet with Churchill?

Like many foreign visitors, Davies found the Elizabethan manor
house cold and drafty. The weather-beaten redbrick pile still bore signs of
wartime camouflage against German bombing. The main entrance was
closed. Grass covered the circular driveway. But a cheerful fire was blazing in the Great Hall. Winston and Clementine arrived twenty minutes
after Davies, full of stories about kissing babies on the hustings. Churchill
insisted on showing the presidential envoy to his room, where he was
greeted by another fire, "a huge, exaggerated, burnished copper tea pot,"
and "many other indications of English country life." Dinner was served
at eight-thirty. Ever sensitive to his health, Davies had stipulated that
he retire to bed early, but the routines of Chequers were not to be disturbed. There were other guests to be entertained: dinner was followed by
a movie, cigars, and brandy. It was not until eleven that Churchill finally

invited Davies to join him in his small private library for a confidential conversation. They stayed up talking until nearly dawn in front of the inevitable log fire.

"The prime minister is one of the greatest men of our time," Davies reported later to Truman, "but he is first and foremost an Englishman. He is still the King's Minister who will not liquidate the Empire. He is still the great Briton of Runnymede and Dunkirk. . . . I could not escape the impression that he was basically more concerned over preserving England's position in Europe than in preserving peace."

Churchill took immediate offense when Davies proposed a Truman-Stalin meeting prior to a conference of the Big Three. As Davies explained it, the president was "at a disadvantage" because he had never met the Soviet leader. It was important to dispel the impression that the capitalist countries were "ganging up" against their Communist ally. Churchill viewed the matter very differently. He disliked the term "ganging up" when applied to meetings of an American president and a British prime minister. Their countries shared many common ideals, including a commitment to political freedom, that were anathema to the leaders of the Soviet Union. It was only natural they would coordinate their positions with each other. Churchill was "surprised and hurt" that he would be excluded from the first meeting with Stalin after the victory. He would "never, never consent" to such an arrangement, which smacked of a Russo-American "deal."

Now Davies was upset. He got up and walked over to the fireplace, saying he resented Churchill's aspersions against the president of the United States. Although he was the prime minister's guest, he might "feel impelled to leave his house." Churchill soothed the envoy, insisting he never intended to impugn the president's honor. He ordered another brandy for himself and a cup of soup ("a chemical synthetic but very nutritious") for his guest.

More difficult for Davies to digest was Churchill's hostility toward Stalin and Russia. "I found it difficult to believe my ears," he complained later to his journal. "I thought I was listening to GOEBBELS, GOERING, and HITLER. It was their old thread-bare arguments that Europe had to be saved from the Bolsheviks, and the Communist menace; that Germany and HITLER were the saviors of Europe, etc." He tactlessly suggested that Churchill would have been better off dying "at the zenith of his contribution to freedom and liberty, before he reached the conclusion that HITLER was right." Churchill's response was not recorded. "It was strong stuff," Davies recalled. "But he had pulled no punches—neither did I. We were both much moved."

Escorting his guest to his bedroom at 4:30 a.m., Churchill expressed his pleasure in talking with someone "with so unusual a perspective on events." The sarcasm was lost on Davies, who was easily flattered. He delved into his stock of superlatives to pay back the compliment: "Goodnight to you, Sir, the Greatest Englishman of all Time, who lives what Shakespeare dreamed, and who translates into deeds what England's greatest have taught." Churchill told associates later that he "needed a bath in order to get rid of the ooze and slime" emitted by the American.

Davies had a restless night. Searching for a bathroom, he stumbled into someone else's bedroom. He wandered around the darkened corridors with a candle before he finally discovered a toilet, hidden behind a tapestry. At eleven the following morning, still in his dressing gown, he was summoned to the prime minister's bedroom. Churchill was propped up in bed, reading cables. He was "still irked and troubled" by the conversation of the previous night. He predicted disaster if American troops were withdrawn from Europe. Davies was treated to yet another "monologue berating the Russians" at lunch, with dark warnings about "police methods behind the Iron Curtain." This time, Truman's envoy chose to keep silent. At a loss to explain Churchill's mistrust of Stalin, he concluded that it was somehow connected to "the coming election."

For his part, Churchill was so distressed by his discussions with Davies that he wrote a long letter of protest to Truman reminding him of the special relationship between the two English-speaking countries. He refused to accept the idea that America should treat Britain and Russia impartially as "just two foreign powers, six of one and half a dozen of the other, with whom the troubles of the late war have to be adjusted." For the British prime minister, the "great causes and principles for which Britain and the United States have suffered and triumphed are not mere matters of the balance of power. They in fact involve the salvation of the world."

While Joe Davies was heading across the Atlantic to confer with Churchill, Harry Hopkins was en route to the Soviet Union for his meeting with Stalin. His party included Averell Harriman, returning to his post in Moscow, and Chip Bohlen, who would serve as interpreter. They were now hopelessly lost, after taking off from Orly Field in Paris soon after breakfast and flying eastward for three hours over a succession of shattered cities, each more devastated than the previous one. By the navigator's calculations they were somewhere over Poland.

As the C-87 transport plane darted in and out of the low-lying clouds at an altitude of one thousand feet, the passengers spotted what looked like one of Hitler's huge, multilane autobahns. Passing over several lakes and a large palace with a bomb-sized hole in the roof, they approached a ruined, seemingly deserted city. There were no signs of life other than a huge fire burning in the distance. None of the buildings appeared inhabitable. The navigator announced that the city down below was Poznan. Harriman and Bohlen, who had visited Germany before the war, recognized the ruins of the Brandenburg Gate and the Unter den Linden. They were over Berlin. The gutted palace they had spotted ten minutes earlier was Sanssouci, the Potsdam palace of Frederick the Great.

"It's another Carthage," murmured an awed Hopkins, gazing down at the rubble of the Third Reich.

After picking up a Russian navigator, the Americans reached Moscow on the evening of May 25. The following night, as Davies began his fireside chat with Churchill at Chequers, Hopkins was ushered into Stalin's Kremlin study. They greeted each other like old friends. Struggling to recover from stomach cancer, Hopkins described the stroke that had struck down FDR two months after his meeting with Stalin at Yalta. A "quick, easy death" was preferable to lingering on as a "helpless invalid." The *vozhd* listened sympathetically, recalling that Lenin had also died from a cerebral hemorrhage following a previous stroke that had paralyzed his hand.

The special envoy then got to the point of his visit: the sharp deterioration in relations between America and Russia. Truman had authorized Hopkins to use either "diplomatic language" or the "baseball bat" in dealing with Stalin, depending on his reading of the situation. He chose the soft approach. Seated across the usual baize-covered table from the dictator, he attempted to explain how politics operated in the United States. An American president was obliged to pay attention to public opinion. Without such support, it would be very difficult for Truman to continue Roosevelt's policy of cooperation with the Soviet Union. Many Americans, including millions of people who had supported the wartime alliance with Russia, were disturbed by recent events. Particularly bewildering was the inability to solve the Polish question along the lines agreed at Yalta. If present trends continued, the "entire structure of world cooperation . . . which President Roosevelt and the Marshal had labored so hard to build would be destroyed."

Stalin blamed the impasse on Churchill. British "conservatives" refused to accept "a Poland friendly to the Soviet Union" and wanted to revive a cordon sanitaire system around Russia. Despite his mistrust of the British, Stalin showed no interest in the Davies proposal for a bilateral summit with Truman in Alaska or Siberia. He had no intention of celebrating the victory over Nazi Germany in an insignificant, faraway place. Instead, he proposed a Big Three meeting in Berlin itself. Like Hopkins, Stalin struck a reasonable tone at this first Kremlin meeting. The two men were sparring with each other. They preferred to speak in vague generalities rather than accuse each other of bad faith. The real negotiations would come later.

But Stalin did fire the opening shot in what turned into a long drawn-out Soviet misinformation campaign. In reply to a query from Hopkins, he expressed the surprising opinion that "Hitler was not dead but hiding somewhere." He speculated that the Nazi leader might have escaped to Japan in a German submarine with large quantities of gold and some of his closest associates, including Joseph Goebbels and Martin Bormann. Stalin told Hopkins that he "did not believe" reports that doctors had succeeded in identifying the bodies of Goebbels, his wife, and their six young children.

Later versions of the Hitler myth deliberately propagated by Stalin raised the possibility that the führer had fled to Spain or Argentina or that he was still in Germany, hiding in the British occupation zone. In fact, Soviet intelligence agents had recovered Hitler's charred body and jaws from the ruins of the Reich Chancellery in Berlin. They flew the jawbone to Moscow in a satin-lined box, along with dental records showing identical gold bridgework on the teeth of the führer. Despite the inevitable confusion surrounding the precise circumstances of Hitler's death on April 30, the Soviet autopsy team had no doubt that they had found their man. The official SMERSH autopsy on Hitler, reporting "suicide by swallowing cyanide compounds," was submitted to Stalin on May 27. He refused to endorse the conclusions of his own experts and insisted on launching an alternative version of history.

The Soviet leader may have simply enjoyed sending western intelligence services on what a CIA historian later termed "a never-ending wild goose chase." But the conspiracy theory was also politically convenient to Stalin, providing him with a trump card he could use at some later stage. If relations with America and Britain continued to sour, he could blame the führer's disappearance on western politicians. The suggestion that Hitler might have fled to Latin America through Spain was designed in part to justify Allied action against Franco, thereby avenging the Communist defeat in the Spanish Civil War.

There was also a domestic dimension to Stalin's disinformation campaign. Generations of Russian parents had scared their children with talk of the mythical *buka*—a monster hiding under the bed who would gobble them up if they misbehaved. Hitler was the perfect *buka*. Rumors of his imminent return could be used to frighten Russians to unite against a common enemy. To stoke popular fear of the *buka*, Stalin made sure that his subordinates spread word of Hitler's miraculous escape. On instructions from the *vozhd*, Marshal Zhukov revised his original statement that Hitler had died in his bunker. He told western reporters on June 9 that Hitler "could have taken off [from Berlin] at the very last minute," adding pointedly, "It is up to you British and Americans to find him."

Stalin was toying with allies and potential rivals alike, forcing them to accept his version of history, just as he had forced the British and the Americans to swallow his lies about the Katyn massacre and forced the purge trial victims to confess to absurd charges of espionage and treason. In both cases, the machinery of the Soviet state could be relied upon to fabricate the necessary evidence. People who contradicted "the great leader and teacher" were beaten until they changed their opinion. "Hitler is alive!" yelled a Russian interrogator when the führer's former valet, Heinz Linge, attempted to describe his master's suicide. "Hitler is alive!"

Whether Stalin was cunning, paranoid, mischievous, or simply delusional, he failed to share the facts of Hitler's death with western leaders or even his own generals. Instead, he went out of his way to promote an extraordinary web of deceit that Soviet intelligence dubbed "Operation Myth."

At the peak of his power and prestige, Stalin sensed danger everywhere. His country was in ruins, its economy shattered by four years of war. Millions of ordinary Soviet citizens had been exposed to foreign propaganda. As Kennan had divined, the *vozhd* was far from confident about his ability to control his new eastern European empire. He doubted the loyalty of numerous non-Russian nations living within the Soviet Union. Much of his animus was directed against small nations like the Crimean

Tatars and Chechens, who were subject to wholesale deportations for suspected treachery. But the deportations were expanded to include representatives of other, larger ethnic groups, such as Ukrainians, Balts, and
Belorussians.

Stalin both needed the West and recoiled from it. Credits from the
United States would assist in rebuilding the Soviet Union. Western recognition of the regimes installed by the Red Army would simplify the
task of asserting Soviet political control over eastern Europe. A diplomatic understanding with Truman and Churchill would allow Russia to
focus on internal reconstruction, freeing resources that would otherwise
be spent on the military. At the same time, there were risks in getting
too close to the capitalist camp. The world's first workers state must not
relax its ideological guard. While it was important to be flexible, Stalin
would not make any concessions that undermined his own political control, either at home or in the new vassal states. The Bolsheviks had always
drawn a sharp distinction between tactics and strategy. Stalin was ready
to take one step back on occasion, if his retreat made it possible to take
two steps forward in the future.

The most immediate challenge was repairing the devastation of the
war, which was far greater than officially acknowledged. With great reluctance, Stalin eventually accepted a figure of 7.5 million combat casualties
and a similar number of civilian dead. In fact, total Soviet losses from all
causes were probably in the region of 26 to 27 million, of whom 10 million
had fallen on the field of battle or died in captivity. The Soviet Union had
lost around 14 percent of its prewar population, a quarter of its physical
assets, and nearly a third of its national wealth. The catalog of destruction
included more than seventeen hundred towns, seventy thousand villages,
forty thousand miles of railroad track, and one hundred thousand collective farms. Many cities had been reduced to rubble: in Stalingrad, only
one building had been left intact. Steel production was down 33 percent,
oil 38 percent, tractors 76 percent. In effect, Russia had to begin its forced
industrialization all over again. The gains achieved at enormous cost in
the thirties had turned to ashes.

After decades of sacrifice, Stalin had to prepare the survivors of the
Great Patriotic War for further hardship and penury. Real wages had
declined some 60 percent from already low prewar levels. Harvests had
been cut by half. Famine once again threatened the land. Beria sent Stalin
regular reports of starvation in the provinces, including an account of
a peasant woman murdering her daughter and eating her corpse. From

Siberia came reports of people eating the bark of fallen trees. The death of so many young men in the war had created a serious population imbalance. Factories and farms relied on women and adolescents to keep running. The streets of Moscow and other big cities were full of armless and legless cripples, wheeling themselves around on homemade pushcarts. In the nationwide victory celebrations on May 9, women danced with one another to make up for the lack of able-bodied men.

If the shattered economy was one Achilles' heel of the Soviet system, the other was repressed nationalism. Even after defeating Nazi Germany, Stalin's armies were still fighting an undeclared, unacknowledged war against insurgents in Poland, western Ukraine, and the Baltic States. Nearly six hundred Red Army soldiers had been killed in Poland alone in battles with remnants of the Home Army loyal to the government-in-exile in London. On May 17, the *vozhd* had received a troubling report from Beria describing the extent of the Polish insurrection. Home Army units were "continuing fighting in many parts of Poland, attacking prisons, militia units, state security posts, banks, factories, democratic organizations." The NKVD had counted thirty-nine separate "armed bands" made up of more than ten thousand insurgents. The Communist-dominated provisional government was unable to deal effectively with the situation. During the first ten days of May, an entire battalion of Polish Interior Ministry troops had defected to the Home Army on rumors that they were about to be disarmed. Seven NKVD regiments—around ten thousand elite troops—were already combating the insurgency. Beria recommended the deployment of an additional three border-guard regiments.

The news from Poland confirmed Stalin's gloomiest assumptions about the precarious nature of his hold over eastern Europe. It would obviously not be possible to maintain control over the newly conquered territories by adhering to principles of free elections and majority rule enshrined in the Yalta agreements. A "strong, independent Poland friendly to the Soviet Union" was a contradiction in terms, at least as Stalin interpreted the word "friendly." Left to their own devices, Poles would never willingly submit to their huge neighbor to the east. Soviet power in a country like Poland could not be guaranteed on the basis of popular consent. To impose his will on his eastern European empire, Stalin was forced from the very beginning to rely on the support of a minority.

However threatened the *vozhd* may have felt in private, he projected an image of supreme self-confidence and strength in his public appearances.

On May 24, the day before Hopkins arrived in Moscow, he presided over a glittering victory reception in the Grand Kremlin Palace. Dressed in his marshal's uniform, he descended the broad marble staircase to the Hall of St. George at 8:00 p.m. precisely to a deafening roar of "Hoorah!" from a thousand throats. Arrayed in homage in front of him, at a series of banquet tables, were generals, admirals, government and party leaders, outstanding actors, scientists, writers, inventors, heroes from all walks of life. The names of Russia's most distinguished regiments were engraved on plaques on the walls, linking the Communist present to the tsarist past. Standing beneath the brilliant chandeliers in the cavernous chamber decked with golden pillars, the son of the Georgian shoemaker drank in the applause of the Russian and Soviet elite. During his sixty-five years, he had gone from seminarian to Caucasian brigand to scheming apparatchik to ruler of an empire that now stretched halfway across the world. Pockmarked, small of stature, lacking either conventional charisma or intellectual brilliance, he had outshone his tsarist predecessors, both in territorial acquisitions and in the number of people he had slaughtered, which was on an industrial scale. "Genghis Khan with a telephone," one of his victims had called him. He had grabbed the mantle of Lenin, murdered Bukharin and millions of others, hunted down Trotsky, vanquished Hitler, and outmaneuvered Churchill and Roosevelt. It was one of history's most extraordinary performances.

Asked once to describe the pleasantest experience imaginable, Stalin talked about the enjoyment he derived from laying a trap for an enemy. After selecting his target, he would "prepare the coup, drive the blow home, and then drink a bottle of red wine and go to bed." The execution would be swift, but the planning process could never be rushed. He proceeded step by step, lulling his victims into a sense of false security before delivering the fatal blow. An embrace from the dictator could be a token of esteem—but could also be a prelude to a sudden fall. As Stalin looked around the snow-white hall adorned with golden pillars, he saw the faces of potential rivals flushed with pride in their common victory. He was already planning his next entertainment.

His political number two, Vyacheslav Molotov, served as master of ceremonies. The foreign affairs commissar invited Zhukov and the other marshals to join the political leadership at the head table. One by one, the officers rose from their seats in other parts of the hall, their chests weighed down by clanging medals. Waves of applause swept across the hall as the marshals were assigned places of honor next to the *vozhd*.

Although Molotov praised the leaders of the Red Army, he depicted Stalin himself as the architect of victory "who led and leads the entire struggle."

Stalin singled two men out for special praise. About "our Vyacheslav" he remarked, "A good foreign policy is sometimes worth more than two or three frontline armies." He then raised his glass to Zhukov, the deputy supreme commander. "Down with Hitler's Berlin, long live Zhukov's Berlin." His words were greeted with laughter and cheers but were mysteriously dropped from the official record of the proceedings published in the newspapers the following day. Instead, the press focused on Stalin's last, and most significant, toast at the victory banquet, "to the Russian people." He recalled the "mistakes" of the Soviet government and the dark days of 1941 to 1942, when the Red Army reeled back before the onslaught of the Germans, "because there was no other option." Speaking in his thick southern accent, he depicted Russians as the "leading nation" of the Soviet Union, the essential bulwark of the state.

> Another people could have said to the government: "You have not justified our expectations, we will replace you with another government that will negotiate with Germany and secure us peace." But the Russian people did not take this step. They believed in the correctness of the policy of their government and sacrificed themselves in order to ensure the defeat of Germany. This trust of the Russian people toward the Soviet government proved to be the decisive factor that guaranteed the historic victory over the enemy of mankind, over Fascism. Thanks to the Russian people for this trust.

A roar filled the hall, continuing for several minutes. The celebrations had lasted more than nine hours: as the guests departed, the Kremlin's golden domes were lit up by the first rays of dawn. Stalin's tribute to the Russian people could be interpreted in various ways. On one level, it was a remarkable mea culpa from a supposedly infallible leader who had refused to believe the multiple warnings of a Nazi invasion and retreated in panic to his dacha during the first days of the war. On another, it marked the apotheosis of Stalin's transformation from Bolshevik revolutionary to Russian nationalist. He no longer distinguished between the Soviet Union as the homeland of international socialism and the Russia of Ivan the Terrible and Catherine the Great. The Soviet Communist Party, under the leadership of an apostate Georgian seminarian, had restored Mother Russia to its true greatness. On yet another level, the speech could be read as a warning to the "traitor nations"—the Balts, Tatars, Chechens, and others. Anybody who had failed to put their complete trust in the *vozhd* would face a terrible revenge.

Finally, and most important, Stalin's words were designed to emphasize his own unbreakable link with the mystical, long-suffering *narod*. By raising up the common man, he was diminishing the contribution of the military and civilian elite assembled in the Kremlin. Ultimate credit for winning the greatest victory in Russian history would not go to the marshals and admirals and commissars arrayed before him but to ordinary Russians, united around their leader.

Stalin and Hopkins had seven separate meetings in the Kremlin over the course of two weeks in late May and early June. The experience of negotiating face-to-face with the Soviet dictator seemed to revive the ghost-like American who had been barely able to lift himself from his sickbed just a few weeks before. Stalin was friendly enough, but unwilling to make any serious concessions. He went onto the offensive in their second meeting, on May 27, lecturing Hopkins for a series of American misdeeds, ranging from the sudden cancellation of lend-lease to the admission of Fascist Argentina to the United Nations. But it was the political setup in Poland that concerned him most. He poured scorn on the American claim that the Yalta agreement provided for the creation of an entirely new government.

"Anyone with any common sense should see that the new government must be formed on the basis of the present government," he fumed. "Russians are a simple people, but they should not be regarded as fools. That's a mistake that is frequently made in the West."

The *vozhd* contemptuously brushed aside the notion, advanced by Hopkins, that American public opinion made it difficult for Truman to settle the Polish question on Russian terms. He would not attempt to use Soviet public opinion as "a screen" for his arguments. Getting down to business, he said it might be possible to include "four or five" non-Lublin Poles in the provisional government. This would still leave the Communists and their allies with fifteen or sixteen ministries, an overwhelming majority. At this point, Molotov whispered something in Russian to Stalin, who immediately corrected himself. The Lublin Poles were prepared to accept "no more than four ministers from other democratic groups."

Unable to make much headway on the formation of a new government,

Hopkins reminded Stalin of his promises at Yalta to guarantee fundamental freedoms in Poland and other eastern European countries. He mentioned freedom of speech, freedom of assembly, freedom of movement, and freedom of religious worship. The dictator balked. Such freedoms, he told Hopkins, "could only be applied in full in peacetime, and even then with certain limitations." Any government, including the American government, reserved the right to restrict such freedoms "when they were threatened by war." Furthermore, even in peacetime, "Fascist parties" seeking to overthrow a "democratic government" would not enjoy freedoms granted to the non-Fascist parties.

Stalin was a master at carving out caveats to the sweeping statements of principle dear to the hearts of American statesmen. Since he reserved the right to define who was Fascist and who was democratic, the exceptions permitted him to do pretty much as he pleased. It took a trained ear to catch all the nuances. When Hopkins asked whether the Soviet Union was prepared to honor other provisions of the Yalta agreements, Stalin prevaricated.

"The Soviet Union always honors its word," he protested. He then mumbled something in Russian that his interpreter, Vladimir Pavlov, failed to translate.

"I believe there is a little more, Pavlov," murmured Bohlen, who was interpreting for Hopkins.

Embarrassed, Pavlov added the catch-all qualification. "Except in case of extreme necessity."

Stalin had refused to compromise on the key question of ultimate political control over the Polish government. But he offered a face-saving solution to his western Allies. One of the non-Communist ministers in the government would be Stanisław Mikołajczyk, the peasant party leader viewed by the Americans as the most reasonable of the London Poles. The soft-spoken, round-faced Mikołajczyk would become the guarantor of democratic liberties in Poland. Mistrusting the Russians, he was deeply pessimistic about his chances of success. Nevertheless, he felt compelled to accept Stalin's offer. By returning to Warsaw, he would become a rallying point for the Poles opposed to communism, a vast majority of the nation. He might be able to obtain some relaxation in the persecution of the Home Army and the arrests and deportations of anti-Moscow Poles. At the very least, he would be an independent voice.

The final deal over Poland was much closer to Stalin's initial demands at Yalta than the western counterproposals. In return for Mikołajczyk's appointment as a deputy prime minister, the Americans and the British were obliged to sever ties with the Polish government-in-exile in London. They granted the enlarged Warsaw government full diplomatic recognition on July 5. Churchill ruefully acknowledged that the non-Communist ministers were "in a hopeless minority" and there was little prospect for truly free elections. But he was worn out by months of diplomatic wrangling and felt obliged to accept whatever arrangement Hopkins could work out. He urged Mikolajczyk to seize "this last opportunity to get not only your foot but your leg in the door."

On a personal level, Stalin went out of his way to be hospitable to Hopkins, who had visited Moscow during the dark days of July 1941, soon after the Nazi invasion. As Roosevelt's closest aide and the architect of lend-lease, Hopkins symbolized the halcyon days of Russian-American relations. He was accompanied by his wife, a trained nurse who was taken on a tour of Moscow hospitals. Back in Spaso House, Louise Hopkins regaled other guests with blow-by-blow accounts of a revolutionary Russian technique for restoring severed penises. Cocktail party conversations screeched to a halt as she described the miraculous operation in a voice that carried to the far corners of the room. "And he continued to have sex with his wife!"

Stalin laid on entertainments for Hopkins and his wife every night, culminating in a gala dinner in the Kremlin on June 1, at which they got a close-up look at the Soviet elite. Kathleen Harriman described the scene in a letter to her sister:

There were 40 guests, seated at one long table that took up the long length of the Catherine the Great ballroom. The Russians were divided into two very distinct types: the educated, fine looking variety, usually with tiny beards (all in uniform) and the big fat sinister type with pig eyes and pince nez. Louie classified them as the "unhappy pansies." They were in the vast majority. The terrifying thing is visualizing them as ever cooperating with foreigners.

After dinner, Stalin took Hopkins off to an adjoining room, where the American envoy raised the issue of the sixteen anti-Lublin Poles incarcerated in the Lubyanka on charges of organizing resistance to the Red Army. Hopkins attempted, once again, to explain the importance of public opinion in shaping American foreign policy. If the Poles were subjected to an elaborate show trial, the entire edifice of American-Soviet relations could be threatened, jeopardizing the progress that had been made on the formation of a new Polish government. Stalin promised to look into the matter. The men would still have to go on trial, but he would do what he could to see they were treated "leniently."

The following day, Stalin sent his emissaries round to Spaso House with a truckload of expensive gifts for Louise Hopkins. A dazzling selection of furs, fabrics, and jewelry was laid out in the drawing room of the ambassador's residence. Louise was urged to take anything she wanted back to America. Sensitive to accusations of impropriety, Hopkins insisted that his wife return everything, apart from one relatively modest semiprecious stone from the Urals. He contented himself with two huge cans of caviar. Averell Harriman had fewer qualms about receiving gifts from his Soviet hosts. During the Kremlin dinner, he mentioned to Stalin that he was a keen horseman and expressed admiration for a magnificent brown stallion ridden by the Red Army chief of staff during the May Day parade. The *vozhd* promptly gave the horse to Harriman, along with a second horse for Kathleen. The multimillionaire ambassador accepted the horses as "reverse Lend-Lease" but did not modify his hard-line views.

"When they want to, the Soviets can do things up proud," his normally acerbic aide, Robert Meiklejohn, noted in his diary.

The American press hailed the agreement over the new Polish government as a diplomatic triumph for Truman's special envoy. But Hopkins felt little of the euphoria he had experienced at the conclusion of the Yalta conference when he was convinced that the "dawn of the new day" had arrived. Next to Joe Davies, he had been the American official most identified with Rooseveltian policies toward the Soviet Union. He had accused the Russian experts at the State Department of forming an "anti-Soviet clique." Long hours of negotiations with Stalin were causing him to revise his views about the prospects for Russian-American cooperation. He now believed that the relationship was likely to be "stormy," largely because of diametrically opposed views on the question of "human liberty."

Hopkins understood that ideology played at least as important a role in the shaping of American foreign policy as it did in the shaping of Soviet foreign policy. Ideology provided both political systems with their fundamental raison d'être: freedom in the case of the United States, the construction of a Communist utopia in the case of the Soviet Union. America and Russia shared a messianic, proselytizing streak, a desire to spread their own political values around the world. After his talks with Stalin, Hopkins told Bohlen that the "American belief in freedom" could "lead to serious differences over affairs in third countries." As he later wrote, "the American people want not only freedom for themselves . . . they want freedom throughout the world for other people as well . . . they simply do not like the notion that you cannot say what you please when you want to say it."

Central to the differences between America and Russia was the role played by public opinion. The autocratic Stalin reacted impatiently when American politicians stressed the need to secure popular support for major foreign policy initiatives. He considered such talk a shameless negotiating ploy. In fact, it went to the heart of the way the American political system operated. No American leader could afford to ignore the moods of the American public. FDR was a master at getting ahead of public opinion, steering it in the direction he himself wanted to go, but he was always attuned to its whimsical, sometimes irrational, demands. His negotiating strategy at Yalta was determined in large measure by the need to convince the American people that he would deliver a just and lasting peace. If Americans came to believe that the Soviets were reneging on their promises in eastern Europe, the basis of the postwar order could be seriously undermined.

Like his former boss, Hopkins was an accomplished political juggler. His goal in traveling to Moscow was to continue to keep all the American balls in the air at once, if only for a short time. The agreement on a new Polish government preserved the illusion of an understanding between the victors over Nazi Germany. In fact, there was no agreement at all on such basic matters as the meaning of democracy and free elections.

Prior to leaving Moscow, Hopkins sought the opinion of George Kennan. The Russia expert had followed the protracted negotiations over Poland "with boredom and disgust," convinced that the very idea of a free and independent Poland friendly to the Soviet Union was "a lost cause." He felt it was pointless to haggle with the Soviets over such matters. Stalin would do whatever he wanted to do in Poland anyway. Kennan told Hopkins that America should "accept no share of the responsibility for what the Russians proposed to do in Poland."

"Then you think it's just sin, and we should be agin it," Hopkins persisted.

"That's just about right."

"I respect your opinion," the special envoy concluded sadly. "But I am not at liberty to accept it."

14

Atomic Poker

June 1

At the same time Stalin and Hopkins were negotiating the fate of Poland in the Kremlin, a drama of a different kind was unfolding back in the United States. In office for just six weeks, Harry Truman found himself swept up in a series of history-making events: the defeat of Nazi Germany, the rise of a Communist superpower, the division of Europe, the death throes of imperial Japan. The most terrifying decisions of all involved an entirely new kind of weapon that promised to unleash the hidden power of the universe, changing the relationship between man and nature. The atomic bomb had been developed at enormous cost and effort for fear that the Nazis might acquire it first. That fear, it turned out, had been exaggerated, but the project had acquired a momentum of its own. The first atomic test was scheduled for July. The new president had to decide whether to use the revolutionary new weapon against Japan. He also had to grapple with much larger issues, such as whether to share nuclear technology with potential rivals, most notably Russia, in the hope of forestalling a ruinous new arms race.

To help sort through these agonizing questions, Truman turned to a man who could easily have been occupying the White House in his place.

A precocious South Carolina country boy who left school at the age of fourteen, Jimmy Byrnes had vast political experience, ranging across all three branches of government. He had spent fourteen years in the House of Representatives and ten in the Senate. He had climbed up the legal ladder from court stenographer to associate justice of the Supreme Court. Most important of all, he was very close to Roosevelt, first as a fundraiser, then as a speechwriter, and finally as his director of war mobilization. Byrnes supervised the economy and domestic policy, leaving the president free to attend to the great international issues. The self-styled "assistant president" had long considered himself—and was viewed by many insiders—as the rightful successor to FDR.

Roosevelt led Byrnes to believe that he would be his running mate in 1944, replacing Vice President Henry Wallace, who was viewed as too mystical and left-wing to be an acceptable president. As was his custom, however, FDR made no firm commitment. He preferred to let events take their course before revealing his hand. In the end, domestic political considerations prevented the ambitious South Carolinian from winning the highest prize. Byrnes had antagonized important voting blocs in the Democratic coalition. He had offended his fellow Catholics by marrying an Episcopalian and leaving the Church. Trade union leaders were upset with him for making it difficult to organize strikes in wartime. Most troubling of all, black voters remembered his record as a southern segregationist and his vehement opposition to a federal antilynching bill. In a close election, such considerations could be decisive, offsetting Roosevelt's huge appeal to African Americans. Harry Truman, a middle-of-the-road senator from a border state who got on well with everybody, was a safer bet. Without a word of explanation to Byrnes, FDR ended up endorsing the relatively unknown senator from Missouri.

Byrnes was "hurt" by the president's decision. A small, wiry man, he exuded a nervous, coiled-up energy. He dressed smartly and wore his homburg hats at a jaunty angle. Downward-slanting eyebrows gave his sharp-angled face a perpetually quizzical expression. He could be petulant when he did not get his way, as Anna Roosevelt discovered at Yalta, when he was excluded from the opening session of the Big Three conference. In addition to being angry at FDR, Byrnes felt betrayed by Truman, who had promised to nominate him formally for vice president at the Democratic Party convention in Chicago. Whatever Truman did to make amends, he always had the feeling that his old friend harbored a grudge.

As he later reminisced, "After I got to be President, I knew every time Jimmy and I talked that he thought it ought to be the other way around. He ought to be sitting where I was sitting."

For the moment, however, Truman relied on his former Senate colleague to educate him in the ways of the world. Soon after becoming president, he offered Byrnes the post of secretary of state, which would also put him first in line of presidential succession under the constitutional arrangements in force at the time. (There was no provision to select a new vice president, so Truman served without one.) The pleasant but ineffectual Stettinius would be permitted to make a dignified exit after the San Francisco conference. Truman entrusted Byrnes with coordination of policy on the atomic bomb while he was waiting for his new appointment to be announced.

One of his first tasks was to receive a delegation of Los Alamos scientists campaigning for a nuclear-free world. They were led by one of the fathers of the Manhattan Project, Leo Szilard, who had been investigating the possibility of a nuclear chain reaction since 1933. The Hungarian-born physicist had also patented a neutronic reactor that would turn mass into energy, a concept dismissed as "moonshine" by rival researchers. As his theories became reality, Szilard began to question "the wisdom of testing bombs and using bombs," particularly now that Germany had been defeated. His greatest fear was that the successful testing of an American atomic bomb would prompt Russia to accelerate its own nuclear program in a desperate effort to catch up. As Szilard saw it, the only way for America to retain her claim to moral superiority, as well as her scientific lead, was to refrain from testing the bomb at all. He had sought an interview with Truman to explain his views but was told to speak to Byrnes instead. Since Byrnes was still a private citizen, he invited Szilard and his two companions to meet with him at his home in Spartanburg, South Carolina, on May 28.

Their conversation got off to a bad start. Szilard submitted a written memorandum arguing that the risks of a nuclear arms race could only be properly understood "by men who have first-hand knowledge of the facts involved, that is, by the small group of scientists who are actively involved in this work." He called for the formation of a scientific committee to advise the president on nuclear policy. Byrnes bristled at the suggestion that political leaders were unqualified to make decisions about the atomic bomb. The two men represented two very different worlds: practical politics and theoretical physics. Byrnes saw the bomb as a military weapon but also as a diplomatic weapon that promised to give the United

States a decisive advantage in dealing with an increasingly recalcitrant Russia. Szilard's focus was on the dangers of nuclear proliferation and the destruction of mankind.

They could not even agree on the technical details. Byrnes objected to Szilard's claim that Russia could catch up with America relatively quickly. He thought that a Soviet atomic bomb was at least a decade away.

"General Groves tells me there is no uranium in Russia."

Szilard agreed that high-grade uranium ore was scarce and might be difficult to find in Russia. The largest proven deposits, from the Belgian Congo, were under American and British control. On the other hand, the Russians had access to small amounts of rich uranium ore in Czechoslovakia. In addition, they would almost certainly be able to draw on plentiful reserves of low-grade uranium, which could also be used to build a bomb.

Byrnes reacted scornfully to Szilard's call for the United States to refrain from testing a weapon it had spent more than $2 billion developing ($24 billion in 2010 dollars). To the former senator, this made no sense at all. "How would you get Congress to appropriate money for atomic energy research if you do not show results for the money that has been spent already?" he demanded.

The physicist and the politician also found themselves at odds over whether the demonstration of American technological might would encourage Stalin to make political concessions. "You come from Hungary," Byrnes reminded Szilard, "you would not want Russia to stay in Hungary indefinitely." Szilard was "completely flabbergasted" at the suggestion that "rattling the bomb might make Russia more manageable." He thought the risk of an atomic arms race between America and Russia far outweighed any worries he might have about the fate of his native country under Soviet occupation.

It had been a dialogue of the deaf. Walking back to the railroad station, Szilard felt deeply depressed. He wished he had never dreamed up the idea of nuclear chain reactions. He should have gone into politics, not physics. Byrnes was happy to be rid of his argumentative visitor. "His general demeanor and his desire to participate in policy-making made an unfavorable impression on me," he later wrote.

There was widespread agreement within the administration that the atomic bomb could be a diplomatic master card if played right. Byrnes himself had told the president back in April that the bomb would allow the United States to "dictate terms" at the end of the war. Its use against Japan could save the lives of hundreds of thousands of American servicemen preparing to invade the Japanese home islands. The demonstration of American technological prowess would also serve to counterbalance the land-based power of the Soviet Union. In the opinion of Secretary of War Henry Stimson, "This was a place where we held all the cards." America now possessed "a royal straight flush, and we mustn't be a fool about the way we play it." The poker-playing analogy was calculated to appeal to Truman, who liked nothing better than to sit around the card table in the evening with his friends.

Soon after his meeting with Szilard, Byrnes traveled to Washington for a two-day conference on the atomic bomb, which opened at the Pentagon on May 31. Truman had established the Interim Committee to coordinate nuclear decision making, with the secretary of state designate as his "personal representative." The meeting was chaired by Stimson and included top scientists, such as Robert Oppenheimer and Enrico Fermi, and senior generals like Marshall and Groves. At the top of the agenda was a review of the work of a military committee that had selected three possible targets for the first atomic bomb: Kyoto, Hiroshima, and Niigata. The Target Committee recommended that "the gadget" be placed in "the center of selected city" rather than aimed at specific military and industrial facilities, which were "quite dispersed" and located on the outskirts of cities. The shortage of atomic devices made it impossible to drop bombs on different neighborhoods: one bomb would have to be sufficient to destroy an entire urban conglomeration. Although the term "precision bombing" had already entered the military lexicon, it was quite impractical for a first-generation atomic bomb.

The idea of using the new bomb as a terror weapon appalled Stimson, who viewed himself as an upholder of "international law and morality," even in time of "total war." He had been upset by the firebombing of Tokyo a few days earlier by the massed B-29 bombers of Curtis LeMay, resulting in the deaths of tens of thousands of Japanese civilians. Stimson had visited Kyoto before the war and understood the cultural and historical importance of the former imperial capital, with its hundreds of Buddhist temples and Shinto shrines. He made it very clear he would not permit the city to be destroyed, even though it was an attractive target from the military point of view, as it had suffered little previous bomb damage. "This is one time I'm going to be the final deciding authority," he told an unhappy Groves. "On this matter, I am the kingpin."

It was equally clear to Stimson that the bomb represented a revolution not just in military affairs but in the "relationship of man to the universe." He told Interim Committee members that the new weapon could be used to "perfect international civilization," or it could turn into "a Frankenstein." A chronic insomniac, the secretary of war had just experienced "a pretty barbaric night as far as sleeping was concerned." He had tossed and turned as he tried to think through the implications of the bomb, not just for the war with Japan but for relations with Russia and for the entire postwar era.

Stimson understood the inevitability of the bomb. Unlike Szilard, he did not think the atomic project could be halted or even slowed down. He believed that America should share its technological achievements with other countries, notably Russia, but on the basis of strict quid pro quos, such as political liberalization and a transparent inspection regime. The lure of access to atomic secrets could encourage Stalin to cooperate with the West, along with American assistance for Russia's battered economy.

Support for Stimson's position came from several other committee members, including Marshall and Oppenheimer. The Los Alamos director had always been in favor of international controls over atomic energy, to the point of being suspected of disloyalty by some American spy catchers. Choosing his words carefully, he now called for a "tentative" discussion with Russia on future cooperation "in the most general terms without giving them any details of our productive effort." It was important not to "prejudge" the Russian attitude.

The army chief of staff went significantly further in advocating an opening toward Moscow. In Marshall's view, the Russians had always fulfilled their military commitments to their allies, whatever their record on political questions. Their reluctance to cooperate on military matters could often be explained by simple paranoia, "the necessity of maintaining security." The Russians could be trusted not to pass American atomic secrets on to the Japanese. The general wondered "whether it might be desirable to invite two prominent Russian scientists" to witness the first atomic test.

The time had come for Byrnes to assert his authority. The hardheaded Senate deal maker had no intention of trading away America's nuclear secrets without being assured of something very concrete, and enormously valuable, in return. He feared that any sharing of information, "even in general terms," could lead Stalin to demand a partnership. That would cause endless trouble. Better to simply push ahead as fast as possible with the production of atomic weapons while making a parallel effort to improve relations with Russia. Once Truman's representative made his position clear, the other committee members fell into line.

Byrnes also succeeded in imposing his views on what to do with the bomb, once it had been successfully tested. He opposed the proposal of some scientists for a publicly announced demonstration to shock the Japanese into submission. There was always a chance that the bomb would fail to explode, which would give "aid and comfort" to the enemy. Byrnes insisted that the bomb be "used against Japan as soon as possible" and that it be "used without prior warning." His only concession to Stimson's concerns about the morality of killing large numbers of civilians was a modification of the language suggested by the Target Committee. The aim point would be "a war plant surrounded by workers' homes," not the center of a city. It was a semantic distinction that soothed the consciences of decision makers but made little practical difference. Many Japanese worked at home producing military matériel. In the words of the unsentimental Curtis LeMay, "The entire population got into the act and worked to make those airplanes or munitions of war . . . men, women, children. We knew we were going to kill a lot of women and kids when we burned [a] town. Had to be done."

Byrnes hurried to the White House as soon as the Interim Committee meeting was over to present Truman with its recommendations. The two politicians reviewed the options for forcing a Japanese surrender. By some estimates, a hundred thousand Americans could be killed in the event of a D-day–style invasion of the Japanese home islands. The choice ended up being pretty straightforward, revolving around the chance of saving American lives. Despite some internal agonizing, the inexperienced president was not disposed to argue with the conclusions of his own more seasoned advisers. He reluctantly told Byrnes that "he could think of no alternative." The decision to drop the atomic bomb on Japan was effectively made on June 1, 1945, the day of Stalin's gala dinner for Hopkins in Moscow. Fewer than four weeks had passed since the surrender of Germany. While not yet irrevocable, it would take the full force of presidential will to achieve a different outcome. As Groves saw it, Truman was like "a little boy on a toboggan," careening down the snow slope of history, astride an invention that would change everything.

Events were acquiring a momentum of their own. If the atomic bomb was on the point of becoming unstoppable, the idea of inaugurating the new era with a gentlemen's agreement with the Russians was fast becoming an illusion. The scientists, the politicians, and even the generals might dream of cooperation, but at the operational level, where it counted, an intense competition was already under way. The defeat of Nazi Germany had unlocked a treasure trove of nuclear scientists, rocket inventors, uranium supplies, and missile parts. The victors were all desperate to gain control over this priceless arsenal and, equally important, deny possession to anyone else. World war allies were turning into Cold War rivals.

It had been far from inevitable at the outset of the war that the United States would become the first country to build an atomic bomb. Scientists in many countries had been engaged in nuclear research prior to 1939, and they shared their knowledge freely. A Polish-French chemist, Marie Curie, discovered the basic principle of radioactivity. A German-born Jew, Albert Einstein, conceived the theory of relativity that underpinned the subsequent development of nuclear physics. An Italian, Enrico Fermi, followed up on the pioneering research of the Hungarian-born Szilard into chain reactions. An Austrian Jew, Otto Frisch, explained how a uranium atom could be split in two, coining the term "fission" to describe the process. The Dane Niels Bohr showed how the uranium isotope U-235 could become the basis for the atomic bomb. It was only after the Nazis marched into Poland in September 1939 that nuclear research became a jealously guarded military secret.

If there was an early leader in the nuclear race, it was the Third Reich. Many leading physicists and chemists remained in Germany, even though many others had been driven out of Europe by the Nazis because of their Jewish ancestry. The Germans also controlled the rich uranium reserves that the Belgian mining concern Union Minière had extracted from the Congo, with the exception of a portion shipped to America at the beginning of the war. The physicist Werner Heisenberg was believed to be hard at work building a "uranium machine," the German term for a nuclear reactor, using heavy water from Norway as a moderator. The German atomic project had failed to live up to its potential due to infighting among the scientists and a lack of interest from Nazi officials, who did not believe that a workable weapon could be produced in time to win the war. Nevertheless, the essential components were all in place, scattered across a no-man's-land between the advancing American and Russian armies.

Anticipating the scramble for Germany's nuclear legacy, General Groves had established an intelligence unit that bore the code name Alsos (the Greek word for "grove"). The group was led by the flamboyant Boris

Pash, the scion of a prominent White Russian émigré family that had fought against the Reds during the Russian civil war. His father, Theodor Pashkovsky, was the leader of the Russian Orthodox Church in North America. A bulldoglike man with rimless glasses, Pash had already won a reputation for himself as a relentless hunter of Communists by conducting a series of national security interrogations of Oppenheimer and other Los Alamos scientists. The former seminarian turned U.S. Army colonel was put in charge of tracking down German scientists and their bomb-making materials. When a trove of documents was found in an abandoned German physics laboratory in Strasbourg in late 1944, Pash and his men rushed to the scene. They quickly realized they had hit pay dirt. "We studied the papers for two days and nights until our eyes began to hurt," an American investigator recalled. The documents provided the Alsos team with a road map to the abortive German nuclear effort.

One of the first items on the Alsos list was the Auer chemical plant at Oranienburg, some fifteen miles north of Berlin, where uranium ore was being processed into metal. Since Oranienburg lay well inside the designated Russian occupation zone, there was no chance that Americans or British troops could get there first. The only solution was to destroy the plant from the air. Groves sent a courier to explain the problem to General Carl Spaatz, the commander of U.S. strategic air forces in Europe. Spaatz was told that the plant was manufacturing "certain special metals for the production of as-yet-unused secret weapons of untold potentialities." On the afternoon of March 15, the Eighth Air Force sent 1,347 heavy bombers, escorted by 762 fighters, to destroy the plant and some nearby railway marshaling yards. Oranienburg was hit with 1,784 tons of bombs and incendiaries. Spaatz reported "the virtual destruction" of the target. Ostensibly the bombing raid was aimed against the Germans, but the Alsos men understood very well by this time that the German atomic project was not an immediate threat; the real purpose of the operation was to deny uranium to the Russians.

Documents seized by Alsos suggested that the largest cache of uranium ore from the Belgian Congo was hidden in a factory at Stassfurt, near the northern German town of Magdeburg. Like Oranienburg, Stassfurt was in the future Russian occupation zone but was close enough to the demarcation line to make a dash for the uranium feasible. American officers "foresaw all kinds of difficulties with the Russians" if an Alsos team moved into the area, but they were overruled by General Omar Bradley. At this point, American and Russian forces had still not linked up on the Elbe.

"To hell with the Russians," snapped the Twelfth Army group commander when asked for his opinion by a subordinate.

On April 17, the Alsos team discovered 1,100 tons of uranium ore at a salt mine near Stassfurt. The uranium was stored aboveground in wooden barrels stacked in open-sided sheds. Many of the barrels were either rotten or broken open, suggesting that they had been there for a long time. The slabs of silvery-gray rock would obviously have to be repacked before they could be transported. The Americans scoured surrounding towns for suitable packing material and located a factory that manufactured heavy cardboard bags. They also found a mill producing wire that could be used to sew up the bags. By April 19, hundreds of press-ganged German workers were repackaging the ore and loading it onto trucks. Over the next three days and nights, twenty thousand barrels of uranium had been transported a hundred miles by road to an airport hangar near Hanover, well inside the British zone. From there, it was moved by ship and air to England.

Pash, meanwhile, was hunting down the physicists. He received a tip that they were holed up in the picturesque hilltop town of Haigerloch, in the Swabian Alps south of Stuttgart. Reaching the town on April 22, he was greeted by a sea of white bedsheets, towels, and pillowcases fluttering from flagpoles and window shutters. The war-weary inhabitants were desperate to surrender to the western Allies, but Pash had no time for that. He headed for a church on top of a cliff, where he discovered a cave protected by a padlocked steel door. He summoned the manager of the facility, who claimed he was just an accountant. He seemed reluctant to unlock the door.

"Shoot the lock off," Pash ordered his men. "If he gets in the way, shoot him."

The manager quickly opened the door to reveal a ten-foot-wide concrete pit. At the center of the pit was a thick metal cylinder containing a "pot-shaped vessel, also of heavy metal, about four feet below the floor level." They had found the German "uranium machine." It was still in the experimental stage, an impressive scientific achievement but too small and too crude to produce the self-sustaining chain reaction necessary for an atomic explosion. Pash breathed a sigh of relief. He now had definitive proof that there was no Nazi bomb. As he later wrote, "the fact that the German atom bomb was not an immediate threat was probably the most significant single piece of military intelligence developed throughout the war. Alone, that information was enough to justify Alsos."

The Alsos team rounded up the key German physicists over the course of the next few days, a preemptive victory over the Soviets at the very time Russian and American troops were shaking hands on the Elbe. Most were captured in the Haigerloch area, in the town of Hechingen. One man still eluded them: Werner Heisenberg. In the opinion of General Groves, the leader of the Nazi nuclear effort was "worth more to us than ten divisions of Germans." It was essential to prevent him from falling into Russian hands. Pash immediately set off on his trail.

Interrogations revealed that Heisenberg had left Hechingen by bicycle on April 20, shortly before the arrival of the Alsos unit, heading east toward his native Bavaria. This was a dangerous time to be trekking across Germany: bands of fanatical SS men were summarily executing suspected deserters; American and British warplanes were bombing the roads; hordes of hungry refugees and foreign workers were scouring the countryside for food. The forty-four-year-old scientist proceeded cautiously, sleeping in hedgerows by day and traveling by night. At one point, he managed to hitch a ride on a train. It took him three days to cover the one-hundred-fifty-mile route until he reached the lakeside village of Urfeld, where he had a vacation home. His wife was astonished to see the former Nobel laureate "climbing wearily up the mountain, half-starved and dirty with the grime of the road."

Pash entered Urfeld in the late afternoon of May 2, well ahead of advance units of the U.S. Seventh Army. The entire area was still in the hands of German troops. The commanding general asked Pash to accept the surrender of several thousand men, but the Alsos chief was after more important prey. He was also worried about the lack of military support. He played for time, claiming that his own general was in the vicinity, but could not be disturbed with such formalities. The Germans "would have to wait until morning to have their surrender officially accepted." Deciding that discretion was the better part of valor, he then withdrew to the American lines, returning at dawn the next day with an infantry battalion. Heisenberg greeted Pash's arrival with relief. As he later wrote, he felt like "an utterly exhausted swimmer setting foot on firm land."

"I have been expecting you," he told the American.

A stream of intelligence information had been reaching Stalin and Beria about the Manhattan Project since March 1943. It came from spies and Communist sympathizers in Britain and the United States who believed that Russia deserved to share the secrets of the bomb as the country that was doing most of the actual fighting against Nazi Germany. The NKVD security police passed the intelligence on to Igor Kurchatov, the scientist in charge of the Soviet Union's own fledgling atomic bomb program. Kurchatov, in turn, used the information to suggest new lines of research to his subordinates, without revealing the source of his extraordinary insights. The bearded physicist was impressed, from the very start, by the value of the intelligence, which had "huge, inestimable significance for our state and science." The steady stream of documents enabled Soviet scientists to take many shortcuts and avoid the long detours that had sidetracked their western counterparts.

As the Third Reich collapsed, the NKVD formed its own specialized search groups to salvage whatever they could from the wreckage of the German nuclear project. The nuclear teams were modeled on the trophy brigades that were already hard at work dismantling German factories and shipping them back to the Soviet Union. They operated in a very similar manner to the American Alsos units: collecting intelligence, rounding up German scientists, swooping down on suspected nuclear facilities before their rivals. The most important trophy of all, from the Soviet perspective, was uranium. As the Americans had already guessed, the Soviet Union had very limited supplies of the radioactive metal. Without more uranium, it would be impossible to build a Russian bomb. Thanks to their spies in London, the Russians knew that the Nazis controlled a large portion of the uranium from the Belgian Congo, which had been transferred to "eastern areas of Germany."

A team of thirty Russian scientists led by an NKVD general flew into Berlin on May 3, just one day after the fall of the German capital to Zhukov's forces. The team included many outstanding physicists dressed, for conspiratorial purposes, in the uniform of NKVD colonels. Yuri Khariton, a Cambridge-educated physicist who went on to design the first Soviet atomic bomb, cut a particularly ludicrous figure. Kurchatov's top assistant was wearing a military cap that was several sizes too large for him. Fortunately, he had large ears, which kept the cap from swallowing the entire upper half of his thin, scholarly head. On arrival in Berlin, Khariton and the other "colonels" headed straight for the Kaiser Wilhelm Institute of Physics in the southwestern suburb of Dahlem. There, amid the wreckage of the whitewashed three-story building, they discovered the blueprints of the German nuclear project. It revealed that the Germans were well behind the Soviets, let alone the Americans, in their progress toward an atomic bomb. The top scientists, including Heisenberg, had been evacuated to Haigerloch two years earlier, along with most of their equipment. In addition to extremely valuable documents, the Russian physicists stripped the institute of everything that remained, down to the "water faucets, doorknobs, and washbowls." It was necessary to act quickly, before the arrival of the western Allies, as Dahlem had been designated part of the American sector of Berlin.

The "colonels" split into smaller groups to scour Soviet-occupied Germany for bomb-making materials. They were upset to learn that the Americans had beaten them to the most important stockpile of uranium ore at Stassfurt, inside the Russian sector. This forced them to look for smaller caches, based on a meticulous study of the documents and interrogations of German scientists. It was a cross-country detective chase. By questioning a plant manager in Potsdam, Khariton discovered that the Germans had hidden several hundred tons of uranium in a town called Neustadt. Unfortunately, there were twenty towns with that name in Germany, including ten in Soviet-controlled eastern Germany. His team visited the first nine towns before reaching Neustadt am Glewe, a hundred and fifty miles northwest of Berlin, just inside the Soviet zone. There they discovered a hundred tons of processed uranium oxide in the warehouse of a leather-tanning plant. This find alone provided Khariton and Kurchatov with sufficient uranium metal to build Russia's first experimental uranium-graphite reactor in December 1946. Prior to May 1945, total Russian reserves of uranium oxide amounted to no more than seven tons.

Meanwhile, another physicist-turned-NKVD colonel, Georgi Flerov, took charge of the uranium-processing plant at Oranienburg that had been bombed by American warplanes back in March. An excitable man with a shock of unruly black hair underneath his military cap, Flerov had been one of the fathers of the Soviet atomic bomb project. He had written to Stalin in April 1942 to warn him that the Americans were almost certainly working on a nuclear device. When he wrote the letter, he was serving near the front lines as a military engineer, aged twenty-nine, without access to any special intelligence information. Flerov had based his startling insight on a hunch; poring over American physics journals at a local library, he noticed there were no articles about nuclear fission, which had previously been very much in the news. Leading nuclear physicists in America and Britain had stopped publishing the results of their work. The conclusion was obvious: the scientists had been recruited to work on a top-secret military project and were being muzzled by censorship. It was the scientific equivalent of the "dog that didn't bark" in the Sherlock Holmes story.

Flerov used his investigative skills to track down the chief scientist of the Auer Company, which specialized in the processing of uranium ore. In mid-May, shortly after the Nazi surrender, he found Nikolaus Riehl in his country home outside Berlin and invited him for a "few days" of scientific discussions. As Riehl later wrote, "The few days lasted for 10 years." Encouraged by promises of excellent research facilities and living conditions, as well as fear of what might happen if they refused, several dozen German scientists "half voluntarily, half-non-voluntarily" agreed to join the Soviet atomic bomb program. While not quite the caliber of the physicists rounded up by Alsos in western Germany, the east German group included some prominent nuclear chemists and engineers. Riehl became director of a uranium-processing laboratory in the Black Sea resort of Sukhumi, returning home only in 1955, two years after Stalin's death. Before leaving Germany, he accompanied Flerov and another "colonel" to the Auer factory at Oranienburg bombed by the Americans on March 15. At the time, the attacks had "made no sense at all" to Riehl. The Oranienburg plant was not contributing in any significant way to the German war effort, which had virtually collapsed in any case. As he watched his new Russian colleagues pick their way grimly through the wreckage, Riehl suddenly understood the purpose of the massive bombing raid. "The bombings were directed not against the Germans, but against them."

As it turned out, the Flying Fortresses and Liberators had failed to complete their most important mission, despite the claims of virtually complete success. The factory itself had been destroyed, but a stash of nearly a hundred tons of high-grade uranium oxide was still intact. It was immediately packed up and shipped to Moscow. Together with the uranium recovered from Neustadt by Khariton, the Russians now had enough uranium to build a full-scale plutonium-producing nuclear reactor, in addition to the experimental reactor. Kurchatov later estimated that the uranium found in Germany in the weeks immediately after VE-day "saved the Soviet atomic project one year" of work.

The Americans may have been correct in believing that they had been dealt a royal straight flush in the form of the world's first atomic bomb. But the nuclear poker tournament was far from over. In fact, it had barely begun.

15

Red Empire

June 24

As the Soviet Union hurled back the Nazi invaders, Stalin had developed an avid interest in political geography. He had a huge globe installed in the annex to his Kremlin office on which he explained his military strategy to visitors ranging from Molotov to Churchill to Khrushchev. He liked to trace the movement of his armies with the stem of his pipe, looking for opportunities and points of vulnerability. His goal was to reassemble all the territories lost by the tsars and the Bolsheviks at moments of weakness. In redressing past humiliations, he wanted to ensure that Russia would never again be as vulnerable to foreign invasion as it had been in June 1941.

The rapidly expanding borders of the Red empire required a constant updating of maps. One day, soon after the end of the war, a new map was brought to the dictator for his approval. He pinned it to the wall of his Kuntsevo dacha and began examining it. "Let's see what the result is for us," he mused to Molotov. The two men looked first at the border with Finland where, in the otherwise disastrous Winter War of 1940, the Red Army had succeeded in annexing the Karelian Isthmus and the northern shores of Lake Ladoga. Stalin expressed satisfaction.

"In the north, everything is as it should be. Fine. Finland greatly offended us, and we have moved the border back from Leningrad."

He then turned to the Baltic States, acquired for Russia by Peter the Great at the Battle of Poltava in the early eighteenth century. They were back under Russian control, thanks in part to the deal that Stalin had struck with Hitler in 1939. So too was a vast one-hundred-fifty-mile band of territory, stretching from the former East Prussia in the north to the Balkans in the south. The *vozhd* could see there was no danger from that direction.

"The Baltic coast—Russian land for centuries—is ours again. The Belo-russians are all now living together with us, the Ukrainians are together, the Moldavians are together. In the west, everything is fine."

The eastern borders of the Soviet Union presented a similar happy picture. Under the deal struck with FDR at Yalta, confirmed by Truman, Russia would regain the southern half of Sakhalin Island and establish sovereignty over the Kurile Islands in return for declaring war against Japan. The Chinese port cities of Port Arthur and Dairen would come under Soviet control, along with the Manchurian railway system. Stalin waved his pipe over Asia.

"China, Mongolia, everything is in order."

He switched his attention to the bottom of the map. A frown appeared on his pockmarked face as he pointed the pipe stem southward, beyond the Caucasus Mountains, toward Iran and Turkey. This was the part of the world that had first formed him, growing up in Georgia.

"But here I don't like our border."

The fledgling Soviet state had been forced to surrender the southern district of Kars and Ardahan to Turkey soon after the revolution. The population of the region was mainly Turks, Armenians, and Kurds, and it had only been part of the Russian empire since 1878, but Stalin regarded it as rightfully his. As a young revolutionary, he had robbed banks in Kars when it was an extension of his Georgia. Like the tsarist politicians, Stalin was also upset by the situation in the Dardanelles and the Bosporus, the narrow channels connecting the Black and Aegean Seas. The 1936 Montreux Convention had declared the straits an international shipping lane but left them under the effective control of Turkey. The Russian navy was bottled up in the Black Sea. The Dardanelles formed a natural passageway into Russia through what Churchill called "the soft underbelly of Europe." A British naval fleet had sailed through the straits in 1854 to

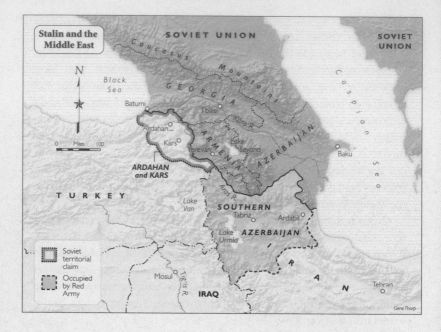

lay siege to Sevastopol and attack Russia during the Crimean War. The British and French had used the same route to intervene in the Russian civil war on the side of the Whites in 1918. As Stalin told his associates, "Historically, this is where the threat has always originated." He had little respect for Turkey, which he viewed as an unnatural conglomeration of nations, including Georgians, Armenians, and Kurds, under Turkish tutelage. The Soviet Union was also a multiethnic state, but the different nations were held together by a common ideology.

"Go ahead," he instructed Molotov, outlining his demands for shared control over the Dardanelles with the Turks. "Press them for joint possession!"

On most foreign policy matters, Molotov was happy to implement the wishes of his master. This was a rare occasion when he felt the *vozhd* was going too far. He knew that territorial claims against Turkey would be vigorously opposed, not only by the Turks but also by the British and the Americans.

"They won't allow it," he stuttered.

"Demand it."

Molotov waited until the day after Hopkins flew back to the United

States to make his move. On June 7, he summoned the Turkish ambassador, Selim Sarper, to his Kremlin office to discuss a new "treaty of friendship" between the two countries. He mentioned in passing that the Soviet Union had been forced to cede the Kars and Ardahan region to Turkey in 1921 at a time when "we were very weak." Molotov wanted to know whether Turkey was willing to make amends now that Russia had regained its strength. As a condition for signing a new treaty, he also demanded security guarantees in the form of Soviet military bases along the Dardanelles. "We must defend the straits together," he told Sarper. His lack of subtlety shocked the ambassador, who rejected the Russian proposals out of hand. "The Soviet Union has no need for either more territory or a few thousand more inhabitants."

Sarper reminded Molotov that the 1921 agreement had been signed by Lenin and confirmed by Stalin. The commissar pointed out that Lenin, under duress, had also signed an "unjust" treaty with Poland. The lands surrendered to Poland, including the city of Lwów, had now been returned. Poland could serve as a "positive model" for relations between Turkey and the Soviet Union.

In pushing for territorial concessions from Turkey, Stalin was following the old Leninist dictum: "Probe with bayonets: if you encounter mush, proceed; if you encounter steel, withdraw." He still had every interest in maintaining good, or at least tolerable, relations with the United States and Britain. At the same time, he wanted to extract maximum political advantage from Russia's sacrifices during the war and the position of strength in which she now found herself. The negotiations with Hopkins over Poland suggested to Stalin that it was possible to square the circle. He could present the West with an unending series of territorial demands without triggering a new global confrontation. It was a fatal miscalculation.

Forcing Turkey to accept Russian demands was difficult, even for Stalin, as there were no Soviet troops in the country. Although he never gave up his claim to a military presence along the Dardanelles, he had no physical means of implementing his will, other than waging a long-range war of nerves. Neighboring Iran represented a somewhat easier challenge. The Red Army had occupied the northern part of the country in 1941 at the same time as the British moved into southern Iran. The goal was to deny strategically important supply routes to Germany and ensure the delivery of lend-lease supplies from the United States to the Soviet Union. The Russians had promised to leave Iran within six months of the end of the war along with the British but were already dragging their feet.

A twentieth-century version of the Great Game was already under way in Iran, pitting Russia, Britain, and America against one another. The objective this time was not land routes to India but access to the vast oil reserves of the Middle East. Because they had gotten there first, the British had a head start in the Great Game as it related to Persia, which they naturally sought to protect. They already had their oil concessions in the south of the country. The Americans presented themselves as an honest broker between the British and the Russians, interested in an "open door" policy. This, of course, was not how Stalin saw the matter. He suspected an Anglo-American conspiracy designed to deny Russia access to strategic resources. He told his oil minister that the western Allies would "crush us if they see such a possibility." Without oil, Stalin explained, it would be impossible to operate the tanks, planes, and other equipment required by a modern army. "Oil is the life force of military technology," the *vozhd* liked to repeat.

Stalin's paranoia was fed by Beria, who reported in August 1944 that "the British, and possibly the Americans, secretly work against a transfer of oil fields in northern Iran to the Soviet Union." One of Molotov's deputies, Sergey Kavtaradze, was dispatched to Tehran to demand oil concessions but came back empty-handed. Encouraged by the United States, the Iranian government refused to negotiate new deals until all foreign troops had withdrawn from Iranian territory. When he heard the news, Kavtaradze remarked that it would have "unhappy consequences." He accused the Iranian prime minister of being "disloyal" and "unfriendly." The Iranian decision represented a serious setback for Stalin; in addition to oil rights, he wanted to secure his southern borders by establishing a buffer zone in northern Iran similar to the one he was creating in eastern Europe.

Rebuffed by the Iranians, Stalin set about achieving his goals in his usual manner. A former commissar for nationalities, he understood better than anyone how to play the ethnic card in national and international politics. He had vast experience in redrawing boundaries, inciting ethnic groups against one another, fomenting secessionist movements, deporting disobedient nations, and inventing irredentist claims. The rights and wrongs of a particular ethnic conflict were largely irrelevant to him. What mattered was the pursuit of supreme power and the strengthening of the Soviet Union as a huge multiethnic state.

Finding an ethnic card to play in Iran was simple. The northern part of the country was home to millions of Azeris with ethnic origins virtually identical to the Azeris across the border in the Soviet republic of Azerbaijan. Russians referred to this region of Iran, around the city of Tabriz, as "Southern Azerbaijan." The easiest way to apply political pressure on Iran was to fan the flames of Azeri nationalism. Iranian Azeris would be encouraged to demand autonomy from the central government in Tehran. The declaration of a Southern Azerbaijan Autonomous Republic was the first step to the incorporation of the region into the Soviet Union. Stalin could count on the leaders of Soviet Azerbaijan to enthusiastically support a policy that, as Molotov pointed out, "would almost double the size of their republic at the expense of Iran." The separation of Southern Azerbaijan from Iran would be followed by the detachment of the Kurdish region bordering Turkey and Iraq.

The campaign to unite the two parts of Azerbaijan under Soviet control got under way on June 10 when Stalin issued a secret directive establishing industrial plants in Tabriz and other northern Iranian cities. Hundreds of Soviet geologists were dispatched to the region to search for oil. On July 7, the Kremlin ordered the creation of a "separatist movement" for Southern Azerbaijan, to be controlled from Baku, the capital of Soviet Azerbaijan. A new political party, the Azerbaijan Democratic Party, was established to spearhead the movement, along with newspapers, publishing houses, and an extensive network of local committees. Party activists were instructed to organize "meetings, demonstrations, strikes, and the disbanding of electoral commissions unsuitable for us." The nationalist party was designed to appeal to a broader section of the Azeri population than the Marxist-Leninist Tudeh Party that had been the vehicle for Soviet propaganda efforts in the past. Stalin counted on the support of "progressive clergymen, landlords, merchants, and intelligentsia," in addition to committed Communists. He understood very well that nationalism was a more powerful motivating force than communism, at least in Iran and his native Caucasus.

Stalin's choice to head the new political party was a former journalist and Communist Party activist named Jafar Pishevari. A report to the Soviet Politburo noted with approval that he had worked for a long time in Soviet Azerbaijan and had been sent to Iran as a Comintern agent in 1927. He had spent ten years in the shah's prisons and was only released in 1941, following the Russian invasion. Two of his brothers were Soviet citizens, including one who was a doctor with the Red Army. Pishevari was summoned to Baku to receive his instructions from the Communist Party boss of Azerbaijan.

Events proceeded according to the scenario drawn up by the puppet masters in Moscow and Baku. The script was familiar to anyone who had witnessed similar events in Bucharest or Warsaw, Riga or Sofia. Distribute "20,000 rifles and 2,000,000 bullets" to political sympathizers, making sure that they are not made in the USSR. Form popular committees, or soviets, to replace the existing administration. Win over the peasants with promises of sweeping land reform. Infiltrate agents into northern Iran from Soviet Azerbaijan to prepare for an armed uprising. Establish printing presses and control the mass media. Propaganda was particularly important. As the British consul in Tabriz noted in one of his monthly reports, "no Russian act in Azerbaijan is performed without its prologue and epilogue of propaganda. The Azerbaijanis have become adept at predicting the act from the prologue. Every Soviet official is, of course, a propagandist: the most seemingly casual remark let fall in private conversation smells of the Directive."

The first act of the drama—the seizure of power in northern Iran—was completed by November 1945. Armed Democratic Party activists captured one local police post after another. Soon, they controlled all the main roads. The Red Army prevented the central Iranian authorities from dispatching reinforcements to the north. Magistrates and landowners who tried to resist the occupation of farms and public buildings were killed. A "People's Congress" was convened to form an "autonomous republic," with Pishevari as "prime minister." Its program included the creation of a "national people's army," the establishment of Turki rather than Farsi as the official language, the distribution of land, employment for all, and freedom of religion.

Reputed to be the largest city in the world at the time of Marco Polo, Tabriz was now a provincial backwater. A few imperial buildings rose above the sea of dried mud huts, offering reminders of past glory when the city was the gateway to the Orient. The new prime minister moved into a grandiose palace surrounded by formal gardens that had previously belonged to the Iranian governor-general. He received visitors in a vast reception room, decorated only by a few Louis Seize chairs. Outside his window, Russian cavalrymen galloped through the unpaved streets in groups of four and eight. According to the American vice-consul Robert

Rossow, Pishevari looked "deceptively unlike a ruthless Communist gauleiter. He stood about five feet five inches tall, had steely gray hair and a small brush mustache under a sharp hooked nose, a shiny blue serge suit and a colored shirt, frayed at the cuffs and noticeably soiled at the collar, which was buttoned but tieless. His hands were the rough, horney hands of the peasant, and the fingernails were dirty."

The power behind the throne, Rossow believed, was the minister of propaganda, Mohammed Biriya, who headed the Society of Friends of Soviet Azerbaijan. A former flute player and leader of the Communist-run Tabriz street cleaners' union, the dapper, diminutive Biriya was a "Master of Terror." On the pretext of recruiting new members to the Society of Friends, his "armed goons" roamed the countryside, collecting signatures to a petition demanding unification with Soviet Azerbaijan. Anyone who refused to sign was "badly beaten."

Western diplomats in Iran had no doubt who was pulling the strings behind the scene. The British ambassador to Tehran, Reader Bullard, reported on July 23 that the Russians were "making great efforts to obtain mastery over Persia before the time should come to remove their troops. . . . Behavior of Soviet ambassador in general resembles that of a Commissar in a Baltic State rather than of a diplomat in a foreign independent country." From Tabriz, the British consul, John Wall, sent a steady stream of reports chronicling the progress of the slow motion coup. He concluded in August that "the Russians are more determined than ever to maintain their hold on this province." Instead of withdrawing their troops, they were reinforcing them. Pishevari was known to "spend hours every day at the Soviet Consulate-General." Articles in the Democratic Party newspaper were written in the Baku rather than Tabriz dialect of the Turki language, suggesting that the paper was produced in the Soviet Union.

"There is no railway to Tehran, but there is a perfectly good one to Baku, and at the moment it looks as though that is where Autonomous Azerbaijan is heading," Wall reported at the end of December 1945. "Autonomous Azerbaijan feels much more like a part of Russia than of Iran."

The most serious threat to the cohesion of Stalin's eastern European empire in the weeks after VE-day came from a pledge he had rashly made to FDR at Yalta. He would soon have to deliver on his promise of "free elections"—or risk a rift with his wartime allies. The Communists were the only political force that could be relied upon to do Moscow's bidding across most of the region, but they lacked a solid basis of popular support. The only way for them to gain a majority was to form Popular Front–type alliances with other left-wing parties. Operating under the protective shadow of the Red Army, the Communists already controlled the all-important power ministries in countries like Poland and Romania and Bulgaria, overseeing the security forces and the administration of justice. They would consolidate their power gradually, employing what came to be known as the salami tactic, slice by inconspicuous slice. By the time the rest of the world woke up to what was happening, the Communists would have consumed the entire sausage.

"Delicious, it was very tasty," Molotov recalled with satisfaction late in life. "We still haven't thought of a better policy."

Since Stalin and Molotov did not want to leave anything to chance, they insisted that coalitions be formed *before* an election rather than *after* an election. The "progressive" parties would fight the elections as a united bloc. Parliamentary seats and ministries were distributed beforehand, guaranteeing the Communists control over the government, whatever the outcome of the popular vote. In order for this strategy to work, the cooperation of other left-wing leaders was required. In return for surrendering their independence, these politicians were granted a share of power, under the leadership of the Communists. But there were always those who refused to compromise. A variety of methods was used to bring the obdurate into line, ranging from bullying to bribery to blackmail. If all else failed, they could be arrested, exiled, or physically eliminated.

One of the earliest such holdouts was the Bulgarian opposition leader Georgi Dimitrov. He was known to everyone in Bulgaria as Gemeto, a play on his initials, to distinguish him from the other Georgi Dimitrov, the leader of the Comintern and a trusted member of Stalin's inner circle. As the head of the Agrarian Party, Gemeto commanded the loyalty of millions of Bulgarian peasants, making him the most popular politician in the country. He had been imprisoned and tortured by the right-wing regime of Tsar Boris III, which allied itself with Hitler during World War II. A charismatic speaker, he was unwilling to subordinate his party to the Communist-led Fatherland Front. His defiance resulted in his house arrest and a propaganda campaign against "Gemetovists." Anyone suspected of Gemetovism—which quickly became synonymous with "fascism" and "treason"—was expelled from the ranks of a purged, subservient Agrarian Party.

Ill with bronchial pneumonia, Gemeto escaped his house arrest on May 23 and made his way to the apartment of a British diplomat. The British were in a difficult position. Churchill had promised Stalin an 80 percent stake in Bulgaria as part of a deal that gave Britain a free hand in Greece. Unwilling to upset this arrangement, the British took the ostracized opposition leader to the residence of the American representative, in the foothills of Mount Vitosha, three miles outside Sofia. The diplomat, Maynard Barnes, was sound asleep, having "drunk a bit too much" the previous evening. When he finally awoke, he escorted his unexpected visitor to the guest bedroom and handed him a pair of pajamas. The issue, as the envoy saw it, was now very simple. Stalin was attempting to establish a one-party system in Bulgaria and other eastern European countries. The time had come for America to demonstrate "maximum resistance to Russian designs in all areas of interest to us with respect to the maintenance of peace and opposition to aggression."

When the Communist interior minister discovered where Dimitrov had gone, he was predictably furious. He sent armed militia units to surround the American residence, with orders to search anyone who left or entered. In response, Barnes rustled up a half-dozen American soldiers serving with the Allied Control Commission and posted them around his estate. The downstairs shutters were drawn. Gemeto was handed a rifle and stationed by a second-story window. As he later wrote, at that moment "I was ready to die with rifle in hand fighting our occupiers, the tyrants who had destroyed the freedom and independence of my people! Shoulder to shoulder with American fighters in defense of freedom and democracy!" Barnes cabled Washington for instructions. The State Department approved his decision to offer protection to Gemeto but warned him not to resist "an attempt to take Dimitrov by force."

As the city buzzed with rumors over Gemeto's fate, anyone suspected of helping him escape was arrested and interrogated. On May 30, the Interior Ministry announced that his former secretary, Mara Racheva, had committed suicide by jumping out of the fourth-story window of the central police station. A doctor who examined her body reported that it bore numerous marks of torture inconsistent with a fall from a window:

- All the nails on both feet had been torn out;
- Three fingers of the left hand had been hacked off at the second joint;
- Both ears cut off;

- Right breast excised;
- Tongue torn out and all teeth extracted;
- Flaying of a strip of skin about two inches wide through one quadrant of the waist.

The standoff over Gemeto continued for two and a half months. Barnes began to tire of "the man who came for breakfast." The constant companionship of a "Bulgarian political refugee (no matter charming and interesting) and two or more American soldiers" eventually became irksome, causing his house to be transformed into "a miniature fortress." The stalemate was eventually broken on September 5 when the Bulgarian government allowed the dissident Agrarian leader to fly out of Sofia on an American plane, escorted by Barnes. Parliamentary elections were finally held two months later. The Communist-dominated Fatherland Front ended up with nearly 90 percent of the vote. The other Georgi Dimitrov—Stalin's friend—was appointed prime minister.

There were many inconvenient people just like Gemeto all over eastern Europe who had to be dealt with, one way or the other. On June 18, the trial opened in Moscow of the sixteen Polish underground leaders arrested two months previously by the Red Army. Armored cars brought the men from Lubyanka Prison to the nearby Hall of Columns in central Moscow. Prior to the revolution, the brilliantly lit hall had hosted the glittering balls of the Russian aristocracy, but now served as the venue for Stalinist show trials. Batteries of movie cameras and klieg lights shone on the crudely built wooden picket-fence dock where the prisoners sat in four rows of seats. To a western reporter observing the scene, they seemed like members of "a small-town Rotary Club reduced to a condition of bewilderment and fright." The president of the court was the notorious military judge Colonel General Vasily Ulrich, "a round-faced, double-chinned man with twinkling eyes and a merry grin which sometimes seemed on the verge of becoming a sneer." His jovial appearance belied a ferocious reputation for sending tens of thousands of his former comrades to their deaths during the 1937 purge of the Red Army. The audience consisted of row after row of uniformed officers festooned with medals and gold braid, plus a smattering of foreign diplomats and journalists in dark suits.

The chief defendant was General Leopold Okulicki, the former commander in chief of the Polish Home Army, which had remained loyal to the government-in-exile in London. Known in the underground as Bear Cub, Okulicki had been one of the leaders of the doomed Warsaw Uprising against the Nazis. He was now charged with crimes ranging from organizing armed resistance in the rear of the Red Army to operating illegal radio transmitters to acts of sabotage that had resulted in the deaths of at least five hundred ninety-four Soviet soldiers. Testifying in his own defense, he sought to walk a fine line between denying that he had ordered specific acts of terrorism and assuming responsibility for the actions of his subordinates. Dignified to the end, he presented himself as "a soldier obeying the instructions of his government." Under questioning, he agreed that he had maintained the Home Army "on a secret footing" and failed to surrender "ammunition, arms, and radio stations" to the Soviet occupation forces.

PROSECUTOR: How do you describe that?
OKULICKI: I describe it as a failure to carry out the order of the Red Army Command.
PROSECUTOR: With what purpose?
OKULICKI: With the object of preserving everything for the future.
PROSECUTOR: For what ultimate purpose?
OKULICKI: For a future struggle, in the event of a threat to Poland.
PROSECUTOR: Against whom?
OKULICKI: Against those who threatened.
PROSECUTOR: What country did you have in mind?
OKULICKI: The Soviet Union . . .
PROSECUTOR: My last question. Do you admit that all your activities were directed against the Red Army and the Soviet Union?
OKULICKI: I admit it, but it was all done because we believed that the Soviet Union was a threat to Poland's independence.

The guilty verdicts were a foregone conclusion. To placate the Allies, the sentences were lighter than usual: ten years for Okulicki, five to eight years for other members of the underground government, shorter prison terms for the less important prisoners. Three defendants were acquitted. By pushing ahead with the trial over western protests, Stalin had achieved his goal of showing he would permit no serious challenge to the Russian domination of Poland. At the same time, he managed to avoid an open break with the Americans and the British. Dismay over the trial of the sixteen Poles in western capitals was balanced by relief over the formation of a Polish coalition government that included Mikołajczyk. The new deputy prime minister soon discovered that his political influence was minimal. His Communist colleagues brushed aside his pleas to petition the Kremlin for the release of the convicted underground leaders.

"It would make Stalin angry," insisted Polish president Bolesław Bierut, a former Comintern operative. "Besides, we don't need these people in Poland now."

Stalin's list of inconvenient people was not limited to foreign enemies. He understood that he would have to deal with the marshals and generals who had shot to prominence during the war, sharing credit for the final victory. A man like Zhukov could easily emerge as an alternate source of authority to the Politburo, just as Bonaparte had set himself up against the Directorate in the aftermath of the French Revolution. The marshal enjoyed huge popularity, not only in the army, but among ordinary Soviet citizens who saw him as the savior who had chased the Germans away from the gates of Moscow, Leningrad, and Stalingrad.

The *vozhd* had already taken steps to put the leaders of the Red Army in their place. He appointed Zhukov commander of the Soviet occupation zone in Germany but made sure that he was surrounded by political advisers and NKVD agents. The Kremlin's ubiquitous diplomatic troubleshooter, Andrei Vyshinsky, was constantly at Zhukov's side while Beria's deputy, Ivan Serov, served as chief of the civilian administration for the Soviet zone. Serov sent a steady stream of derogatory reports back to Moscow, complaining that Zhukov was "boasting about his victories and even that he was planning a military conspiracy." Zhukov lacked the freedom of action that his western counterparts took for granted. The Americans quickly concluded that "it was Vyshinsky, a civilian, and not Zhukov who was deciding matters with political implications, decisions of a type which Eisenhower could and did make on his own authority." Zhukov often did not know what was going on in his own zone of operations. He was stunned to learn, many years later, that Hitler's remains were under the control of the NKVD at the very time he was telling western journalists that the former führer was probably on the run.

At Yalta, Stalin had pointedly reminded the military leaders that the time would come, after the war, when they would be "quickly forgotten."

That day was fast approaching. But first he would permit them one final moment of glory.

Stalin had been making plans for a triumphant victory parade through Red Square on June 24, seven weeks after the fall of Berlin. Each army that had taken part in the assault on Nazi Germany would be represented by a full combat regiment. The Russian tradition, going back to the time of the tsars, was for the commander in chief to review the troops on horseback. A magnificent white stallion had been specially selected for Stalin, but the *vozhd* was no horseman. When he mounted Kumir for a trial run, the horse reared in protest and threw him to the ground. A furious Stalin summoned Zhukov to his dacha and asked him if he still knew how to ride.

"No, I haven't forgotten," replied Zhukov, an accomplished cavalryman in his youth. "I still ride sometimes."

"Fine, you review the Victory Parade."

"Thanks for the honor, but wouldn't it be better if you reviewed the parade? You are the supreme commander. By right and by duty, you should review the parade."

"I'm too old to review parades. You are younger. You review it."

A few days later, Vasily Stalin let Zhukov in on the "big secret." His father had planned to review the parade himself but backed out after "the horse bolted." It was a friendly warning to the conqueror of Berlin not to disgrace himself on the big day. Zhukov's "heart beat faster" as he mounted Kumir at the Spassky Gate at the appointed hour. The cobblestones of Red Square were slick from heavy rain. Dressed in his army greatcoat, Stalin ascended the steps of the Lenin mausoleum, followed by Beria and the other Politburo potentates. As the clock on the Spassky Gate struck ten, Zhukov galloped onto the square, fully in control of the gleaming white stallion. Rokossovsky, the vanquisher of Poland and East Prussia and onetime purge victim, galloped toward him from the opposite direction on an equally imposing black horse. Each marshal was accompanied a few steps behind by an aide, on a seemingly identical steed. A mighty hurrah rose from ten thousand voices across the square as they met in front of the mausoleum, oblivious to the rain, which soon became a downpour. The band played Glinka's patriotic hymn "Slavsya," or "Glory."

Unlike the impromptu popular celebrations on May 9, this was a private parade, for the exclusive enjoyment of a few hundred top officials. Red Square was festooned with portraits of Stalin alongside Lenin. The

"Man of Steel" seemed a deity to his followers marching across the slick paving stones beneath.

"Do you see him?" the war correspondent Alexander Avdeenko called out to his son, perched high on his shoulders.

"Aha," the boy shouted in excitement. "Standing in the rain. The old man. Is he getting wet?"

"Tempered steel does not fear rain."

"Is he a man of steel? Is that why he is called Stalin?"

"An ordinary man, but with a will of steel."

The little boy noticed a frown darkening the brow of the "father of the people."

"Papa, why is he not happy? Is he mad at somebody?"

"At God probably, who didn't send us good weather."

"So why didn't Stalin order God to send us good weather?"

The climax of the ceremony came as two hundred goose-stepping officers in dress uniform hurled captured German standards and Nazi banners onto the ground in front of Stalin. At a Kremlin reception later that evening, the marshals proposed that Stalin be promoted to generalissimo, a rank that had never previously existed in the Red Army. The *vozhd* made a show of modesty, saying he did not deserve such an honor, but his acolytes noted that he did not veto the idea. Generalissimo he became. Once again, as he had on May 24, Stalin raised his glass to the common man. He praised the "little screws and bolts" of the military machine "without whom all of us, marshals and commanders of fronts and armies, would not be worth a damn." It was his way of reminding the generals that they were nothing compared with the *narod* as represented by the Communist Party, in the person of its general secretary. Moscow was soon buzzing with jokes, evidently planted by the NKVD, about the uppity ways of the new "military caste."

The people, of course, had no voice of their own. Ordinary Muscovites were tired of the war, tired of the Terror, and hoping desperately for some kind of normality. When a British diplomat, Hugh Lunghi, returned to Red Square much later in the day, he found a small group of Russians gazing at the rain-sodden Nazi banners, which had been dumped unceremoniously in front of the mausoleum. There was no triumphant gloating, no stomping on the banners. Instead, there was merely a solemn grief for the staggering losses of the war.

"That's the end of that, then," commented an old woman as she stared at the symbols of German defeat. "What we need now is a new beginning."

As he shook hands with the woman, Lunghi was deeply moved. He sensed that victory and tragedy were inextricably intertwined. There would be no "new beginning" for the Russian people. Stalin's vindictiveness was about to display itself with extraordinary force.

Americans got a firsthand glimpse of the terror inspired by Stalin's regime less than a week after the victory parade in Red Square. On June 28, the State Department announced that one hundred fifty-four Soviet citizens held as prisoners of war in Fort Dix, New Jersey, would be sent back to Russia in accordance with the Yalta agreements. They had all been wearing German uniforms at the time of their capture by the U.S. Army but were a motley group in other respects. Some of the POWs were former Red Army men who had deserted to the Wehrmacht because of their hatred of communism, men like Lieutenant Karalbi Baschew, whose father and brother had been shot by the NKVD. Others, like Private Wassily Tarrasuk, a former partisan from Belorussia, had been forced to join the German army against their will. Such details made little difference to Stalin. He regarded them all as "traitors to the Motherland." His Order No. 270, issued in August 1941 soon after the German invasion, specified that Soviet soldiers "falling into encirclement are to fight to the last." Those who surrendered were "to be destroyed by any available means while their families are to be deprived of assistance."

The Fort Dix prisoners were well aware of the fate in store for them if they were forcibly returned to the Soviet Union. A forty-year-old Wehrmacht officer told his American captors, "I knew I was a traitor because when I was a commander in the Red Army, I myself read those orders to my troops." Overnight, the POWs came up with a plan to commit mass suicide. They dismantled the metal beds in their barracks and refashioned them into crude clubs. They also armed themselves with knives they had stolen from the mess, which they concealed in their clothes. At 9:00 a.m. the following morning, the camp superintendent ordered them, in German, out of the barracks into the courtyard to prepare for a transfer.

"*Nein, nein,*" shouted the prisoners.

The prisoners barricaded themselves inside their rooms and refused all appeals to come out. Smoke was observed coming from a window. The guards were issued gas masks and tear-gas grenades and ordered to attack the barracks. A large number of prisoners rushed out a rear door, wielding their makeshift weapons.

"Shoot at us," they cried, pointing to their hearts as they attacked the guards.

The guards eventually succeeded in restoring order through the use of tear gas and gunfire. When they entered the building, they discovered the corpses of three Russian prisoners, who had hung themselves. Another fifteen nooses had been strung up on doors and window frames, ready for use.

The Fort Dix riot made grim headlines the following day, prompting a round of soul-searching in the Truman administration over the policy of forcible repatriation. No one was under any illusion about what lay in store for the prisoners if they were sent back to Russia. A stream of disturbing reports had reached Washington from western diplomats describing the horrifying treatment meted out to former Russian POWs and slave laborers forced to work in German factories and mines. There were documented cases of prisoners being marched behind a warehouse as soon as they disembarked at Odessa and shot on the spot. If they escaped summary execution, they could expect long sentences in the Gulag. A June 11 cable from the U.S. Embassy in Moscow described "trainloads of repatriates" passing through Moscow and heading eastward, to unknown destinations. "Given Soviet attitude toward surrender, it is probable that prisoners are assumed guilty of desertion unless they can present convincing evidence of mitigating circumstances." The embassy believed that the "great bulk of repatriates" on the sealed trains were being assigned to "forced labor battalions" in Siberia or central Asia.

The compulsory repatriations horrified Secretary of War Henry Stimson. "First thing you know we will be responsible for a big killing by the Russians," he scrawled in one memo. A group of U.S. Army officers in Europe predicted "a wave of unfavorable public opinion" if they were forced to go ahead with the repatriation operation. The State Department legal adviser, Richard Flournoy, also objected strongly. He argued that the policy violated both the "spirit and intent" of the Geneva convention on the treatment of prisoners of war. "I find nothing in the Convention which either requires or justifies this Government in sending the unfortunate Soviet nationals in question to Russia, where they will almost certainly be liquidated," he wrote. Flournoy was, however, overruled by more-senior State Department officials who feared Soviet retaliation against American POWs, not just in Europe but also in Asia. Thousands of American prisoners held by the Japanese in Manchuria were likely to fall under the control of the Red Army once the Soviet Union went to war with Japan.

The tragedy of the POWs went back to the Yalta agreement that equated "United States citizens freed by forces operating under Soviet command" with "Soviet citizens freed by forces operating under United States command." In fact, the two groups were not analogous. The question of forcibly repatriating the American prisoners did not arise, as they were desperate to return home to the United States. Securing the return of these men was a top humanitarian priority for the U.S. government. This was not the case with the Russian prisoners, particularly those who had joined the Wehrmacht, whether voluntarily or against their will. While many were anxious to return to their families, others were terrified of the security police. Stalin wanted them back not for humanitarian reasons but to make an example of them. On May 11, less than a week after VE-day, he issued an order for the creation of ninety-three prison camps in Central Europe to process former Soviet POWs, sorting out the traitors from the cowards. In many cases, the NKVD simply took over camps that had originally been built by the Nazis to house Jews, political opponents, or other "degenerates."

Stalin understood very well the importance western governments attached to the return of their prisoners and used this as a bargaining chip. He played his hand with skill and cynicism. Allied protests about delays in fulfilling the Yalta agreement on POWs were invariably met with Kremlin counterprotests. Soviet officials complained about "unbearable" living conditions in Allied transit camps, mass cases of food and alcohol poisoning, and murders of Russian POWs. In the end, the Americans and the British felt obliged to go along with the Russian demands. Seven of the Fort Dix prisoners were reprieved after it was determined that they never had been Soviet citizens. The remainder were secretly shipped to Europe and transferred to Soviet control at the end of August after being put on suicide watch for two months. They were permitted mattresses but no bunks: bed parts could be used as "implements of self-destruction." Nothing was heard from them again. They joined an estimated 1.8 million former POWs assigned to the NKVD for special processing. This figure represented roughly a third of the total number of Soviet survivors of the German prison camp system. Around a million former prisoners were either executed immediately or sentenced to twenty-five-year terms in labor camps. Others received shorter sentences. Many committed suicide. Those who were reprieved and allowed home without being screened by the NKVD often found it impossible to find jobs: they were permanently stigmatized as "socially dangerous."

Stalin's motivation in insisting on the return of the despised POWs can be explained in part by realpolitik. He wanted to eliminate "undesirable witnesses against communism," meaning anyone who had experienced life outside the Soviet Union, and deter other potential "traitors." But he was also driven by an elemental thirst for revenge. According to his daughter, Svetlana, a "psychological metamorphosis" would come over him when he suspected that someone had somehow betrayed him or let down the cause. At this point, an "inner demon" would whisper, "I don't even know you any more." Years of friendship, even family intimacy, were subordinated to the demands of politics.

What Svetlana saw as Stalin's "cruel, implacable nature" was demonstrated by the way he treated his son Yakov, a thirty-three-year-old artillery lieutenant taken prisoner by the Germans at the beginning of the war. The *vozhd* immediately had his Jewish daughter-in-law thrown into jail, in accordance with Order No. 270. Asked about Yakov following his capture by the Nazis, he replied, "I have no son called Yakov." He refused a German offer to exchange Yakov for the German field marshal who surrendered at Stalingrad. He told intimates that he pitied his son but had no other choice. If he agreed to the German offer, "I'd no longer be 'Stalin.'"

Around the time of the Fort Dix incident, a British-American intelligence team captured the German dossier on Yakov, including the records of his internment at the Sachsenhausen prison camp. The documents showed that Yakov had been at the center of frequent fights between British and Russian POWs. A Russian cell mate testified that he was tormented by his father's refusal to exchange him for Field Marshal Friedrich Paulus.

On the evening of April 14, 1943, Yakov was observed picking his way between the trip wires that surrounded the concentration camp. When he reached the electrified fence, he called out to an SS guard, "Don't be a coward. Shoot, shoot." The guard fired a single bullet at his head. The son of the Russian despot seized the high-tension wire at precisely the same moment.

State Department officials debated whether to show Stalin the documents about Yakov but decided that they were too "unpleasant," and possibly "embarrassing," to share. In fact, the *vozhd* gained a measure of satisfaction from the news of his son's suicide, when the story eventually became public. By choosing to die, the "traitor to the Motherland" had finally lived up to his father's expectations.

Part Three

A Peace
That Is No Peace

—George Orwell

JULY–AUGUST 1945

16

Berlin

July 4

It's got to look democratic," Walter Ulbricht instructed his followers in his thick Saxon accent. "But we must have everything in our control."

They called themselves the Ulbricht Group, a small band of German Communists who had fled to Russia after the rise of Hitler. They spent the war years in Moscow, interrogating Wehrmacht prisoners and making propaganda broadcasts. After more than a decade outside the country, they were now back in Berlin, equipped with impressive-looking Red Army passes and the ration cards of Russian majors. Their mission was to establish a new German government along lines approved by Stalin. For the moment, they had been instructed to keep in the background. "Representatives of the bourgeoisie" with proven "anti-Fascist" credentials would be appointed to the most visible posts in the new city administration, along with Social Democrats persecuted by the Nazis before the war. But the key positions in each district, including those in charge of police and personnel matters, must be held by "completely reliable comrades." In private conversations, Russian officers made clear they regarded the Ulbricht Group as the future rulers of Germany.

A semblance of normality had returned to Berlin two months after its capture by the Red Army. The capital was still littered with burned-out military vehicles and huge piles of rubble, but life was visible in the ruins. Apartment buildings that seemed totally destroyed were illuminated by the dim glow of electric bulbs. Washing lines were strung across the debris. Primitive shops were springing up along the banks of the river Spree despite "the sour smell of death and corruption" spilling out of the "open sewer." There were outsize Cyrillic street signs for the benefit of the Soviet occupation forces. Female Russian soldiers dressed like Communist drum majorettes in boots and leather belts stood at the main intersections directing the meager traffic with red and yellow flags. A red banner proclaiming "Hail to the Soviet Conquerors of Berlin" fluttered from the top of the Brandenburg Gate. Billboards were emblazoned with quotes from Stalin's speeches, including one that had become a reassuring propaganda message: "Hitlers come and go, but the German nation and the German state remains." Giant portraits of Stalin, Truman, and Churchill had been erected in the Tiergarten where Hitler had celebrated his fiftieth birthday in 1939 in front of 2 million adoring Berliners.

The terror of the early days of the occupation, when drunken Red Army men roamed the city raping and killing, had subsided. "The pistol stopped being the language of love," in the phrase of the infantryman Grigory Pomerants: Russian soldiers now used rationed food and clothing to gain the affections of German women. They were no longer driven primarily by thoughts of revenge though looting remained a problem. An employee of the Swiss legation reported in early July that it was "still entirely unsafe to wear a watch on the streets of the Russian sector." Bicycles were another prized possession subject to seizure at any time.

Stalin knew that Ulbricht and his followers had no hope of winning a free election. "Communism on a German is like a saddle on a cow," he scoffed. His political strategy in Germany was similar to the strategy he was pursuing elsewhere in eastern Europe, to build up a coalition of "progressive" parties, with the Communists in key positions. On June 10, the Soviet occupation authorities issued Order No. 2 authorizing the resumption of political activity in the Russian sector of Germany under carefully controlled conditions. Stalin hoped to tap into the popularity of the Social Democrats, who had long claimed the strongest following in Berlin. At the appropriate time, the Social Democrats would be forced to merge with the Communists to form a single "workers' party," following the precedent set in Bulgaria, where the Communists were absorbing the Agrarians. Stalin ordered the Ulbricht Group to adopt a political program designed to appeal to the maximum number of voters. Marx and Engels were banished from the Communist Party charter, together with any mention of socialism. The party program called for "complete and unrestricted development of free commerce and private enterprise on the basis of private property."

Ideological lapses were overlooked, as long as party members did what they were told. Ulbricht, like Stalin, regarded obedience as the supreme virtue. The son of a tailor who had organized assassinations of Berlin police officers during the final months of the Weimar Republic, he was held in low regard by Soviet leaders. Beria considered him a "complete imbecile" and "a scoundrel capable of killing his father and mother," which was a little rich coming from the depraved secret police chief. Ulbricht had spent his Moscow years intriguing and informing on his fellow exiles. This did not trouble Stalin in the least. Informed that Ulbricht's only talent was "writing denunciations," the *vozhd* had only one question: "Does he write without making mistakes?" Whatever his failings, the narrow-minded Ulbricht could be trusted to follow orders. As a Comintern operative, he had loyally implemented every twist and turn in Kremlin policy, from the persecution of anti-Stalinist Republicans in the Spanish Civil War to the promotion of the Molotov-Ribbentrop Pact in 1939. He had great organizational ability and an exceptional capacity for hard work.

One of Ulbricht's top priorities after returning to Berlin in May 1945 was to stifle political initiatives from below. Anti-Fascist committees had sprung up spontaneously in many German cities following the defeat of Hitler. Many of the committees were led by Communists who had gone underground during the Nazi years or been liberated from concentration camps. Stalin, who had nothing but disdain for independent activists running around with red armbands, instructed Ulbricht to clamp down. He fulfilled the task with his usual zeal, describing the committees as "a comic show."

"They are to be dissolved, and at once," he told his subordinates. "Provisional or not, the whole show must be broken up."

To control the population, the Ulbricht Group revived a much-hated Nazi institution, known as the *Blockleiter,* or "block leader," extending it down to the level of individual "house leaders." The *Blockleiters* were responsible for organizing the removal of rubbish, the administration of ration cards, and the enforcement of health regulations. But they also functioned as a network of "snoopers, strong-arm men and petty tyrants," in the words of an American officer. The *Blockleiter* system permitted the Russians to retain a grip on the western sectors of Berlin following their transfer to the United States and Britain.

There was other business to complete before the Americans and British moved in. "Take everything out of Western Berlin," ordered a Red Army reparations officer, Vladimir Yurasov. "All of it! What you can't take, destroy. Only leave nothing for the allies: no machine, not even a single bed; not even a chamber pot." The Americans estimated that the Russians hauled away 80 percent of the industrial machinery in their sector. "They had dismantled the refrigeration plant at the abattoir, torn stoves and pipes out of restaurant kitchens, stripped machinery from mills and factories and were completing the theft of the American Singer Sewing Machine plant when we arrived," complained an American occupation official. Much of the S-Bahn overground rail network and rolling stock had been similarly disassembled, along with one line of the Berlin–Potsdam railway and most of the city's central telephone exchanges. Thousands of horses and cattle had been driven away to the Russian sector.

The Russians could justifiably claim some positive accomplishments during the early occupation of Berlin. They had cleaned up the city, restored water, electricity, and other basic services, and established a civil government. Newspapers were back on the streets. The opera house had reopened, along with cinemas and sports halls. These achievements were outweighed, however, in the minds of most Germans by personal experiences of Soviet brutality. A more humane occupation policy might have succeeded in winning over the bulk of the defeated population. Berliners blamed the western Allies, not Russia, for the air raids that had reduced their city to rubble long before the arrival of the Red Army. "The Russians were our enemy, but at least they did not bomb us" was a frequently expressed opinion. But the opportunity to build goodwill at the expense of the western Allies was squandered in the initial orgy of raping and looting. When it came to public relations, the Red Army was its own worst enemy.

By the end of June, a Soviet intelligence report acknowledged the obvious. "Apart from a few genuine anti-Fascists, the entire population is unhappy with the presence of the Red Army on German soil, and hope and pray for the arrival of the Americans or English." That day was fast approaching.

The first advance unit of the U.S. Army set out for Berlin at daybreak on June 17. It was led by Colonel Frank Howley, a former advertising man from Philadelphia who had been selected to head the American military government in the German capital. An excitable Irishman, Howley had arrived in Germany as an evangelist for the "Anglo-Saxon judicial creed" and the American way of life. He thought of Russians as "big, jolly, balalaika-playing fellows, who drank prodigious quantities of vodka and liked to wrestle in the drawing room." Full of confidence in his own abilities and the power of the United States, he did not expect much trouble from such clumsy oafs. Problems were sure to arise, but they would be resolved in the spirit of Allied friendship.

The Stars and Stripes fluttered from the right fender of Howley's black limousine as he drove across the Elbe River on a pontoon bridge decorated with huge pictures of Lenin and Stalin and a sign that read "Welcome to the Motherland." The colonel had decided to make his grand entrance into the German capital in a Horch roadster, "the biggest and best car in Germany," commandeered from a former Nazi leader. He was supported by a reconnaissance force of some five hundred officers and men in one hundred twenty military vehicles, including armored personnel carriers bristling with machine guns. The impressive-looking convoy was halted barely a mile into the Russian zone by "a red and white pole leaning across the road." Howley listened impatiently as his Red Army escort explained that there were a few "formalities" to observe. After several rounds of drinks and toasts, the Russians claimed that "the Berlin agreement" limited the American contingent to "37 officers, 50 vehicles and 175 men." No heavy weapons were permitted. Howley had never heard of this agreement but was unable to persuade his hosts to back down. It took a full six hours to rearrange baggage and send the unauthorized vehicles back to the American-occupied zone.

When the convoy eventually got back on the road in midafternoon, the Americans were startled by the sight of "gypsy-like detachments of Soviet troops guarding livestock in the fields." As they approached Berlin, the American jeeps and trucks were held up by "horse-drawn convoys of Asiatic wagons looking like boats on wheels." Howley was reminded of the faded photographs of U.S. Army supply trains during the Civil War. "They were the poorest troops I have ever seen," he later recalled. "The men wore shabby cotton, a strong contrast to the smart uniforms of my convoy. And were they dirty! A third had distinctly Mongolian features." Contrary to Howley's expectations, the Americans were not permitted into Berlin. Instead they were directed toward a place called Babelsberg, about ten miles from the city center, near the imperial town of Potsdam. Before the war, Babelsberg had been the center of the German movie industry, a Prussian version of Hollywood.

Howley had come to Berlin expecting to make logistical arrangements for the American occupation of the city. His new mission, he learned with disgust, was to fix up villas that would be used to accommodate delegates attending the forthcoming conference of the Big Three, due to open in Potsdam in the middle of July. The Babelsberg compound was surrounded by armed NKVD soldiers with orders to let no one pass. Howley and his men were "virtual prisoners." Their frustration only intensified when the U.S. Army issued a long list of rules on fraternizing with Russians. It consisted mainly of prohibitions:

- Never have a buffet dinner when entertaining Russians. (The food would disappear in the first few minutes.)
- Never offer a Russian a drink without food.
- Never argue politics with a Russian and never criticize his government.
- Don't be too inquisitive.
- Don't ask about Russia fighting Japan.
- Try in every way to get along amicably with the Russians. They are our allies.

"Should we genuflect before asking permission to speak to a Russian?" Howley asked sarcastically.

A week after his arrival in Babelsberg, Howley was permitted to make a quick tour of Berlin on the pretext of visiting Tempelhof Airport. Although he was accustomed to death and destruction, he was shocked by what he found. The city resembled the landscape for an apocalyptic movie, with shards of bombed-out buildings sticking out in unlikely directions. Berliners seemed "licked physically and mentally." Except for the main thoroughfares, "streets were filled with rubble and in many cases, not discernible at all." Howley found it difficult to understand why the United States was still insisting on a share of the ruined city. It would be better to leave Berlin to the Russians and retain the rich agricultural lands of Saxony and Thuringia that had been seized by the Americans in the final weeks of the war, even though they were part of the Soviet-designated zone.

"Berlin is a shambles," the colonel told his men. "It's not worth an acre of good land with cattle on it. I think the smart thing is to keep what we've got and let the Russians keep what they've got."

His superiors had other ideas. From Truman down, the leaders of the United States still had an optimistic vision of East-West cooperation after the war. The new president vetoed a suggestion from Churchill to use the lands west of the Elbe as a bargaining chip with Stalin. The Englishman was alarmed by the projection of Soviet power into "the heart of Western Europe and the descent of an iron curtain between us and everything to the eastward." He wanted to link the American retreat, "if it has to be made," to "the settlement of many great things which would be the true foundation of world peace." Truman took the view that territorial agreements should be respected by all sides. He feared that Churchill's approach would be "highly disadvantageous to our relations with the Soviets." On June 29, senior U.S. generals met with Marshal Zhukov to make the final arrangements for the American move into Berlin and the simultaneous evacuation of Saxony and Thuringia.

The lines of the occupation zones in Germany and Berlin had been drawn back in 1943, at a time when the Red Army was making rapid advances and the much-rumored second front existed only on paper. The job of working out postwar arrangements had been assigned to an obscure bureaucratic body called the European Advisory Commission, which met in secret in London. The Roosevelt administration showed little interest in the work of the commission, and the British ended up taking the lead. The Foreign Office proposed a united Germany divided, for administrative purposes, into British, American, and Russian zones. To secure Stalin's cooperation, the British planners offered the Russians 40 percent of German territory, 36 percent of the population, and 33 percent of the productive resources. Berlin was part of the Soviet zone, as it was in the eastern part of the country, but it would be occupied jointly by all three powers. The planners used the old German administrative lines to divide the city, awarding eight boroughs to the Russians and six each to the Americans and British. (The British later gave two of their boroughs to the French.) The Brandenburg Gate and the Unter den Linden fell just inside the Russian sector.

The American side was represented at the June 29 meeting at Zhukov's Karlshorst headquarters by General Lucius Clay. A chain-smoking workaholic who drank twenty cups of coffee a day, Clay was Eisenhower's point man for the occupation of Germany. He had made his reputation as a problem solver. He came highly recommended by Jimmy Byrnes, who remarked that his former subordinate in the Office of War Mobilization could learn how to run "General Motors or US Steel" in six months. Clay quickly reached agreement with Zhukov on the logistics of moving thirty thousand troops from the 2nd Armored Division (motto: "Hell on Wheels") to Berlin. The two commanders negotiated a temporary arrangement that permitted British and American troops to use the main Halle–Berlin highway, a railway line, and two air corridors.

Little thought was given to the issue of permanent access to the western sectors of Berlin. It seemed a somewhat academic point. The three wartime Allies intended to run the city together through a joint body, to be known as the Kommandatura. Such matters would surely be resolved with goodwill on both sides. Clay did not want to put anything in writing that might jeopardize the principle of unrestricted access that he considered implicit in the 1943 agreement. He did not feel he had the authority to link the access route question to the American withdrawal from a large swath of eastern Germany. It was an oversight that would haunt the western Allies for decades to come.

The main body of U.S. troops rolled up the autobahn from Halle on July 1 as the Red Army moved in the opposite direction. "The high road to Bedlam," as Howley called it, became a massive tangle of tanks, trucks, carts, and assorted military vehicles. Some of the Russians were welcoming, wanting only to exchange vodka toasts with their American allies. Others "behaved like little commissars." Howley was delighted to see an American general push "one particularly obstreperous Red Army officer" into a ditch after his men were halted at a Russian roadblock. A heavy rain began to fall as the Americans reached Berlin. Confined to Babelsberg, Howley had been unable to arrange quarters for the occupying troops, so they were forced to camp out in the Grunewald in pup tents, under the forest's dripping trees. "It was undoubtedly the most unimpressive entry in history to the capital of a defeated enemy nation by the armed forces of a great conquering power," an aide later recalled. "Right then and there in the feelings of the US forces to a man, there was instilled a feeling of resentment against the Russians that was really never to disappear."

A refugee crisis of biblical proportions awaited the newly arrived American and British troops. Berlin was awash with multitudes of lost souls, forced out of their homes in the final weeks of the war, drifting pointlessly from one place to another. "The wanderers" could be seen at every street corner, resting their heads on pathetic bundles of possessions wrapped in sackcloth. Whether it was cold or hot, they were often dressed in ragged overcoats they would otherwise have to carry. Many bore a haunted look, their bulging eyes expressing bewilderment and resignation. Others had outsize heads and distended limbs, signs that they were on the verge of starvation after traipsing hundreds of miles from the burning towns and villages of Silesia and the Sudetenland. There were many orphans, prematurely aged from the horrors they had experienced. Mingled with the refugees were crowds of "displaced persons," Russian, Polish, French, and Belgian slave laborers who had been forced to serve the Reich during the war and were now trying to make their way home.

The refugee tragedy was most visible in the bombed-out railway stations of Berlin, which had become home to seething masses of desperate, uprooted people. Every day, trainloads of cattle cars arrived from the east, packed with "blind mutilated soldiers, homeless boys, starving verminous mothers, infants." Families squatted on the roofs of the cattle cars. Wrinkled old men and women in kerchiefs clung precariously to the sides, sometimes falling off from exhaustion. Every day Red Cross workers removed dozens of corpses from the trains, covering their noses against the stench of death. For Robert Murphy, the U.S. political advisor for Germany, the scenes at the railway stations evoked images of Dachau and Buchenwald. "Here is retribution on a large scale," he wrote the State Department, "but practiced not on the *Parteibonzen* [Nazi Party activists], but on women and children, the poor, the infirm." There was no timetable for the trains, which ran at halting intervals as the Russians had removed long stretches of track. It could take up to a week to make the two-hundred-fifty-mile trip from Danzig to Berlin.

The wanderers came in waves, breaking across the overcrowded city in a rolling tide of misery. The first wave had fled in terror in advance of the Red Army, which swept through East Prussia and Pomerania in late 1944 and early 1945. The second wave came from the Sudetenland at the end of the war as Czechs took their revenge against a minority that had enthusiastically greeted Hitler in 1938. A final wave came from Poland as the new, Communist-led government took over German-inhabited Silesia in exchange for territory ceded to the Soviet Union in the East. By the time the flights and expulsions were over, at least 12 million Germans had been uprooted from their homes. Some 2 million perished during the exodus, from disease and hunger and forced death marches. The successive waves of ethnic cleansing permanently changed the map of Europe. An area of forty-four thousand square miles, nearly the size of England, had been lopped off the Germany that Hitler inherited in January 1933.

Redrawing ethnic lines was one of Stalin's specialties, but the Czechs and the Poles and the Yugoslavs needed little encouragement when it came to redressing the wrongs of the war. Sensing an opportunity to resolve centuries-old ethnic disputes once and for all, they set about the task of expelling Germans with a ferocity that startled even their Russian patrons. The persecuted became the persecutors almost overnight.

In Czechoslovakia, the government simply took over anti-Jewish regulations drawn up by the Nazis and applied them to Sudetenland Germans. The Germans were ordered to wear patches of cloth that bore the letter *N* (for *Niemiec*, the Czech for "German") on their left breast. Anyone who had been affiliated with Nazi organizations was required to wear the sign on their backs as well. Germans were only permitted to visit shops in the final hour before closing, after Czechs had been served. They were forbidden to ride public transport, visit parks, or leave their homes after 8:00 p.m. Germans passing a Russian or Czechoslovak officer on the street were instructed to "remove their hats or caps and pass by at an appropriate distance." The Nazi internment camp at Theresienstadt, used to process Jews en route to Auschwitz, became a camp for Germans awaiting deportation. There was little attempt to distinguish "bad Germans" from "good Germans." In the eyes of the government of Edvard Beneš, they were all guilty. The Catholic Church adopted a similar position. The canon of Vysehrad, Monsignor Bohumil Stasek, was exultant. "Once in a thousand years the time has come to settle accounts with the Germans, who are evil and to whom the commandment to 'love thy neighbor' therefore does not apply."

Like the Jews before them, the Germans were given as little as fifteen minutes to prepare for their deportation. They had to surrender the keys of their houses and leave most of their valuables behind. Anybody who displayed any signs of hesitation was brutally beaten, often killed. An American academic study found that "Germans were hung by their heels from trees, doused in petrol, and set on fire. In outright pogroms, Czech militia rampaged through towns and villages, shooting Germans at will." The entire German population of Brno was ordered to assemble in the street on the night of May 30, 1945. The able-bodied men had already been expelled, leaving behind some thirty thousand women and children, sick and elderly. Flanked by armed guards, the Germans were herded, like cattle, toward the Austrian border, thirty-five miles away. Anyone who failed to keep up was pushed into a ditch to die. Around seventeen hundred people failed to survive the death march.

Although Stalin had given the go-ahead for the expulsions, the NKVD complained on July 4 that the deportations were taking place in "a disorganized manner without advance warning to our commanders." In a message to Beria from Berlin, General Serov reported that five thousand Germans were arriving from Czechoslovakia every day, "the majority of them women, old men, and children." He noted that many deportees chose to "commit suicide by cutting their wrists." A Soviet officer had counted "seventy-one corpses with slit wrists" in one incident alone. In their despair, Germans ended up looking to the Red Army for protection against the even more brutal Czechs.

Western governments were uncertain how to react to the mass expulsions of Germans from eastern Europe. Both Roosevelt and Churchill had endorsed the principle of large-scale population exchanges to create ethnically homogeneous states, along the lines of the Greek-Turkish transfers that had followed the dissolution of the Ottoman Empire. In a House of Commons speech in December 1944, Churchill said that expulsions were preferable to a "mixture of populations" as in Alsace-Lorraine, which had caused "endless trouble" between French and Germans. "A clean sweep will be made," he predicted. "I am not alarmed at the prospect of the disentanglement of population, nor am I alarmed by these large transferences, which are more possible than they were before through modern conditions." Western officials worried that they would lose the battle for public opinion in countries like Czechoslovakia and Poland if they opposed the expulsions, which had the support of ordinary Czechs and Poles.

On the other hand, the manner in which the expulsions were carried out offended the consciences of many in the West. Harrowing photographs of starving German refugees began appearing in newspapers and magazines in the summer of 1945, prompting British and American soul-searching. A U.S. military intelligence officer who succeeded in traveling behind what Churchill was already calling the iron curtain sent back wrenching accounts of the brutal treatment of Sudetenland Germans. "The Czech treatment of the Germans is very similar to the German treatment of the Jews," wrote Lieutenant John Backer, in a widely circulated report. "*Two wrongs do not make a right.* Injustices and economic instability in one of the sore spots of Europe may lay the groundwork for dangerous political developments." The bottom line was that western governments accepted the inevitability of massive ethnic cleansing, but wanted it to take place in a civilized and orderly manner.

None of this was any comfort to the millions of refugees pouring into Berlin and other German cities. They were harassed and robbed at every stage of their journey. An American general in Berlin noted that the refugees were able to "carry very little with them and naturally burden themselves with only the articles which they consider most valuable. These people throng in the railroad stations and naturally are of considerable interest to looters." By chance, most of the big Berlin railroad stations were in the American sector, close to the border with the Russian sector. The wanderers were easy prey for any thug with a gun.

Russian and American commanders had originally set July 4 as the date for the U.S. Army to assume responsibility for its sector of Berlin. A hitch arose at the last minute when Zhukov announced that the transfer of authority would have to await the formation of the Kommandatura, the unified Allied command. Infuriated, the Americans decided to simply take over the city halls in their six boroughs, as planned. "We move in at daybreak and set up Military Government," Howley told his subordinates. "The Russians don't get up until noon."

A confrontation quickly ensued. Howley's men put up posters announcing the formation of an American military government; Zhukov's men tore them down. When a Red Army colonel tried to force his way into a bank in the American sector to collect some "missing property," he found tanks from the 2nd Armored Division blocking his way. Berliners gloated: they had long predicted a falling-out between the occupiers. For a few days there were "two military governments in the sector—American and Russian." Howley gained a small victory when the Russians stopped pulling down American posters. He congratulated himself on mastering the art of the "*fait accompli,* the favorite Russian technique," but was soon swept up in bigger, more important battles.

On July 7, Zhukov summoned American and British commanders to a meeting in his Karlshorst headquarters, where he had accepted the German surrender just two months before. The westerners thought they had been invited for a social event, but the marshal had other matters on his mind. Flanked by his economic experts, he announced that food reserves were running critically low. Flour and sugar supplies would be depleted in five days, cereals in six days, meat in a week. Coal stocks were also almost exhausted. When existing supplies ran out, each occupying army would be responsible for meeting the food and energy needs of its own sector.

"The difficult food problem must be solved immediately," Zhukov warned. "Otherwise, people will starve."

The Americans and the British were stunned by the unexpected Russian ultimatum. They had assumed that Berlin would continue to import food from the rich farmlands to the east, in Pomerania, which were under the control of the Red Army. Coal had traditionally come from the eastern German province of Silesia. Without warning, and without making any preparations, the western Allies found themselves responsible for supplying nearly 2 million Berliners with food and fuel. They would have to scrounge twenty-one thousand tons of food a month from western Europe—where supplies were already critically low—and transport it hundreds of miles across Soviet-controlled territory over bombed-out bridges and torn-up railroads. To make matters worse, they had just given up the rich agricultural lands west of the Elbe, another obvious source of food for the capital. It suddenly dawned on the Americans that they faced "an almost impossible supply problem."

The senior American representative at the meeting was General Clay, the U.S. Army's logistical wizard. He told Zhukov that there were food shortages in the American zone as well. "There are difficulties of transport and organization. Even if we were willing to bring in food and coal, it would be difficult, because there is no big bridge across the Elbe."

The Russians were unmoved. Zhukov explained that the huge demographic changes wrought by the war made it impossible for Berlin to rely on its traditional suppliers. Pomerania and Silesia were now part of Poland. The Germans who used to live in these provinces had all "run away" and had flooded into the Soviet zone, along with 4 million Soviet citizens repatriated from the west. There was no food surplus. The Russians had found a way to hold the population of west Berlin hostage at virtually any time by delaying deliveries of food and fuel.

"Our governments agreed that Germany must feed itself," Clay's political adviser, Robert Murphy, protested feebly. "The country must be treated as a single unit." As far as the Americans were concerned, Silesia still belonged to the Soviet occupation zone of Germany.

It was left to Zhukov to point out the harsh political reality. "Germany does not exist. Germans must be fed through the efforts of the Allied governments." Having outlined the dire food situation, he invited the Allied generals to "tea." "Of course, it wasn't tea at all that Zhukov provided," Howley commented sourly, "just mountains of caviar and rivers of vodka, beer, and other drinks the Russians call tea because they flow around four or five o'clock."

The American problems were exacerbated by still-secret policy instructions on the postwar treatment of Germany. A Pentagon document known as JCS 1067 directed the U.S. occupation forces to "take no steps" toward the economic rehabilitation of the country. Germany was to be treated as "a defeated nation" that must never again become "a threat to the peace of the world." This meant strict controls on heavy industry and the development of a self-sufficient, predominantly pastoral, economy. Quotas were established for the production of iron, steel, chemicals, machine tools, and automobiles. Fraternization between Americans and Germans was banned. Former Nazi Party members were excluded from employment not only as executives but also as skilled workers. The denazification process made it difficult to find qualified workers to run the railways, forcing the Americans to place incompetent people in key positions.

The purpose of the restrictions was to make a military revival impossible, but the practical effect was to stifle the most productive sectors of the German economy. The cost of importing sufficient food to prevent mass starvation in Berlin and other German cities fell on the American taxpayer. Clay and his advisers understood very quickly that JCS 1067 was tying their hands, but they could not disobey a directive that had been endorsed by the president. "This thing was assembled by economic idiots," complained Lewis Douglas, Clay's top economic expert. "It makes no sense to forbid the most skilled workers in Europe from producing as much as they can for a continent which is desperately short of everything!" Needless to say, none of the other Allies felt constrained by the prohibitions enshrined in the Pentagon directive. In the Russian sector, former Nazis were already flocking to join the newly legalized Communist Party. The Russians were busy cultivating the Germans that the Americans had been directed to shun.

The contrast between the intentions of the political leaders and diplomats back in Washington and the ground-level reality in conquered Berlin was becoming starker by the day. The statesmen had decreed that there was to be a single governing structure for Germany, to be known as the Allied Control Council, to include representatives of the United States, the Soviet Union, Britain, and France. Decisions would be made by consensus. The same political and economic policies would be applied to all four occupation zones. It did not take long for everyone to discover that there was no unanimity on fundamental questions of how the German economy should be organized and how the country should be governed.

The ruins of Berlin had become a petri dish for one of the most extraordinary social experiments ever conceived—merging American notions of the free market with the Russian philosophy of a centrally directed, command economy. The dispute over food supplies provided a glimpse of the problems ahead. As the *Economist* reported on July 14, "The chances that the Allies will be willing and able, between them, to evolve a satisfactory and workable policy for Germany were never very large. And they are visibly shrinking." Senior generals had to do everything in their power to ensure the success of a joint occupation, even as their subordinates joined western reporters in expressing grave doubts.

Clay glared at Howley when he dared suggest that there were many questions on which Americans and Russians would never agree.

"You are entirely wrong," the American proconsul said coldly. "I have just come from Washington, and it certainly is the intention of our government to administer Berlin on a unanimous basis."

The aftershocks of a geopolitical earthquake were being felt from Warsaw to Vienna, from Budapest to Bucharest. It was as if two tectonic plates—representing two competing ideologies—had collided, sending gigantic tremors across a war-torn continent. Western observers had difficulty following events in many of the Soviet-controlled territories as they were barred from traveling freely in countries like Poland and Hungary. Berlin, by contrast, had become an open city with the arrival of tens of thousands of American and British troops and civilian administrators. It was here that the clash between the rival political and economic systems was sharpest and most obvious, revealed in a multitude of everyday encounters between the different occupation armies.

"Russians are still occupying the U.S. Zone and are systematically looting everything like a horde of locusts," reported an American officer in mid-July, two months after VE-day. It was difficult to go anywhere in Berlin and not be confronted with signs of Russian vandalism and gratuitous violence. Robert Murphy moved into a new house in Dahlem that previously had been occupied by Russian officers. According to the aged housekeeper, the former residents had drunk their way through a magnificent wine cellar of two thousand bottles. They amused themselves "by shooting up the place every night. Ceilings, walls and family portraits were full of holes. The Russians especially enjoyed shooting at the crystal chandeliers." The housekeeper claimed that the officers had found a badly wounded German soldier lying on a divan the night they arrived, "and promptly shot him." Even the office building that served as American headquarters bore signs that the Red Army had got there first. The furniture included a set of beautiful leather-upholstered chairs with gaping holes in the seats and backs. It turned out that Russian soldiers had cut swaths of upholstery from each of the chairs to make boots.

The British were as offended as the Americans by Russian behavior. Richard Brett-Smith was taken aback by the swift deterioration in relations between the Allies. "Disappointment, dismay, disillusionment, dislike, bitterness, and even positive hatred were bred in a few weeks between the great majority of both sides," the army officer wrote later. "Most British soldiers came to Berlin with an open mind about the Russians, or if not an open mind one that had been prejudiced *in their favor* by the reiterative panegyrics of the popular press. Not one British soldier whom I knew left Berlin with any feeling warmer than distrust for the Russians. Almost all were far more rabid about them." According to Goronwy Rees, an intelligence officer who had flirted with Marxist ideas in his youth, a visit to Germany was a sure antidote for "any possible sympathy with anything that savoured of communism." Rees ended up a six-day tour of the British zone in July 1945 by concluding that "the war between the Russians and the democracies is approaching, and indeed has already begun."

Like Truman, Stalin had publicly embraced the idea of a united Germany governed by a joint Allied occupation authority. He had abandoned an earlier proposal, advanced at Yalta five months previously, to dismember the Reich. He hoped that the defeated country would become a "democratic, anti-Fascist" state ruled by a coalition of left-wing parties dominated by the Communists and their Social Democrat allies. As long as there was any possibility of extracting large-scale reparations from the Germans—a figure of $10 billion had been mentioned at Yalta—Stalin had every incentive to insist on the principle of a single Germany. The Soviet dictator stressed the importance of "the unity of Germany" as late as February 1946. "Unity is correct," he told Ulbricht.

On the other hand, Stalin was also a supreme realist. Whatever else happened, he was determined to maintain personal control over territories conquered by the Red Army. While it was not his preferred outcome, there was a very real possibility, even probability, that the western and eastern sectors of Germany would drift apart. Stalin hinted as much during a meeting with Ulbricht and other German Communists in June 1945.

"There will be two Germanies," he predicted, "notwithstanding the unity between the allies."

17

Terminal

July 16

As was his custom, Harry Truman woke early on the morning of Monday, July 16, on his ninety-sixth day as president. He found himself in a narrow bed in a strange house by the side of a lake. There was no netting on the windows and swarms of mosquitoes had been bothering him for much of the night. He shared a bathroom with Admiral Leahy, his chief of staff, whose bedroom was down the corridor. The second-floor Presidential Suite included a living room, complete with grand piano, a breakfast room, and a large office from which he could stroll out onto the sundeck overlooking the lake. The entire three-story house was furnished in expensive but hideous taste. Nothing seemed to match. Art deco armchairs had been placed arbitrarily alongside heavy baroque furniture. The multicolored rugs clashed with the floral wallpaper, which had nothing in common with the dark velvet drapes. "French or Chippendale table and chairs—maybe a mixture of both" had been set up in the downstairs dining room next to "a two ton German sideboard." Truman decided that the whole place was an interior decorator's "nightmare." But apart from the mosquitoes, it was "comfortable enough all round."

He got out of bed at 6:30 a.m. and ate breakfast. Then he explored his surroundings, noting with disapproval that the "Berlin White House" was a "dirty yellow and red." He detected elements of a French château, but any semblance of a uniform architectural style had been "ruined by German endeavor to cover up the French. They erected a couple of tombstone chimneys on either side of the porch facing the lake so they would cover up the beautiful château roof and tower." The overall effect reminded Truman of the Kansas City railway station. "Made the place look like hell but purely German." The redeeming feature was a beautifully secluded garden, with fir trees and weeping willows, stretching down to a narrow lake, Griebnitzsee. The Stars and Stripes fluttered from the top of a tall flagstaff next to the water, which bent around the corner to the right. A thick pine forest covered the opposite bank of the lake, about a hundred yards away, creating a wonderfully peaceful vista.

The U.S. Army had erected eighteen guard posts around the house, manned by military policemen with gleaming white belts and leggings. The lakefront alone was protected by five military posts and a motorboat patrol. Truman strolled out through the front gate of 2 Kaiserstrasse and walked briskly down the street, trailed by his Secret Service detail. The street was lined with attractive two-story and three-story villas, built in the late nineteenth century for wealthy industrialists and aristocrats. Babelsberg had survived the war miraculously unscathed, making it the perfect place to accommodate the political leaders, diplomats, and generals invited to the Big Three conference in nearby Potsdam. The previous month, the Russians had made more than a hundred homes available to the Americans, after giving the previous owners thirty minutes to clear out. A huge military machine existed to cater to the everyday needs of the new residents, from overnight dry-cleaning and shoe polishing to barbers and pedicurists and twice-daily postal service.

Back from his morning walk, the president waited in his office for his first meeting with Winston Churchill. The prime minister was staying six hundred yards down the road, in a pink, Tuscan-style villa overlooking the lake. He appeared at the gates of 2 Kaiserstrasse at 11:00 a.m. in a crumpled white tropical suit, sprinkling cigar ash. Truman was amused to hear that this was the earliest the legendary warlord had risen from his bed in ten years. He recorded his first impressions of Churchill in his diary later that day:

> We had a most pleasant conversation. He is a most charming and very clever person—meaning clever in the English not the Kentucky sense. He gave me a lot of hooey about how great my country is and how he

loved Roosevelt and he intended to love me etc. etc. Well. I gave him as cordial a reception as I could—being naturally (I hope) a polite and agreeable person. I am sure we can get along if he doesn't give me too much soft soap.

Churchill brushed aside Truman's attempts to discuss an agenda for the conference, saying, "I don't need one." True to form, he believed that he could make things up as he went along. He had spent the past week on a painting holiday in southern France, refusing to look at his briefing books and the endless telegrams from London. "I'm very depressed," he told his doctor. "I don't want to do anything. I have no energy. I wonder if it will come back." His sour mood stemmed in part from worry about the outcome of the parliamentary elections in Britain, which would determine his own future as prime minister. The poll had been held on July 5. It would be another three weeks before the results were announced, because of logistical complications counting the votes of soldiers stationed in Europe. Most observers were predicting a Conservative victory, but Churchill was unsure. "I will be half a man until the result of the poll," he said. "I hear the women are for me, but the men have turned against me." His wife reminded him that he had bitterly opposed votes for women as Home Secretary during the suffragette movement. "Quite true," he conceded morosely.

As Churchill walked back to his residence, he told his daughter that he "liked the president immensely" and was sure they could work together. He was impressed with Truman's "gay, precise, sparkling manner, and obvious power of decision." Mary "nearly wept for joy and thankfulness." Her father had recovered from his latest encounter with the "Black Dog." He was "relieved and confident" once again.

Since Stalin's whereabouts were still mysterious, both leaders used the afternoon to do some sightseeing. Truman left Babelsberg in an open Lincoln at 3:40 p.m. He was preceded by a two-star general with a couple of Secret Service men in a closed car, in order "to fool 'em if they wanted to do any target practice of consequence on the Pres." The fresh breezes provided some relief from a stifling hot day. Assembled along the autobahn were the tanks and men of the 2nd Armored Division which had stormed into western Czechoslovakia with Patton. Truman and his top aides piled into a truck that reminded the president of "a hoodlum wagon minus the top." It took them twenty-two minutes to ride slowly past the twelve hundred Sherman tanks and half-tracks, next to the woods of the Grunewald.

General Eisenhower and Marshal Zhukov watch a ceremonial flyover during Zhukov's visit to Allied military headquarters in Frankfurt on June 10, 1945.

U.S. Army officers inspect a Nazi "uranium machine" in Haigerloch, Germany, discovered by the Alsos Mission.

A Russian officer enjoys black-market treats at the Femina nightclub in Berlin, July 1945.

A favorite spot for black-market activity in Berlin was the corner in front of the Reichstag. It became a gathering point for Red Army soldiers buying watches and cigarettes from American GIs, and German civilians selling clothing and cameras.

Joseph Davies, former U.S. ambassador to Moscow and Truman's special envoy to Churchill. Davies was awarded the Order of Lenin in May 1945 for his contribution to "friendly Soviet-American relations."

Byrnes (left) and Harriman at the Potsdam conference, with Bohlen in background smoking a cigarette.

Churchill, Truman and Stalin pose for a formal photograph at the Potsdam conference. Churchill has moved his chair to be closer to his American ally.

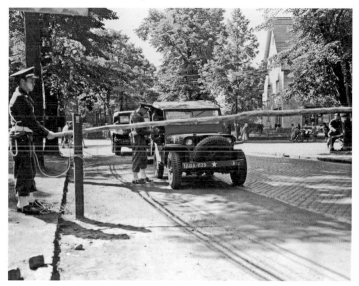

U.S. soldiers man the checkpoint to the suburb of Babelsberg, used to house President Truman and other delegates to the Potsdam conference.

Truman leaves Cecilienhof Palace, followed by Stalin, who is trailed by his bodyguard, General Nikolai Vlasik (at right), later accused of black-market activities in Potsdam.

The square in front of the Brandenburg Gate in Berlin, which still bore signs of war damage when the Americans arrived in July 1945.

Secretary Byrnes (left) with Andrei Gromyko (center) and Andrei Vyshinsky at Gatow airfield in Berlin.

On the balcony of Stalin's residence at 27 Kaiserstrasse in Babelsberg on July 18, 1945. From left to right: Byrnes, Gromyko, Truman, Stalin, Molotov.

Hiroshima after the bomb.

Truman learned about the successful bombing of Hiroshima on board the USS *Augusta* around 1200 on August 6, while returning home from Potsdam. In this photograph, he is seen lunching with the crew moments before he heard the news.

"This is the most powerful land force I have ever seen," marveled Leahy, a five-star admiral. "I don't see how anybody could stop them if they really wanted to go somewhere."

"Nobody has stopped them yet," the commanding general replied proudly.

The vegetation changed dramatically along the eighteen-mile drive into Berlin. The trees were thick and luxurious in Babelsberg but thinned out in the Grunewald. By the time Truman reached the Tiergarten, the grand park in the center of the city, all that remained were miserable stumps, shorn of bark. The foliage had been systematically stripped away, first by bombing, then by ravaging for firewood. On the Siegesallee, the president's party passed a garden bench that still bore the sign NICHT FÜR JÜDEN, "Not for Jews." They hurried on to the ruins of the Reichstag and the Brandenburg Gate, at the entrance to the Russian sector, taking a salute from Red Army commanders. Finally, they pulled up outside the Reich Chancellery on Wilhelmstrasse, where the leaders of Europe had come to pay homage to Hitler. Seated in his open limousine, alongside Byrnes and Leahy, Truman stared at the stone balcony from which the führer had whipped his followers into frenzies of nationalism. A huge

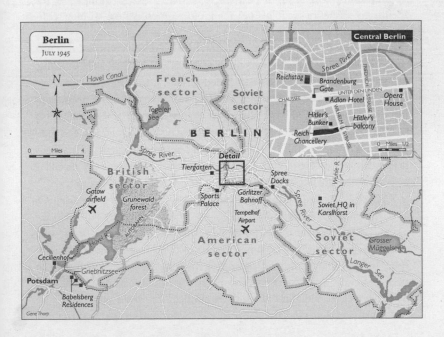

mound of rubble—topped, incongruously, by an empty armchair—was piled on the street where tens of thousands of Nazis had marched in torchlight processions. The president did not feel like getting out of his car. Instead he thought somberly of cities like "Carthage, Baalbek, Jerusalem, Rome, Atlantis, Peking, Babylon, Nineveh" and conquerors like "Rameses II, Titus, Herman, Sherman, Jenghis Khan, Alexander, Darius the Great." Never before had he seen such destruction.

"They brought it on themselves," he told the reporters crowding around his car. "It just demonstrates what man can do when he overreaches himself."

The president took a different route back to Babelsberg, passing the bombed-out Sports Palace on Potsdamerstrasse, where Hitler had given his first speech as chancellor in February 1933. "The German nation must be built up from the ground anew," the führer had declared then. Ten years later, after the disaster at Stalingrad, Goebbels had used the same venue to ask Germans if they were ready for "a war more total and radical than anything that we can ever yet imagine." Were they willing to do anything Hitler ordered? "Führer, command, we follow," they had screamed back.

Even more distressing to Truman than the ruined buildings was the seemingly endless parade of "old men, old women, young women, children from tots to teens carrying packs, pushing carts, pulling carts" along the back roads of Berlin. There was a notable absence of young men. It was unclear where the refugees had come from, or where they were heading, other than away from Soviet-controlled territory, toward anywhere they could find food and shelter. Few showed any interest in the president's motorcade as it roared past. "The most sorrowful part of the situation is the deluded Hitlerian populace," Truman recorded. "Of course the Russians have kidnapped the able bodied and I suppose have made involuntary workmen of them. They have also looted every house left standing and have sent the loot to Russia. But Hitler did the same thing to them."

Churchill arrived at the devastated Reich Chancellery ten minutes after the president left, riding in an open jeep with Anthony Eden. Unlike Truman, he was determined to explore the macabre scene. To his surprise, a small crowd of Germans "began to cheer" as he walked toward them in his military uniform, chomping his cigar. "My hate had died with their surrender and I was much moved by their demonstrations, and also by their haggard looks and threadbare clothes," he wrote later.

Russian soldiers escorted the prime minister and his party through a courtyard littered with burned armored cars, tanks, and other battlefield debris. They marched up the steps into the Chancellery, picking their way through piles of shattered mosaic and fallen chandeliers. Albert Speer had designed the gallery to be twice as long as the Hall of Mirrors at Versailles, in order to give Hitler's visitors a foretaste of "the power and grandeur of the German Reich." "A most elegant crater" now adorned the center of the gallery, "revealing two floors below an abundance of ruptured pipes and some dangling machinery." Passing through the rubble-filled hall, Churchill inspected the remains of Hitler's once-grandiose study. His interpreter noted the Russian graffiti on the wall, much of it written in "highly unparliamentary language." Russian guards had smashed the führer's marble desk into tiny pieces, which they were handing out as souvenirs. Eden recalled that Hitler had entertained him at a dinner in a nearby room in 1935, shortly before German troops marched into the demilitarized Rhineland. Churchill could not resist a sly dig at his foreign secretary.

"You certainly paid for that dinner, Anthony," he growled.

The party then descended seven flights of stairs into the bunker where Hitler was rumored to have committed suicide with Eva Braun. It was dark and dank, and they had to grope around by torchlight. The floor was covered with "broken furniture, strewn books and papers, personal belongings from desks, broken doors to safes, broken lighting fixtures and broken glass." The debris was six feet high in places and emitted an odor of moldering corpses. When they returned to the surface, Churchill sat down in a gilt chair and wiped the perspiration off his forehead. "Hitler must have come out here to get some air, and heard the guns getting nearer and nearer," he murmured.

He stared at the spot where Hitler's body was rumored to have been burned, before turning away, chin down, his right hand flashing a grim V sign. He suddenly felt a flash of empathy for the dead dictator. "This is what would have happened to us if *they* had won the war. We would have been the bunker."

At the temporary White House on Kaiserstrasse, dinner was served in a large room overlooking the lake. The band of the 2nd Armored Division was assembled outside on the neatly cropped lawn to provide musical entertainment. Truman's guests included Averell Harriman and Joe Davies, who represented the twin antipodes of his confused Russia policy.

The proud recipient of the Order of Lenin, Davies worried that the president was surrounded by people who were spreading derogatory rumors about the Soviets. He suspected Harriman of wanting an "immediate war" with Russia. Harriman, for his part, regarded the millionaire attorney with contempt. He was upset when he learned that his rival was using his own back channels to set up a meeting between the president and Stalin. It turned out that the *vozhd* had arrived in Potsdam secretly that morning and expressed a desire—relayed through Vyshinsky and Davies—to call on Truman as soon as possible. Such arrangements should be made through the present ambassador, not a former one, Harriman felt.

The president was sipping coffee after dinner when he was told that the secretary of war wished to see him "on an important matter." Henry Stimson had come to Potsdam on his own initiative because he sensed that momentous decisions were about to be taken concerning the war in Japan. He wanted to personally inform Truman of the results of the first ever atomic test, which had been scheduled for 5:30 that morning in the desert of New Mexico (2:30 p.m., Berlin time). Stimson waited impatiently for news in his own villa in Babelsberg, a block and a half away from the Little White House. At 7:30 p.m., he finally received a telegram from Washington that he took directly to the president. It was signed by George Harrison, an insurance company executive who served as his special assistant for all matters relating to the Manhattan Project.

TOP SECRET

EYES ONLY FROM HARRISON FOR STIMSON

OPERATED ON THIS MORNING. DIAGNOSIS NOT YET COMPLETE BUT RESULTS SEEM SATISFACTORY AND ALREADY EXCEED EXPECTATIONS. LOCAL PRESS RELEASE NECESSARY AS INTEREST EXTENDS GREAT DISTANCE. DR. GROVES PLEASED. HE RETURNS TOMORROW. I WILL KEEP YOU POSTED.

Truman seemed relieved but tired when he returned to his guests. The message was obscurely worded, but he understood exactly what it meant. The world had entered the nuclear age.

"Everything all right?" Davies asked.

"Yes, fine."

"Over here or back home?"

"Back home."

Davies urged the president to agree to Stalin's request for a meeting that evening. He had told Vyshinsky that Truman would "willingly" accept, but he would have to check. To his "astonishment," Truman had no interest in a late-night session with Stalin. It had been a full, exhausting day capped by the news about the atomic bomb. He was accustomed to getting to bed early. He told Davies to try to delay the meeting until the morning.

Dismayed by this turn of events, the special envoy shuttled back and forth between the Little White House and the Russian headquarters, a three-minute drive down the road. The normally friendly Vyshinsky was "as cold as ice" as he explained the change of plans. It was now well after ten o'clock. Davies had another of his "heart-to-heart" chats with the president, telling him that he risked antagonizing his Soviet counterpart. Truman relented and agreed to see Stalin immediately. By this time the generalissimo had changed his mind. A meeting the following day would be fine.

Truman still had to calm down the histrionic Davies, who had begun "to wonder about the policy [the president] wished to follow with the Soviets." He feared that the "little men"—his derisory term for Harriman and the State Department—were now in charge. Davies offered to go home "without a word" if he had lost the president's confidence.

"You won't even see my dust."

"I am trying my best to save the peace," Truman replied earnestly. "I want you by my elbow at the Conference table."

A 1949 Soviet propaganda movie, *The Fall of Berlin,* shows Stalin arriving in the German capital in a gigantic civilian airplane escorted by four small fighters. As the plane flies over Berlin, jubilant Red Army soldiers race through the streets to welcome the *vozhd.* Joined by happy Germans, they surge onto the airfield clutching red banners, a scene reminiscent of Eisenstein's depiction of the storming of the Winter Palace. Stalin, played by his favorite Georgian actor, Mikheil Gelovani, steps from the plane in a gleaming white military tunic, a God-like figure descending from the heavens. Former concentration camp inmates, still dressed in their striped prison jackets, hail their liberator. A half smile plays across the generalissimo's handsome features as he acknowledges the cheering masses.

Of course, it did not happen that way. Stalin was terrified of traveling by plane and never set foot in Berlin. An armored train brought him direct to the Potsdam railway station following an overnight journey from Moscow. He arrived at noon on July 16 and was met by Marshal Zhukov and a few close aides. He had made it very clear that there were to be no "honor guards with bands" on hand for his arrival. After greeting the welcoming party "with a curt wave of his hand," he was driven to his Babelsberg residence in a Packard limousine with thick bulletproof windows, identical to the car that he had used at Yalta. Unlike Truman and Churchill, Stalin showed no interest in touring the devastated German capital.

Planning the 1,195-mile rail trip from Moscow to Potsdam had taken many weeks. The 516-mile portion of track through Germany and Poland was entirely rebuilt to the broader Russian gauge to save the dictator the inconvenience of changing trains at Brest-Litovsk. Security was even tighter than at Yalta, due to the risks Stalin was running by traveling out of the Soviet Union, through territory where anti-Communist partisans were still active. The route was guarded by seventeen thousand elite NKVD security troops and thousands more regular soldiers. Thirty men were posted along every mile of track in Poland and Germany to ensure against sabotage. Eight armored trains with NKVD troops were on constant patrol.

The villa colony in Babelsberg resembled a mini-Berlin, divided into Russian, American, and British sectors, each protected and patrolled by its own national army. Russian soldiers strolled into the American and British sectors whenever it suited them but did not allow their allies into the Soviet sector. "One has to walk rather like a tiger, round and round one's cage," the British diplomat Alexander Cadogan complained in a letter to his wife. "If one goes outside the British sector, one is challenged at every yard by Russian sentries with tommy-guns." The three heads of government had villas alongside the Griebnitzsee. Stalin's house, at 27 Kaiserstrasse, was smaller than either Truman's or Churchill's but boasted a pleasant semicircular porch at the back. Like Truman, Stalin could wander out of his second-floor office onto a deck overlooking the lake. The style was art nouveau functional: the architect, Alfred Grenander, had made his reputation designing Berlin subway stations. The previous owner was a wealthy department store boss who had been thrown into the street to make way for Stalin.

"The house is completely equipped," Beria reported to Stalin two weeks prior to his arrival. "It has a communications center. Stocks of game, poultry, delicacies, groceries and drink have been laid in. Three supplementary sources of supply have been established seven kilometers from Potsdam with livestock and poultry farms and vegetable stores. There are two bakeries at work. All the staff is from Moscow."

The former inhabitants of Babelsberg disappeared from view during the conference. Most were living in "miserable surroundings" nearby, having moved in with anyone prepared to offer them shelter. They were warned not to go out into the street and kept under virtual house arrest. The ordeal of the owners of the Little White House, just down the road from Stalin's residence, was typical enough. Truman was informed that the villa was previously occupied by the head of the Nazi movie industry "who is now with a labor battalion somewhere in Russia." In fact, it belonged to a prominent publisher, Gustav Müller-Grote, whose father had built the house in 1896. In a letter to Truman many years later, the publisher's son described what happened after the arrival of the Red Army:

> Ten weeks before you entered this house, its tenants were living in constant fright and fear. By day and by night plundering Russian soldiers went in and out, raping my sisters before their own parents and children, beating up my parents. All furniture, wardrobes, trunks etc. were smashed with bayonets and rifle butts, their contents spilled and destroyed in an indescribable manner. The wealth of a cultivated house was destroyed within hours. . . . In the middle of May, well after the capitulation, the owners of this house as well as their tenants were put on an hour's notice. They were permitted to take along just the barest necessities of life.

The Russians stripped the Müller-Grote house of its original furniture and old-master paintings and refurnished it with a hodgepodge of items confiscated from nearby villas and castles. This allowed them to plant listening equipment in the most important rooms of the house, including the president's office. Eavesdropping "was still on the program," noted Sergo Beria. As at Yalta, Stalin was intimately familiar with American and British negotiating positions at Potsdam. The eavesdropping reports were supplemented by purloined State Department and Foreign Office cables obtained by Soviet spies in Washington and London. In some cases, Stalin knew more about western policies than western leaders themselves, making a mockery of their valiant attempts at secrecy.

A roar of motorcycle outriders announced Stalin's arrival at the temporary White House at noon on Tuesday, July 17, in his bulletproof Packard.
The president's military aide, General Harry Vaughan, bounded down
the steps to greet the dictator like a "fellow Rotarian." The Russian security men seemed taken aback by this display of backslapping familiarity,
but they permitted Vaughan to escort their boss upstairs. Truman was
waiting to receive his visitor in his second-floor office, overlooking the
lake. As his visitor entered the room, he got up from his ornately carved
wooden desk. A still life with fruit and a dead duck hung morosely on the
wall above the marble-framed fireplace.

There were the usual awkward greetings. Like FDR before him, Truman
tried out an "Uncle Joe" joke, but "it did not draw even a hint of a smile,"
according to Chip Bohlen, who was serving as interpreter. Byrnes made
a jocular reference to Stalin's habit of rising late, as Molotov squirmed in
the background. The cobbler's son from Georgia was dressed in a plain
khaki uniform with red stripes down the pants and a buttoned-up tunic;
the former Missouri haberdasher wore a light double-breasted suit with
two-tone shoes, polka-dot bow tie, and matching handkerchief.

The two leaders wasted little time getting down to business. Stalin
said he intended to stick to his promise at Yalta to declare war on Japan
and invade Japanese-occupied Manchuria. "He'll be in the Jap War on
August 15," Truman noted in his diary that night. "Fini Japs when that
comes about." In return, the *vozhd* had a series of geopolitical demands
of his own. Upset that a Fascist dictator was still in power in Spain, he
wanted the United States to join Russia in breaking relations with Francisco Franco. He also expressed an interest in Italian colonies in Africa,
such as Libya and Eritrea. "It is dynamite," Truman dutifully recorded,
"but I have some dynamite too which I'm not exploding now." All things
considered, he felt he could "deal with Stalin. He is honest—but smart as
hell." He was favorably impressed by Stalin's politeness, good humor, and
the fact that the dictator "looked you in the eye as he talked to you."

On the spur of the moment, Truman invited his new friend to stay for
lunch. Stalin said that he was busy but allowed himself to be persuaded.
There was no time to prepare anything special, so the kitchen staff scrambled to "increase the quantities of liver and bacon" they had planned to
serve the president as a main course. The first course was creamed spinach
soup and pumpernickel bread. Worried about the success of the potluck
lunch, the Americans were delighted to see Stalin stroking his mustache
with satisfaction over the liver and bacon. He liked the wines so much

that he "made a point of asking where we got them." Truman took the hint and sent around thirty bottles of Niersteiner, Moselle, and port to the generalissimo's quarters.

The conversation at lunch drifted from topic to topic. Asked how he thought Hitler had died, Stalin stuck to the story he had told Harry Hopkins. He said the führer was probably still alive and hiding "either in Spain or Argentina." He did not mention the Soviet autopsy report that concluded that he had committed suicide in his bunker. Instead, he claimed that a careful search had failed to find "any trace of Hitler's remains" or positive evidence for his death. It was the first of many lies that he would tell Truman.

The opening plenary session of the Potsdam conference was scheduled for 5:00 p.m. that Tuesday afternoon. The Russians had selected the country estate of the German royal family as the venue for the conference. Known as Cecilienhof, the palace was described by a British official as "a stockbroker's idea of paradise." It was built at great expense between 1914 and 1917 for Crown Prince Wilhelm, a passionate Anglophile. The architectural style was mock Tudor, with exposed beams, overhanging gables, and tall chimneys, plus a few pseudo-Gothic spires and stained-glass windows. The Russians had planted thousands of begonias in the courtyard to form a gigantic red star. Surrounding the palace was a well-landscaped park that contained the headstones of the crown prince's pet dogs and cats and the rough graves of German soldiers killed during the Russian assault on Potsdam.

In order to reach Cecilienhof, Truman had to drive past Stalin's residence at 27 Kaiserstrasse, and cross a rickety, one-lane pontoon bridge that had been placed across the Griebnitzsee, into the American sector of Berlin. He then swung back into the Russian-controlled zone, via a temporary wooden bridge that had been constructed across the Havel River from Berlin to Potsdam, parallel to a steel suspension bridge that had been blown up during the final days of the war. Like royal potentates of old, each leader was provided with his own entrance to the one-hundred-seventy-six-room palace. Truman entered through the front lobby. Churchill used the courtyard entrance, with its sweeping circular drive. Stalin was taken around to the back. An archway had been hastily slapped onto the French doors leading out onto the veranda to provide the *vozhd* with his own ceremonial entryway. The palace itself was divided

up into Russian, American, and British sectors, along the already familiar pattern of Babelsberg and Berlin. Each leader was allocated a study,
dining room, and separate door leading into the conference chamber, a
grand two-story banquet hall. Because of the labyrinthine layout of the
palace, Churchill's door required an inconvenient detour along a gloomy
corridor. British officials tried to persuade the Russian commandant to
allow the prime minister to use a set of double doors that led directly
into the chamber from his suite. "Not possible" was the reply. "They use
the three smaller doors, one each." The double doors were kept firmly
locked. Protocol required that the heads of delegation make their exits
and entrances through doors of precisely the same size.

At the appointed hour, the three leaders walked into the cavernous,
oak-paneled room, decorated with the flags of the victorious Allies. A
twelve-foot-wide, baize-covered round table, specially ordered from the
Luks furniture factory in Moscow, had been placed in the center of the
room, together with fifteen chairs. Three identical armchairs, decorated
with miniature cupids, were reserved for the principals, each of whom
was flanked by his interpreter and three top aides. The delegates were
"almost blinded by a battery of klieg lights and moving picture cameras"
as they milled around, waiting for the proceedings to start. The photo
session was a minor concession to the thousands of reporters who had
arrived in Berlin to cover the Big Three summit, which had been given the
code name Terminal. The journalists spent the rest of the conference in
Berlin bars, working themselves up into what Churchill called "a furious
state of indignation" over the news blackout. After ten minutes, the photographers retired, and Stalin called the conference to order. As at Yalta,
he proposed that the president chair the meetings.

Much of the first session was devoted to discussing the agenda. Truman and Stalin kept their remarks succinct and to the point. Churchill
insisted on making long, flowery speeches, to the dismay of his aides.
"He butts in on every occasion and talks the most irrelevant rubbish,"
Cadogan informed his wife. "Truman is most quick and businesslike. He
was only trying, at this first meeting, to establish a list of the questions
we must deal with. Every mention of a topic started Winston off on a
wild rampage from which the combined efforts of Truman and Anthony
[Eden] with difficulty restrained him."

Once again, Stalin proved a master debater. An admiring Davies
watched him "sitting in his chair, listening, with eyes almost closed.
When he speaks, it is tersely. Each sentence is a naked idea, stated in as

few words as possible. He clips off ideas like a machine gun. His mind has strong retentive power. In taking up the opposing argument, he analyses and states the points made. Then, seriatim, he takes them up one by one and answers them with counter-facts." Truman's main strengths were his modesty and his decisiveness. "He is alert, keen, clear-headed, positive and frank," noted Davies.

In his straightforward manner, the president made clear that action was more important than words. "I don't want just to discuss," he told the others. "I want to decide." Furthermore, he wanted to meet at 4:00 p.m. every day, rather than 5:00 p.m.

"I will obey your orders," replied Churchill, who was wearing his colonel's uniform.

This prompted Stalin to get down to business. The salvageable portion of the German navy—three cruisers, fifteen destroyers, and a dozen torpedo boats—was now in the hands of the British. The generalissimo wanted his share of the spoils.

"If you are in such an obedient mood today, Mr. Prime Minister, I should like to know whether you will share with us the German fleet."

The fleet would either be shared or destroyed, Churchill replied. Weapons of war were "terrible things."

"The navy should be divided," Stalin insisted. "If Mr. Churchill prefers to sink the navy, he is free to sink his share of it. I have no intention of sinking mine."

To the Americans and the British, there were moments when the Russian ambitions seemed limitless. During a break in the conference, Harriman remarked to Stalin that he must feel "great satisfaction to be in Berlin." The *vozhd* looked at him with disdain. "Czar Alexander," he eventually replied, "got to Paris."

A second telegram arrived overnight from Harrison at the Pentagon providing a few more details of the mysterious "operation" that had grabbed the attention of Truman and his top aides. It made little sense to the decoding clerks manning the army message center.

DOCTOR HAS JUST RETURNED MOST ENTHUSIASTIC AND CONFIDENT THAT THE LITTLE BOY IS AS HUSKY AS HIS BIG BROTHER. THE LIGHT IN HIS EYES DISCERNIBLE FROM HERE TO HIGHHOLD AND I COULD HAVE HEARD HIS SCREAMS FROM HERE TO MY FARM.

An excited Stimson walked the message across the street to the Little White House on the morning of Wednesday, July 18. He explained its meaning to Truman. The plutonium bomb tested near Alamogordo, New Mexico, had exceeded all expectations. Groves (the "doctor") believed that it was at least as powerful as its older "brother," the still untested uranium bomb. The flash from the atomic blast on July 16 had been visible for two hundred fifty miles, the distance between Washington and Highhold, Stimson's country estate on Long Island. The explosion itself could be heard fifty miles away, the distance to Harrison's farm in Virginia. The president was "highly delighted."

Truman had a luncheon appointment with Churchill. He stuffed Harrison's telegram in his pocket to show the prime minister and marched briskly up the road to 23 Ringstrasse, a six-minute walk. The two leaders lunched alone, discussing the bomb. The big question was whether to let Stalin in on the secret—and, if so, when. Truman thought it best to wait until the end of the conference. Churchill felt it was better to inform Stalin sooner rather than later, to avoid the question, "Why didn't you tell us this before?" This logic impressed Truman. He agreed with Churchill that he should reveal only the basic fact of the atomic bomb's existence, without going into details.

"I had better just tell him after one of our meetings that we have an entirely novel form of bomb, something quite out of the ordinary, which we think will have quite decisive effects upon the Japanese will to continue the war."

Truman was scheduled to pay a return courtesy call on Stalin later that afternoon. His motorcade pulled up at the generalissimo's residence at 3:04 p.m. following the two-minute drive from Churchill's villa. The president was dismayed to find another feast awaiting him, even though he had just left the luncheon table. There were the usual elaborate toasts, after which the two leaders adjourned for a private talk. Stalin handed Truman a copy of a Japanese government note, transmitted via the ambassador in Moscow, stating that the emperor wanted to negotiate an end to the war. He pointed out that Russia was not yet at war with Japan. It might be best to "lull the Japanese to sleep" by asking them to provide more details of the surrender terms. This time, it was Truman's turn to dissemble. He was already aware of the peace feeler from Tokyo, as American cryptographers had broken the Japanese diplomatic code. But he feigned ignorance.

A vaguely worded reply would be quite "satisfactory," he told Stalin.

The conference dragged on slowly. The Big Three could not even agree on such basic matters as the postwar shape of Germany. Stalin had lopped off a large chunk of Germany and given it to Poland without reaching agreement with the Allies. He insisted that Germany "is what has become of her after the war. No other Germany exists."

"Why not say the Germany of 1937?" asked Truman.

"Minus what she has lost," countered Stalin. "We cannot get away from the results of the war."

"But we must have a starting point."

Pushed into a corner, Stalin agreed reluctantly to take the "Germany of 1937" as a "point of departure." But he was quick to add a qualification. "It's merely a working hypothesis."

"So it is agreed that the Germany of 1937 should be the starting point," said Truman, anxious for any kind of progress.

After only three days in Berlin, Truman was "sick of the whole business" but still confident that he could "bring home the bacon." He was determined to prevent Stalin and Churchill from taking the United States for a ride and remained committed to the goal of a "lasting peace" enunciated by FDR. "I reared up on my hind legs and told 'em where to get off and they got off," he wrote to Bess, after an unproductive session on July 19. "I have to make it perfectly plain to them at least once a day that so far as this President is concerned Santa Claus is dead and that my first interest is U.S.A. Then I want the Jap War won and I want 'em both in it. Then I want peace—world peace—and will do what can be done by us to get it. But certainly am not going to set up another Govt here in Europe, pay reparations, feed the world and get nothing for it but a nose thumbing."

On a personal level, the three leaders got on excellently. Truman hosted a dinner at the Little White House later that evening. When it came time for the toasts, Stalin and Churchill engaged in a good-humored competition to praise the common man. Stalin gave a speech insisting that the "toiling masses" deserved the credit for winning the war. This had become one of his favorite themes, a not-so-subtle way of denigrating the contributions of Zhukov and the other marshals. He pointed out that the term "toiling masses" included "common soldiers and sailors." Churchill threw up his hands in mock surrender. He proposed his own "toast to the toiling masses, whether they be soldiers, sailors or workers, conservative or liberal, black or white, Tory or Republican, or even Communist." Stalin grinned.

After dinner, the president led his guests out onto the porch overlooking the lake. It was still light: Berlin was now on the same time as Moscow, and the summer sun did not go down until midnight. Truman had flown in a professional pianist to play a selection of pieces by Chopin, Shostakovich, and Tchaikovsky. He joined in the recital, playing a Paderewski minuet on the piano and serving as page turner for Sergeant Eugene List. He pronounced the evening a great success in his letter to Bess. "Stalin felt so friendly that he toasted the pianist when he played a Tskowsky (you spell it) piece especially for him. The old man loves music. He told me he'd import the greatest Russian pianist for me tomorrow. Our boy was good."

A Pentagon courier arrived in Babelsberg on the morning of Saturday, July 21, with the detailed report on the Alamogordo test. Stimson arranged to see the president in the Little White House at 3:30 p.m. Once again, he insisted on reading the entire twelve-page document aloud. General Groves described the "huge ball of fire" that rose from the test site, pulverizing a steel tower designed to simulate a twenty-story building. "The blast tore the tower from its foundations, twisted it, ripped it apart and left it flat on the ground." The fireball mushroomed into a cloud of smoke ten thousand feet high that could clearly be seen in Albuquerque and El Paso, nearly two hundred miles away. Groves then quoted from a memorandum written by his deputy, Brigadier General Thomas Farrell, who was stationed at the control shelter, six miles south of the explosion.

The scene inside the shelter was dramatic beyond words. . . . All seemed to sense immediately that the explosion had far exceeded the most optimistic expectations and wildest hopes of the scientists. All seemed to feel that they had been present at the birth of a new age. . . . The effects could well be called unprecedented, magnificent, beautiful, stupendous and terrifying. No man-made phenomenon of such tremendous power had ever occurred before. The lighting effects beggared description. The whole country was lighted by a searing light with the intensity many times that of the midday sun. It was golden, purple, violet, and blue. It lighted every peak, crevasse and ridge of the nearby mountain range with a clarity and beauty that cannot be described but must be seen to be imagined. It was that beauty the great poets dream about but describe most poorly and inadequately. Thirty seconds after the explosion came first the air blast pressing hard against the people and things, to be followed almost immediately by the strong, sustained, awesome roar which warned of doomsday.

"We are all fully conscious that our real goal is still before us," Groves concluded. "The battle test is what counts in the war against Japan."

The report left Truman "tremendously pepped up," according to Stimson. After one hundred days in office, he now controlled "the most terrible bomb in the history of the world." It was an enormous responsibility, but it gave him "an entirely new feeling of confidence." The secretary of war obtained a similar reaction from Churchill after reading the report to him the following day. "Stimson, what was gunpowder? Trivial," the prime minister enthused. "What was electricity? Meaningless. This atomic bomb is the Second Coming in Wrath." Churchill was sure that the new weapon "would redress the balance with the Russians" and completely change the "diplomatic equilibrium" at the conference. He dreamed of laying down terms to Stalin. "If you insist on doing this or that, well we can just blot out Moscow, then Stalingrad, then Kiev, then Kuibyshev."

The boost in American and British spirits was apparent immediately inside the conference chamber at Cecilienhof. Assistant Secretary of War John McCloy noted in his diary that Truman and Churchill behaved "like little boys with a big red apple secreted on their persons." Churchill thought that Truman became "a changed man" after hearing Stimson read the report. "He stood up to the Russians in a most dramatic and decisive manner. He told the Russians just where they got on and off and generally bossed the whole meeting." Robert Murphy agreed. "We noticed a decided change in the President's manner," he recorded in his memoir, referring to the late-afternoon plenary session of July 21. "He seemed much more sure of himself, more inclined to participate vigorously in the discussions, to challenge some of Stalin's statements. It was apparent that something had happened."

Truman opened the meeting by warning that the United States would refuse to recognize the governments of Romania, Bulgaria, Hungary, and Finland until they were "established on a proper basis" following free elections. For good measure, he also reminded Stalin of his commitment to hold free elections in Poland. He then complained that the Russians were attempting to present him with a fait accompli regarding Poland's western borders. Roosevelt and Churchill had agreed at Yalta to compensate Poland for territory lost to the Soviet Union, but there had been no agreement on where the new boundary line with Germany would be drawn. Six months later, American negotiators had finally grasped the distinction between the Western and Eastern Neisse Rivers (see map on page 65). The territory between the two rivers was roughly the size of Massachusetts. It included the Silesian capital Breslau, which had been in German hands for centuries, as well as some of the country's most productive coal mines and large farms.

The transfer of Silesia and Pomerania to Poland changed the economic calculations of the postwar planners. Traditionally, these regions had supplied the German capital with coal and food. The shortfall would now have to come from western Germany—together with billions of dollars of reparations for the Soviet Union. Based on what had happened after World War I, Truman feared that Uncle Sam would end up paying the bill. To make matters worse, refugees from the eastern part of Germany were flooding into areas controlled by the western Allies. Feeding these people would become the responsibility of America and Britain.

"We cannot agree on reparations if parts of Germany are given away," Truman said bluntly. He reminded Stalin of the agreement to use the "Germany of 1937" as the "starting point" for the negotiation of postwar arrangements.

The *vozhd* attempted to inject a dose of geopolitical reality into the debate. "Not a single German remains in the territory to be given Poland. . . . They have all run away." These territories were now inhabited by Poles.

Admiral Leahy leaned over to the president. Of course there were no Germans east of the Oder-Neisse line, he whispered. "The Bolshies have killed them all."

Seated on the other side of Truman from Leahy, Joe Davies was alarmed by the acrimonious turn in the discussion. He scribbled a note on a piece of paper and handed it to the president.

"I think Stalin's feelings are hurt. Please be nice to him."

Churchill jumped into the debate in support of Truman. He expressed the hope that the refugees would return once conditions improved. Stalin reacted with scorn.

"The Poles will hang them if they return." He had no sympathy for "scoundrels and war criminals."

"Surely eight and a half million people can't be war criminals," Churchill rejoined. Like Truman, he did not want to be saddled with "masses of starving people in Germany."

Feeding hungry Germans was an irrelevance to Stalin. He gave his capitalist interlocutors a brisk lecture on the Marxist theory of imperialism. "The less industry there is in Germany, the larger the market there will be for your goods. We have destroyed your competitor."

The session ended on a discordant note. Truman had laid down a red line. If Russia continued to do as she pleased in her part of Germany, America and Britain would treat their portion of the country as a separate entity. There would be no reparations payments to Russia from the West in the absence of food and energy deliveries from the East. The Yalta vision of a defeated but united Germany occupied and administered jointly by the wartime Allies was fading away.

18

Loot

July 23

Edwin Pauley ordered his driver to head for the sprawling freight yard and docks on the northern bank of the river Spree in the Russian sector of Berlin. The former oilman and Democratic Party operative had received a detailed report from his staff on the looting of German industrial equipment and household goods by the Red Army. His assistants had observed convoys of American lend-lease trucks entering a vast fenced-in compound crammed with "woodworking machines, bakery ovens, textile looms, electric generators, transformers, telephone equipment." Thousands of Russian soldiers, helped by press-ganged German laborers, were said to be loading the booty onto railcars headed for the Soviet Union. The plunder ranged from large items of industrial machinery, such as printing presses and stamping mills, to piles of furniture and bales of clothing. Pauley wanted to see for himself what was going on.

A six-foot-three-inch Californian with slicked-back dark hair, Pauley combined the roles of political insider and man of action. A career as a roughneck and oil-field driller had ended in an airplane crash, which left him with a broken back, broken neck, thirty broken bones, and nineteen thousand dollars in medical bills. Inspired by FDR's example in combating polio, he put the accident behind him and set about establishing his own oil company. He raised funds for Roosevelt's presidential campaigns and helped engineer Truman's nomination as vice president in 1944. When Truman succeeded Roosevelt as president, he repaid his debt to Pauley by appointing him the American representative on the Allied Reparations Commission. The tough, smooth-talking businessman had the job of negotiating a reparations agreement with the Russians.

"Just deal with the Russians the same way you deal with me at poker, and we'll be all right," the president had instructed.

Leaving his military escort behind, the forty-two-year-old Pauley scrambled on top of a brick wall overlooking the freight yard and railroad tracks. From his vantage point on top of the wall, he could see hundreds of freight cars loaded with industrial equipment. He began filming the scene with a sixteen-millimeter motion picture camera but was quickly interrupted by shouts and frantic gestures from a Russian sergeant, who came sprinting toward him. Deciding that discretion was the better part of valor, Pauley climbed down from the wall, only to be confronted by the red-faced sergeant, who emerged through a gate in the fence. Pauley noted that he was of "Mongolian" appearance and "clearly understood no English."

The Russian made jabbing motions at Pauley with a bayoneted rifle with one hand while grabbing his camera with the other. He then grabbed Pauley himself, attempting to arrest him. Pauley yelled for help, but his escort, an American colonel, was several blocks down the street.

As Truman's special envoy was being led away by the sergeant, the colonel finally realized what was happening. He ran to Pauley's rescue, brandishing a loaded .45 automatic and a Russian military pass. The sergeant understood that he was outranked and ran off to find a superior officer. "Needless to say, we did not wait," Pauley later recalled. "We began putting the freight yard behind us—fast."

Pauley had read many reports suggesting that the Russians had no interest in restoring Germany's economic potential, but it was a different matter to observe the pillaging with his own eyes. He was shocked to discover that machinery had been disassembled and carted away from several American-owned factories. Red Army reparations teams had stripped the west Berlin plant of the International Telephone and Telegraph Company of all its machinery "down to even small tools" days before the U.S. Army entered the city on July 4. They were now focusing their attention on a General Electric subsidiary in Soviet-controlled east Berlin. The street next to the plant "is blocked off for some two blocks and guarded," Pauley's aides reported. "It is full of small lathes, winding equipment and other machinery all of which is being wrapped in oil paper or crated. . . . While we passed [the plant], a wagon of good-looking office furniture was driven out of the main gateway from the administration building."

"It would appear that all these removals were in complete violation of all efforts to maintain 'non-war potential' industries in Germany," Pauley complained in a July 27 memorandum to Secretary Byrnes. "The effect of these removals will be the complete destruction of employment opportunities in the area. What we saw amounts to organized vandalism not alone against Germany, but against the U.S. forces of occupation." Pauley's aides later drew up a list of twenty American companies whose plants and machinery had been seized by the Red Army, including International Business Machines, Gillette, the Ford Motor Company, F. W. Woolworth, and Paramount Pictures.

Intellectually, Pauley could understand the motivations for the Soviet position on reparations, even though he was repelled by the manner in which it was being implemented. He had just returned from a monthlong trip to Russia during which he had friendly talks with his Soviet counterpart, Ivan Maisky. A former journalist and ambassador to Great Britain, Maisky was fluent in English and "completely acceptable on the English social scene." He knew how to talk to capitalists and imperialists in their own language. His goatee beard, impeccable manners, and somewhat pudgy appearance gave him the air of an "imperturbable literary intellectual." Pauley regarded Maisky as "just about as pleasant a man as one could have hoped for to represent the USSR in the Allied Commission of Reparations."

In addition to lavishing hospitality on Pauley and introducing him to the Bolshoi Ballet, Maisky insisted that he visit Stalingrad, where the Red Army had turned back the Hitlerite hordes in 1942. From the Russian point of view, Stalingrad had been the decisive battle of the war. As their plane circled the devastated city on the Volga, Pauley got an unforgettable sense of the epic scale of the fighting, involving millions of men, tens of thousands of tanks, and fleets of fighter jets. Piles of rubble, twisted metal, and shattered vegetation stretched in all directions, as far as the eye could see. By taking Pauley to Stalingrad, Maisky was making the not-so-subtle point that his country had "suffered so terribly at the hands of the Germans that almost any kind of retribution was justified." Stalin had turned Russia into an industrialized country by exacting untold sacrifices from the Russian people, only to see his life's work destroyed by the Nazi war machine. Reparations represented a second chance for the dictator to make good on his promise to close the gap with the West. As Stalin saw it, there was no choice. "We are 100 years behind the advanced countries," he had told his industrial managers in 1931. "We must make good this lag in ten years. Either we do it or they crush us!"

As a hardheaded businessman, Pauley did not allow his sympathy for the Russian people to interfere with his determination to defend American economic interests. He explained his position to Maisky by comparing Germany to a cow. America and Russia both had an interest in ensuring that the cow produced plenty of milk. To achieve this goal, the cow had to be provided with a certain amount of fodder, which would be paid for with some of the milk. Any milk left over could then be used for reparations. The United States was not prepared to accept a situation in which Russia collected all the milk while America provided the fodder. Nor was she willing to allow the cow to starve to death. Pauley's argument was simple: the wartime Allies had to agree on how the cow was to be fed *before dividing up her milk.*

Maisky was unimpressed by the American argument that German economic growth was key to the payment of reparations: Communists had always been more interested in the redistribution of wealth than the creation of wealth. He reminded Pauley that FDR had agreed at Yalta to use a figure of $20 billion as a "basis for discussion" for postwar reparations. It was understood that Russia would be entitled to 50 percent of total reparations, which would work out to the equivalent of $10 billion. For Maisky, everything was very simple: the Americans were backing away from their Yalta commitments. He regarded Pauley's bovine comparisons as a trick, designed to shift the negotiations away from a specific dollar amount to a nebulous percentage figure. The Americans were still willing to offer the Russians 50 percent or even 55 percent of total reparations but were not prepared to specify a concrete sum. Furthermore, they were now insisting that the cost of imports to keep German factories in business—"fodder" in the cow analogy—be regarded as a "prior charge" on the German economy that took precedence over reparations to Russia. By the time such imports were paid for, there might be nothing left to divvy up. It did not take a mathematical genius to figure out that 55 percent of zero was zero. The impasse was total.

At first blush, it seemed that Stalin had won a considerable victory by persuading Truman and Churchill to meet him in Potsdam, in the heart of Soviet-occupied Germany. Having conquered half of Europe, the *vozhd* was receiving his western counterparts on his own turf, with the Red Army providing security. Like medieval princes summoned to meet the emperor, they were traveling to him, rather than he to them.

In fact, it was a Pyrrhic victory. By inviting western leaders to Berlin, he was offering them a glimpse behind the "iron curtain" that he had installed around his empire. Thousands of American and British diplomats and military officers were confronted for the first time in their lives with the reality of Soviet tyranny. Many Allied officials arrived in Berlin admiring the Russians and hating the Germans, having witnessed the horror of Nazi concentration camps. But they changed their views very quickly once they saw what was happening in the Soviet occupation zone. Western officials who had been sickened by the sight of Buchenwald now exchanged stories about the looting of German factories by Soviet troops and the mass rapes of German women.

The sense of outrage at Russian behavior extended to some senior American officials who had previously been inclined to give their Soviet allies the benefit of the doubt. Henry Stimson was revising his earlier view about sharing the fruits of atomic research with the Russians. "It is becoming more and more evident to me," he wrote sadly on July 19, "that a nation whose system rests upon free speech and all the elements of freedom, as ours does, cannot be sure of getting on permanently with a nation where speech is strictly controlled and where the Government uses the iron hand of the secret police." In the third-person autobiography that he wrote years later, he said he was "deeply disturbed . . . by his first direct observation of the Russian police state in action. Partly at first hand and partly through the reports of Army officers who had observed the Russians closely during the first months of the occupation, Stimson now saw clearly the massive brutality of the Soviet system and the total suppression of freedom inflicted by the Russian leaders first on their own people and then on those whose lands they occupied. The words 'police state' acquired for him a direct and terrible meaning. What manner of men were these with whom to build a peace in the atomic age?"

Although Truman got on reasonably well with Stalin—"I liked the little son-of-a-bitch," he acknowledged—he came to think of Russians as "people from the wrong side of the tracks." In an interview for his memoir, he recalled that Soviet soldiers ransacked German homes, hauling away everything from beds to stoves to grandfather clocks. "They destroyed most of the things. Russian soldiers had never seen a comfortable bed and they didn't know how to handle it or what to do with it." The president's willingness to believe such stories dismayed the die-hard Russophile Joe Davies. "It is being sedulously circulated," he complained to his diary on July 21. "The whole atmosphere is being poisoned by it."

The reports of looting came as little surprise to American diplomats who had arrived in Berlin from Moscow. Averell Harriman told anyone who would listen that Russia was "a vacuum into which all movable goods would be sucked." Concluding that there was "nothing we could do to stop the Russians from taking whatever they wanted out of their own zone," he was adamant that "we ought to give them nothing from the Western Zones. Otherwise the American taxpayer would have to pay the bill for feeding the Germans, who could not possibly support themselves with all their industrial machinery transported to Russia." The ambassador's aide, Robert Meiklejohn, noted with satisfaction that American reparations officials were "learning fast about dealing with the Russians." After listening to one of Harriman's presentations, U.S. Navy secretary James Forrestal confided to his diary that "all hands" were disturbed by the Russian position on reparations. "They are stripping every area they are in of all movable goods, and at the same time asking reparations and designating the goods they take as war booty. They are shooting and impressing Germans out of the American district."

The sight of Russian soldiers helping themselves to anything of value in Berlin caused U.S. officials to rethink their policy on the Ruhr, Germany's industrial heartland, which was now part of the British occupation zone. Stalin and Maisky were demanding the "internationalization" of the Ruhr. The economic resources—coal mines, steel mills, chemical plants—that had fueled Nazi militarism should not be left under German control. Truman administration officials had been willing to consider at least some of the Soviet demands just a few weeks earlier. They had been toying with a plan for the "pastoralization" of Germany devised by Henry Morgenthau, FDR's treasury secretary. Stripping the western part of Germany of its industrial potential no longer seemed such a good idea now that they were confronted by the challenge of feeding millions of starving Germans. Dividing the country into separate economic zones, and stopping the Russians from taking reparations from western zones, would be contrary to the Yalta agreements and lead inevitably to a divided Germany and a divided Europe. But it might prove to be the lesser of two evils. John McCloy noted in his diary on July 23 that the division of Germany was preferable to the "constant distrust and difficulty we would have with the Russians over their being in our zones, knowing what goes on, and we not being in theirs."

> It is better to have a clear line of distinction and negotiate across that line. It has tremendous significance for Europe, but the other arrangement has more sinister and not entirely favorable considerations when one considers the atmosphere in which negotiations are conducted in Berlin today. . . . . There are such diversities and lack of understanding that I cannot see how it can work out any other way.

Whatever their sense of moral superiority over the Russians, the American occupiers of Berlin had to come to terms with an uncomfortable fact. It had been the Red Army—not the U.S. Army—that had fought its way into the fiercely defended city at a horrific cost in Russian lives. The Red Army suffered nearly eighty thousand dead and missing in the battle for Berlin alone. By contrast, the U.S. Army lost just nine thousand men in the final weeks of the war as it advanced, with little effective opposition, from the Rhine to the Elbe. Out of the 5.5 million German soldiers who perished during the war, an estimated 3.5 million had been killed on the eastern front, compared with just under a million who died in western Europe, Italy, and North Africa. (The remainder was killed in the partisan wars of the Balkans or as prisoners of war.)

In conversations in mess rooms, many U.S. officers spoke disparagingly of the Red Army, which they viewed as unkempt, ill equipped, and frequently undisciplined. At the same time, when they were being honest, Americans were obliged to concede that Stalin's troops had borne the brunt of the fighting against Hitler. The deputy chief of staff of the U.S. occupation force in Berlin, General John Whitelaw, felt sickened by the tone of "sarcasm or contempt or ridicule" employed by many Americans in talking about the Russians. "Of course they stink, have poor staff work and do a little hijacking," he wrote privately to his wife back home in America. "But these same stinking Cossacks with all of their poor staff work made the teeth of the Wehrmacht rattle when we were playing around in Tennessee with wooden weapons. Later, when they got help from us, they destroyed Hitler's army."

A string of military victories, combined with wartime sacrifices beyond the comprehension of most Americans, imbued Red Army generals and privates alike with a powerful sense of entitlement. Soviet military commanders set a rapacious example for their soldiers, amassing vast hauls of personal loot. After Zhukov fell out of favor, the NKVD secret police recovered dozens of boxes of silverware and crystal from his dacha, along with forty-four rugs, fifty-five "valuable classical paintings," three hundred twenty-three furs, and four hundred meters of velvet and silk. Zhukov claimed that he had paid for the goods out of his Red Army salary, with the intention of giving them as gifts to his relatives. An NKVD report noted that the dacha was entirely furnished with "every kind of foreign luxury" and that "a huge canvas depicting two naked women" hung over the marshal's bed. With the exception of the mat outside the front door, there was not a single item that had been manufactured inside the Soviet Union.

Stalin was undoubtedly aware of the looting by his subordinates, which he saw as a means to reward them and possibly use against them in the future. His own chief bodyguard, General Vlasik, used his time at Potsdam to extract some personal reparations from Germany. Vlasik returned to Moscow with a one-hundred-piece porcelain set, along with dozens of crystal vases and wine goblets. After his arrest in 1952, he claimed that senior Russian security officers attending the conference had all received similar china services, while the crystal ware had been inserted into his luggage without his knowledge. More difficult to explain were the two cows, bull, and horse that ended up in his ancestral home in Belorussia. Vlasik described the livestock as "a gift from the Red Army," in recompense for animals that had been seized from his relatives by the Germans during their occupation of Belorussia. The farm animals privatized by Vlasik had been confiscated from German farms and transferred to an NKVD agricultural reserve set up to meet the food needs of the Potsdam delegates.

"The time is over when packages to Germany were stuffed to overflowing with our Russian things," exulted a platoon commander. "Now it will be the other way around. Women with simple Russian names—Nina, Marusia, Tonia, and many others—will receive packages from beloved husbands, fiancés, and friends. They will rejoice in the victories of the Red Army and curse our enemies." The higher the rank, the greater the rewards. A June 1945 decree signed by Stalin authorized every Red Army general and admiral to receive a "trophy automobile," such as a Mercedes or an Opel, while lower-ranking soldiers were given motorcycles or bicycles.

Soviet statisticians kept meticulous records of everything that was removed from Germany, filing detailed reports every two weeks to the Kremlin. During the first months of the Soviet occupation, 400,000 railway wagons of war booty were dispatched from Germany to Russia, containing, among other things, 60,149 pianos, 458,612 radios, 188,071 carpets, 941,605 pieces of furniture, 3,338,348 pairs of shoes, and 1,052,503 hats. Interspersed with these household items were 24 railway wagons of museum pieces, 154 wagons of furs and valuable glassware, more than 2 million tons of grain, and 20 million liters of alcohol. A total of 2,885 German factories were slated to be dismantled and shipped to Russia by 1946. In the words of the Russian historian Vladislav Zubok, "for the Soviets, Germany was a giant shopping mall where they did not pay for anything."

Challenged by the Allies to explain Soviet looting, Zhukov drew up his own list of American and British misdeeds, ranging from the dismantling of scientific laboratories and the removal of railway stock to the disappearance of German scientists and vital technical documents. In a report to Truman, Pauley conceded that the Soviet list was "probably largely correct" but argued that the American expropriations were limited to "recent German technical advances for immediate use in war and war production," which were "clearly war booty." By contrast, the Russians were also removing equipment needed to rebuild the civilian economy, such as farm machinery and textile machines. Some western historians have conceded that Zhukov had a point, at least as far as the exploitation of German technical know-how was concerned. Thousands of prominent German scientists and technicians were spirited away to the United States in a top-secret operation known as Project Paperclip, designed, at least in part, to deny their services to Soviet Russia. By some calculations, the value of these unreported "intellectual reparations" approached the $10 billion figure that formed the basis of the Soviet reparations claim in Germany. But the Paperclip transfers were less obvious, and therefore less shocking to ordinary Germans, than the depredations of the Red Army trophy brigades.

The zeal of the trophy brigades embarrassed some Russian officers, particularly those responsible for running the Soviet zone of Germany. They understood very clearly that a harsh occupation regime would undermine any remaining goodwill toward the Soviet Union among ordinary Germans and harm the economy of a prospective client. The NKVD reported sympathetically on protests by German workers against particularly outrageous behavior by Soviet troops, including an incident in the town of Plauen "when machinery and parts that were not even slated for removal were so badly damaged by the dismantling team that they could not be used again." To add insult to injury, Soviet soldiers often press-ganged German workers into dismantling their own factories and sending them off to Russia. The NKVD cited the example of the Ninth Trophy Brigade, which surrounded a soccer stadium, stopped the game in midmatch, and hauled the spectators away to disassemble a factory. Movies and even dances were halted to round up labor for the reparations operation. Germans expressed their unhappiness with their occupiers in a popular ditty, which came to the attention of the Soviet military government:

> *Welcome, liberators!*
> *You take from us eggs,*
> *Meat and butter, cattle and feed,*
> *And also watches, rings, and other things.*
> *You liberate us from everything, from cars and machines.*
> *You take along with you train cars and rail installations.*
> *From all of this rubbish—you've liberated us!*
> *We cry for joy.*

Officers of the Soviet military government complained that the actions of the trophy teams undercut their attempts to build popular support for the occupation regime. A Red Army political officer pointed out a group of new residential homes to a prominent German Communist, Wolfgang Leonhard, while they were touring Berlin.

"That's where the enemy lives."

"Who—the Nazis?" asked a surprised Leonhard.

"No, worse still—our own reparations gang."

Other Russians found themselves torn between a complex mix of emotions: pride in what their country had accomplished, envy at the superior living standards of western Europe, resentment at American moralizing, and desire for greater personal freedom. The political schizophrenia was exemplified by the celebrated war photographer Yevgeny Khaldei, who had taken the iconic photograph of Soviet soldiers raising the red flag on top of the Reichstag. Khaldei could never forget that "the Fascists killed my mother and three sisters. They did not just shoot them. They threw them alive with 75,000 other people into a pit." As he moved through the ruined, smoldering city, Khaldei was struck by the extent of the damage caused by American and British bombing raids. He felt that the western Allies had no right to lecture the heroic Red Army about brutality toward civilians. As for all the reports of Russians raping German women, he thought "there was no need to rape them because they offered themselves."

At the same time, like his Red Army counterparts, Khaldei was intensely curious about the outside world. He believed he had earned the right to be trusted by his own regime. When American reporters covering the Potsdam conference invited Soviet journalists to their hotel for drinks, his immediate impulse was to accept. He checked with the press attaché for the Soviet embassy, who told him to seek permission from deputy foreign minister Vyshinsky.

Vyshinsky said it was fine with him, but he should ask Molotov. The foreign minister was asleep.

"Nobody was going to wake Molotov up," Khaldei recalled decades later. "So we didn't go. It was very sad."

If delegates to the Potsdam conference needed a lesson in the incompatibility of the clashing economic systems proposed for Germany, all they had to do was take a stroll through the center of Berlin. The parks and boulevards surrounding the once fashionable Tiergarten had been turned into what one delegate termed "the black market to end all such markets," dedicated to profiting from the contradictions between American capitalism and the Soviet-style command economy. In the opinion of a disillusioned U.S. Army chaplain, Berlin had become the "most immoral city in the world," corrupting whoever set foot in it. "Here crowds of soldiers gather daily for trade, both legal and illegal," reported *Life* magazine, introducing a four-page photo spread of furtive-looking Red Army soldiers buying watches and cigarettes from happy American GIs. "Germans, who traipse hopefully to the Tiergarten with their household goods in prams and rucksacks, want food, cigarets and foreign currency. Red Army men, who lug along suitcases of bills representing their back pay for several years, want cameras, clothing, and especially watches. The Americans, British and French, who drive up with pockets bulging with salable gadgets, want money."

For Americans on occupation duty, fantastic profits were to be made through the sale of consumer items purchased at U.S. Army Post

Exchanges. A carton of Lucky Strikes cigarettes went for a hundred dollars (in 1945 prices), a hundredfold markup over the original price. Mickey Mouse watches, sold at the PX for three dollars and ninety-five cents, were snapped up by Russian soldiers for five hundred dollars apiece. Cameras could fetch a thousand dollars or even more. Americans could afford to buy a car back home in the United States out of the profits from selling their watches to Russian soldiers. The U.S. military shipped vast quantities of watches, cigarettes, and candy to Berlin to keep pace with the exploding demand, which far exceeded the consumption patterns of American servicemen anywhere else in the world. PX officers complained that members of Truman's Secret Service detail "cleaned out" much of the stock, "buying watches, cameras, and such items by the dozen."

The mechanisms of all this black-market activity were initially a mystery to U.S. Army finance officers, but they eventually figured out what was going on. Acting in a spirit of Allied cooperation, the Americans had shared the plates of the new occupation currency with the Soviets. Each side printed its own banknotes, which were practically indistinguishable from each other. American soldiers could convert the funny money back into real money at the official rate of exchange of ten occupation marks to one dollar. Red Army soldiers were paid with wads of the same occupation marks, but these marks became worthless as soon as they returned home, as they could not be converted back into rubles. The Russians spent their entire salaries in the streets of Berlin, splurging on watches and dining at expensive nightclubs. Prices around the Tiergarten shot up in accordance with the laws of supply and demand. Everything was for sale, from chewing gum to army jeeps.

The hapless U.S. Army was effectively supplying both ends of the black-market chain. It provided the original raw materials in the form of cigarettes and other consumer goods and purchased otherwise valueless paper bills for real dollars. For a time, everybody was happy. But then finance officers noticed that American GIs were sending much more money to relatives back home than they could have possibly earned from their military salaries. In the words of a military bureaucrat, "After entry into Berlin the volume of Russian printed Allied Marks presented for transmission to the United States increased to amazing proportions. . . . Transmissions of funds out of the theater [by U.S. troops] exceeded the amount of pay and allowances at a ratio of *six* or *seven* to *one.*" Someone, it seemed, was ripping off Uncle Sam. The bifurcated nature of the currency system, answering to two very different masters, was a recipe for speculation. Adding to the chaos was the worthlessness of the old Reich mark, which elevated cigarettes into the true occupation currency.

Barter represented the only way for Berliners to meet their daily needs. "The trouble," noted a U.S. officer, "is that American cigarets, as a medium of exchange, bring prices out of all proportion when Americans are dealing with Germans; a couple of cartons of cigarets would buy a piano if the buyer had any way of transporting it."

Military authorities made several halfhearted attempts to crack down on the black market in Berlin during the opening week of the Potsdam conference. Military police were instructed to jot down the license plates of American military vehicles in the vicinity of the Tiergarten, which was in the British sector of the city. German civilian policemen were dispatched to the park on July 20 and 21 to check identification papers and arrest suspected black marketers. Dressed in old-style Prussian tunics, with spikes on top of their rounded caps, the unarmed gendarmes looked as if they had stepped off the stage of a comic opera. They were not a particularly effective security force, although they did manage to round up some three thousand suspects, including a dozen GIs. The black marketeering was proving too profitable to Allied soldiers, right up the chain of command, for an unarmed German police force to put a stop to it.

Almost everyone, except the most regulation-conscious top brass, found a way to make some extra money. General Whitelaw got a foretaste of the temptations facing his troops when his staff car was stopped by "a Russian with a bank roll big enough to choke an ox" while driving into Berlin on the autobahn. The Russian offered him the occupation mark equivalent of five hundred dollars for his watch and five dollars per pack of cigarettes. "And he had the cash in hand," the general marveled in a letter to his wife. "He was very annoyed when we didn't do business. I'm told that we were lucky that he wasn't armed."

Savvy GIs used German civilians to do their black marketeering for them, offering them a cut of the proceeds. They also looked for trading spots in the Soviet sector, where prices were consistently 20 percent higher than in the western sectors. Large-scale black marketers were known as BTOs, or "big time operators." Black-market activities overlapped with the gathering of intelligence. In return for being allowed to continue trading, German black marketers provided valuable information to western intelligence officials about their high-ranking Red Army contacts. An officer serving with the U.S. Army's Criminal Investigation

Division gained a reputation for extracting kickbacks from speculators and terrorizing pretty women dabbling in the black market into having sex with him.

The tentacles of the vast black-market operation even extended into the Little White House in Babelsberg. The president's military aide, General Vaughan, who had greeted Stalin so effusively on the first day of the conference, traded his spare clothes with a Russian soldier for "a couple of thousand bucks." The crew of the presidential plane, the *Sacred Cow*, used their down time to compete for business with the local BTOs. The president's baggage plane was loaded up with black-market loot, including "a completely disassembled small German airplane" and "at least one motorcycle." One crew member boasted that he had earned sixty-five hundred dollars, roughly twice his annual salary, through the sale of watches and other goodies. Even Truman was tempted by rock-bottom prices at the American PX stores. In a letter home, he told Bess that her favorite brand of perfume, Chanel No. 5, was sold out, but he had "managed to get some other kind" for six dollars an ounce. "They said it is equal to #5 and sells for $35.00 an ounce at home. So if you don't like it a profit can be made on it."

Harry Truman prided himself on being a shrewd "Missouri horse trader." He believed in driving a hard bargain, whether at the PX or in negotiations with the Russians. At Potsdam, however, he left much of the day-to-day haggling to his secretary of state, who had vast experience negotiating with fellow politicians and papering over differences. The "able and conniving" Byrnes excelled in the art of backdoor deal-making, grinding down opponents with clever sleights of hand before offering them a face-saving way out. He seemed the ideal man to penetrate the defenses of the "ruthless automaton" Vyacheslav Molotov.

Byrnes was mistrusted by some of Truman's aides, who considered him primarily driven by his own personal interests. A "horse's ass" was Leahy's succinct description. Harriman felt that he was too willing to compromise with the Soviets. "He seemed to have gone to Potsdam with the idea that it was going to be a good deal like the Senate," the ambassador complained. "When there was controversy, he would pour oil on the waters." But he still had the confidence of the president. The two politicians had crossed the Atlantic together, occupying adjoining staterooms and posing for photographs arm in arm. "My but he has a keen mind,"

Truman wrote admiringly in his diary on July 7, after a discussion of the reparations issue. "And he is honest. But all country politicians are alike. They are sure all other politicians are circuitous in their dealings. When they are told the straight truth, unvarnished, it is never believed, an asset *sometimes.*"

Byrnes asked Molotov to meet him, accompanied only by interpreters, in the crown prince's book-lined study in Cecilienhof on the morning of Monday, July 23. He deftly set the stage for an American retreat from the $10 billion reparations promise made to Stalin at Yalta by noting that the Soviets wanted to transfer a sizable chunk of Germany to Poland. Such a step, he observed, would "expose the British and Americans in their zones to serious dangers in connection with an overall reparations plan." Since the Germany of 1937 was no more, he "wondered whether it might not be better" for each occupying power to take reparations from its own zone. By American calculations, about 50 percent of German wealth lay in the Soviet zone, so Stalin would not be losing anything through this arrangement. If the Russians wanted equipment or machinery from the Ruhr, they could exchange it for coal from Silesia.

The new American negotiating position effectively linked the reparations issue to the question of Poland's future western borders, which was itself tied to the Soviet annexation of Polish lands in the East, around the city of Lwów. In the American view, reparations were merely part of a much larger diplomatic package agreed at Yalta that included various political commitments, such as free elections in liberated countries and a fair resolution of border issues. Determined not to give up territory, Molotov began to retreat on reparations. Marshal Stalin, he told Byrnes, remained strongly in favor of an overall reparations plan for Germany but was prepared to reduce the Soviet claim for $10 billion in the interest of an agreement.

Molotov retreated even further that afternoon, during the foreign ministers' meeting, which was also attended by Pauley and Maisky. Byrnes asked him whether it was true, as American officials had observed, that Soviet reparations teams had been removing large quantities of equipment and materials from their zone, in addition to "household equipment, such as plumbing, silver and furniture."

The man known to his Kremlin colleagues as Stone Ass acknowledged, reluctantly, that "a certain quantity of property" had been removed. Striking a tone of magnanimity, he offered to "knock off $300 million for miscellaneous removals."

This did not satisfy Byrnes, who noted that the United States had spent $400 billion so far in support of the Allied cause in World War II.

"The Soviet Union is prepared to reduce its claims from $10 billion to $9 billion to cover removals already made and thus dispose of the question," Molotov countered.

Internal memos showed that neither Byrnes, nor Molotov, was being entirely honest with each other in their calculations. Byrnes had liberally rounded up American estimates of the relative wealth of the Soviet zone. Basing their calculations on the country's 1937 borders, American economists believed that the Soviet zone accounted for 39 percent of German industry and mining and 48 percent of German agriculture, not 50 percent overall, as claimed Byrnes. Soviet experts, meanwhile, had informed Molotov that the Soviet Union had extracted roughly $1.5 billion in war booty from Germany through July 8, 1945, or roughly five times the figure he provided Byrnes.

Byrnes was still not prepared to reach a deal with Molotov. Since the end of the war, nearly 5 million German refugees had flowed into the American zone. American economists had calculated that it would cost $1.5 billion to feed all these people—in the first year alone.

Molotov was becoming more accommodating but determined to draw the line somewhere. "We are prepared to cut our reparations figure to $8.5 billion, even $8 billion, but we have to insist on a fixed amount from the Ruhr," he pleaded. "Let's say $2 billion."

Anthony Eden chimed in to say that the western Allies were confronted with the specter of "wholesale starvation" in their zones over the coming winter. It had become apparent that the Soviets were "unwilling to turn over food and coal from the zone which they wished to give to Poland."

Stone Ass squirmed some more. "That is a question that can be discussed."

19

"FINIS"

July 26

Winston Churchill was in an anxious, even irascible mood. The British general election—"this bloody election" was his preferred term—"hung like a veil over the future." He would fly back to London on July 25 to hear the result of the vote count, which had been under way for the last three weeks. His aides assured him that his Conservative Party would retain a comfortable majority in the House of Commons, but the prime minister could not rule out an electoral upset. The previous Saturday, his Labour Party rival, Clement Attlee, had been greeted effusively by British troops assembled in the Tiergarten for a victory parade. At first, Churchill thought the cheers were for him and raised his hand in the V salute. When he heard the shouts of "Attlee," he dropped his hand and "glowered straight ahead." It struck his aides as "decidedly odd" that "the great war leader but for whom we should never have been in Berlin at all got a markedly less vociferous cheer" than the colorless Attlee. But they were too polite to mention the incident.

Churchill had spent the last ten days in Potsdam struggling to come to terms with his own increasing irrelevance. Truman and Stalin listened politely to his long-winded interventions and laughed at his jokes, but paid little attention to his concerns. They behaved like grown-ups who allowed themselves to be entertained by the outbursts of a precocious child even as they remained focused on their own adult pursuits. For all his jingoistic showmanship, Churchill was painfully aware that the war had left Great Britain deeply in debt to the United States, dependent on the generosity of its onetime colony. The British Empire was racked by ethnic turmoil and nationalist insurrection and in danger of falling apart. The Royal Navy remained a formidable force, but the overstretched British Army was no match for the Red Army. Without a permanent American military presence, western Europe lay defenseless before the Russian bear.

Personal discomforts added to the ill humor of the king's first minister. Like Truman and Stalin, Churchill had been assigned a large villa over-looking the lake. The hobnailed shoes of British sentries echoing across the courtyard outside his window had disturbed his sleep. He demanded that they be issued rubber soles and kept out of earshot. On the evening of July 22, a storm had swept through Babelsberg, leaving the streets "lit-tered with trees." A century-old lime tree right outside Churchill's resi-dence at 23 Ringstrasse was bent over by the gale, uprooting a water pipe beneath. "PM very annoyed at not being able to have a bath," a senior British diplomat noted in his diary. "He says it is 'a most unwarranted act of Providence.'"

The storm came at a particularly inconvenient time for the prime minister, who had arranged to host a ceremonial dinner for Truman and Stalin on the evening of July 23. He was mischievously looking forward to the occasion as it would allow him to "get even" with the other two statesmen for the "musical marathons" they had inflicted on him earlier in the conference. Stalin had responded to Truman's opening bid of one pianist and one violinist by upping the stakes and producing two pianists and two violinists, who were flown in from Moscow to provide entertain-ment for his guests. The president was impressed by their musical abili-ties, if not by their looks. "They were excellent," he conceded, in a letter to his mother and sister. "They had dirty faces though and the girls were rather fat." The prime minister, by contrast, was "bored to tears." He pre-ferred rousing military marches to delicate piano concertos. He skulked in the corner with Admiral Leahy, grumbling and plotting his revenge, which would come in the form of the entire Royal Air Force orchestra. He selected a distinctly lowbrow program, opening with "Ay-Ay-Ay," a Mexican serenade, and concluding with "Irish Reels" and the "Skye Boat Song."

Churchill's dinner was on a grander scale than either Truman's or

Stalin's. If the empire was in retreat, at least it would go out in style. The prime minister had British Army engineers construct a special table that could comfortably seat twenty-eight guests, including the chiefs of staff of all three Allied armies. He stationed a Scots Regiment honor guard with rifles and fixed bayonets in front of the entrance to the villa to salute the guests, most of whom were in military uniform.

Heavily armed Russian soldiers took up positions around the villa half an hour before Stalin's arrival. To avoid an incident, Churchill's outnumbered bodyguards withdrew to the terrace. The *vozhd* drove up in a convoy of huge limousines following the one-minute journey from his own residence around the corner. He was dressed in a new generalissimo's uniform, which consisted of a sparkling white jacket with a gold-braided collar, a Hero of the Soviet Union gold star, and blue dress pants with a double red stripe down the center, a departure from his previously modest style. The outfit made him look "like the emperor of Austria in a bad musical comedy," in the opinion of a British official, but his gun-toting security men projected an image of raw power. Stalin replied to the salute of Churchill's honor guard by raising his arm stiffly. Truman, meanwhile, had made an unostentatious entrance on foot, having walked from the Little White House. The three leaders stood together for a few seconds on the porch, staging a three-way handshake for the benefit of the photographers.

The dinner itself consisted of the usual string of effusive toasts, with everybody showering compliments on one another, when they were not drowned out by the RAF band in the next room. Churchill praised Truman's "sincerity, frankness, and powers of decision." The president struck a tone of humility, depicting himself as a timid "country boy from Missouri" who felt overwhelmed by being in the company of "such great figures as the Prime Minister and Marshal Stalin." Stalin replied that such personal modesty was a "real indication of character," combined, as it was, with "strength" and "honesty of purpose."

Stalin seemed to genuinely enjoy himself. His eyes twinkling with good humor, he told Churchill's interpreter, Arthur Birse, that he liked the "dignified" style of English dinners, and compared American and British generals favorably with Soviet generals.

"Ours still lack breeding," he complained, glancing down the table at Marshal Zhukov. "Their manners are bad. Our people have a long way to go."

Territorial aggrandizement was clearly on Stalin's mind at the dinner.

Rebuffed by Churchill in his demand for a fortified position in the Sea of Marmora, adjoining the Dardanelles, he requested a military base on the Aegean Sea. Not wanting to be rude to his guest, the prime minister replied diplomatically, "I will always support Russia in her claim to the freedom of the seas all year round." The generalissimo made no secret of his ambitions in the Far East. He surprised Churchill and Truman by revealing his plans to attack Japan in the presence of a phalanx of stewards and waitresses, not to mention the RAF band next door. The Soviet Union had not yet declared war on Japan and was still—at least in theory—bound by the terms of a nonaggression pact that did not expire until April 1946.

There was much jollity as the guests changed places every so often to encourage more conversation. At the end of the meal, Stalin got up from his seat and walked around the table collecting signatures on his menu card. "I never thought to see him as an autograph hunter," Churchill recalled later. Soon everybody was requesting autographs from everyone else, as a souvenir of the Big Three meeting. Both Stalin and Truman wandered into the adjoining room to toast the orchestra and request their favorite tunes.

Churchill was thinking about the election, and his own political fate. Raising a glass to Attlee, he called for a toast to "the next leader of the opposition—whoever that may be."

The telegram that Harry Truman had been eagerly anticipating arrived in Babelsberg on the evening of Monday, July 23, while he was exchanging toasts with Stalin and Churchill. It was couched in the euphemistic language that American officials had developed to discuss the most terrifying weapon in history. The atomic bomb had become "the patient." Extending the medical terminology, its use over Japan was now described as "the operation." Topping the War Department's list of possible targets was the city of Hiroshima, which had been spared from the worst of Curtis LeMay's bombing raids.

OPERATION MAY BE POSSIBLE ANY TIME FROM AUGUST 1 DEPENDING ON STATE OF PREPARATION OF PATIENT AND CONDITION OF ATMOSPHERE. FROM POINT OF VIEW OF PATIENT ONLY, SOME CHANCE AUGUST 1 TO 3, GOOD CHANCE AUGUST 4 TO 5 AND BARRING UNEXPECTED RELAPSE ALMOST CERTAIN BEFORE AUGUST 10.

The telegram was addressed to the secretary of war. At 9:20 a.m. the following morning, Henry Stimson strolled down Kaiserstrasse to deliver the message to the president in the Little White House. He found Truman in his study on the second floor of the "nightmare house," overlooking the lake. Truman pronounced himself "highly delighted" with the news. He could now issue a formal ultimatum to the Japanese government, offering them a choice between "unconditional surrender" and "prompt and utter destruction."

"Just what I wanted," enthused the president.

Both men felt that the military equation in the Far East had been transformed by the atomic bomb. Soviet participation in the war against Japan—which had once seemed the only way to avoid hundreds of thousands of American casualties—was no longer essential or even desirable. The president and his advisers hoped that the bomb would compel the Japanese to surrender, preventing the Russians from getting in "on the kill" and claiming sweeping territorial concessions. "We should get the Japanese affair over with before the Russians get in" was how Byrnes put it. "Once they are in, it will not be easy to get them out." Briefed by Byrnes on the latest developments, Churchill concluded that "the United States do not at the present time desire Russian participation in the war against Japan." The push for Japan's final surrender was turning into a race between American airpower and technological ingenuity and the land power of the Red Army, massing on the border with China.

Stimson persuaded Truman that the bomb should not be dropped on the ancient Japanese capital of Kyoto, a city of unique historical importance. The president noted in his diary that the weapon would be used against "soldiers and sailors" rather than "women and children." America would not descend to the level of its enemies. "Even if the Japs are savages, ruthless, merciless and fanatic, we as the leader of the world for the common welfare cannot drop this terrible bomb on the old Capitol or the new."

"He & I are in accord," wrote Truman, referring to Stimson. "The target will be a purely military one and we will issue a warning statement asking the Japs to surrender and save lives. I'm sure they will not do that, but we will have given them the chance. It is certainly a good thing for the world that Hitler's crowd or Stalin's did not discover this atomic bomb. It seems to be the most terrible thing ever discovered, but it can be made the most useful."

Hiroshima was hardly the "purely military" target that Truman claimed. While it was an important naval base, it was impossible for the American bombardiers to distinguish between factories serving the military and civilian homes. The targeting instructions specified hitting an "urban industrial area," with the object of "obtaining the greatest psychological effects against Japan." It was anticipated that the bomb would "almost totally destroy an area three miles across." Hiroshima was a particularly attractive target because "it was of such a size that a large part of the city could be extensively damaged." Adjacent hills were likely to produce "a focusing effect which would considerably increase the blast damage."

Although Truman later depicted July 24 as the "day of decision" on the atomic bomb, he never issued a formal presidential order for the destruction of Hiroshima. The S-1 program had acquired a momentum of its own, employing one hundred thirty thousand workers across more than thirty sites at a cost of $2 billion. The president was just one cog in a gigantic machine that rolled inexorably on. From the moment that Truman was first briefed on the new weapon, two weeks after becoming president, he had assumed it would be used to "bring about the earliest possible surrender of Japan." The only question in his mind was whether it would work, but that issue had now been settled, thanks to the test in New Mexico. In the words of his military aide, George Elsey, there was "no decision to be made" about the bomb. Truman "could no more have stopped it" than he could have stopped "a train moving down a track."

The order to drop a series of atomic bombs on Japan was drafted by General Groves in Washington and sent to Stimson and General Marshall in Potsdam for their approval. It was issued in the name of the secretary of war and the chief of staff of the U.S. Army. The targets were listed in the following order: Hiroshima, Kokura, Niigata, Nagasaki.

Fortified by the knowledge that the "most terrible bomb in the history of the world" was now a military reality, Truman headed into one of his most acrimonious sessions with Stalin. The toasting of the night before had given way to hardheaded bargaining about the future of Europe. Both Truman and Churchill were worried by the creation of a string of Soviet satellites from Poland in the north to Bulgaria in the south. They had recognized the Communist-dominated government in Poland in return for the inclusion of several London Poles but were demanding larger concessions from Hungary, Romania, and Bulgaria. The president informed the generalissimo that the governments of the other satellite countries had to be reorganized "along democratic lines," as agreed at Yalta.

Stalin insisted that the Soviet satellites were "more democratic" than Italy, where the Americans and British were running the show. He pointed out that no elections had been held in Italy since the overthrow of Hitler's ally, Benito Mussolini. As far as Stalin was concerned, "if a government is not Fascist, it is democratic."

Churchill defended the Italians. There was no censorship in Italy: he himself was often attacked in Italian newspapers. "Democratic elections" would soon be held. Russian officials were "welcome to come to Italy and go anywhere." By contrast, western representatives were prevented from traveling freely in Bulgaria and Romania. Complaining that members of the British military mission in Bucharest had been "penned up with a closeness approaching internment," he trotted out a phrase that he was still polishing.

"An iron fence has come down around them."

"All fairy tales," snapped Stalin.

"Statesmen may call one another's statements fairy tales if they wish."

"The same situation prevails in Italy."

"That is not accurate. You can go where you like in Italy."

Seated two chairs down from Truman, Admiral Leahy felt the conference had reached "a complete impasse." Reflecting on what had happened in his day-by-day account of Big Three diplomacy, he concluded that the moment represented "the beginning of the Cold War between the United States and Russia."

Truman was more upbeat, telling his wife, Bess, that "we have accomplished a very great deal" after "going at it hammer and tongs in the last few days." He cited the establishment of a council of foreign ministers and "a government for Germany." Nevertheless, he acknowledged that there were "some things we can't agree to. We have unalterably opposed the recognition of police governments in the Germany Axis countries. I told Stalin that until we had free access to those countries and our nationals had their property rights restored, so far as we were concerned there'd never be recognition. He seems to like it when I hit him with a hammer."

Stalin upset the president by impatiently dismissing his pet idea for the internationalization of major European waterways. The former World War I artillery captain was convinced that Europeans would stop fighting one another if they could trade freely with one another. "I do not want to fight another war in twenty years because of a quarrel on the Danube," he had told Stalin and Churchill on July 23. "We want a prosperous, self-supporting Europe. A bankrupt Europe is of no advantage to any country, or to the peace of the world." The prospect of American ships steaming up the Danube through Soviet-controlled Romania, Yugoslavia, and Hungary was unappealing to Stalin.

To bait Churchill, and divert attention from the Danube, Stalin broadened the discussion to include the sea approaches to India, the jewel in the British Empire.

"What will be done about the Suez Canal?" he demanded.

The English bulldog suddenly found himself on the defensive.

"It will be open."

"What about international control?"

"That question has not been raised."

"I am raising it."

Churchill gamely insisted that there had been "no complaints" about the existing arrangement, which envisaged British control over the canal until at least 1956. Stalin had made his point about the hypocrisy of the western powers, who were in favor of international control when it suited their purposes, but not otherwise. He rested his case.

The waterway question, he told Truman and Churchill, was "not ripe for discussion."

It had been a tense and irritable session, but there was one last piece of business to conduct. When the meeting ended at 7:30 p.m., Truman strolled over to Stalin, without his interpreter, as if to exchange a few meaningless pleasantries. To protect himself from charges of duplicity, the president had decided to inform his Soviet ally about the existence of the atomic bomb, without revealing any details. Speaking through Stalin's interpreter, Vladimir Pavlov, he mentioned—in as casual a tone as he could muster—that the United States had discovered "a weapon of unusual destructive force."

"Glad to hear it," the generalissimo replied. "I hope you will make good use of it against the Japanese."

Churchill watched the "momentous talk" unfold across the room. He had been briefed on Truman's intentions and paid close attention to Stalin's reactions. The dictator's face remained "gay and genial." It seemed that he had failed to comprehend the "revolution in world affairs" that was under way. Churchill was convinced that the Soviet leader had "no idea of the significance of what he had been told." Truman and his closest aides came away with a similar impression. Had Stalin been even remotely aware of the power of the atomic bomb, he would surely have pressed the Americans for further details. Instead, he seemed almost uninterested.

"How did it go?" Churchill asked the president as they waited for their cars outside the Cecilienhof Palace.

"He never asked a question."

The look of bafflement on Stalin's face was a ruse. He had been waiting for Truman to disclose the secret of the atom bomb ever since arriving in Potsdam—and was half irritated, half amused by the president's indirect approach. Thanks to a network of atomic spies across the United States, he knew considerably more about the Manhattan Project than Truman himself had known prior to becoming president. Soviet foreign intelligence had succeeded in recruiting three agents in Los Alamos alone and had already acquired rough blueprints of the bomb. One of these agents, the German physicist Klaus Fuchs, had informed his Soviet control officer that the first test of the atomic bomb would take place "around July 10." The test was subsequently postponed until July 16.

The *vozhd* had given considerable thought to the question of how to react if the president informed him about the bomb. After weighing his various options, he decided to "pretend not to understand" and display no curiosity at all. He did not want the Americans to conclude that he was impressed by their new weapon and therefore susceptible to political intimidation. Stalin had little doubt that the U.S. government intended to use the atomic weapon to bargain from a position of strength. He would not allow himself to be bullied or blackmailed.

Although he acted as if nothing significant had happened, Stalin was the ultimate political realist, constantly calculating what Marxist-Leninists liked to call "the correlation of forces." He understood immediately that the worldwide balance of power had shifted: America and Britain now had a way of neutralizing the huge Soviet advantage in conventional forces even if they continued to demobilize their own armies.

Returning to his Babelsberg residence after the conversation with Truman, Stalin telephoned the director of the Soviet atomic project, Igor Kurchatov. Russian scientists had been carrying out nuclear research for more than two years on a relatively modest scale since there was no guarantee of success. The *vozhd* feared that some of the espionage materials gushing out of Los Alamos could be disinformation, designed to divert Soviet resources away from more useful military projects. He now ordered Kurchatov "to speed things up." A Soviet atomic bomb was at least two years away, but he knew from his spies that the Americans only had enough fissile material for two or three bombs. This gave Russia an opportunity to close the gap.

In private, surrounded by a few close aides, Stalin launched into a tirade about the insincerity of his western partners. He was convinced that the tough tone adopted by Truman and Churchill in rejecting Soviet plans for eastern Europe and postwar reparations was connected to the development of the new superweapon. The Americans had the nerve to complain about Soviet looting while shipping the "best equipment, complete with all its documentation" back to the United States.

"The Soviet Union is being cheated," he fumed. "Truman doesn't even know the meaning of justice."

"The Americans have been doing all this work on the atom bomb without telling us," said Molotov.

"We were supposed to be allies," Stalin added bitterly.

At first, he spoke calmly, but then started cursing Truman, Churchill, and even Roosevelt "in ripe language." The Anglo-American strategy was clear to Stalin. The imperialists wanted to use the American monopoly over nuclear weapons to browbeat Mother Russia.

"They want to force us to accept their plans on questions affecting Europe and the world. Well, that's not going to happen."

His aides attempted to calm him down by making jokes about the other leaders. Andrei Gromyko, the Soviet ambassador to Washington, painted a lecherous portrait of the British prime minister. "Churchill was so riveted by our women traffic police in their marvelous uniforms that he dropped his cigar ash all over his suit."

For the first time in the meeting, the dictator allowed himself a smile.

There was little Stalin could do to pry the riches of the Ruhr away from Truman and Churchill. But he was in a position to get his way on Poland, where the Red Army was in full control. He had decided months ago that Poland would be allowed, even encouraged, to absorb forty thousand square miles of German territory, establishing its western borders on the Oder and Western Neisse Rivers. He was also determined to ensure that the government in Warsaw remain in the hands of Moscow-trained Polish Communists who owed him their full loyalty. The Americans and the British could demand free elections and freedom of the press as much as they liked, but Stalin would not permit Poland to slip from his grasp. His position was virtually identical to that of his tsarist predecessor, Alexander

I, at the Congress of Vienna in 1815, who told western statesmen that the Polish question "could end only in one way, as he was in possession."

Stalin produced a delegation of Polish leaders to echo his views on the shape of the new Poland. They were led by a veteran Communist, Bolesław Bierut, a longtime NKVD agent who had survived the Great Purge that eliminated most of his comrades. Now acting president, Bierut was already known to the western politicians for his sycophancy toward Stalin; he had proven his loyalty by vociferously demanding that Poland's eastern territories, around the city of Lwów, be surrendered to the Soviet Union. Trailing along behind was the sorrowful figure of Stanisław Mikołajczyk, the former prime minister-in-exile now reduced to providing a fig leaf of respectability to the Bierut regime.

The Poles were not invited to join the Big Three in the plenary sessions at Cecilienhof. Instead they made their rounds of the foreign ministers and senior officials, reciting long lists of statistics justifying their claim to large chunks of Germany. Churchill, happy to have a captive audience, gave them nearly two hours of his time. Truman dismissed them after fifteen minutes, before rushing off to rejoin the prime minister and generalissimo.

In his talks with the British, Bierut scoffed at Churchill's concerns that democracy was in jeopardy in Poland. He pointed out that prior to the war Poland had "23 political parties, which is even more than Great Britain has." They would all be permitted to take part in the elections, which would be conducted under the eyes of foreign journalists. Privately, Mikołajczyk told the British that Bierut was trying "to establish a one-party system." Free elections were impossible as long as the Soviet army and NKVD remained in the country, and there was no sign of them leaving. Leadership positions in the Polish army from major upward were held by "Russians in Polish uniform," many of whom did not speak Polish. Tens of thousands of Polish partisans remained in the woods of eastern Poland, afraid to emerge for fear of being swept up in a wave of mass arrests. But Mikołajczyk wholeheartedly supported Bierut's claim to German territories in Silesia and Pomerania.

Dealing with the Poles left western officials, particularly the British, disillusioned and dispirited. "Dreadful people, all of them, except Mikołajczyk," Cadogan complained to his diary. Even Churchill, who liked to remind Stalin that Britain had gone to war against Hitler because of Poland, had lost his appetite for the endless diplomatic squabbling.

"I'm sick of the bloody Poles," he told his doctor, Charles Moran. In private conversation, he referred to the three most prominent Polish leaders as "the Fox, the Snake, and the Skunk." His official biography acknowledged the sad geopolitical truth: "The Poland for which Britain had gone to war in 1939 no longer existed."

Churchill had a vivid and disturbing dream the night after his meeting with the Poles. "I dreamed that life was over," he told Moran on the morning of Wednesday, July 25. "I saw—it was very vivid—my dead body under a white sheet on a table in an empty room. I recognized my bare feet projecting from under the sheet. It was very life-like." He paused to consider what the dream meant. "Perhaps this is the end."

Contrary to his usual practice, he had got out of bed early to attend to some last-minute business before flying back to London to await the election results. He received Bierut for a second time at 10:00 a.m., lecturing him about the importance of "free elections." The Communist leader nodded earnestly, assuring Churchill that Poland had no desire "to copy the Soviet system." Asked when the Soviet secret police would leave Poland, Bierut replied that "the NKVD played no part in Poland," which had its own, independent security police. Churchill was unconvinced but too worn down to argue. He urged the Polish leader "to make the most of the present opportunities" and "get on well" with Mikołajczyk.

The three leaders were greeted by a phalanx of movie cameramen and photographers when they arrived at Cecilienhof at 10:45 a.m. They had agreed to a group photo in the garden of the palace before a plenary session scheduled for eleven. Three wicker chairs had been placed on the sun-splashed lawn so they were exactly one foot away from one another. As chairman of the conference, Truman sat down in the middle chair, equidistant from his fellow leaders. Stalin, resplendent in his cream generalissimo jacket, settled into the chair to the president's left. Churchill, who was dressed in his colonel's uniform, did not care for the seating arrangements. Turning to face the photographers, he surreptitiously grabbed the chair, which was now behind him, and moved it a foot to the left. The leaders of the two democracies were now visually—and symbolically—united while the Soviet dictator was seated by himself, a foot away. Taken aback, Truman attempted to shift his chair back to the middle. Since it now contained his full body weight, it scarcely budged.

Churchill looked pleased with himself, like a schoolboy who has pulled one over on the teacher. His chair trick was executed so deftly that no one apart from Truman seemed to notice. Stalin gazed stolidly ahead.

The plenary session turned into a dialogue of the deaf between Churchill and Stalin, with Truman doing his best to adjudicate. Everybody rehearsed their previous lines, like actors sticking doggedly to the script. Churchill complained about the Russian-Polish land grab along the Western Neisse and the interruption in food supplies to Berlin. The Poles and Russians were "throwing the Germans into the American and British zones to be fed." Stalin countered by asking about deliveries of steel and coal from the Ruhr to the Russian zone of Germany, an issue he deemed of "much greater importance" than the feeding of German refugees. There had to be some kind of reciprocity, Churchill replied: if the miners of the Ruhr did not get fed, they would be unable to produce coal.

"There is still a great deal of fat left in Germany," Stalin scoffed, ruling out food deliveries from the rich agricultural lands of Pomerania, "because that territory goes to Poland."

Ground down by the same arguments, Churchill tried a different tack, telling Stalin that England faced the prospect of a "fireless winter." Stalin was unsympathetic, noting that Russia was short of coal and practically everything else. The prime minister would "weep" if he knew the desperate situation of the Soviet people.

"I am finished," Churchill said finally, raising his hands in mock surrender.

"What a pity" was Stalin's comment.

"We shall adjourn until Friday at five p.m.," said Truman briskly.

There was no need for formal farewells; everybody expected Churchill to be back in Potsdam within forty-eight hours. Stalin gestured toward the diminutive figure of Clement Attlee, hunched in his chair next to the Soviet delegation. With his bald pate, trim mustache, and rounded eyeglasses, the Labour Party leader looked more like a bank manager than a future prime minister. "A sheep in sheep's clothing," Churchill liked to joke. The supreme leader of Russia was equally dismissive.

"Mr. Attlee does not look to me like a man who is hungry for power."

The plenary session over, Churchill hurried to Gatow airfield after a brief stop at his villa. He was met at Northolt RAF base in Britain by his wife, his brother, and his political aide, Jock Colville. Everybody was still upbeat about the likely result of the election. Colville noted in his diary that evening that Labour Party insiders "expected a Government majority of 30." This was less than earlier estimates, but still respectable. Churchill went to bed in 10 Downing Street "in the belief that the British people would wish me to continue my work." He planned to invite Attlee to join another national coalition government, with seats allocated in proportion to representation in the new House of Commons.

He woke up just before dawn the following morning, Thursday, July 26, with "a stab of almost physical pain." He was suddenly seized by a sense of panic. "A hitherto subconscious conviction that we were beaten broke forth and dominated my mind," he recalled later. "The power to shape the future would be denied me. The knowledge and experience I had gathered, the authority and goodwill I had gained in so many countries, would vanish." He turned over and went back to sleep, not waking until 9:00 a.m.

His staff had set up an election result hub in the Map Room in the Downing Street Annex, where he had spent the last four years tracking the movements of Allied and enemy armies. The Map Room chief, Captain Pim, had plastered the walls with an alphabetical list of all parliamentary constituencies as well as the names of ministers in Churchill's government, awaiting ticks or crosses to show whether they had been reelected. Scoreboards kept track of gains, losses, and total seats of the major political parties. When Churchill walked in soon after 10:00 a.m., dressed in his wartime boiler suit, Map Room staff were already tearing messages from the tape machine and chalking up the first results. One Tory constituency after another was falling to Labour. At first, Churchill displayed "no visible sign of surprise or emotion," acknowledging each result with a nod of his head, even though they were completely counter to all the newspaper predictions. His aides assured him that the tide would swing back in his direction once the votes were counted in the rural constituencies, but it never did.

By lunch, it was all over. The Churchill family sat "in Stygian gloom" around the dining table. The silence was interrupted by Clementine.

"Winston, it may be a blessing in disguise."

The old warhorse looked at his wife with a wry smile.

"At the moment it certainly is very well disguised."

He kept repeating that the results represented "the will of the people" but could not hide a sense of deep betrayal. "I wooed them and they spurned me," he told his ministers. "I ought to have seen it in their eyes."

The Churchills spent a final weekend at Chequers, the prime minister's country house. Winston "made valiant efforts to be cheerful," playing cards and croquet with his houseguests. He watched an American propaganda movie and a documentary film on the early stages of the Potsdam conference. But "a cloud of black gloom" soon descended. There were no top-secret communications to review, no messengers bearing red boxes. "No work, nothing to do," he grumbled. His daughters played gramophone records for him, including his favorite tunes from Gilbert and Sullivan, to little avail. Finally, long after midnight, they trooped off to bed. The following day, before departing, everybody signed the Chequers visitors' book.

Churchill insisted on signing last. Beneath his signature, at the bottom of the page, he wrote a single word:

FINIS

20

Hiroshima

August 6

The *vozhd* suspected a double cross. He was determined to join the war against Japan, keeping a promise he had made to Roosevelt at Yalta. In return for delivering the knockout blow against the Japanese militarists, the Soviet Union would be rewarded with a series of territorial concessions, ranging from the island of Sakhalin to control over the principal ports of Manchuria. Stalin even had hopes for a joint occupation of the Japanese mainland—with a Soviet officer serving as deputy to General MacArthur as the supreme Allied commander.

Suddenly, without explanation, everything had changed. Truman no longer seemed as eager to secure Soviet participation in the war as when he first arrived in Potsdam, just two weeks before. The latest version of the Allied ultimatum to Japan omitted a reference to the "vast military might of the Soviet Union" that had been part of an earlier draft. Instead, it hinted at the existence of a new weapon that would ensure "the utter devastation of the Japanese homeland," in addition to the "complete destruction of the Japanese armed forces." The cryptic references to the atomic bomb may have been obscure to the Japanese, but they were crystal clear to Stalin, thanks to his spies in Los Alamos. He understood that the Soviet Union and the United States were now engaged in a vast geostrategic competition, unfolding across Europe and Asia. The imme-diate focus was the surrender of Japan. Would America succeed in finish-ing off Japan with its new explosive device before the Red Army stormed into Japanese-occupied Manchuria?

Molotov received the text of the Potsdam proclamation from Byrnes in the late evening of July 26. The document bore the signatures of Tru-man, Churchill, and the Chinese nationalist president, Chiang Kai-shek, who had given his assent by telegram. The Russians had no problem recognizing Chiang as the legitimate leader of China—overlooking the claims of the Communist Mao Tse-tung—but they wanted to have a say in dictating Japan's surrender. Molotov's aides immediately got to work on the text of an alternative four-power declaration, confirming that the Soviet Union was ready to join in the war against the "Japanese milita-rists." "Japan must understand that further resistance is futile," the Soviet draft declared. "Japan must end the war, lay down its arms and surrender unconditionally."

A Molotov aide, Vladimir Pavlov, telephoned the U.S. delegation five minutes before midnight on July 26 to request a three-day delay in issuing the document to allow for consultations. His American contact rang back fifteen minutes later to say it was too late. U.S. radio stations based on the West Coast had begun broadcasting the full text of the proclamation in English, and highlights in Japanese, at 11:00 p.m. Berlin time. By the time the proclamation was issued, one of the signatories was no longer in office. The British Broadcasting Corporation had announced Churchill's resignation as prime minister on the 9:00 p.m. evening news—10:00 p.m. Berlin time.

There was no Big Three meeting on July 27, as the British had not yet returned from London. Truman flew to Frankfurt for the day to inspect American troops. When Molotov called on Byrnes at 6:00 p.m., he imme-diately broached the subject of Stalin's exclusion from the Potsdam proc-lamation. Byrnes produced a rather lame excuse. "We did not consult the Soviet government because you are not at war with Japan. We did not want to embarrass you."

"I am not authorized to discuss the matter any further," Molotov replied stiffly.

The next plenary session, on July 28, was delayed until 10:30 p.m. to allow Clement Attlee time to reach Berlin. The new British prime minis-ter sank deep down in his chair, puffing at his pipe. He was accompanied by his foreign secretary, Ernest Bevin, who did most of the talking. The president and the generalissimo were unimpressed. A couple of "sour-pusses" was how Truman described Attlee and Bevin in a letter to his daughter. He had become comfortable with "fat old Winston" despite his windy oratory. "He knew his English language, and after he'd talked half an hour, there'd be at least one gem of a sentence and two thoughts maybe, which could have been expressed in four minutes." With Churchill gone, Truman could not wait to get home.

Stalin eyed Attlee and Bevin suspiciously, shocked not only by the ingratitude of the British electorate but also by Churchill's failure to fix the result. He had privately told Churchill that he expected him to be reelected with a comfortable majority of "about eighty" seats. "This queer manifestation of our British democracy is quite beyond the grasp of Russians," noted Archibald Clark Kerr, the British ambassador to Moscow, in a condolence letter to Clementine Churchill. "To a Russian it is inexplicable that a people should be allowed to deliberately put out of office a man who has led them through the darkest day of their history to a thumping victory." Clark Kerr found himself surrounded by "a bunch of gibbering and bewildered Russians" demanding explanations. Molotov, in particular, was "clearly much upset" by the election result, "throwing up his fat hands and asking 'why, why?'"

With malicious delight, Clark Kerr imagined Stalin going home that night, getting out of "his latest (and rather pansy) uniform," and pondering "where a free and unfettered popular vote in Russia would leave him." Via a Polish official, he learned that Stalin's first reaction to Churchill's defeat was to pronounce the British people "tired of war. They are turning their minds away from the beating of Japan to internal problems. This may make them softer about the Germans." The *vozhd* did not intend to permit his own people to get similarly distracted.

Stalin wasted no time emphasizing his unhappiness over the Potsdam declaration. He began by saying that he had received a new peace feeler from the Japanese government. He felt a "duty" to keep the Allies informed—despite their failure to inform him in advance about the ultimatum to Japan. The Soviet Union, Stalin announced stiffly, would refuse the Japanese request for mediation. The gesture of Allied solidarity was not as magnanimous as he tried to make it sound. He knew the Americans had succeeded in breaking the Japanese diplomatic code—and were able to read communications between Tokyo and Moscow.

A truer indication of Stalin's changing attitude toward the United States was his decision to speed up his own preparations for attacking

Japan. Soviet generals had told their American counterparts that the Red Army would be ready to invade Manchuria in the second half of August. Determined not to be beaten by the Americans, Stalin now gave secret orders for hostilities to be advanced by ten to fourteen days. He also appointed Marshal Alexander Vasilevskii supreme commander of all Soviet forces in the Far East. The race to finish off Japan was under way in earnest.

Stalin's displeasure with his western Allies went far beyond his concerns over Japan. He was convinced that Truman was reneging on promises made at Yalta by FDR. In conversations with Davies, their most sympathetic American interlocutor, Stalin's aides complained that Russia was being robbed of the fruits of its hard-won victory. Molotov wanted to know why the United States had changed its position on reparations. In a rare display of emotion, he described how Hitler's armies had "despoiled everything of value" in Russia. "They enslaved women and children in barbaric death chambers. They tortured and killed thousands upon thousands. They destroyed whole cities." It seemed to Molotov that the Americans were more concerned with the welfare of the defeated Germans than their long-suffering Russian allies. He could not understand why there had been such "a marked change of attitude since Yalta."

"We trusted President Roosevelt and we believed in him," Molotov said grimly. "It is not easy for us to understand your new president."

Jimmy Byrnes sensed the time had come to make a deal. "I know how to deal with the Russians," he boasted to his staff. "It's just like the U.S. Senate. You build a post office in their state, and they'll build a post office in our state."

The outline of the probable Potsdam agreement was as clear as it was cynical. All three parties would hold on to what they already had, making only token concessions to grand but nebulous concepts such as "Allied cooperation," a "united Germany," and the "spirit of Yalta." Stalin would not permit any threat to the stability and cohesion of his new eastern European empire. Nor would he compromise on the borders of Poland, which were under the full control of the Red Army. Similarly, Truman had no intention of relaxing his hold over the parts of Germany that were under American or British occupation. He would not permit Stalin to get his way on reparations, whatever the hints and promises made to Russia by FDR.

As far as Truman was concerned, there would be "no reparations" at all if the Russians continued to strip their part of the country bare.

Truman and Byrnes invited Stalin and Molotov to a private negotiating session on Sunday, July 29, at the Little White House in Babelsberg. Molotov showed up by himself and was escorted to the president's study on the second floor, overlooking the lake. He explained that his boss had "caught a cold and his doctors would not let him leave the house." The Americans had no way of determining the gravity of the generalissimo's illness or whether it was real or diplomatic. Truman was sufficiently alarmed to reflect on the likely political consequences of Stalin's death. "It would end the original Big Three," he mused in a diary entry the following day. "First Roosevelt by death, then Churchill by political failure and then Stalin. . . . If some demagogue on horseback gained control of the efficient Russian military machine, he could play havoc with European peace for a while. I also wonder if there is a man with the necessary strength and following to step into Stalin's place and maintain peace and solidarity at home. It isn't customary for dictators to train leaders to follow them in power." On balance, the president felt the West was better off with the devil it knew than someone else.

Anxious to get out of "this Godforsaken country" as soon as possible, Truman let Byrnes do most of the bargaining. The secretary outlined the two most important outstanding issues: Poland's western boundary and reparations. Once these matters were settled, it would be possible to wind up the conference. To open the negotiations, he offered his Russian counterpart 25 percent of German industrial equipment "available for reparations" in the Ruhr and a Polish frontier that followed the line of the Eastern Neisse River. This did not satisfy the equally canny Molotov. He pointed out that "25 per cent of an undetermined figure meant very little." He asked for a "fixed sum," equivalent to $2 billion. He also insisted on a Polish frontier along the Western Neisse, an arrangement that would give Poland an additional eight thousand square miles of German territory. Having rejected the initial American bid, Molotov drove the quarter mile up Kaiserstrasse to consult with Stalin.

Byrnes and Molotov met again at 4:30 p.m. on July 30, this time in the Cecilienhof Palace. Truman chose not to attend; Stalin remained "indisposed." The secretary announced he was prepared to agree to the Western Neisse border. He also held out the possibility of a compromise on western diplomatic recognition for the governments of Romania, Hungary,

Bulgaria, and Finland. But he made clear these concessions had to be part of a package that included an agreement on reparations.

The haggling continued at the foreign ministers' meeting at 5:00 p.m. in the grand hall of the crown prince's palace. Sensing that he had to make a concession of his own, Molotov lowered his demand for industrial equipment from the Ruhr from $2 billion to $800 million.

Byrnes repeated that it was "impossible" to name any kind of fixed sum. "We have no information about the amount of equipment that will be available for the payment of reparations."

Realizing that he had hit a brick wall, Molotov shifted direction. He wanted to know who would determine how much equipment would be "available for reparations." The Russians wanted to vest this authority in a central "Control Council," representing all the occupying powers. The Americans and British were determined to retain the final say on how much equipment was removed from the territory they controlled.

"We cannot agree to take away the right of veto from the commander of the zone," Byrnes insisted. He reminded Molotov that the United States had made a big concession to the Soviet Union on the Western Neisse.

"That was a concession to Poland, not to us," rejoined the Russian.

Final agreement was left to the Big Three, or the "Big 2½," as a British wit labeled the Churchill-less troika. Stalin returned to the negotiating table on the afternoon of July 31, apparently none the worse for his "indisposition." The *vozhd* succeeded in clarifying the language on reparations. Most of the German reparations payable to the Soviet Union would come from the Soviet-controlled zone, but an unspecified amount of industrial equipment could be removed from the western zones once the needs of the "German peace economy" had been met. The Soviet Union would have the right to acquire "10 per cent of such industrial equipment" on its reparations account "without payment or exchange of any kind." The Russians could also trade food and raw materials from their zone for a further 15 percent of surplus industrial equipment in western Germany. The amount of available industrial equipment would be determined by the Control Council subject to the "final approval of the Zone Commander in the Zone from which the equipment is to be removed." The western Allies had preserved the right of veto.

Truman finessed a plea from Stalin for a formal invitation to join the war against Japan. He watered down the Russian draft to eliminate any suggestion that the United States was the *demandeur,* in diplomatic parlance. The furthest he was prepared to go was to sign a letter stating that the Russians had an obligation under the newly drafted United Nations charter to "consult and cooperate with other great powers" in eliminating the Japanese security threat. The president refused to beg. Instead, in the phrase of a Potsdam historian, "he sounded more like a teacher reminding a forgetful pupil of his chores."

In the meantime, a top-secret telegram had arrived in Babelsberg from Stimson, who was now back in Washington. The secretary of war notified Truman that preparations for an atomic attack against Japan were almost in place. The Japanese government had declared it intended to "ignore" the Allied ultimatum. The president had already given the verbal go-ahead for the bomb. His only remaining task was to authorize release of the accompanying press announcement "as soon as necessary." He told his aide George Elsey that the news must not break before his departure from Potsdam, now scheduled for the early morning of August 2. "I don't want to have to answer any questions from Stalin," he explained. He scribbled out a reply to Stimson and handed it to Elsey for transmission to Washington.

"Release when ready but not sooner than August 2. HST"

The Potsdam conference wrapped up with two final plenary sessions on August 1. The disposal of Germany's foreign assets was settled in a way that foreshadowed the political division of Europe. Stalin and Truman had little difficulty agreeing to an imaginary dividing line "running from the Baltic to the Adriatic," corresponding to the reach of the different Allied armies. All German assets to the east of the line would go to the Soviet Union; everything to the west would belong to America and Britain.

The president had one final matter he was determined to raise before leaving Potsdam. He wanted to demonstrate forward movement on his favorite diplomatic obsession—the proposal for a Europe-wide inland waterway system under international control. Stalin had already dismissed the idea as impractical, but Truman wanted some mention of it in the final communiqué. The self-described "innocent idealist" was convinced that canals and rivers had been key to the economic development of the United States and could do the same for war-torn Europe. Noting that he had "accepted a number of compromises during this conference," he addressed a "personal request" to Stalin to at least acknowledge that the free navigation idea had been "discussed" at Potsdam. Truman's earnestness left the generalissimo unmoved.

"That question was not discussed," he said coldly.

"But I raised it at length on three different occasions."

Stalin pointed out that there was nothing in the communiqué about his demand for Russian forts along the Dardanelles, which he regarded as much more vital to his country's national security than the internationalization of waterways. When Truman offered to include both subjects in the statement, Stalin became visibly irritated.

"Nyet," he snapped. He then uttered the only English words that anybody at Potsdam ever heard him use. "No. I say no."

Truman's face flushed at the rebuff. "I cannot understand that man," he muttered to himself. He turned to his secretary of state, who was seated immediately to his right. "Jimmy, do you realize we have been here seventeen whole days? Why, in seventeen days, you can decide anything!"

All that remained was to wrap up the conference with the customary expressions of gratitude and friendship. Shortly after midnight, Stalin expressed his personal thanks to Byrnes, "who has worked harder perhaps than any one of us to make this conference a success." Truman, who had privately decided that he never wanted to experience such a diplomatic ordeal again, said he hoped to host the next meeting in Washington.

"God willing," said the leader of the world's first atheist state.

The president and the generalissimo shook hands, never to meet again.

On paper, the Potsdam conference preserved a united German state. The leaders gathered in Cecilienhof decreed that occupied "Germany shall be treated as a single economic unit" and called for "uniformity of treatment of the German population throughout Germany." The practice, however, was very different. The Potsdam decisions led inexorably to the division of the country into two rival entities—guided by competing ideologies, geopolitical ties, and economic and political systems. The goal of unification was undermined from the start by the decision to make national military commanders ultimately responsible for occupation policies in their particular zone. The Control Council was powerless to act without the consent of the national commanders, who were sovereign within their own bailiwicks.

American and Russian policy makers were never able to agree on the most basic question, whether to feed the defeated German people or let them go hungry. The answer to that question determined everything else: the resources required for the functioning of the German "peacetime economy," the revival of German industry, and the creation of democratic institutions. The British intelligence official Noel Annan came to believe that the reparations decision shaped "the future of Germany. All talk about a central government—reunification, denazification, frontiers and the rest—was secondary to the decision about reparations. The decision determined that the Western powers would be responsible for the German economy in their zones." The Americans and the British never made more than symbolic transfers of industrial equipment to the Soviet zone. Stalin lost interest in the idea of a united Germany once he understood that he would receive little in return.

Differences over reparations and supplying Berlin had the effect of creating an "economic iron curtain splitting Europe in two," in the phrase of one of Truman's economic advisers. Western commanders were now responsible for feeding 2 million refugees who had fled to the American and British zones of Germany for a mixture of political and economic reasons. There was no way they were going to dismantle German factories and ship the contents eastward when they were struggling to provide basic necessities to the population in their zones. Complaints that the other side had failed to keep its promises became more and more common. Western military officers responsible for handling day-to-day economic crises quickly concluded that there was no surplus to be handed over to the Russians. "We are preventing Germany from having any economy at all and at the same time are filling the press and the air with a lot of prating about democratic principles," grumbled the deputy American commander in Berlin. Implementing the economic provisions of the Potsdam agreements was like "sticking bayonets into a dead man."

Delivering food and raw materials to Berlin became a logistical nightmare for the western Allies after the Russians cut off the traditional sources of supply in mid-July. Flour had to be shipped in from Holland, coal from the Ruhr, potatoes from Hanover. Cargo trains backed up at Magdeburg, the sole transit point between the American and Russian zones, due to the dismantling of railway tracks by the Red Army. To feed Berliners, the Americans drove cattle across the border into the Russian zone but were unable to find Soviet troops authorized "to receive the cattle, which were without food and water." A Pentagon memo noted dryly that "German farmers in the U.S. Zone were obviously not enthused about delivering cattle" to Berlin. Coal deliveries to the western sectors of Berlin became "a continuous source of friction and argument." It took many months to build up stable reserves.

The complaints of lower-level officers gradually made their way up to General Lucius Clay, who was in overall charge of the occupation. At first, Clay loyally tried to implement the Potsdam provisions on a united Germany, but the task was beyond him. "After one year of occupation, zones represent airtight territories with almost no free exchange of commodities, persons and ideas," he reported to his superiors in May 1946. "Germany now consists of four small economic units which can deal with each other only through treaties." Without free trade and a free market, implementation of the reparations plan was "absolutely impossible." It would lead to "economic chaos."

Fewer than a hundred days had passed since American and Russian soldiers exchanged hugs and vows of eternal friendship on the banks of the Elbe River, but it already seemed like a different age. Representatives of the rival occupation armies in Berlin were shooting at each other even as their supreme commanders posed for family photographs and issued triumphant communiqués, just fifteen miles down the road, in Potsdam. The dream of a defeated but united Germany jointly occupied by her conquerors was giving way to the reality of superpower competition. Nowhere were the two armies in closer proximity—and more intense contention—than in the ruins of Hitler's capital.

On the afternoon of July 31, as Truman and Stalin haggled over the terms of German reparations in the Cecilienhof Palace, American military police received a report of looting by Russian troops at the Görlitzer railroad station in Berlin. It was a familiar story. Red Army soldiers preyed on the hundreds of thousands of refugees who were flooding into the city from Silesia in trains so overcrowded that people had to cling to the roofs and outside doors. When the trains reached Berlin, the passengers were frisked at gunpoint by Russian soldiers, looking for jewelry, watches, and other valuables. Since the Görlitzer Bahnhof was in the American sector of the city, the Americans felt an obligation to protect the refugees.

By the time military police showed up at 5:00 p.m., the Russians had commandeered a room in the station hotel. The Soviet officers refused to allow the Americans to search the room. They claimed they were "resting" prior to catching a train. Reinforcements were summoned—and the hotel was soon surrounded by American armored vehicles. At this point, three of the Russians decided to leave, ignoring attempts to arrest them.

"Halt!" shouted an American soldier who had just arrived on the scene.

He pointed his pistol at the Russians, two of whom stopped in their tracks. The third Russian, Major Mikhail Kolomets, kept on walking. The American shouted "Halt!" again and grabbed Kolomets by the shoulder. He saw the Russian reach for his hip pocket and "look at me kind of funny."

"No," yelled the American, firing his pistol at the Red Army major and wounding him in the stomach. Kolomets died two days later.

Such incidents became increasingly common as the Americans and British sought to impose their authority on their sectors of Berlin. Virtually every day brought fresh reports of looting by Russian soldiers, abductions of political opponents, rapes, shootings, armed robberies, and countless cases of drunkenness. The only remaining nightclub in Berlin had to be closed following a clash between heavily armed American and Red Army soldiers. Many of the confrontations ended in bloodshed and high-level recriminations.

"You must control and discipline your troops," the American commanding general lectured his Soviet counterpart. "You can't expect us to let them run wild in our sector, looting and shooting, without doing something about it."

"Maybe they had a few drinks and the wine caused them to get out of hand," conceded the Russian general. "But we don't shoot Americans when they come into our sector."

The American general explained that shooting first was "an American tradition, growing out of frontier days" when "the man who shot first lived." History does not record what the Russians made of this patently self-serving explanation.

The fault did not lie entirely on the Russian side. In letters home, a senior American officer acknowledged that some of his men were "triggerhappy." General Jack Whitelaw complained that the quality of the average American soldier had declined sharply since the end of the war. "We have no army over here. The Army is just a lot of homesick boys with a liberal sprinkling of rascals." In other letters, he told his wife that "too many Russian marauders are being killed in our district. . . . Russia is not going to give up anything that she considers essential to her wellbeing without a fight and I mean a *fight*. If we want that, we had better get ready for it. I don't think that America wants to fight the only nation left with whom we have never been at war. But I may be wrong. Certainly I see all around me rascals and idiots who seem hell bent on stirring up trouble."

Germans as well as Russians complained about the American habit of shooting first and asking questions later. Tales of random shootings by

American soldiers filled the censorship reports compiled by the military government from intercepted German correspondence. "Some [Americans] act like gangsters," was a typical complaint from a resident of the middle-class suburb of Zehlendorf. "Here in our district they drag some into the woods, beat them up and rob them." A Steglitz man described how two of his friends were attacked by five American soldiers. "They were punched, thrown down, and their heads knocked against a wall. Then they were kicked in the ribs." The most notorious incident involved the conductor of the Berlin Philharmonic Orchestra, Leo Borchard, who was killed at an American military checkpoint. The conductor was being driven home late at night by a music-loving British colonel who had invited him to dinner. The colonel was unaware of the existence of the checkpoint. His headlights blinded the American sentry who failed to recognize the British staff car. Although he aimed for the tires, he ended up shooting Borchard through the head. The musician died instantly.

During their first five months in Berlin, American troops shot dead ten Russians and wounded another seven, with zero casualties on their own side. The head of the U.S. military government, Colonel Howley, attempted to explain the disparity:

- The Russians draw their weapons as a persuader, without the intention of shooting;
- Even when they shoot, they are inclined to shoot in the air rather than shoot at the Allied soldier;
- The short Russian pistol, no bigger than the palm, is a very inaccurate weapon;
- In most cases, the Russian officer or soldier was so drunk that careful aim was out of the question.

American officers suspected the Germans of doing everything in their power to pit one occupying army against another. "They get the troops bitching and blaming all their difficulties on the Russians," complained Major General James Gavin, commander of the 102nd Airborne Division, which moved into the city in early August. "The Germans will be disappointed, and I believe surprised, if we do not come to blows with the Russians before the winter is over."

Truman was delighted to finally leave Potsdam immediately after breakfast on Thursday, August 2. He flew to Plymouth in southwest England, where he boarded the cruiser *Augusta* for the five-day voyage back across the Atlantic. The first three days of the journey were uneventful, the sea unusually calm. The president took the opportunity to relax and listen to his favorite classical tunes played by the ship's orchestra. He spent the evening of August 5 watching *The Thin Man Goes Home,* the latest hit movie from Metro-Goldwyn-Mayer, starring William Powell and Myrna Loy. The cruiser maintained a steady speed of 26.5 knots.

The following day, Monday, August 6, Truman decided to eat lunch with the crew, belowdecks. The *Augusta* was now some two hundred miles south of Nova Scotia, just a day out from Newport News in Virginia. Shortly before noon, one of the Map Room watch officers, Captain Frank Graham, handed the president an urgent message that had just arrived from the War Department in Washington. Truman's face broke out into a broad grin as he perused the contents. An atomic bomb had been dropped on Japan sixteen hours earlier. "Hiroshima was bombed visually with only one tenth cloud cover at seven fifteen PM Washington time August five," the message read. "There was no fighter opposition and no flak . . . results clear cut successful in all respects. Visible effects greater than in any test."

"This is the greatest thing in history!" exulted Truman, clasping the messenger by the hand.

A second message arrived a few minutes later from Stimson, confirming the contents of the first message. "First reports indicate complete success which was even more conspicuous than earlier test."

The president jumped to his feet, calling out across the mess room to Byrnes. "It's time for us to get on home." He waved the decoded message triumphantly in front of him as he addressed the crew. He was in no doubt that the war with Japan was effectively over. Pearl Harbor had been avenged.

"Please keep your seats and listen for a moment. I have an announcement to make. We have dropped a new bomb on Japan which has more power than twenty thousand tons of TNT. It has been an overwhelming success."

The crew responded with clapping and cheers, pounding the tables in front of them. "Mr. President, I guess that means I'll get home sooner now!" one sailor shouted out. The ship's radio system began broadcasting excited news bulletins from Washington. A presidential statement described the Manhattan Project as "the greatest scientific gamble in history."

It is a harnessing of the basic power of the universe. The force from which the sun draws its power has been loosed against those who brought war to the Far East. . . . We are now prepared to obliterate more rapidly and completely every productive enterprise the Japanese have above ground in any city. . . . It was to spare the Japanese people from utter destruction that the ultimatum of July 26 was issued at Potsdam. Their leaders rejected that ultimatum. If they do not now accept our terms they may expect a rain of ruin from the air, the like of which has never been seen on this earth.

The statement made clear that the Americans and the British would not be sharing the secrets of the bomb with their Russian allies, at least for the foreseeable future. "Under present circumstances it is not intended to divulge the technical processes of production or all the military applications, pending further examination of possible methods of protecting us and the rest of the world from the danger of sudden destruction."

For many Americans, jubilation over the seemingly imminent defeat of Japan was tinged with foreboding. The discovery of atomic energy was "the greatest scientific achievement of this war and could be the greatest in history," editorialized the *Chicago Tribune*. "It may also mean the obliteration of the civilization that makes such discoveries possible." The *Washington Post* described the sense of "bewildered awe" that had greeted the news. "We must love one another or die," the newspaper cautioned. "Otherwise the story of homo sapiens will become, as the late Lord Balfour once said, 'a brief and unpleasant episode in the history of one of the minor planets.'" The military analyst of the *New York Times*, Hanson Baldwin, warned that the "secondary effects" of the bomb—he was not yet familiar with the term "radiation"—could leave survivors of the initial blast "marred or maimed, blinded, deafened, diseased."

Yesterday man unleashed the atom to destroy man, and another chapter in human history opened, a chapter in which the weird, the strange, the horrible becomes the trite and the obvious. Yesterday we clinched victory in the Pacific, but we sowed the whirlwind.

The reaction in Europe and Britain was equally ambivalent. The British diplomat Pierson Dixon summed up the startling possibilities in a laconic diary entry later that day. "It is the dawn of utopia or the end of the world."

Stalin traveled back to Moscow by heavily guarded armored train across Poland, a country that had been unceremoniously moved, as if on a railway carriage, nearly two hundred miles to the west. He heard the news about the destruction of Hiroshima at his Kuntsevo dacha, on the evening of August 6, the day after his return from Berlin. (Moscow time was seven hours in advance of Washington time, and six hours behind Tokyo time.) His daughter, Svetlana, arrived at the dacha to show off her newborn son, whom she had named Joseph, in honor of her father. But Stalin was too preoccupied to pay much attention to either his first grandson or his only daughter. He was constantly interrupted by the "usual visitors" bearing reports about the atomic bomb.

There was little doubt in the minds of Stalin and his senior aides about Truman's real intentions. The *vozhd* observed that Hiroshima "has shaken the whole world. The balance has been destroyed." Molotov shared his master's belief that the atomic bomb was "not aimed at Japan but rather at the Soviet Union." The Americans were saying, in effect, "Bear in mind you don't have an atomic bomb and we do, and this is what the consequences will be like if you make a wrong move!"

Stalin responded to the bombing of Hiroshima by further accelerating his plans for attacking Japan. On the evening of August 7, he ordered Marshal Vasilevskii to commence operations against Japanese-occupied Manchuria at midnight local time on August 9. At 10:10 p.m., he received a Chinese delegation led by Foreign Minister T. V. Soong, in his Kremlin study. Time was running out to reach an agreement with the Chinese on Soviet operations in Manchuria prior to the invasion. The nationalist government was still resisting Russian demands for control over Port Arthur, Dairen, and a tsarist-era railroad connecting the Chinese ports with Harbin and Vladivostok. Stalin calculated that the Chinese would become more reasonable once Soviet tanks drove the Japanese out of Manchuria. He was determined to extract all the territorial concessions promised by FDR at Yalta in return for joining the war in the Far East. It was vitally important that Soviet forces occupied Manchuria *before* Japan was bludgeoned into submission by American bombs.

The Soviet media were awaiting instructions on how to report the news of the atomic bomb. *Pravda* carried a five-paragraph summary of Truman's statement on the bottom of page 4 of its August 8 edition, next to a much longer article, "Leninism and Progressive Russian Culture in the 19th Century." The front-page headlines focused on the harvest in Ukraine, but Soviet citizens had long been trained to ferret out the real news in obscure places in the paper. A twenty-four-year-old physicist by the name of Andrei Sakharov glanced at the newspaper on his way to the bakery. He was so stunned that his legs "practically gave way. There could be no doubt that my fate and the fate of many others, perhaps of the entire world, had changed overnight. Something new and awesome had entered our lives, a product of the greatest of the sciences, of the discipline I revered."

Despite the lack of information, ordinary Russians grasped the significance of the atomic bomb as quickly as their leaders. The British journalist Alexander Werth reported that the bomb was the only subject Muscovites talked about all day. "The news had an acutely depressing effect on everybody. It was clearly realized that this was a New Fact in the world's power politics, that the bomb constituted a threat to Russia, and some Russian pessimists I talked to that day dismally remarked that Russia's desperately hard victory over Germany was now 'as good as wasted.'" From top to bottom, Russians were convinced that the bomb's "real purpose was . . . to intimidate Russia."

Stalin also took steps to vastly expand the Soviet Union's own nuclear weapons program. He assigned responsibility for Task Number One, the code name for the atomic project, to his secret police chief, Lavrenty Beria, who had demonstrated his organizational skills by running the gulag. The *vozhd* made clear that no expense was to be spared to end the American monopoly. An army of half a million slave laborers would be assigned to building the facilities and processing the uranium needed to produce a Soviet bomb. Stalin brushed aside Kurchatov's qualms about diverting resources from the shattered civilian economy. "If the baby doesn't cry, the mother doesn't know what he needs," he snapped. "Ask for anything you need. There will be no refusals." He had just one demand in return. "Provide us with atomic weapons in the shortest possible time."

A million and a half Soviet troops poured across the 2,730-mile border into China in the predawn hours of August 9, attacking from half a dozen different directions. They swept through the Gobi Desert toward Peking, across the mountains and rivers of Manchuria toward Harbin, and along the heavily forested coast of the Sea of Japan. It was the last major set-piece operation of World War II. The Soviet troops enjoyed "a paper superiority of two to one in men, five to one in tanks and artillery, two to one in aircraft." The Russian troops advanced behind a massive barrage from *katyusha* rocket launchers and tanks that overwhelmed the Japanese defenders. Unable to motivate their soldiers with stories of recent Japanese atrocities against Russian civilians, Soviet commanders invoked memories of the humiliating defeat in the 1905 Russo-Japanese War. The time had come, political officers told their troops, "to erase the black stain of history against our homeland."

As in Europe, the invading armies were followed by reparations teams who dismantled industrial plants and government buildings for shipment back to Russia. Truman's reparations chief, Edwin Pauley, who arrived on an inspection tour soon afterward, estimated the resulting damage to the Manchurian economy at around $2 billion. What Pauley termed "Operation Locust" was ostensibly targeted against Japanese property owners in Manchuria, but in practice there was "little distinction" between the treatment meted out to the Japanese and the Chinese.

Reeling before the Russian onslaught, the outnumbered Japanese army

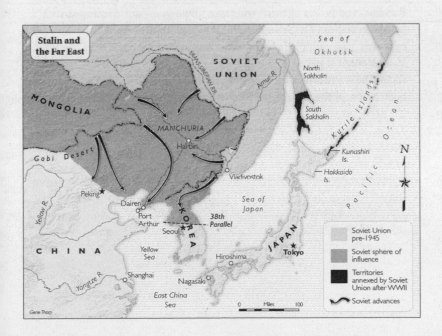

soon found itself split into several different pieces. The Japanese retreat was so rapid that the occupiers were unable to honor a promise to evacuate the puppet Chinese emperor, Pu Yi, who was captured by the Red Army and taken to Russia. After capturing eastern Manchuria, the Russian invaders swept down the Korean peninsula. They stopped at the thirty-eighth parallel, just to the north of the city of Seoul, in accordance with an agreement with the United States. (A few days earlier, after consulting a *National Geographic* map late one night in the Pentagon, two U.S. Army colonels had suggested the thirty-eighth parallel as a "convenient dividing line" between Allied operations on the Korean peninsula.)

After pushing hard for Soviet participation in the war against Japan, Truman was not at all pleased by the manner in which it came about. "They're jumping the gun, aren't they?" he observed to his chief of staff when he heard the news from Manchuria.

"Yes, damn it," Admiral Leahy replied. "The bomb did it. They want to get in before it's all over."

Stalin acted just in time. Ten hours after the Red Army launched its attack on Manchuria, a U.S. Air Force B-29 dropped a second atomic bomb on the city of Nagasaki. Japan surrendered six days later, on August 15. The race to deliver the final knockout punch to Japan—pitting Russian land power against American airpower—had concluded with a virtual dead heat. The Second World War had finally ended, to be replaced by a new type of global conflict that would consume the lives, energies, and ideological passions of an entire generation of Americans and Russians. The transformation of World War II Allies into Cold War rivals had been accomplished in a period of just six months.

21

After the Bomb

No single event defined the start of the Cold War in the way that the fall of the Berlin Wall, on November 9, 1989, came to symbolize its end. Historians have assigned different starting dates to the conflict that brought the world to the brink of nuclear destruction, depending on their ideological preferences and personal interpretation of events. Some have pointed to the Communist coup in Czechoslovakia in February 1948 as the moment when Europe was irrevocably divided into two rival camps. Others have cited Truman's decision in March 1947 to provide military aid to Greece and Turkey in line with his pledge to support "free peoples who are resisting attempted subjugation by armed minorities or by outside pressures." Traditionalist historians view Stalin's refusal to honor an earlier commitment to pull his troops out of northern Iran in March 1946 as the first major Cold War confrontation. Revisionists argue that Truman triggered decades of superpower rivalry through his embrace of "atomic diplomacy" against the Soviet Union, beginning with the bombing of Hiroshima in August 1945.

The premise behind many of these competing versions of history is that a political leader, of one or another ideological stripe, was responsible for the Cold War. By placing the politicians at the heart of their story, diplomatic historians assume that larger-than-life individuals determine the course of great events. Sometimes this may be the case. But sometimes history has a mind of its own, riding roughshod over the decisions of the most charismatic personalities and moving in directions contrary to their desires. History can be hijacked by chance events, such as the assassination of a grand duke, a ruler falling in love, or a sudden change in the weather. Sometimes, it follows an internal logic that is bewildering to those who are caught up in its contradictory currents but makes complete sense from a distance.

The Cold War is the perfect example of a historical event that was foreseen more than a century in advance but still took contemporaries by surprise. As long as they were both fighting Nazi Germany, Tocqueville's "two great nations" had reason to preserve their alliance and paper over any disagreements. But as soon as their common enemy was defeated, and they came into direct contact with each other, their political and ideological interests diverged sharply. The logic of events was often clearer to outsiders than to the principals themselves. With his twisted but occasionally brilliant grasp of historical forces, Hitler got it right when he concluded that the defeat of the Third Reich would leave "only two great Powers capable of confronting each other—the United States and Soviet Russia." He went on to predict that "the laws of both history and geography will compel these two Powers to a trial of strength, either military or in the fields of economics and ideology. . . . It is equally certain that both these Powers will sooner or later find it desirable to seek the support of the sole surviving great nation in Europe, the German people."

Virtually all of the watershed events of the early Cold War can be traced back to the six-month period between February and August 1945 that spanned the death of FDR, the end of World War II, the disintegration of the anti-Hitler alliance, and the division of Europe into rival political blocs. The Czechoslovak coup followed a pattern established in Romania in the weeks immediately following Yalta, with the Communists using their control over the police and security forces to seize complete power. Truman's support for prowestern governments in Greece and Turkey followed inexorably from his earlier resistance to Soviet plans to acquire military bases along the Dardanelles and in the Mediterranean. The 1949 Berlin blockade had its origins in the squabbles over western access rights to the city at the time of the Potsdam conference. In the meantime, Stalin came to understand that the Soviet Union would receive little help from the West for its postwar recovery. He was left with only one option:

to demand more sacrifices from the long-suffering Russian people. This all coincided with Europe's largest ever bout of ethnic cleansing, with the forcible expulsion or resettlement of some 20 million people, mainly Germans but also Poles, Jews, Hungarians, and others. The result was a deepening in the geopolitical divide. Poland became dependent on the Soviet Union to guarantee its new western border. West Germany was overwhelmed by refugees from the east, forcing the western Allies to give up any idea of handing over promised reparations to the Soviet Union.

The temporary territorial arrangements hammered out by the Big Three at Yalta and Potsdam congealed into the front lines of the Cold War. The Brandenburg Gate came to symbolize the division of Germany. The Glienicke Bridge across the Havel River that formed part of the daily twenty-minute commute of Truman, Stalin, and Churchill between Babelsberg and Potsdam became the site of Cold War spy swaps. A mile-wide no-man's-land bristling with guard posts and coils of barbed wire snaked across the continent, marking what Churchill (and Joseph Goebbels) had already dubbed "the iron curtain." In Asia, Stalin succeeded in incorporating Sakhalin and the Kurile Islands into the Soviet Union, setting the stage for a new round of territorial disputes with Japan. On the Korean peninsula, the thirty-eighth parallel became the Asian equivalent of the Berlin Wall, separating the Communist North from the capitalist South. The most significant change to the East-West standoff in the immediate aftermath of World War II occurred in northern Iran. Sensing that the Red Army was overextended, and under heavy pressure from a suddenly aroused Truman administration, Stalin abruptly withdrew support for "Southern Azerbaijan." The autonomous republic collapsed soon after the last Soviet troops left northern Iran in May 1946, three months behind schedule.

The phrase "Cold War" did not enter the political lexicon until 1947 when it was popularized by the American financier Bernard Baruch and the commentator Walter Lippmann. But its usage can be traced back to an October 1945 essay by George Orwell, author of the recently published anti-Communist satire *Animal Farm*. Writing about the advent of the atomic age, Orwell warned of a standoff between rival superpowers, each of which possessed the ability to blow up the world. Once a country possessed an atomic bomb, it would become unconquerable. The result would be "an epoch as horribly stable as the slave empires of antiquity," "a peace that is no peace" characterized by a permanent state of "cold war."

The politicians had only limited ability to shape the course of events.

The cruelest and most willful of them all, Joseph Stalin, was also the prisoner of the forces that had created him. There is ample evidence that he would have preferred a period of détente with the capitalist powers, if only to prepare for a new war in ten or twenty years' time. He was prepared to make some concessions to keep his options open, but would not sacrifice any of his core interests: consolidation of his newly acquired empire, survival of the Soviet regime, and elimination of any threats to his own authority as Russia's supreme leader. The fact that he was a tyrant did not mean, however, that he could do whatever he liked. The American who knew him best, Averell Harriman, thought it was "absurd to suggest that Stalin sat in the Kremlin and issued orders, as if he were Hitler. It was a different form of control that he exercised." The ambassador cited the example of eastern Europe where national Communist leaders depended on Soviet support for protection against their own populations which were "at least seventy to eighty percent anti-Russian and anti-Communist." He had no doubt about the advice these leaders were providing Stalin: "If you dare to hold free elections, you will lose the country."

Stalin disavowed any intention of imposing carbon copies of his own Soviet regime on eastern Europe. He came up with a new term, "people's democracies," that would allow each part of his empire to move toward socialism at a pace that accorded with its own national traditions. The Communists were in a minority everywhere. They would rule by forming a coalition with other "progressive" forces. As long as these new regimes acknowledged the primacy of the Soviet Union, they would be permitted a degree of political autonomy. Stalin was perfectly willing to do business with a bourgeois politician like Edvard Beneš of Czechoslovakia, provided he got his way on the matters he deemed essential. The problem with this attempt to square the circle was that ordinary Poles, Hungarians, Czechs, and Romanians could never reconcile themselves to Russian domination. Given a chance to express their views freely, they rejected the limited sovereignty variant offered by the Kremlin. Stalin allowed a relatively free parliamentary election in Hungary in November 1945, only to see his Communist allies end up with a derisory 17 percent of the vote. Unable to command the support of the majority, the Soviets and their eastern European acolytes were forced to rely on an ever-dwindling minority. One side or the other had to emerge on top. As the logic of events became apparent, there was less and less room for political maneuver. Communist dictatorships, from Warsaw to Prague to Budapest to Sofia, became the only solution.

Stalin's failure to permit free elections in eastern Europe exacerbated his difficulties with the West. In their own fashion, American leaders were at least as ideological as Soviet leaders. They were committed to the Wilsonian proposition that the world had to be made "safe for democracy." America was the "shining city upon a hill" whose beacon would light up the rest of mankind. Whether explicitly or not, the Americans behaved as if their amalgam of free peoples, free markets, and free speech should be adopted by every country in the world. The belief in the universality of liberal democracy was deeply rooted in the American national psyche but was unacceptable to Stalin because it struck at the very source of his power. "This war is not as in the past," he told the Yugoslav Communist Milovan Djilas. "Whoever occupies a territory also imposes on it his own social system. Everyone imposes his own system as far as his army can reach. It cannot be otherwise." By demanding free elections in lands they had never conquered, Americans were attempting to circumvent the *vozhd*'s iron law of Great Power politics.

By the summer of 1945, Americans and Russians had accumulated plenty of evidence that the other side was failing to live up to its obligations under the Yalta agreements. The Soviets were violating their pledges on eastern Europe; the Americans were wriggling out of their promises on reparations. The laborious attempt to disguise deep-seated divisions between the wartime Allies with reassuring rhetoric and ambiguously worded communiqués succeeded only in providing them with ammunition to attack each other when a suitable moment came.

Relations between Russia and the western Allies deteriorated sharply in the aftermath of the Potsdam conference. Molotov met his fellow foreign ministers in London in September, but an impasse developed after the United States rejected Soviet demands for a substantial role in the affairs of postwar Japan. Stalin had already decided that the time had come to strip away the "veil of amity" with the West, "some semblance of which the Americans are so eager to preserve." He instructed Molotov to "stand firm" on eastern Europe. "The Allies are pressing on you to break your will and make concessions," he wrote Stone Ass in a coded cable from Moscow. "It is obvious that you should display complete obduracy." Stalin felt it was better to let the London conference end in failure, as it eventually did, than another agreement that simply papered over the irreconcilable differences with the people "who call themselves our allies."

Stalin and Harriman met for the last time on October 24. The exhausted Soviet leader was taking a long-delayed "rest-vacation" at his seaside retreat at Gagra in the mountains of northern Georgia but agreed to see Truman's emissary. On a personal level, the meeting went smoothly enough, although Stalin grumbled about the lack of consultation over Japan. He felt it would be more honest "if the Soviet Union were to quit Japan than to remain there as a piece of furniture." Ominously, however, he raised the possibility of an isolationist tack in Soviet foreign policy. He told Harriman that he had never been in favor of such a policy but now believed there was "nothing wrong with it." Harriman understood him to mean isolationism not in the classic American sense, of a Great Power concerning itself exclusively with its own affairs, but a "policy of increased militancy and self-reliance."

Attitudes were hardening on the American side as well. They found expression in a February 1946 dispatch from George Kennan in Moscow that came to be known as the "Long Telegram." Left in charge of the Moscow embassy following Harriman's departure, Kennan set himself the goal of educating his superiors in Washington about the nature of Soviet communism. His 5,350-word missive contained little he had not said many times before in largely unread memoranda gathering dust in his State Department files. The difference, this time around, was that he had a receptive audience. Galvanized into action by the crisis over northern Iran, senior Truman officials finally paid attention to the diplomat crying in the wilderness. Kennan painted a bleak picture of a malignant, totalitarian force determined to destroy the "international authority of our state" and "the internal harmony of our society," but he also offered a way out. The Kremlin, he observed, "does not take unnecessary risks. Impervious to logic of reason, it is highly sensitive to logic of force. For this reason it can easily withdraw—and usually does—when strong resistance is encountered at any point." Kennan's prescriptions became the basis for a new U.S. foreign policy doctrine known as containment.

Reaching an amicable compromise on dividing the spoils of World War II might have been possible had the results of the conflict been clearcut, but this was not the case. Russian and American interests overlapped in many parts of the world. Stalin resented being excluded from any say in the postwar arrangements in Japan; Truman was unwilling to recognize the Soviet-dominated regimes of Hungary, Romania, and Bulgaria. Stalin staked a claim to a "trusteeship," or semi-colony, in Libya; Truman was determined to hang on to the American foothold in Berlin. In diplomatic negotiations, both sides abided by the dictum "What's mine is mine; what's yours is up for grabs." Potential flashpoints abounded, from the Korean peninsula to northern Iran to the Balkans to the heart of the vanquished Third Reich.

The dramatic confrontations of 1947 to 1949 followed the euphoria, disappointments, and turmoil of 1945 as night follows dusk. The historical record shows that none of the principals wanted a Cold War. In their different ways, Roosevelt, Stalin, Churchill, and Truman all struggled to prevent the division of the globe into rival ideological-military camps. But even the most powerful warlords were unable to sway what Alexis de Tocqueville, more than a century before, had called the "will of Heaven."

Acknowledgments

I am—almost literally—a child of the Cold War. I first went to Russia at the age of eight weeks, courtesy of my diplomat parents, in 1950, when Josef Stalin was still at the height of his power, hurling verbal thunderbolts against evil imperialists. Childhood memories include watching military parades in Red Square, being shadowed by the KGB, and waiting for nuclear war to break out during the Cuban missile crisis. I still associate certain colors and smells with Soviet communism, just as I vividly recall the startling reawakening of the senses triggered by the journey back to the other side of the "Iron Curtain." In one way or the other, I have been thinking about the Cold War all my life, either as a boy growing up in places like Moscow and Warsaw, or as a journalist covering the collapse of communism, or as a historian poring over documents prepared for leaders like Churchill and Truman, Kennedy and Khrushchev, Reagan and Gorbachev.

The present book completes a "Cold War trilogy." I began at the end, relating the extraordinary story of the fall of the Soviet empire in *Down with Big Brother* (1997). In my last book, *One Minute to Midnight* (2008), I examined the peak of the Cold War, the moment when the world stood on the edge of nuclear annihilation in October 1962. *Six Months in 1945* describes how it all started, focusing on the history-shaping events that transformed World War II allies into Cold War rivals. Together the three books are intended to capture the arc of the defining ideological conflict of the twentieth century, spanning the division and reunification of the European continent over a forty-four-year period.

A project such as this would not have been possible without a lot of help and encouragement along the way. I have my parents to thank for introducing me to Russia and eastern Europe and setting me on the path to becoming a reporter and a writer. I am grateful to various employers, particularly *The Washington Post,* for sponsoring my reporting behind the Iron Curtain, culminating in a five-year stint in Moscow between 1988 and 1993. My understanding of the Cold War has been greatly enhanced by time spent at outstanding American universities, including Harvard, Princeton, and the University of Michigan. Most recently, I am indebted to the Woodrow Wilson International Center for Scholars and the U.S. Institute of Peace, both in Washington, D.C., for supporting my research through fellowships and grants.

One of the joys of researching narrative history is the opportunity to follow in the footsteps of your characters, imagining yourself gazing down from the ceiling as they make momentous decisions. Sometimes you want to applaud, at other times you shake your head at their blunders and miscalculations, but always you are fascinated. In one guise or another, I have visited most of the places described in this book, from the Livadia Palace in Yalta and Cecilienhof in Potsdam to the Kremlin in Moscow and the White House in Washington. I am grateful to William Drozdiak, Gary Smith, and the late Richard Holbrooke for helping to arrange a fellowship at the American Academy of Berlin that permitted me to explore the sites described in the last four chapters of this book. Ulrike Graalfs and Stephanie Buri organized visits to the Babelsberg residences of Stalin and Truman, in addition to the Soviet military museum at Karlshorst, site of the Nazi surrender in May 1945. While I was in Berlin, I also spent a wonderful day along the Elbe, tracing the routes taken by the American and Soviet frontline units that met near Torgau during the final weeks of World War II.

The archival trail has taken me from the Bundesarchiv in Berlin to the Churchill Archives in Cambridge, England, to the National Archives in London to the Truman Library in Independence, Missouri, and the FDR Library in Hyde Park, New York. Closer to home, I have also spent long and happy hours in the National Archives in College Park, Maryland, the Manuscripts Division of the Library of Congress, and the Military History Institute in Carlisle, Pennsylvania. It is impossible to list everyone who helped me by name but I would particularly like to single out Sam Rushay of the Truman Library, David Keough of the Military History Institute, John Haynes of the Library of Congress, and Allen Packwood of the Churchill Archives. My talented and hard-working research assistant at the Woodrow Wilson Center, Oleksandr Chornyy, helped me track down documents relating to the ill-fated mission of American airmen in Poltava held in the archives of the Ukrainian security services.

I have greatly benefited from bouncing ideas off fellow Cold War enthusiasts and friends, including Marty Sherwin, David Holloway, Melvyn Leffler, Ronald Suny, Masha Lipman, and Sergei Ivanov. Tom Blanton and Svetlana Savranskaya of the National Security Archive have been an invaluable source of encouragement and support, as with my previous books. I have fond memories of our visit together to the Stalin museum in Gori, which features the railway carriage that carried the Soviet dictator to Yalta and Berlin. Rick Atkinson has provided invaluable expertise on the final battles of World War II. Avis and Celestine Bohlen shared memories of their father, Charles Bohlen, one of the characters in this book. I am grateful for the hospitality and friendship of our neighbors, Paul and Stephanie Taylor, as well as David and Anita Ensor, kindred spirits from the Soviet Union and eastern Europe.

My namesake and distant cousin, known in our family as the "false Michael Dobbs" but better known as the author of the hit television series *House of Cards,* has patiently forwarded e-mails intended for me but sent to him. He will be pleased to know that I now I have my own Web site, www.coldwartrilogy.com, through which readers can get in touch with me directly. In addition to a shared interest in exploring our Irish roots, Michael and I share a fascination with Winston Churchill. I am grateful to my brother Geoffrey Dobbs, founder of the hugely successful Galle Literary Festival in Sri Lanka, for bringing us together to talk about Churchill through the eyes of a fiction and nonfiction writer. While on the subject of family, I must also mention my talented niece, Rachel Dobbs, who has helped me create social media networks to promote my Cold War books. And of course, my mother, Marie Dobbs, who first went to Moscow in 1947 as a wide-eyed young Australian and stayed a good deal longer than she ever intended. My understanding of Russia in the immediate postwar period is shaped in considerable part by conversations with her and my late father.

A special debt of gratitude goes to Knopf, the publisher of my three Cold War books. My first editor at Knopf was the legendary Ashbel Green, publisher of Andrei Sakharov and Milovan Djilas. Andrew Miller has proved a more than worthy replacement for Ash, a source of much excellent advice and meticulous attention to detail. Andrew Carlson and Marc Chiusano shepherded the book through production with the help of production manager Lisa Montebello, production editor Maria Massey, designer Maggie Hinders, and copy editor Sue Betz. I thank Jason Booher for the wonderful jacket (reminiscent of his best-selling hit with *One Minute to Midnight*) and Michelle Somers for her help with the publicity. My former *Washington Post* colleague, Gene Thorp, has done an excellent job with the maps. I am grateful, as always, to my agent Rafe Sagalyn, who has steered me in the right direction countless times, along with a host of other former *Washington Post* reporters.

Most of all, I am grateful to my wife, Lisa, and children for making this all possible and putting up with my obsessions and frequent absences. This book is dedicated to my son, Joseph Samuel, named after his Irish grandfather and his Russian-Jewish great-grandfather. With a heritage like that, the world is open to him.

Notes

WSC TT Winston S. Churchill, *Triumph and Tragedy*, vol. 6 of *The Second World War*

WSC7 Martin Gilbert, *Road to Victory*, vol. 7 of *Winston S. Churchill*

WSC8 Martin Gilbert, *Never Despair*, vol. 8 of *Winston S. Churchill*

1 ROOSEVELT

3 "I never authorized": Jim Bishop, *FDR's Last Year*, 300; William Leahy, *I Was There*, 295–96.

4 boarded the *Sacred Cow*: Anna Roosevelt Boettiger diary, FDRL; Robert Meiklejohn diary, 620, LCH.

5 "I had no idea": Robert H. Ferrell, *The Dying President*, 89.

5 "terribly wrong": Doris Kearns Goodwin, *No Ordinary Time*, 494–95; Jean Edward Smith, *FDR*, 602–5.

5 "slept rather poorly": Howard Bruenn notes, February 4, 1945, FDRL; Ferrell, *Dying President*, 104.

6 "beautiful sunrise": ARB diary, February 3, 1945, FDRL; Michael F. Reilly, *Reilly of the White House*, 211–12.

6 "bumping the full length": Averell Harriman and Elie Abel, *Special Envoy to Churchill and Stalin*, 391.

7 "world bully": Harriman and Abel, 346.

7 "divide Europe frankly": Kennan letter to Bohlen, January 26, 1945, Princeton Mudd Library.

8 "frail and ill": WSC7, 1171.

9 "The PM walked by the side": Charles Moran, *Churchill at War, 1940–1945*, 267.

9 "a bit worried": ARB diary, February 3, 1945, FDRL; Secret Service report on FDR's trip to Yalta, July 5, 1945, FDRL.

9 "desolate steppe": Pierson Dixon, *Double Diploma*, 137.

9 "ten years on research": Harry Hopkins to FDR, January 24, 1945, FDRL; Winston Churchill to FDR, January 26, 1945, FDRL.

9 "those worn": Laurence S. Kuter, *Airman at Yalta*, 114.

10 "immense, tough": Maureen Clark notes on Yalta, Ralph Edwards Papers, REDW 2/20, WSC CC.

10 "get even": ARB letter to husband, John Boettiger, February 4, 1945, Boettiger Papers, FDRL. See also FDR report to Congress, March 1, 1945.

10 "how long have": Sarah Churchill, *Keep On Dancing*, 74.

10 "another dingy town": Meiklejohn diary, 613, LCH.

10 "this part of the country": ARB diary, February 3, 1945, FDRL.

11 "the curves were short": Admiral Wilson Brown, unpublished manuscript, 185, FDRL.

12 "another country": Alexander Cadogan, *The Diaries of Sir Alexander Cadogan, O.M., 1938–1945*, 702.

12 "I can't understand": Reilly, 212.

12 "with many bows": ARB diary, February 3, 1945, FDRL.

12 thousands of NKVD: "Sekretnaya Operatsiya Argonavt," *ForPost* (Sevastopol online newspaper), June 10, 2009.

12 "early Pullman car": Norris Houghton, "That Was Yalta, Worm's Eye View," *New Yorker*, May 23, 1953.

14 "ordered him to eat": Kathleen Harriman letter to Pamela Churchill, February 7, 1945, cited in Jon Meacham, *Franklin and Winston*, 316.

14 "They hurt me": Frank McNaughton notes, March 1, 1945, HSTL.

15 Alexandra ordered: Greg King, *The Court of the Last Tsar*, 440–51.

16 "In St. Petersburg": King, 437.

17 "billeted bed to bed": Meiklejohn diary, 625, LCH.

17 "for God's sake": ARB diary, February 4, 1945, FDRL.

17 "for dear life": ARB diary, January 25, 1945, FDRL.

18 "a dictatorship as absolute": FDR address to American Youth Congress, February 11, 1941.

18 "I know you will not": FDR to Churchill, March 18, 1942, FDRL.

18 Hitler had deployed. Georg Tessin and Christian Zweng, *Verbände und Truppen der deutschen Wehrmacht und Waffen-SS im Zweiten Weltkrieg, 1939–1945*.

19 "every mile of front": Max Hastings, *Armageddon*, 97–98.

19 casualty figures: Rüdiger Overmans, *Deutsche militärische Verluste im Zweiten Weltkrieg*, 336.

19 "done the main work": Speech to the House of Commons, August 2, 1944.

20 "Take a method": Speech to Oglethorpe University, May 22, 1932.

20 "tremendously interested": FDR letter to Edgar Snow, January 2, 1945, PSF, Russia, FDRL.

20 "that old buzzard": John Gunther, *Roosevelt in Retrospect*, 356.

20 "spent his life": Charles Moran, *Churchill: The Struggle for Survival, 1940–1965*, 143.

20 "has no conception": Harriman and Abel, 369–70.

21 "all roads are now closed": Houghton, "That Was Yalta."

2 STALIN

22 arrived in the Crimea: Many historians have reported erroneously that Stalin arrived in Yalta on the night of February 3–4. But Stalin himself cabled Churchill on February 1 that he had arrived "at the rendezvous," see Fleece 77. PREM 4/78/1, PRO.

22 terrible nosebleed: Kathleen Harriman interview, *Cold War* (CNN TV series), CNN CW; Dmitri Volkogonov, *Stalin*, 488; Harriman memo, September 24, 1944, FRUS YALTA, 5.

22 "Stations all down": A. H. Birse, *Memoirs of an Interpreter*, 178. The railway car is on display at the Stalin museum in Gori, Stalin's birthplace.

23 "unfriendly elements": Beria report to Stalin, January 8–27, 1945, reprinted in *Istoricheskii Arkhiv*, No. 5, 116–31, 1993.

24 "The noise and the shouting": Laurence Rees, *World War II Behind Closed Doors*, 253.

24 "crematoria on wheels": Norman M. Naimark, *Fires of Hatred*, 102; Rees, 267–71.

25 "could not resist": Gerard Pawle and C. R. Thompson, *The War and Colonel Warden*, 357–58.

25 "carried out on": Beria, January 27, 1945, *Istoricheskii Arkhiv*.

26 "We are surrounded": Quoted in Robert Tucker, *Stalin as Revolutionary,* 460.

26 "Georgians are fools!": Svetlana Alliluyeva, *Only One Year,* 359–61, 372.

26 "You have to control": Melvyn Leffler, *For the Soul of Mankind,* 29.

26 psychological portraits: Pavel Sudoplatov et al., *Special Tasks,* 222.

27 "Even cowards become": U.S. Department of State, *Conferences in Cairo and Tehran,* 583; Harriman and Abel, 276.

27 Fifty-three German divisions: FRUS YALTA, 582.

27 "Your order": Zhukov to Stalin, January 29, 1945, LCV.

27 just thirty-nine miles: NYT, Feb. 5, 1945.

27 Zhukov had made preliminary: Tony Le Tissier, *Zhukov at the Oder,* 40.

29 "Not bad at all": Russian minutes, in Andrei A. Gromyko, ed., *Sovetskii Soyuz na Mezhdunarodnikh Konferentsiyakh Perioda Velikoi Otechestvennoi Voiny,* vol. 4, 48–49.

29 "We shall follow": WSC TT, 347–49.

29 "For him, only": Volkogonov, *Stalin,* 475.

30 "You cannot wage war": Vladimir Pavlov, autobiographical notes, *Novaya i Noveishaya Istoriya,* no. 4 (2000), 109.

30 "every shrub and every bush": Charles H. Donnelly, unpublished manuscripts, 719, MHI.

31 "one of his rare": Charles E. Bohlen, *Witness to History,* 180.

31 "like men and brothers": Frances Perkins, *The Roosevelt I Knew,* 85.

32 "more bloodthirsty": Bohlen minutes, FRUS YALTA, 570–73; Gromyko, ed., *Sovetskii Soyuz,* 49–51. Unless otherwise noted, Yalta conference quotes are from FRUS YALTA. In some cases, I have changed reported speech to direct speech.

33 "change of climate": Harriman to FDR, September 24, 1944; FRUS YALTA, 5.

33 "approximately 13,842 miles": Secret Service log, FDRL.

34 "a perfect night": King, 451.

34 "sit on their fannies": ARB to John Boettiger, February 9, 1945, FDRL; Wilson Brown manuscripts, 185, FDRL.

34 "He is very thin": Contemporaneous diary quoted by Denis Richards, *The Life of Marshal of the Royal Air Force, Viscount Portal of Hungerford,* 287.

35 "the kind of man": Milovan Djilas, *Conversations with Stalin,* 61.

35 "a puzzled porcupine": Richards, 288.

35 "a long procession": Kuter, 138; Houghton, "That Was Yalta."

36 "funereal hush": Houghton, "That Was Yalta."

36 "an extreme case": Harriman and Abel, 395; ARB Yalta diary, FDRL.

37 "Where's Stalin?": Bohlen, 174; Edward R. Stettinius Jr., *Roosevelt and the Russians,* 111; Kathleen Harriman to Pamela Churchill, February 7, 1945, quoted in Geoffrey Roberts, *Stalin's Wars,* 238. Pamela Digby Churchill later married Averell Harriman.

37 "as a republican": Field Marshal Lord Alanbrooke, *War Diaries, 1939–1945,* 657; John Martin, unpublished diary, WSC CC.

37 "Yugoslavia, Albania": Bohlen notes, FRUS YALTA, 589–91; Stettinius, 111–15. A copy of the dinner menu can be found in FDRL.

39 "You do not mind": WSC7, 1175.

39 "Dinner with Americans": Anthony Eden, *The Reckoning,* 593.

40 his teacher: Edvard Radzinskii, *Stalin,* 470. Stalin scribbled the word "teacher" on his copy of Alexey Tolstoy's play *Ivan the Terrible,* which was published in 1942.

40 "even more decisively": Maureen Perrie, *The Cult of Ivan the Terrible in Stalin's Russia,* 87.

3 CHURCHILL

42 "Great dissatisfaction": Message from John Martin to Private Office, Jason 117, February 4, 1945, PRO.

42 "colonel, drenched in scent": Pawle and Thompson, 352.

43 The prime minister dictated: Fleece 139, Jason 137, PREM 4/78/1, PRO.

43 "Bed's not right". Jean Edward Smith, *FDR,* 543.

43 "Sawyers, Sawyers": Charles Moran, *Churchill at War, 1940–1945,* 274.

44 "What a hole": Marian Holmes Spicer diary, February 3, 1945, WSC CC.

44 Lunch was served: Churchill appointment diary, WSC CC.

44 "press a day and a half's": Winston Churchill, *The Gathering Storm,* 421.

45 "a giant refreshed": Mary Soames, *Clementine Churchill,* 317.

45 "You never saw": Cadogan, 703.

45 "quite fantastic": Sarah Churchill, 75.

45 married a Herbert: Churchill gives an inaccurate version of the Vorontsov-Herbert connection in the sixth volume of his autobiography, *Triumph and Tragedy.* Ekaterina Vorontsova, daughter of Count Semyon Vorontsov and only sister of Mikhail Vorontsov, married George Herbert, eleventh earl of Pembroke, in 1808.

46 "the flesh only": Moran, *Churchill at War, 1940–1945,* 264.

46 "We must just KBO": Martin Gilbert, *Finest Hour,* 1273.

47 "a small lion": John R. Colville, *The Fringes of Power,* 564.

47 "Formidable questions": WSC TT, 353.

48 "No, you keep": WSC TT, 226–28.

49 "Nazi war machine": WSC broadcast, June 22, 1941, see Richard Langworth, ed., *Churchill by Himself,* 146.

49 "like wooing a crocodile". January 24, 1944, Downing Street, WSC; Langworth, ed., 144.

49 "the descendant of the Duke": Isaac Deutscher, *Stalin,* 490.

49 "I have had very nice": Soames, *Clementine Churchill,* 399.

49 "dine with Stalin": WSC7, 664.

50 "his own extreme": George F. Kennan, *Memoirs, 1925–1950,* 524–26.

50 "a riddle wrapped": October 1, 1939 (radio broadcast); Langworth, ed., 145.

50 "If you have a motor car": FRUS YALTA, 621; see also James Byrnes, *Speaking Frankly,* 27. A trained court stenographer, Byrnes kept his own notes of the Yalta meeting, which are sometimes more complete than the official notes.

50 "It's always the same": Cadogan, 704.

50 "to hear Colonel Kent": Martin Papers, WSC CC.

51 "I don't know why": Maureen Clark Papers, REDW2, WSC CC.

51 "luxuriousness and even": Dixon, 137–38; Joan Bright Astley, *The Inner Circle,*

194–95. I have also drawn on the diaries of Maureen Clark and Elizabeth Onslow, WSC CC.

51 "anti-social people": Richards, 286–87.

52 "most generally discussed subject": Kuter, 122.

52 "I am clearly convinced": WSC7, 1167.

52 "I do not suppose": Sarah Churchill, 76.

53 "dead, blank walls": Joint press conference with FDR, Quebec, Canada, September 16, 1944.

53 "strange ways of fate": WSC TT, 343.

53 "Bullets are not": Brian Lavery, *Churchill Goes to War*, 8.

53 "Faithful Servant": Bohlen, 174.

54 "I am taking it": Robert Hopkins, *American Heritage*, June/July 2005.

54 "Every word": Winston Churchill, *The Grand Alliance*, 432.

55 "completely starkers": Patrick Kinna, OH, WSC CC; Warren F. Kimball, ed., *Churchill and Roosevelt*, vols. 1, 4.

55 "no lover": Colville, 624; Moran, *Churchill at War*, 277.

55 "Quite agreeable": Cadogan, 705; ARB to John Boettiger, February 7, 1945, FDRL.

56 "You tell Harry Hopkins": William M. Rigdon, *White House Sailor*, 150–51. Hopkins had sent a sarcastic message to FDR about Watson on January 24, saying that he was sorry to hear that the president's military aide was "seasick as usual," Map Room files, FDRL.

4 POLAND

58 "like soldiers at drill": Jean Edward Smith, *FDR*, 591.

58 "nearly cost us": WSC TT, 368.

59 "unusual fervor": Maisky diary, published in O. A. Rzheshevskii, *Stalin i Cherchill*, 506.

59 "Mr. President": FRUS YALTA, 686; see also Eden, 593–94.

59 "enough democratic feeling": Bohlen, 188.

60 a "snifter": ARB to John Boettiger, February 7, 1945, FDRL.

60 "Winston's fault": Byrnes, *Speaking Frankly*, 59.

60 "the unnecessary people": ARB to John Boettiger, February 7, 1945, FDRL.

61 recorded casualty rates: Seweryn Bialer, ed., *Stalin and His Generals*, 619.

62 "genius of dosage": Stephen F. Cohen, *Bukharin and the Bolshevik Revolution*, 346.

63 "What are you doing?": V. I. Chuikov, *The Fall of Berlin*, 120. In an earlier article for a Soviet magazine, Chuikov said this conversation occurred on February 4. He changed the date after the accuracy of the original account was challenged by Zhukov.

63 "The Riviera of Hades": WSC7, 1187.

64 "full-fledged Soviet satellite": FRUS YALTA, 232. See also map on population transfers, 233.

64 "The Germans are not human": Alfred M. de Zayas, *Nemesis at Potsdam*, 66; Alexander Werth, *Russia at War*, 965.

65 "much the most impressive": Cadogan, 706.

66 "the Poles never": Feliks Chuev, *Molotov Remembers*, 54.

66 "this destruction of Poles": Alliluyeva, *Only One Year*, 390; Roman Brackman, *The Secret File of Joseph Stalin*, 331.

67 "to offer a rebuff": Rees, 185.

68 "What do you want": Djilas, 61.

68 "could only end": Deutscher, 517.

68 "historically and ethnically": FRUS YALTA, 379–83, 896–97.

68 "It's bizarre": Sergo Beria, *Beria, My Father*, 93, 104–5.

69 "wired for sound": Rigdon, 153.

69 "Good, very good": Andrei Gromyko, *Memoirs*, 89. The State Department paper on the Kuriles was prepared by George H. Blakeslee, December 28, 1944, FRUS YALTA 379–83. See also Tsuyoshi Hasegawa, *Racing the Enemy*, 34–37.

69 "bourgeois ploy": V. M. Berezhkov, *At Stalin's Side*, 240.

69 "no power whatsoever": Bohlen, 195–99.

70 "Let him wait": Donnelly, 721, MHI; FRUS YALTA, 769–71.

70 "was gaunt": Donnelly, 721, MHI.

71 "How long will": Byrnes, *Speaking Frankly*, 32; FRUS YALTA, 790.

71 "sinister appearing": ARB to John Boettiger, February 9, 1945, FDRL.

71 "Can I have": Sarah Churchill, 77.

72 "standard of the speeches": Alanbrooke, 660.

72 "Those dinners": Nikita S. Khrushchev, *Khrushchev Remembers*, 300–301.

73 "wince with embarrassment": Svetlana Alliluyeva, *Twenty Letters to a Friend*, 137; Alliluyeva, *Only One Year*, 384.

73 "that's our Himmler": Gromyko, *Memoirs*, 368.

73 Atlantic salmon: Dinner menu, PSF: Crimean Conference, FDRL.

74 "against kings": WSC TT, 361–64, 391; FRUS YALTA, 797–99.

74 "spoke more tripe": Richards, 288.

74 "Never trust": Kathleen Harriman, OH, CNN CW.

75 "man who looks": Kathleen Harriman to sister, February 9, 1945, LCH.

75 "our three-power alliance": FRUS YALTA, 798; WSC TT, 363.

76 "Interpreters of the world": Richards, 288; Birse, 184. Bohlen claims credit for the joke in his memoir (page 182), which was published twenty-eight years later. I have relied on the contemporaneous notes of Portal, supported by Birse.

76 "The Glory Song": Holmes diary, WSC CC; WSC7, 1195.

76 "Color very poor": Bruenn notes, February 8, 1945, FDRL.

5 GRAND DESIGN

77 "Go back": Stettinius, 204.

78 "By God, that's": Ferrell, *The Dying President*, 85.

78 "Harry is a complete": ARB to John Boettiger, February 9, 1945, FDRL.

78 Brother Ed: Elbridge Durbrow, OH, May 1973, HSTL.

79 "I am a juggler": John Morton Blum, ed., *From the Morgenthau Diaries*, 197.

79 "globaloney": George M. Elsey, *An Unplanned Life*, 42; Leahy, 314.

79 "tyranny and aggression": FDR press conference, April 7, 1944, cited by Bishop, 19.

80 "the best method": FDR press conference, February 23, 1945, FDRL.

80 "big, loud, vain": James Reston, *Deadline*, 164; see also Vandenberg speech to the U.S. Senate, January 10, 1945.

81 "raced with enthusiasm": Stettinius, 204.

82 "got up from": Eden, 595.

83 "I prefer arithmetic": Eden, 337; for Stalin's failure to read the proposed UN charter, see FRUS YALTA, 666; Byrnes, *Speaking Frankly*, 36–37.

83 Declaration on Liberated Europe: FRUS YALTA, 862, 977.

83 "the people who cast": The widely quoted aphorism derives from the memoir of Stalin's former secretary, Boris Bazhanov, *Vospominaniia Byvshego Sekretaria Stalina*, published in Moscow in 2002. Bazhanov quotes Stalin as saying, prior to a Communist Party Congress in 1923, "I consider it completely unimportant who in the party will vote, or how; what is extraordinarily important is who will count the votes, and how."

84 "a great deal of trouble": Kuter, 172.

84 "Spirits are much": Bruenn notes, February 10, 1945, FDRL.

85 "This is so elastic": Leahy, 315–16.

86 "The Russians have given": FRUS YALTA, 920.

86 "a question of etymology": FRUS YALTA, 851, 846.

87 "rubber words": Hugh G. Gallagher, *FDR's Splendid Deception*, 205; Eden, 599.

87 "glittering generalities": ARB to John Boettiger, February 10, 1945, FDRL.

87 "Don't worry": Chuev, 51.

87 "England and the USA": Ralph B Levering et al., *Debating the Origins of the Cold War*, 15.

87 "Roosevelt believed": Chuev, 46.

88 "in this global war": FDR letter to Stalin, October 4, 1944, quoted in Susan Butler, ed., *My Dear Mr. Stalin*, 260.

89 "The war will soon": Djilas, 91.

89 "They locked": WSC TT, 391.

89 "eyeing the Russian": Marian Holmes diary, WSC CC; see also Hugh Lunghi interview, CNN CW; Nina Sturdee Papers, ONSL1, WSC CC.

89 "Are you ready": Stettinius, 206.

90 "One party is": WSC TT, 392.

91 "Stalin looked": Pim recollections, cited in WSC7, 1209.

91 "Too many joints": Stettinius, 279; see also Dixon, 146–47.

92 "blank sheets of paper": Meiklejohn diary, 630, LCH.

92 "Last meeting": *Life*, March 12, 1945.

93 "Why do we": Sarah Churchill, 77–78; Holmes OH, WSC CC.

6 EUPHORIA

94 "almost hysterically": Dixon, 148; WSC7, 1216; Clementine Churchill to WSC, February 13, 1945, WSC CC.

94 "A pretty horrific": Martin diary, February 13, 1945, WSC CC; WSC7, 1214.

95 "The German tanks": WSC TT, 394–95.

95   "lot of horseplay": Robert E. Sherwood, *Roosevelt and Hopkins,* 871.
95   "justify and surpass": Crimea conference folder, FDRL.
95   "We really believed": Sherwood, 870.
96   "meaningless platitude": Kennan memorandum, February 14, 1945, Kennan Papers, Princeton University.
96   "to paralyze the junctions": February 4, 1945, plenary, FRUS YALTA, 583; see also FRUS YALTA, 557, and Hastings, *Armageddon,* 336.
97   "There is no such": Colville, 562.
97   "a great kick": ARB OH, Columbia University; Geoffrey C. Ward, ed., *Closest Companion,* 395–96.
98   "on a scale": WSC7, 1222–23; FRUS YALTA, xi.
99   "deeply depressed": Samuel I. Rosenman, *Working with Roosevelt,* 523–24.
99   "disappointed and even": Sherwood, 874.
99   "the Americans had been": Colville, 560.
100   "They have certainly": Władysław Anders, *An Army in Exile,* 86.
101   "death warrant": HQ Eighth Army memos, February 17 and March 5, 1945, PSF Poland, FDRL; British war office memos, WO 204/5560, PRO.
101   "in a better position": Alanbrooke, 665.
101   "gallant man": WSC TT, 759; Polish communiqué, reported in NYT, February 14, 1945.
101   "It is your own fault": Anders, 256.
102   "Poor Neville": Hugh Dalton, *The Second World War Diary of Hugh Dalton,* 836.
102   "Echo of Munich": Churchill draft, CHAR 9/206 A, WSC CC; *Hansard,* February 27, 1945.
102   "rather depressed": Colville, 562.
103   "make-believe diplomacy": Lord Strang, "Potsdam After Twenty-Five Years," *International Affairs* 46, July 1970.
103   "I felt bound": WSC TT, 400.
104   "committee of commissars": David Reynolds, *From World War to Cold War,* 243.
104   "lose nearly half": *Hansard,* February 27–28, 1945.
105   "do in an hour": Frank McNaughton notes, March 1, 1945, HSTL.
106   "spheres of influence": "Roosevelt Shaped 2 Yalta Solutions," NYT, February 14, 1945.
107   Public opinion surveys: Stettinius memorandum for FDR, March 13, 1945, FDRL.
107   "absolutely contrary": Fraser Harbutt, *Yalta 1945,* 348–49.
108   "Adolf, I didn't": Adolf A. Berle, *Navigating the Rapids,* 477.

7   COMRADE VYSHINSKY

111   "world's premier concourse": *Life,* February 19, 1940, 70.
112   "I became his hostess": Evan Thomas, *The Very Best Men,* 20.
112   "There were parties": Robert Bishop and E. S. Crayfield, *Russia Astride the Balkans,* 96.
113   "Eating, working": Bishop and Crayfield, 101.
113   "a beautiful woman": OSS report on Major Robert Bishop, April 30, 1945, OSS per-

sonnel records, RG 226, NARA; Eduard Mark, "The OSS in Romania, 1944–45," *Intelligence and National Security*, 9, no. 2 (April 1994), 320–44.

114　"pure drivel": Captain L. E. Madison report, May 30, 1945, OSS Bucharest Files, RG 226, NARA.

114　"brutally shocked": Burton Hersh, *The Old Boys*, 208. See also Bishop and Crayfield, 123–28; OSS analysis, "The Rădescu Cabinet," June 1, 1945, Bucharest embassy records, RG 84, NARA.

115　"last vestiges": "The National Democratic Front and the Crimea Conference," *Scânteia*, February 18, 1945.

115　"reactionary clique": Burton Berry, "The Drive for a National Democratic Front Government in Romania," dispatch no. 152, March 13, 1945, U.S. Embassy, Bucharest Confidential Files 800, RG 84, NARA.

115　two newly formed: T. V. Volokitina et al., eds., *Tri Vizita A. Ia. Vyshinskogo v Bukharest*, 123–24.

116　"3,500 armed men": Cortland Schuyler diary, February 23, 1945, LCS.

116　"Citizens of the Capital!": Berry, March 13, 1945, dispatch. This document also contains lists of dead and wounded, government and opposition communiqués, and translations of procès-verbals by Romanian military magistrates. The embassy files include notes and censored dispatches from AP reporter Livius Nasta on the February incidents.

116　"Nation Square": Piața Natiunii, in Romanian; now Piața Unirii. Under the Ceaușescu regime, the square was incorporated into the gigantic development around the Palace of the Parliament. The Royal Palace is now the Romanian National Art Museum. The Ministry of the Interior housed the offices of the Communist Party Central Committee during the Communist period. Palace Square, now Revolution Square, was the site of the first protests against Nicolae Ceaușescu in December 1989 that ultimately brought down his regime. The dictator gave his last public speech from the balcony of the former Interior Ministry and fled by helicopter from the roof.

118　A leading Communist: Silviu Brucan, *The Wasted Generation*, 45.

118　"blood of the people": NDF communiqué, enclosure no. 9, March 13, 1945, report.

118　"special mission": Arkadii Vaksberg and Jan Butler, *Stalin's Prosecutor*, 245–46.

119　"Conservative mayor": Harold Macmillan, *The Blast of War*, 388.

119　"Democracy is like": Macmillan, 392.

119　"deeply respected": Vaksberg and Butler, 71–72.

120　"Shoot these rabid": Trial of Kamenev and Zinoviev, August 1936.

120　"all existing Romanian": Alfred J. Rieber, "The Crack in the Plaster," *Journal of Modern History* 76 (March 2004), 64. See also Perry Biddiscombe, "Prodding the Russian Bear," *European History Quarterly* 23 (1993), 193–232, and Volokitina et al., eds., *Tri Vizita*, 118–21.

120　"Romania, bah!": *Life*, February 19, 1940, 76.

121　"truly democratic": Burton Y. Berry, *Romanian Diaries, 1944–1947*, 89; FRUS 1945 V, 487–88.

121　"resounding crash": Arthur Gould Lee, *Crown Against Sickle*, 107.

122　"putting our finger": FRUS 1945 V, 504.

122　"not to say": Terence Elsberry, *Marie of Romania*, 245.

123 "chirping sparrows": Vyshinsky speech, Arlus reception, March 9, 1945.

123 "Everything in town": Schuyler diary entry, March 9, 1945, LCS.

124 "ate some humble": FRUS 1945 V, 504. King Michael was eventually forced to abdicate on December 30, 1947, when the Communist government declared a People's Republic. He left the country four days later.

124 "a direct clash": Foreign Office minutes and Stevenson cables, FO 371/48538, PRO.

124 Intelligence intercepts: See Eduard Marc comments, *H-Diplo Roundtable Reviews* 10, no. 12 (2009). A March 14, 1945, Foreign Office memo refers cryptically to information gathered by the British that "shows that the Russians may have had some genuine causes for the action they took against General Rădescu's government," FO 371/48538. The German side of the story is contained in Biddiscombe, "Prodding the Russian Bear."

125 "There is no": Foreign Office minutes on "Romania," February 27, 1945, FO 371/48537.

125 "absolutely contrary": Churchill-FDR correspondence on Romania is published in FRUS 1945 V, 505–10.

8 "AN IMPENETRABLE VEIL"

126 "The war is going": Kathleen Harriman to Mary Harriman, March 8, 1945, LCH.

126 "The honeymoon after": Kathleen Harriman to Pamela Digby Churchill, March 20, 1945, LCH.

127 "Stalin needed time": "Yalta at Work," *Time*, March 19, 1945.

128 "I know it will": Walter Isaacson and Evan Thomas, *The Wise Men*, 219; Harriman diary, October 21, 1943, LCH.

128 "In spite of": Harriman and Abel, 302, 327.

128 "ruthless political": Harriman and Abel, 344–45.

128 "This is not": Harriman and Abel, 310.

129 "complete runaround": Harriman and Abel, 291.

129 "representatives of the international": Thomas Brimelow, OH, WSC CC, article 58, paragraph 4.

129 "loosening up program": Kathleen Harriman to Marie and Mary Harriman, November 17, 1943, LCH.

130 "criminal gardener": Birse, 198–99.

130 "tame Russians": Durbrow, OH, May 1973, HSTL; Kathleen Harriman to Mary Harriman, March 8, 1945, LCH.

130 "his favorite subject": Rudy Abramson, *Spanning the Century*, 361.

130 "Yonder balustrade": Frank Stephens memo, January 15, 1945, Moscow Embassy Files, RG 84, NARA.

131 "a regular Jeremiah": C. L. Sulzberger, *A Long Row of Candles*, 253.

132 Harriman filed: Unsent cable, April 10, 1945, LCH.

132 "How can a man": Isaacson and Thomas, 243.

133 "the *real* democratic": Polish Commission minutes, February 27, 1945, LCH; FRUS 1945 V, 135.

133 "every day the Lublin": FRUS 1945 V, 145, 159.

133 "all entry into": FRUS 1945 V, 171–72.

134 "attempting to wear": Unsent Harriman cable, March 21, 1945, LCH.

134 "games of golf": FRUS 1945 V, 813.

135 "I don't think": John R. Deane, *The Strange Alliance*, 192. For overview on American POWs, see Timothy Nenninger, "United States Prisoners of War and the Red Army," *Journal of American Military History*, 66 (July 2002), 761–82.

136 Harriman finally managed: Harriman memo, "Prisoners of War," March 13, 1945, LCH.

136 "The Russians dearly love": Colonel C. E. Hixon memo, April 19, 1945, U.S. Military Mission to Moscow Records, POWS, boxes 22–23, RG 334, NARA.

137 "The Soviet attitude": James D. Wilmeth, "Report on a Visit to Lublin, February 27–March 28, 1945," POWS, boxes 22–23, RG 334, NARA.

137 "no hot water": Wilmeth, "Report on a Visit to Lublin."

138 "German spies": James D. Wilmeth memo to Major General John R. Deane, April 13, 1945, POWS, boxes 22–23, RG 334, NARA.

138 "the tactical situation": Hixon memo, NARA.

139 "cleansing operations": Beria memo to Stalin, April 17, 1945, published in V. N. Khaustov et al., eds., *Lubyanka: Stalin i NKVD, 1939–1946*, 507–9; Hastings, *Armageddon*, 258–59.

140 "to solve very": Zbigniew Stypułkowski, *Invitation to Moscow*, 211. For Russian account, see NKVD reports in A. F. Noskova and T. V. Volokitina, eds., *NKVD i Polskoe Podpole, 1944–45*, 111–29.

141 "All around": Stypułkowski, 226.

141 "Undress": Stypułkowski, 229.

9   DEATH OF A PRESIDENT

143 "spotless cleanliness": Simon Sebag Montefiore, *Stalin*, 369; "Glavdacha SSSR," *AiF Moskva*, February 8, 2006.

144 "Why are your": Deutscher, 596.

144 "usual guns, howitzers": Alliluyeva, *Twenty Letters*, 171.

144 "last vestiges": Alliluyeva, *Only One Year*, 373.

144 "Don't worry": Montefiore, 283.

145 "Ivan the Terrible": Juozas Urbšys memoir excerpted in *Litanus* 34, no. 2 (1989). See also articles on Stalin's Kremlin apartments by Aleksandr Kolesnichenko, *Argumenty i Fakty*, June 17, 2009, and Aleksandr Gamov, *Komsomolskaya Pravda*, March 13, 2008.

146 "with fanatical": Antony Beevor, *Berlin*, 194. For casualty figures, see Janusz Przymanowski, "Novye dokumenty o liudskikh poteriakh vermakhta vo vtoroi mirovoi voine," *Voenno-istoricheskii zhurnal*, no. 12 (1965), 68.

146 "succeeded in shifting": Susan Butler, ed., 305–7; Beevor, 144.

147 "We are fighting": Roberts, 243; Susan Butler, ed., 316–17.

147 "When the Polish": Beevor, 200.

148 "greatest April fool": Beevor, 147.

149   meticulous log: Iurii Gorkov, *Gosudarstvennyi Komitet Oborony Postanovliaet, 1941–1945,* 461. Photocopies of the original Poskrebyshev logs are in LCV. In his memoir, Zhukov erroneously says this meeting took place on March 29. A log of Zhukov's movements published in *Voenno-Istoricheskii Zhurnal,* no. 10 (1991), shows that he left the front on March 29, but his plane made a forced landing in Minsk at 1320. He left for Moscow by train at 2020, arriving on March 31. He remained in Moscow until April 3.

149   "If the division": Bialer, 436–38; Georgi Zhukov, *Marshal Zhukov's Greatest Battles,* 13.

149   "They love and pity": Montefiore, 389.

150   "a prop and a weather vane": Montefiore, 389; Georgi Zhukov, *The Memoirs of Marshal Zhukov,* 283.

150   "collapsed completely": Zhukov, *Memoirs,* 587–90. I have retranslated some quotes from the Russian edition.

150   "Well, who is": Bialer, 516–20.

152   "feeble signature": William D. Hassett, *Off the Record with FDR, 1942–1945,* 328; Reilly, 227.

152   "He could no longer": Eleanor Roosevelt, *This I Remember,* 343.

153   "a few hours": ARB notes, Boettiger Files, FDRL; Joseph Lash, OH, FDRL; Joseph E. Persico, *Franklin and Lucy,* 325.

153   "veins stood out": Ferrell, *The Dying President,* 114.

153   "Averell is right": Arthur M. Schlesinger, *The Cycles of American History,* 167. Schlesinger was citing the testimony of Anna Rosenberg Hoffman, who lunched with FDR in Washington on March 24, before he left for Hyde Park and Warm Springs. For stifling of criticism of Russia, see FDR letter to former presidential envoy George Earle, March 24, 1945, published in New York *Daily News,* December 9, 1947.

154   "There is only one": Alanbrooke, 680.

155   "the coffin": Grace Tully, *F.D.R., My Boss,* 359.

155   "imagining that": Ward, ed., 413; Elizabeth Shoumatoff, *FDR's Unfinished Portrait,* 101–3.

156   "He came back": Ward, ed., 414.

156   "come hell": Hassett, 332.

156   "If something was": Jean Edward Smith, *FDR,* 55.

157   "I would minimize": Kimball, 630. An annotation in the Map Room log for April 11 records that the president "wrote this message," Map Room Files, FDRL.

157   "The president, like": Shoumatoff, 114; Blum, ed., 415–19.

157   "with a slight headache": Ward, ed., 418; Hassett, 333–35; Shoumatoff, 115–18.

158   "Approved": Susan Butler, ed., 320–22. Original cables are in Map Room Files, FDRL.

158   "so used": Meiklejohn diary, 649, LCH; Harriman cable to Stettinius, April 13, 1945, LCH; B. I. Zhilaev et al., *Sovetsko-Amerikanskie Otnosheniia, 1939–1945,* 644.

159   "We have accepted": Unsent Harriman dispatch, April 10, 1945, LCH.

159   "to talk to you": Harriman-Stettinius cables, Stalin meeting notes, April 13, 1945, LCH.

10 THE NEOPHYTE AND THE COMMISSAR

161 "if you ever pray": HST1, 19.

162 "about the war": Margaret Truman, *Letters from Father,* 106.

162 "an obscure vice-president": Bohlen, 212.

162 "contrariest man": Margaret Truman, 141; Frank McNaughton, notes for *Time* cover story, April 14, 1945, HSTL.

162 "clodhopper who has ambitions": Letter to Bess, November 10, 1913, HST3, 143.

163 "coldest man": Thomas Fleming, "Eight Days with Harry Truman," *American Heritage,* July–August 1992.

163 "shrewd poker player": McNaughton, notes for *Time* cover story, HSTL.

163 "see Hitler victorious": NYT, June 24, 1941, 1–7.

164 "see at a glance": HST1, 51.

164 "unpleasant facts": Bohlen minutes, FRUS 1945 V, 231–34; Harriman and Abel, 447–50.

165 "cased the joint": Elbridge Durbrow, OH, HSTL.

166 "very good looking": Interview with Robert Harris, Memoirs File, HSTL.

166 "a complete deadlock": Bohlen notes, FRUS 1945 V, 252–55.

166 "got itself into a mess": Stimson diary entry, April 23, 1945, HSY.

167 "isolated incident": James Forrestal, *The Forrestal Diaries,* 49.

168 "no progress": FRUS 1945 V, 256–58; Leahy, 351–53; NYT, April 24, 1945.

169 "He began talking": Chuev, 55; Bohlen, 213–14.

169 "I gave it": Joseph Davies journal, April 30, 1945, LCD.

169 "I have never": HST1, 82.

169 "Molly [Molotov] told Bohlen": Eben E. Ayers Papers, box 10, HSTL; Truman Memoir Files, HSTL. For further discussion, see Geoffrey Roberts, "Sexing Up the Cold War," *Cold War History,* April 2004, 105–25.

170 "a nuisance": Stimson diary, March 13, 1944, HSY.

171 "development of a new": HST1, 10.

171 "You demand": HST1, 85.

171 "Within four months": Stimson diary, April 25, 1945, HSY; HST1, 87–88.

172 "I don't like": Richard Rhodes, *The Making of the Atomic Bomb,* 625.

172 Truman: "I don't think": HST1, 89.

173 "might well put": HST1, 87, 11.

174 "All 3,167 persons": Volkogonov, *Stalin,* 339; Radzinskii, 461.

174 "greyness, dullness": Donald Rayfield, *Stalin and His Hangmen,* 260; Khrushchev, 58.

174 Iron Ass: Montefiore, 34.

174 "Polinka, darling": Montefiore, 35.

175 "I'm going next door": Gromyko, *Memoirs,* 315.

175 "A man of outstanding": Churchill, *Gathering Storm,* 329–30.

176 "A great victory": Chuev, 46; AP report on Molotov visit, June 21, 1941.

177 "tinged with hoarseness": *Chicago Tribune,* April 26, 1945; HST1, 94–95.

177 "Polinka, my love": Montefiore, 473.

178 "forfeit the friendship": Bohlen, 214; NYT, April 28, 1945.

178 "Communist dictatorships": Harriman and Abel, 456–57.

179 "So these are": Forrestal diary, May 11, 1945, Princeton Mudd Library; Harriman and Abel, 454; Chuev, 71.

179 Real wages had dropped: Jonathan R. Adelman, *Prelude to the Cold War,* 225–27.

180 "By the way": Bohlen, 215; Eden, 620; Noskova and Volokitina, 114.

180 "In a very short": WSC TT, 574–75.

11 LINKUP

181 "to make contact": "The Russian-American Linkup," World War II Operations Reports, RG 407, NARA. Unless otherwise identified, all quotes taken from contemporaneous report written by Captain William J. Fox.

182 "army of misery": AP report by Don Whitehead and Hal Boyle, *Washington Post,* April 28, 1945.

183 Aitkalia Alibekov: Mark Scott and Semyon Krasilschik, eds., *Yanks Meet Reds,* 22.

185 "the most carefree": *Stars and Stripes,* April 28, 1945, reprinted in Scott and Krasilschik, eds., 84.

185 "looked like a disaster": Aronson, OH, CNN CW.

186 "They appear to be": Colonel Walter D. Buie, letter, May 26, 1945, Charles Donnelly Papers, MHI.

186 "Mongoloid appearance": Major Mark Terrel, Report on Task Force 76, May 15, 1945, MHI.

187 "Americans of other": Forrest Pogue, report on "The Meeting with the Russians," World War II Operations Reports, NARA.

187 "the first day": Scott and Krasilschik, 117.

187 "The Americans were": Scott and Krasilschik, 125, 132.

189 more than seventy-eight thousand: John Erickson and David Dilks, eds., *Barbarossa,* 266.

189 "who had won": S. M. Shtemenko, *The Last Six Months,* 36.

190 "How well these parasites": Extracts from wartime diaries cited by Oleg Budnitskii, RFE program, "Mifi i Reputatsii," February 22, 2009; see also Budnitskii, "The Intelligentsia Meets the Enemy," *Kritika,* Summer 2009, 629–82.

190 "home-cured meat": Norman M. Naimark, *The Russians in Germany, 1945–1949,* 78.

190 "how pleasant it is": Nikita V. Petrov, *Pervyj Predsedatel KGB Ivan Serov,* 44.

190 "First let's send": Lev Kopelev, *No Jail for Thought,* 53.

191 "Our people, like": Budnitskii, "Intelligentsia," 657.

191 "Looting everywhere": Georgi Solyus diary, German-Russian Museum, Karlshorst.

191 "great mass of distraught": History of 272nd Infantry Regiment.

192 "the forgotten bastards": Thomas A. Julian, "Operations at the Margin," *Journal of Military History,* October 1993, 647.

192 "Christ, if we": William L. White, *Report on the Russians,* 189.

193 "Why are you going": William R. Kaluta, historical report, April–June 1945, Operation Frantic Files, box 66, RG 334, NARA. All quotes taken from this report unless otherwise indicated.

195 "for ulterior purposes": Harriman memo on conversation with Stalin, April 15, 1945, LCH.

195 "an armed clash": SMERSH report to Stalin, April 2, 1945, LCV.

196 "take the initiative": Stalin Order 11075, April 23, 1945, LCV.

196 "Stalin made": Lieutenant John Backer, "Report on Political Conditions in Czechoslovakia," October 19, 1945, Robert Murphy Files, RG 84, NARA.

196 "You have, of course": Djilas, 87.

197 "The armies must change": Stalin Order 11072, April 20, 1945, LCV.

198 "Comrade Stalin's order": Petrov, 49.

199 "Germany has been": Beria, 337.

12 VICTORY

200 "The war is not": Shtemenko, 409–11.

200 "Who the hell": Marshal N. N. Voronov, memoir, translated in Bialer, 557–58. Contrary to some reports, Susloparov did not disappear into the Gulag. He ended his career as an instructor in the Military Diplomatic Academy.

201 "beaten look": Zhukov, *Memoirs*, 630–31.

201 "overcome with emotion": Deane, 180; R. C. Raack, *Stalin's Drive to the West, 1938–1945*, 117–18.

202 "Everyone is dancing": Vassily Grossman, *A Writer at War*, 340.

202 "One of the greatest": Budnitskii, "Intelligentsia," 660.

202 "recently converted": Wolfgang Leonhard, *Child of the Revolution*, 298.

202 "Before, I thought": David Samoilov, *Podennye Zapisi*, 224.

203 "They were so happy": Werth, 969.

203 "Long live": C. L. Sulzberger, "Moscow Goes Wild over Joyful News," NYT, May 10, 1945.

203 "a little embarrassed": Kennan, *Memoirs*, 242.

204 "They think the war": Kennan, *Memoirs*, 244. The quote is from Ralph Parker, a former *New York Times* reporter who subsequently worked for the Soviets. In his memoir, Kennan described Parker's reporting as "fabricated" but did not specifically challenge this quote, which echoes statements he acknowledged making.

204 "an oddball on campus": Kennan, *Memoirs*, 11.

204 "a fit ally": Kennan, *Memoirs*, 57.

204 "to keep their people": Kennan, *Memoirs*, 74.

205 "a certain histrionic": Kennan, *Memoirs*, 54.

205 "ever-hopeful suitor": Kennan, *Memoirs*, 544.

205 "The idea of a Germany": Kennan, *Memoirs*, 258.

206 "utterly impractical": Bohlen letter to Kennan, February 1945, Kennan Papers, Princeton University.

206 "bearers of some species": Kennan, *Memoirs*, 195.

207 "a man who understood": Isaacson and Thomas, 229.

207 "Russia's International Position": Written in May 1945; reprinted in Kennan, *Memoirs*, 532–46.

208 "doubted if he had": Colville, diary entry, May 14, 1945, 599.

208 "the P.M. can be": Colville, diary entry, May 1, 1945, 595.

208 *Bellum in Pace*: Colville, diary entry, May 17, 1945, 599.

208 "I am profoundly": WSC TT, 572.

208 "iron curtain": Churchill did not invent the "iron curtain" imagery. Joseph Goebbels used the expression in an article in the Nazi newspaper *Das Reich* on February 25, 1945. He predicted that the Yalta accords would lead to an *eiserner Vorhang* falling over the "enormous territory controlled by the Soviet Union, behind which nations would be slaughtered." The term *eiserner Vorhang* referred to the iron safety curtain installed in European theaters to prevent the spread of fire from the stage to the auditorium.

210 "impenetrable veil": WSC TT, 429.

210 "in years I shall not": Marian Holmes Spicer diary entries, May 11–13, 1945, WSC CC.

210 "simple and honorable": Churchill broadcast, May 13, 1945.

211 "very steamed": Montgomery Papers, Imperial War Museum, London, BLM 162; David Reynolds, *In Command of History*, 476.

211 "All reduction": WSC TT, 575.

211 Operation UNTHINKABLE: CAB 120/691/109040, PRO; Alan Brooke diary entry, May 24, 1945, King's College, London.

212 "deadly hiatus": WSC TT, 455–56.

212 "Things have moved": HST to Martha and Mary Truman, May 8, 1945, HSTL.

213 "fat old Prime Minister": HST to Martha and Mary Truman, May 8, 1945, HSTL. The letter is reprinted in HST1, 206, without the adjectives "fat old."

213 "consistent vein": Joseph E. Davies, *Mission to Moscow*, 11, 270, 340–60.

213 "keep the situation": Davies letter to Truman, May 12, 1945, LCD.

214 "These damn sheets": Davies journal, May 13, 1945, LCD; Walter Trohan report, *Chicago Tribune*, May 12, 1945; Eben Ayers diary, May 12, 1945, HSTL.

214 "given Stalin": HST1, 228.

215 "our three ablest": HST2, 35.

215 "enormous samovars": Todd Bennett, "Culture, Power, and Mission to Moscow," *Journal of American History*, September 2001; Bohlen, 123.

215 "gleamed like piano": Frank McNaughton notes, March 1, 1945, HSTL; Elizabeth Kimball MacLean, *Joseph. E. Davies*, 27.

216 "little fellows": Davies diary entry, June 4, 1945, LCD.

216 "sublimely ignorant": Bohlen, 44; Kennan, *Memoirs*, 83.

216 "tough approach": Davies journal, May 13, 1945; letter to HST, May 12, 1945, LCD.

13 "THE SALVATION OF THE WORLD"

218 "promise beer": Clifton Daniel, NYT, May 27, 1945.

219 "There were no": Harold Hobson, *Christian Science Monitor*, May 29, 1945.

219 "see the light": Truman diary entry, May 22, 1945; HST2, 31–35.

219 "vain amateur": Eden, 623–24.

219 "a huge, exaggerated": Davies to wife, May 28, 1945, LCD.

220 "The prime minister is": Davies report to Truman, June 12, 1945. The description of the meeting with Churchill is taken from this report, Davies's letters to his wife, and journal entries, all available at LCD.

221   "needed a bath": David Carlton, *Churchill and the Soviet Union*, 140.
221   "just two foreign": May 27, 1945, memo, WSC TT, 579.
222   "another Carthage": Sherwood, 887. The Sherwood book includes transcripts of the Stalin-Hopkins meetings in Moscow. For description of getting lost over Berlin, see Meiklejohn diary, 672–74, LCH; Kathleen Harriman letter, May 29, 1945, LCH.
222   "diplomatic language": HST2, 31.
223   "suicide by swallowing": Henrik Eberle and Matthias Uhl, eds., *The Hitler Book*, 283.
223   "never-ending wild": Benjamin Fischer, "Hitler, Stalin, and Operation Myth," *CIA Center for Study of Intelligence Bulletin*, no. 11 (Summer 2000).
224   "could have taken off": NYT, June 10, 1945.
224   "Hitler is alive!": Heinz Linge, *With Hitler to the End*, 213.
224   "Operation Myth": Lev Bezymenskii, *Operatsiia "Mif,"* 148.
225   catalog of destruction: Gorkov, 171–72; Adelman, 225–29, Roberts, 325.
225   Beria sent Stalin: Volkogonov, *Stalin*, 504.
226   "continuing fighting": NKVD report submitted to Stalin, May 17, 1945, reprinted in Noskova and Volokitina, 187–90.
227   "prepare the coup": Bohlen, 339.
228   "to the Russian people": NYT, May 25, 1945.
229   "Anyone with any": For a detailed account of the Hopkins visit, see Sherwood, 886–912.
230   "The Soviet Union always": Bohlen, 219.
231   "this last opportunity": Stanisław Mikołajczyk, *The Rape of Poland*, 118; WSC TT, 583–84.
231   "And he continued": Meiklejohn diary, LCH, 679.
231   "There were 40 guests": Kathleen Harriman to Mary Harriman, June 4, 1945, LCH.
232   treated "leniently": Hopkins memo, June 1, 1945, LCH.
232   "reverse Lend-Lease": Meiklejohn, 680; Edward Page memo on caviar, May 29, 1945, LCH.
232   "American belief in freedom": Bohlen, 222; Sherwood, 922.
233   "accept no share": Kennan, *Memoirs*, 212.

14   ATOMIC POKER

235   Byrnes was "hurt": James Byrnes, *All in One Lifetime*, 230.
237   "General Groves tells me": Spencer Weart and Gertrude Szilard, "Leo Szilard, His Version of the Facts," *Bulletin of the Atomic Scientists*, May 1979; Rhodes, *Making of the Atomic Bomb*, 638.
237   "general demeanor": Byrnes, *All in One Lifetime*, 284.
238   "royal straight flush": Stimson diary, May 14, 1945, HSY.
238   "center of selected city": Notes of Target Committee, May 28, 1945, MED; Rhodes, *Making of the Atomic Bomb*, 638.
238   "I am the kingpin": Rhodes, *Making of the Atomic Bomb*, 640.
239   "relationship of man": Notes of Interim Committee, May 31–June 1, 1945, MED; Stimson diary, May 30–June 1, 1945, HSY.

240   "The entire population": Rhodes, *Making of the Atomic Bomb,* 649.

240   "he could think": Len Giovannitti and Fred Freed, *The Decision to Drop the Bomb,* 109.

242   "We studied the papers": Rhodes, *Making of the Atomic Bomb,* 607–9.

242   "certain special metals": Groves memo to Marshall, March 7, 1945, MED.

242   "virtual destruction": Spaatz memo to Marshall, March 19, 1945, MED.

243   "To hell with": Lieutenant Colonel John Lansdale memo, July 10, 1946, MED.

244   "worth more to us": Leslie R. Groves, *Now It Can Be Told,* 243.

244   "climbing wearily": Thomas Powers, *Heisenberg's War,* 425.

244   "I have been expecting": Groves, 243; Powers, 426.

245   "huge, inestimable": David Holloway, *Stalin and the Bomb,* 91.

246   "water faucets, doorknobs": Naimark, *Russians in Germany,* 209.

246   total Russian reserves: Kurchatov notes, early 1946, cited in Vladimir Gubarev, "Bely Arkhipelag," *Nauka y Zhizn,* no. 1 (2004). The first Soviet nuclear reactor went critical in December 1946.

247   "dog that didn't bark": Holloway, 78.

247   "few days": Nikolaus Riehl and Frederick Seitz, *Stalin's Captive,* 71.

247   "saved the Soviet atomic": Pavel V. Oleynikov, "German Scientists in the Soviet Atomic Project," *Nonproliferation Review,* Summer 2000.

15   RED EMPIRE

248   "Let's see what": Holloway, 152.

250   "Historically, this": Georgi Dimitrov, *The Diary of Georgi Dimitrov, 1939–1949,* 136.

250   "Go ahead": Chuev, 73.

251   "The Soviet Union has": Jamil Hasanli, *SSSR—Turtsiya,* 201.

252   "crush us": N. K. Baibaikov, *Ot Stalina do El'tsina,* 81.

252   "the British, and possibly": Vladislav Zubok, *A Failed Empire,* 41.

252   "unhappy consequences": Bruce R. Kuniholm, *The Origins of the Cold War in the Near East,* 195–96.

253   "almost double": Chuev, 74.

253   "progressive clergymen": Jamil Hasanli, *At the Dawn of the Cold War,* 70; an English translation of Stalin's directives was published in CWIHPB, no. 12/13, Fall 2001.

254   "20,000 rifles": Hasanli, *At the Dawn of the Cold War,* 79.

254   "no Russian act": Wall letter to Bullard, August 23, 1945, FO 371/45478, PRO. Wall later became a successful novelist, using the pen name Sarban.

254   "deceptively unlike": Peter Lisagor and Marguerite Higgins, *Overtime in Heaven,* 148.

255   "making great efforts": May 13, 1945, dispatch, printed in Reader Bullard, *Letters from Tehran,* 280.

255   "Russians are more determined": Wall letter to Bullard, August 12, 1945, FO 371/45478, PRO.

255   "spend hours": Tabriz diary, no. 17, October 4–25, 1945, FO 371/45478, PRO.

255   "There is no railway": Tabriz diary, no. 19, November–December 1945, FO 371/52740, PRO.

256   "Delicious, it was": Chuev, 75.

257   80 percent: The original stake was 75 percent, but Molotov negotiated it upward to 80 percent. Roberts, 218–19.

257   "drunk a bit": Charles A. Moser, *Dimitrov of Bulgaria*, 225.

257   one-party system: Barnes to secretary of state, June 23, 1945, copied to Moscow embassy, NARA.

257   "I was ready to die": Moser, 229.

257   "All the nails": Colonel S. W. Bailey to Foreign Office, June 12, 1945, FO 371/48127, PRO, quoted in Moser, 232.

258   "the man who came": Moser, 231–36; FRUS 1945 IV, 314.

258   "a small-town Rotary club": *Time*, July 2, 1945.

259   "on a secret": Trial transcript, published by People's Commissariat of Justice of USSR; see also Werth, 1012–16.

260   "It would make Stalin": Mikołajczyk, *Rape of Poland*, 128.

260   "boasting about his victories": Amy W. Knight, *Beria, Stalin's First Lieutenant*, 128–29.

260   "it was Vyshinsky": Robert Murphy, *Diplomat Among Warriors*, 258.

260   "quickly forgotten": WSC TT, 363.

261   "No, I haven't forgotten": G. K. Zhukov, *Vospominaniia i Razmyshleniia*, 353.

262   "Do you see": E. I. Zubkova, *Russia After the War*, 32–33.

262   "little screws": Werth, 1003.

262   "That's the end": Lunghi interview, CNN CW.

263   "I knew I was": "Fort Dix and the Return of Reluctant Prisoners of War," NYT, November 24, 1980.

264   "Shoot at us": POW records, 1942–45, MLR P 179B, RG 165, NARA.

264   "trainloads of repatriates": U.S. Embassy, Moscow, cable, June 11, 1945, LCH.

264   "spirit and intent": Mark R. Elliott, *Pawns of Yalta*, 87.

265   "United States citizens": FRUS Yalta, 985–87.

265   "unbearable": Deane message to Eisenhower, June 7, 1945, U.S. military mission to Moscow, RG 334, NARA.

265   "implements of self-destruction": Elliott, 89.

265   an estimated 1.8 million: Catherine Merridale, *Ivan's War*, 303.

266   "undesirable witnesses": R. J. Overy, *Russia's War*, 359.

265   "psychological metamorphosis": Alliluyeva, *Twenty Letters*, 78.

266   "I have no son": Alliluyeva, *Only One Year*, 370; Montefiore, 395.

266   "Don't be a coward": "The Death of Stalin's Son," *Time*, March 1, 1968; Radzinskii, 478.

266   "unpleasant," and possibly: State Department memos, 800.1, Stalin File, Robert Murphy Files, RG 84, NARA.

16 BERLIN

269 "It's got to look": Leonhard, *Child of the Revolution*, 303.

270 "open sewer": Richard Brett-Smith, *Berlin '45*, 118.

270 "The pistol stopped": Grigorii Pomerants, *Zapiski Gadkogo Utenka*, 202.

270 "still entirely unsafe": "Conditions in Berlin," July 21, 1945, Perry Laukhuff report to Robert Murphy, Office of the U.S. Political Advisor to Germany, Classified General Correspondence 1945, RG 84, NARA.

270 "Communism on a German": Mikołajczyk, *Rape of Poland*, 79.

271 "complete and unrestricted": Leonhard, *Child of the Revolution*, 329.

271 "complete imbecile": Beria, 89.

271 "They are to be dissolved": Leonhard, *Child of the Revolution*, 319; notes from Initiative Groups meeting with Stalin, June 4, 1945, quoted in Dirk Spilker, *The East German Leadership and the Division of Germany*, 55.

271 "snoopers, strong-arm men": Laukhuff report, Murphy Files, RG 84, NARA.

272 "Take everything": Giles MacDonogh, *After the Reich*, 478.

272 "They had dismantled": Frank L. Howley, *Berlin Command*, 44; report to Murphy, U.S. Political Advisor Classified Correspondence, July 19, 1945, NARA.

272 "The Russians were": Wolfgang Leonhard, OH, CNN CW.

272 "Apart from a few": Merridale, 301.

273 "big, jolly": Howley, *Berlin Command*, 11.

273 "a red and white": Howley, *Berlin Command*, 29.

273 "gypsy-like detachments": John J. Maginnis journal, MHI.

274 "Should we genuflect": Maginnis journal, MHI.

275 "Berlin is a shambles": Howley, *Berlin Command*, 41.

275 "the heart of Western": Churchill to Truman, June 4, 1945, quoted in WSC TT, 603.

275 "highly disadvantageous": Truman to Churchill, June 12, 1945, quoted in Harry S. Truman, *Defending the West*, 119–20.

276 "General Motors": Byrnes, *All in One Lifetime*, 272.

276 "The high road": Howley, *Berlin Command*, 42.

276 "It was undoubtedly": Maginnis journal, July 1, 1945, MHI.

277 "blind mutilated": Alexandra Richie, *Faust's Metropolis*, 637.

277 "Here is retribution": Memo, quoted in Richie, October 12, 1945, 637.

278 "remove their hats": Zayas, *A Terrible Revenge*, 90.

278 "Once in a thousand": Naimark, *Fires of Hatred*, 115.

279 "a disorganized manner": Serov memo to Beria, July 4, 1945, reprinted in T. V. Volokitina et al., eds., *Sovetskij Faktor v Vostochnoj Evrope*, vol. 1, 212.

279 "commit suicide": Serov memo to Beria, June 14, 1945, reprinted in T. V. Volokitina et al., eds., *Vostochnaia Evropa v Dokumentakh Rossiiskikh Arkhivov*, 1 (1944–48), 223.

279 "A clean sweep": Naimark, *Fires of Hatred*, 110.

279 "The Czech treatment": Backer memo, October 19, 1945, U.S. Political Advisor Classified Correspondence, NARA.

280 "carry very little": Brigadier General P. L. Ransom report, November 28, 1945, General Correspondence, AG 250.1, OMGUS, RG 260, NARA.

280 "We move in": Howley, *Berlin Command*, 49.

281 "The difficult food": Minutes of July 7, 1945, meeting, U.S. Political Advisor Classified Correspondence, NARA. See also Murphy memo on meeting, reprinted in FRUS POTSDAM I, 630–33; Howley, *Berlin Command*, 57–60; Murphy, 27–29.

281 "an almost impossible": FRUS POTSDAM I, 632.

282 "Of course, it wasn't": Howley, *Berlin Command*, 60.

282 "take no steps": JCS 1067, revised April 26, 1945, FRUS 1945 III, 484–503.

282 "This thing was": Murphy, 251.

283 "You are entirely": Howley, *Berlin Command*, 54.

283 "Russians are still": W. Alexander Samouce, "Report on Visit to Berlin," July 11, 1945, MHI.

284 "shooting up": Murphy, 264.

284 "Disappointment, dismay": Brett-Smith, 156.

284 "any possible sympathy": Rees tour diary, FO 1056/540, PRO.

284 "Unity is correct": Spilker, 65.

285 "There will be two": Wilhelm Pieck notes, quoted in Spilker, 31.

17 TERMINAL

286 "French or Chippendale": Truman diary entry, July 16, 1945, reprinted in HST2, 50.

287 "We had a most": HST2, 51.

288 "I don't need": FRUS POTSDAM II, 35.

288 "I'm very depressed": Moran, *Churchill at War*, 313.

288 "liked the president": WSC8, 61; WSC TT, 630.

288 "a hoodlum wagon": HST2, 52.

289 "This is the most powerful": Leahy, 395.

290 "They brought it": NYT, July 17, 1945.

290 "The most sorrowful": HST2, 52.

290 "began to cheer": WSC TT, 630.

291 "the power and grandeur": Albert Speer, *Inside the Third Reich*, 103.

291 "A most elegant crater": Meiklejohn diary, 709, LCH; Birse, 205.

291 "You certainly paid": People section, *Time*, July 30, 1945.

291 "Hitler must have": Moran, *Churchill at War*, 333. Moran says that Churchill did not descend all the way to the bunker. Churchill himself says that he did (WSC TT, 631), as do contemporaneous news reports. (See, for example, *Time*, July 30, 1945.) Moran is an unreliable witness, as his memoir, while purportedly a diary, was written three decades after the war; Donnelly diary, July 21, 1945, MHI.

291 "This is what": WSC8, 61; "Minuet at Potsdam," *Time*, July 30, 1945.

292 "immediate war": Davies journal, July 15–17, 1945, LCD.

293 "as cold as ice": Davies journal, July 1945, LCD; for Vyshinsky's version, see *Sovetskii Soyuz na Mezhdunarodnikh Konferentsiyakh Perioda Velikoi Otechestvennoi Voiny*, 6, 723–24.

294 "honor guards with bands": Zhukov, *Memoirs*, 668.

294 "One has to walk": Cadogan, 771.

294 "The house is completely": Volkogonov, *Stalin*, 498.

295   "miserable surroundings": Dietrich Müller-Grote letter, February 10, 1956, Truman Post-Presidential Files, HSTL.

295   "who is now with": Presidential log, FRUS POTSDAM II, 9.

295   "still on the program": Beria, 118. For examples of documents stolen by Soviet spies, see Khaustov et al., eds., 525.

296   "fellow Rotarian": Elsey, 87.

296   "it did not draw": Bohlen, 228; see FRUS POTSDAM II, 43–46, for contemporaneous Bohlen notes; Bohlen 1960 memo is published in FRUS POTSDAM II, 1582–87.

296   "He'll be in the Jap": Truman diary entry, July 17, 1945, HST2, 53.

296   "looked you": Truman interview for memoir, May 1954, HSTL.

296   "increase the quantities": Rigdon, 197.

297   "either in Spain": Byrnes, *Speaking Frankly*, 68; Leahy, 396.

297   "a stockbroker's idea": Birse, 206; Astley, 217.

298   "Not possible": Astley, 218.

298   "almost blinded": Davies letter to wife, July 19, 1945, LCD.

298   "He butts in": Cadogan, 765.

298   "sitting in his": Davies letter to wife, July 19, 1945, LCD.

299   "The navy should": Russian transcript of July 17 session, published in Gromyko, ed., *Sovetskii Soyuz*, 6, 352. The American transcript can be found in FRUS POTSDAM II, 39–63. I have drawn on both sources to create a composite record of the conference.

299   "Czar Alexander": Harriman, OH, Columbia University Oral History Collection.

300   "highly delighted": Stimson diary, July 18, 1945, HSY.

300   "I had better just": WSC TT, 640.

300   "lull the Japanese": Bohlen memo, FRUS POTSDAM II, 1587–58; original Bohlen notes, FRUS POTSDAM II, 87.

301   "sick of the whole": July 20, 1945, letter to Bess, HSTL; HST3, 520.

301   "toiling masses": Davies journal, July 19, 1945, LCD.

302   "huge ball": Groves memo to Stimson, July 18, 1945, MED records, RG 77.

303   "tremendously pepped": Stimson diary, July 21, 1945, HSY; Truman diary, July 25, 1945; HST2, 55.

303   "Stimson, what was": Harvey H. Bundy, *Atlantic Monthly*, March 1957.

303   "redress the balance": Alanbrooke, 709.

303   "like little boys": McCloy diary entry, July 23–24, 1945, Amherst College Archives.

303   "changed man": Stimson diary, July 22, 1945, HSY.

303   "We noticed": Murphy, 273.

304   "The Bolshies have": HST1, 369.

304   "I think Stalin's feelings": H. Freeman Matthews, OH, June 1973, HSTL.

18   LOOT

306   "woodworking machines": Pauley, unpublished memoir, HSTL.

307   "Just deal": Pauley, unpublished memoir, HSTL.

307   "Needless to say": Pauley, unpublished memoir, HSTL.

307   "down to even small": FRUS POTSDAM II, 875, 889.

308 "It would appear": FRUS POTSDAM II, 889, 902–3.

308 "completely acceptable": Pauley, unpublished memoir, HSTL.

308 "suffered so terribly": Pauley, unpublished memoir, HSTL.

309 "prior charge": Pauley letter to Maisky, July 13, 1945, FRUS POTSDAM I, 547–48.

310 "It is becoming": Stimson diary entry, July 19, 1945, HSY.

310 "deeply disturbed": Henry L. Stimson, *On Active Service in Peace and War*, 638.

310 "I liked the little": Unsent letter to Dean Acheson, March 15, 1957, see HST2, 349; interview for memoir, HSTL.

311 "sedulously circulated": Davies diary, July 21, 1945, LCD.

311 "nothing we could do": Harriman and Abel, 484.

311 "all hands": Forrestal, 79; Meiklejohn diary, 707, LCH.

312 "constant distrust": McCloy diary entries, July 23–24, 1945, John J. McCloy papers, Amherst College Archives and Special Collections.

312 The Red Army suffered: Erickson and Dilks, 266.

312 "sarcasm or contempt": John L. Whitelaw letter, August 25, 1945, MHI.

313 "valuable classical paintings": Pavel Knyshevskii, *Dobycha: Tainy Germanskikh Reparatsii*, 126–28.

313 "gift from the Red Army": General Vlasik-Telokhranitel Stalina, *7 dnei*, Belorus magazine online; *Voenno-Istoricheskii, Zhurnal*, no. 12 (1989), 92; Knyshevskii, 134.

313 "The time is over": Budnitskii, "Intelligentsia," 658.

313 "trophy automobile": Knyshevskii, 120.

314 "for the Soviets": Zubok, 9; statistical data from Knyshevskii, 20.

314 "clearly war booty": FRUS POTSDAM II, 905.

314 "intellectual reparations": John Gimbel, *Science, Technology, and Reparations*, 170.

315 "machinery and parts": Naimark, *Russians in Germany*, 180–81.

315 "That's where": Leonhard, *Child of the Revolution*, 345.

316 "Nobody was going": Khaldei interview, CNN CW.

316 "the black market to end": Donnelly diary, July 22, 1945, MHI.

316 "most immoral": Chief of staff diary, July 23, 1945, U.S. HQ Berlin District, RG 260, NARA.

316 "crowds of soldiers": *Life*, September 10, 1945.

317 "cleaned out": Donnelly diary, July 22, 1945, MHI.

317 "Transmissions of funds": Berlin District Finance Officer, Report of Operations, May 8, 1945–September 30, 1945, U.S. HQ Berlin District, RG 260, NARA.

318 "The trouble": Donnelly diary, July 22, 1945, MHI.

318 "big time operators": Leonard Linton, "Kilroy Was Here Too," unpublished MS, 29–30, MHI.

319 "completely disassembled": Meiklejohn diary, 713, LCH; Charles L. Mee, Jr., *Meeting at Potsdam*, 241.

319 "managed to get": Letter to Bess Truman, July 22, 1945, HSTL; HST3 520.

319 "ruthless automaton": Eden, 634.

319 "horse's ass": David G. McCullough, *Truman*, 479; Harriman and Abel, 488.

319 "My but he has": HST diary, July 7, 1945, HST2, 49.

320 "expose the British": FRUS POTSDAM II, 274–75.

320 "household equipment": FRUS POTSDAM II, 295–98.

321 Internal memos: FRUS POTSDAM II, 877–81; M. Z. Saburov et al. note to Molotov, July 10, 1945; G. P. Kynin and Jochen Laufer, *SSSR i Germanskii Vopros, 1941–1949*, vol. 2, 180. The Soviet estimate was based on an average cost calculation of three hundred seventy dollars for one ton of equipment.

19 "FINIS"

322 "this bloody election": Moran, *Churchill at War*, 342–43.

322 "decidedly odd": WSC8, 81; "Minuet in Potsdam," *Time*, July 30, 1945.

323 "PM very annoyed": Cadogan, 770; "Minuet at Potsdam," *Time*, July 30, 1945.

323 "get even": Leahy, 412.

323 "They were excellent": HST letter, July 23, 1945, HSTL.

324 "like the emperor": Hayter, 28; Pawle and Thompson, 396–97.

324 "Ours still lack": Birse, 209.

325 "I will always": WSC8, 93.

325 "Operation may be": FRUS POTSDAM II, 1374.

326 "highly delighted": Stimson diary, July 24, 1945, HSY.

326 "on the kill": Hasegawa, 158.

326 "We should get": Forrestal, 78.

326 "the United States do not": Rohan Butler et al., ed., *Documents on British Policy Overseas*, series 1, vol. 1, 573.

326 "soldiers and sailors": HST diary, July 25, 1945, President's Secretary File, HSTL, HST2 55–56.

327 "urban industrial area": Target Committee minutes, May 10–11, 1945, MED, RG 77, NARA; Rhodes, *Making of the Atomic Bomb*, 700.

327 "day of decision": McCullough, 442.

327 "no decision": McCullough, 442; Elsey, 89.

327 order to drop: Exchange of messages between the War Department and Marshall, July 24–25, 1945, MED, RG 77. The message from Washington arrived in Potsdam in the early morning hours of July 25, following Truman's meeting with Stimson. Authorization for the order was sent at 9:45 a.m. Berlin time (0645 GMT), just prior to a 10:00 a.m. meeting between Truman and Marshall. It seems likely that Marshall informed the president about the order after it had already been sent.

328 "iron fence": FRUS POTSDAM II, 362, 371. There were two American note takers at the meeting.

328 "complete impasse": Leahy, 416.

328 "we have accomplished": Letter to Bess, July 25, 1945, HSTL; HST3, 521.

328 "I do not want": FRUS POTSDAM II, 313.

329 "not ripe for": FRUS POTSDAM II, 373.

329 "Glad to hear it": HST1, 416.

329 "gay and genial": WSC TT, 670; see also Bohlen, 237.

330 "around July 10": Soviet intelligence report, quoted by Joseph Albright and Marcia Kunstel, *Bombshell*, 141.

330 "pretend not to understand": Beria, 118–19.

330   "speed things up": Zhukov, *Memoirs,* 675; Chuev, 56.

331   "The Soviet Union is": Gromyko, *Memoirs,* 109.

332   "could end only": Lord Castlereagh dispatch, Charles K. Webster, ed., *British Diplomacy 1813–1815,* 208.

332   "23 political parties": Mikołajczyk notes from conversation with Eden, July 24, 1945.

332   "establish a one-party": British notes on conversations with Mikołajczyk, FO 934/2, PRO.

332   "Dreadful people": Cadogan, 771.

333   "the Fox": Kathleen Harriman letter, June 18, 1945, LCH; Moran, *Churchill at War,* 349.

333   "no longer existed": WSC8, 103.

333   "I dreamed": Moran, *Churchill at War,* 351.

333   "free elections": WSC8, 101.

334   "There is still": WSC8, 103; Mee, 176.

334   "fireless winter": FRUS POTSDAM II, 390.

334   "sheep in sheep's": Cuthbert Headlam, *Parliament and Politics in the Age of Churchill and Attlee,* 474.

334   "Mr. Attlee": Cadogan, 772.

334   "expected a Government": WSC8, 105.

335   "a stab of almost": WSC TT, 674.

335   "no visible": Pawle and Thompson, 399.

335   "blessing in disguise": Soames, 424.

20 HIROSHIMA

337   "vast military might": FRUS POTSDAM II, 1275.

337   "utter devastation": FRUS POTSDAM II, 1475–76.

338   "Japan must understand": V. P. Safronov, *SSSR, SShA i Iaponskaia agressiia na Dalnem Vostoke i Tikhom okeane, 1931–1945,* 331–32.

338   three-day delay: Vladimir Miasnikov ed., *Russko-Kitaiskie Otnoshenii v XX Veke,* vol. 4, book 2, 146.

338   "We did not consult": FRUS POTSDAM II, 449–50.

339   "sourpusses": HST letter to Margaret Truman, July 29, 1945, HSTL.

339   "about eighty": WSC TT, 634.

339   "This queer manifestation": Letter to Clementine Churchill, July 27, 1945, WSC CC; Birse, 211.

339   Stalin wasted: FRUS POTSDAM II, 459–60, 466–67. For U.S. sharing of MAGIC intercepts with Russia, see Bradley F. Smith, *Sharing Secrets with Stalin,* 238.

340   ten to fourteen days: Hasegawa, 177.

340   "We trusted": Davies journal entries, July 28, 1945, LCD.

340   "I know how": Wilson D. Miscamble, *From Roosevelt to Truman,* 253.

340   "no reparations": Truman diary entry, July 30, 1945, HSTL.

341   "caught a cold": FRUS POTSDAM II, 471.

341   "It would end": Truman diary, July 30, 1945; HST2, 57.

341 "this Godforsaken": HST letter to mother, July 28, 1945, HSTL; Cadogan, 775.

341 "available for reparations": FRUS POTSDAM II, 473.

342 "We have no information": FRUS POTSDAM II, 486.

342 "Big 2½": Cadogan, 778.

342 "German peace economy": See Potsdam final protocol, FRUS POTSDAM II, 1478–98. Reparations paragraphs are on page 1486.

343 "he sounded more": Mee, 258. FRUS POTSDAM II, 1334.

343 "I don't want": Elsey, 90. Elsey donated the handwritten "release" document to the Truman Library in 1979.

343 dividing line "running": FRUS POTSDAM II, 567.

343 "innocent idealist": HST2, 348.

344 "No. I say": Murphy, 279; FRUS POTSDAM II, 577–78.

344 "God willing": FRUS POTSDAM II, 601.

344 "Germany shall be treated": FRUS POTSDAM II, 1481, 1484.

345 "the future of Germany": Noel Annan, *Changing Enemies*, 146.

345 "economic iron curtain": Samuel Lubell memo, quoted by Mee, 190.

345 "sticking bayonets": Whitelaw letters, October 7 and 27, 1945, MHI.

345 "receive the cattle": William H. Draper memo, July 1945, on food situation in Berlin, Floyd Parks Papers, MHI.

346 "After one year": Clay memo to Eisenhower, May 26, 1946, Lucius D. Clay, *The Papers of General Lucius D. Clay: Germany, 1945–1949*, 213.

347 "Halt!": "Incidents-Russian" File, Records of U.S. Occupation Headquarters, Office of the Adjutant General, General Correspondence, box 44, RG 260, NARA.

347 "You must control": Howley, *Berlin Command*, 69.

347 "We have no army": Jack Whitelaw to R. S. Whitelaw, October 27, 1945; see also Whitelaw letters to wife, August 30, 1945, October 8, 1945, MHI.

348 "act like gangsters": William Stivers, "Victors and Vanquished," published in Combat Studies Institute, *Armed Diplomacy*, 160–61.

348 "The Russians draw": Howley diary entry, August 9, 1945, MHI.

348 "They get the troops": Major General James M. Gavin diary, August 8, 1945, MHI.

349 "This is the greatest": Rigdon, 207.

350 "greatest scientific gamble": FRUS POTSDAM II, 1377.

350 "greatest scientific achievement": editorials in *Chicago Tribune*, *Washington Post*, NYT, August 7, 1945.

351 "It is the dawn": Dixon, 177.

351 "usual visitors": Alliluyeva, *Twenty Letters*, 188.

351 "has shaken the": Holloway, 132.

351 "not aimed at Japan": Chuev, 58.

352 "practically gave way": Andrei Sakharov, *Memoirs*, 92.

352 "The news had": Werth, 1037, 1044.

352 "If the baby doesn't": Richard Rhodes, *Dark Sun*, 178–79.

353 "paper superiority": Max Hastings, *Nemesis*, 530.

353 "to erase the black": Hastings, *Nemesis*, 531.

353 "Operation Locust": Pauley, unpublished memoir, HSTL.

354 "convenient dividing": Dean Rusk, *As I Saw It*, 123–24.

354 "They're jumping": Elsey, 92.

21 AFTER THE BOMB

356 "only two great Powers": Hitler political testament, April 2, 1945; see Alan Bullock, *Hitler*, 955.

357 "cold war": George Orwell, "You and the Atomic Bomb," *Tribune*, October 19, 1945.

358 "absurd to suggest": Harriman and Abel, 517.

359 "This war is not": Djilas, 90.

359 "veil of amity": Radzinskii, 511.

359 "stand firm": Vladimir Perchatnov, "The Allies Are Pressing on You to Break Your Will," CWIHP Working Paper No. 26, September 1999.

360 "nothing wrong": Harriman and Abel, 514.

Bibliography

PRIMARY SOURCES—AMERICAN

Berle, Adolf A. *Navigating the Rapids, 1918–1971.* New York: Harcourt, Brace, Jovanovich, 1973.

Berry, Burton Y. *Romanian Diaries 1944–1947.* Edited by Cornelia Bodea. Iaşi: Center for Romanian Studies, 2000.

Bishop, Robert, and E. S. Crayfield. *Russia Astride the Balkans.* New York: R. M. McBride, 1948.

Blum, John M., ed. *From the Morgenthau Diaries: Years of War, 1941–1945.* Boston: Houghton Mifflin, 1967.

Bohlen, Charles E. *Witness to History, 1929–1969.* New York: W. W. Norton, 1973.

Butler, Susan, ed. *My Dear Mr. Stalin.* New Haven, Conn.: Yale University Press, 2005.

Byrnes, James F. *All in One Lifetime.* New York: Harper, 1958.

———. *Speaking Frankly.* Westport, Conn.: Greenwood Press, 1974.

Clay, Lucius D. *The Papers of Lucius D. Clay: Germany, 1945–1949.* Bloomington: Indiana University Press, 1974.

Davies, Joseph E. *Mission to Moscow.* New York: Simon and Schuster, 1941.

Deane, John R. *The Strange Alliance.* New York: Viking, 1947.

Elsey, George M. *An Unplanned Life.* Columbia: University of Missouri Press, 2005.

Forrestal, James. *The Forrestal Diaries.* New York: Viking, 1951.

Groves, Leslie R. *Now It Can Be Told.* New York: Harper, 1962.

Harriman, W. Averell, and Elie Abel. *Special Envoy to Churchill and Stalin.* New York: Random House, 1975.

Hassett, William D. *Off the Record with FDR, 1942–1945.* New Brunswick, N.J.: Rutgers University Press, 1958.

Howley, Frank L. *Berlin Command.* New York: Putnam, 1950.

Kennan, George F. *Memoirs, 1925–1950.* Boston: Little, Brown, 1967.

Kimball, Warren F., ed. *Churchill and Roosevelt*. Princeton, N.J.: Princeton University Press, 1984.

Kuter, Laurence S. *Airman at Yalta*. New York: Duell, Sloan and Pearce, 1955.

Leahy, William P. *I Was There*. New York: Whittlesey House, 1950.

Lisagor, Peter, and Marguerite Higgins. *Overtime in Heaven*. Garden City, N.Y.: Doubleday, 1964.

Murphy, Robert D. *Diplomat Among Warriors*. Garden City, N.Y.: Doubleday, 1964.

Perkins, Frances. *The Roosevelt I Knew*. New York: Viking, 1946.

Reilly, Michael F. *Reilly of the White House*. New York: Simon and Schuster, 1947.

Rigdon, William M. *White House Sailor*. Garden City, N.Y.: Doubleday, 1962.

Roosevelt, Eleanor. *This I Remember*. Westport, Conn.: Greenwood Press, 1975.

Rosenman, Samuel I. *Working with Roosevelt*. New York: Harper, 1952.

Rusk, Dean. *As I Saw It*. New York: W. W. Norton, 1990.

Sherwood, Robert E. *Roosevelt and Hopkins*. New York: Harper, 1948.

Shoumatoff, Elizabeth. *FDR's Unfinished Portrait*. Pittsburgh, Pa.: University of Pittsburgh Press, 1991.

Stettinius, Edward R., Jr. *Roosevelt and the Russians*. Garden City, N.Y.: Doubleday, 1949.

Stimson, Henry L. *On Active Service in Peace and War*. New York: Harper, 1948.

Sulzberger, C. L. *A Long Row of Candles*. New York: Macmillan, 1969.

Truman, Harry S. *Dear Bess: The Letters from Harry to Bess Truman, 1910–1959*. Edited by Robert H. Ferrell. Columbia: University of Missouri Press, 1998.

——. *Defending the West: The Truman-Churchill Correspondence*. Edited by G. W. Sand. Westport, Conn.: Praeger, 2004.

——. *Off the Record*. Edited by Robert H. Ferrell. Columbia: University of Missouri Press, 1997.

——. *Year of Decisions*. Vol. 1 of *Memoirs*. New York: Doubleday, 1955.

Truman, Margaret. *Letters from Father*. New York: Arbor House, 1981.

Tully, Grace. *F.D.R., My Boss*. New York: Scribner's, 1949.

United States Department of State. Foreign Relations of the United States. *1945*. Vols. 3, 4, and 5. Washington, D.C.: GPO, 1967–68.

——. Foreign Relations of the United States: *The Conferences at Malta and Yalta, 1945*. Washington, D.C.: GPO, 1955.

——. Foreign Relations of the United States: *The Conferences at Cairo and Tehran, 1943*. Washington, D.C.: GPO, 1955.

——. Foreign Relations of the United States: *The Conference of Berlin (Potsdam Conference), 1945*. Vols. 1 and 2. Washington, D.C.: GPO, 1960.

Ward, Geoffrey C., ed. *Closest Companion*. New York: Simon and Schuster, 2009.

White, William L. *Report on the Russians*. New York: Harcourt, Brace, 1945.

PRIMARY SOURCES—BRITISH

Alanbrooke, Field Marshal Lord. *War Diaries, 1939–1945*. Berkeley: University of California Press, 2001.

Anders, Władysław. *An Army in Exile*. London: Macmillan, 1949.

Annan, Noel. *Changing Enemies*. London: HarperCollins, 1995.

Astley, Joan Bright. *The Inner Circle*. Boston: Little, Brown, 1971.

Birse, A. H. *Memoirs of an Interpreter*. London: Michael Joseph, 1967.

Brett-Smith, Richard. *Berlin '45*. London: Macmillan, 1966.

Bullard, Reader. *Letters from Tehran*. London: I. B. Tauris, 1991.

Butler, Rohan, et al., eds. *Documents on British Policy Overseas*. London: HMSO, 1984.

Cadogan, Alexander. *The Diaries of Sir Alexander Cadogan, O.M., 1938–1945*. Edited by David Dilks. New York: Putnam, 1972.

Churchill, Sarah. *Keep On Dancing*. London: Weidenfeld and Nicolson, 1981.

Churchill, Winston. *The Gathering Storm*. Vol. 1 of *The Second World War*. Boston: Houghton Mifflin, 1948.

———. *The Grand Alliance*. Vol. 3 of *The Second World War*. Boston: Houghton Mifflin, 1950.

———. *Triumph and Tragedy*. Vol. 6 of *The Second World War*. Boston: Houghton Mifflin, 1953.

Dalton, Hugh. *The Second World War Diary of Hugh Dalton, 1940–45*. Edited by Ben Pimlott. London: Cape, 1986.

Dixon, Pierson. *Double Diploma*. London: Hutchinson, 1968.

Eden, Anthony. *The Reckoning*. Boston: Houghton Mifflin, 1965.

Hayter, William. *The Kremlin and the Embassy*. London: Hodder and Stoughton, 1966.

Langworth, Richard M., ed. *Churchill by Himself*. London: Ebury, 2008.

Macmillan, Harold. *The Blast of War, 1939–1945*. New York: Harper and Row, 1968.

Moran, Charles. *Churchill at War, 1940–1945*. New York: Carroll and Graf, 2002.

———. *Churchill: The Struggle for Survival, 1940–1965*. Boston: Houghton Mifflin, 1966.

Pawle, Gerald, and C. R. Thompson. *The War and Colonel Warden*. New York: Alfred A. Knopf, 1963.

Soames, Mary, ed. *Winston and Clementine: The Personal Letters of the Churchills*. Boston: Houghton Mifflin, 1999.

PRIMARY SOURCES—RUSSIAN/EASTERN EUROPEAN

Alliluyeva, Svetlana. *Only One Year*. New York: Harper and Row, 1969.

———. *Twenty Letters to a Friend*. New York: Harper and Row, 1967.

Baibaikov, N. K. *Ot Stalina do El'tsina.* Moscow: GazOil Press, 1998.

Berezhkov, V. M. *At Stalin's Side.* Secaucus, N.J.: Carol, 1994.

Beria, Sergo. *Beria, My Father.* London: Duckworth, 2001.

Chuev, Feliks. *Molotov Remembers.* Chicago: Ivan R. Dee, 1993.

Chuikov, V. I. *The Fall of Berlin.* New York: Holt, Rinehart and Winston, 1968.

Dimitrov, Georgi. *The Diary of Georgi Dimitrov, 1933–1949.* Edited by Ivo Banac. New Haven, Conn.: Yale University Press, 2003.

Djilas, Milovan. *Conversations with Stalin.* Harmondsworth, U.K.: Penguin, 1969.

Gorkov, Iurii A. *Gosudarstvennyi Komitet Oborony Postanovliaet, 1941–1945.* Moscow: OLMA-Press, 2002.

Gromyko, Andrei A. *Memoirs.* New York: Doubleday, 1989.

Gromyko, Andrei A., ed. *Sovetskii Soyuz na Mezhdunarodnikh Konferentsiyakh Perioda Velikoi Otechestvennoi Voiny,* vols. 4 (Yalta) and 6 (Potsdam). Moscow: Politizdat, 1979–80.

Grossman, Vasily. *A Writer at War.* Edited by Antony Beevor and Luba Vinogradova. New York: Pantheon, 2005.

Khaustov, V. N., et al., eds. *Lubianka: Stalin i NKVD, 1939–1946.* Moscow: Mezhdunarodnyi Fond "Demokratiia," 2006.

Khrushchev, Nikita S. *Khrushchev Remembers.* Boston: Little, Brown, 1970.

Kopelev, Lev. *No Jail for Thought.* London: Secker and Warburg, 1977.

Kynin, G. P., and Jochen Laufer. *SSSR i Germanskii Vopros, 1941–1949.* Moscow: Mezhdunarodnye Otnosheniia, 2000.

Leonhard, Wolfgang. *Child of the Revolution.* Chicago: H. Regnery, 1958.

Linge, Heinz. *With Hitler to the End.* New York: Skyhorse, 2009.

Miasnikov, Vladimir, ed. *Russko-Kitaiskie Otnosheniiav XX Veke.* Moscow: Pamiatniki Istoricheskoi Mysli, 2000.

Mikołajczyk, Stanisław. *The Rape of Poland.* Westport, Conn.: Greenwood Press, 1972.

Noskova, A. F., and T. V. Volokitina, eds. *NKVD i Polskoe Podpole, 1944–1945.* Moscow: RAN, 1994.

Pomerants, Grigorii. *Zapiski Gadkogo Utenka.* Moscow: Moskovskii Rabochii, 1998.

Riehl, Nikolaus, and Frederick Seitz. *Stalin's Captive.* Washington, D.C.: American Chemical Society, 1996.

Rzheshevskii, O. A. *Stalin i Cherchill.* Moscow: Nauka, 2004.

Safronov, V. P. *SSSR, SShA i Iaponskaia Agressiia na Dalnem Vostoke i Tikhom okeanes, 1931–1945 gg.* Moscow: Institut Rossiiskoi Istorii RAN, 2001.

Sakharov, Andrei. *Memoirs.* New York: Alfred A. Knopf, 1990.

Samoilov, David. *Podennye Zapisi.* Moscow: Vremia, 2002.

Shtemenko, S. M. *The Last Six Months.* Garden City, N.Y.: Doubleday, 1977.

Stypułkowski, Zbigniew. *Invitation to Moscow.* New York: Walker, 1950.

Sudoplatov, Pavel, et al. *Special Tasks*. Boston: Little, Brown, 1994.

Volokitina, T. V., et al., eds. *Sovetskij Faktor v Vostochnoj Evrope*. Moscow: Rosspen, 1999.

——. *Tri Vizita A. Ia. Vyshinskogo v Bukharest*. Moscow: Rosspen, 1998.

——. *Vostochnaia Evropa v Dokumentakh Rossiiskikh Arkhivov*. Moscow: Sibirskii Khronograf, 1997.

Zhiliaev, B. I., et al., eds. *Sovetsko-Amerikanskie Otnosheniia, 1939–1945*. Moscow: Materik, 2004.

Zhukov, G. K. *Vospominaniia i Razmyshleniia*. Moscow: Novosti, 1990.

Zhukov, Georgi. *The Memoirs of Marshal Zhukov*. New York: Delacorte, 1971.

SECONDARY SOURCES

Abramson, Rudy. *Spanning the Century: The Life of W. Averell Harriman*. New York: William Morrow, 1992.

Adelman, Jonathan R. *Prelude to the Cold War*. Boulder, Colo.: Rienner, 1988.

Albright, Joseph, and Marcia Kunstel. *Bombshell*. New York: Times Books, 1997.

Beevor, Antony. *Berlin*. London: Penguin, 2003.

Bessel, Richard. *Germany 1945*. New York: Simon and Schuster, 2009.

Bezymenskii, Lev. *Operatsiia "Mif."* Moscow: Mezhdunarodnye Otnosheniia, 1995.

Bialer, Seweryn, ed. *Stalin and His Generals*. New York: Pegasus, 1969.

Bishop, Jim. *FDR's Last Year*. New York: William Morrow, 1974.

Bowie, Beverly Munford. *Operation Bughouse*. New York: Dodd, Mead, 1947.

Brackman, Roman. *The Secret File of Joseph Stalin*. London: Frank Cass, 2001.

Brucan, Silviu. *The Wasted Generation*. Boulder, Colo.: Westview Press, 1993.

Bullock, Alan. *Hitler: A Study in Tyranny*. New York: Harper & Row, 1962.

——. *Hitler and Stalin*. London: Fontana Press, 1993.

Carlton, David. *Churchill and the Soviet Union*. Manchester, U.K.: Manchester University Press, 2000.

Cohen, Stephen F. *Bukharin and the Bolshevik Revolution*. New York: Alfred A. Knopf, 1973.

Colville, John R. *The Fringes of Power*. New York: W. W. Norton, 1985.

Deutscher, Isaac. *Stalin*. Harmondsworth, U.K.: Penguin, 1966.

Eberle, Henrik, and Matthias Uhl, eds. *The Hitler Book*. New York: PublicAffairs, 2009.

Eisenberg, Carolyn. *Drawing the Line*. New York: Cambridge University Press, 1996.

Elliott, Mark R. *Pawns of Yalta*. Urbana: University of Illinois Press, 1982.

Elsberry, Terence. *Marie of Romania*. New York: St. Martin's Press, 1972.

Erickson, John, and David Dilks, eds. *Barbarossa*. Edinburgh: Edinburgh University Press, 1994.

Feis, Herbert. *Between War and Peace.* Princeton, N.J.: Princeton University Press, 1960.

Ferrell, Robert H. *The Dying President.* Columbia: University of Missouri Press, 1998.

Gallagher, Hugh G. *FDR's Splendid Deception.* Arlington, Va.: Vandamere Press, 1994.

Gilbert, Martin. *Finest Hour.* Vol. 6 of *Winston S. Churchill.* London: Heinemann, 1983.

———. *Never Despair.* Vol. 8 of *Winston S. Churchill.* London: Heinemann, 1988.

———. *Road to Victory.* Vol. 7 of *Winston S. Churchill.* London: Heinemann, 1986.

Gimbel, John. *Science, Technology, and Reparations.* Palo Alto, Calif.: Stanford University Press, 1990.

Giovannitti, Len, and Fred Freed. *The Decision to Drop the Bomb.* New York: Coward-McCann, 1965.

Goodwin, Doris Kearns. *No Ordinary Time.* New York: Simon and Schuster, 1994.

Gunther, John. *Roosevelt in Retrospect.* New York: Harper, 1950.

Harbutt, Fraser. *Yalta 1945.* New York: Cambridge University Press, 2010.

Hasanli, Jamil. *At the Dawn of the Cold War.* Lanham, Md.: Rowman and Littlefield, 2006.

———. *SSSR—Turcija: Ot Nejtraliteta k Cholodnoj Vojne.* Moscow: Centr Propagandy, 2008.

Hasegawa, Tsuyoshi. *Racing the Enemy.* Cambridge, Mass.: Harvard University Press, 2005.

Hastings, Max. *Armageddon.* New York: Alfred A. Knopf, 2004.

———. *Nemesis.* London: HarperPerennial, 2007.

Headlam, Cuthbert. *Parliament and Politics in the Age of Churchill and Attlee.* Cambridge: Cambridge University Press, 2000.

Hersh, Burton. *The Old Boys.* New York: Scribner's, 1992.

Holloway, David. *Stalin and the Bomb.* New Haven, Conn.: Yale University Press, 1994.

Isaacson, Walter, and Evan Thomas. *The Wise Men.* New York: Simon and Schuster, 1986.

Ismay, Hastings L. *The Memoirs of General the Lord Ismay.* London: Heinemann, 1960.

King, Greg. *The Court of the Last Tsar.* Hoboken, N.J.: John Wiley, 2006.

Knight, Amy W. *Beria, Stalin's First Lieutenant.* Princeton, N.J.: Princeton University Press, 1993.

Knyshevskii, Pavel. *Dobycha: Tainy Germanskikh Reparatsii.* Moscow: Soratnik, 1994.

Kuniholm, Bruce R. *The Origins of the Cold War in the Near East.* Princeton, N.J.: Princeton University Press, 1979.

Lavery, Brian. *Churchill Goes to War.* Annapolis, Md.: Naval Institute Press, 2007.

Lee, Arthur Gould. *Crown Against Sickle.* London: Hutchinson, 1950.

Leffler, Melvyn P. *For the Soul of Mankind.* New York: Hill and Wang, 2007.

Levering, Ralph B., et al. *Debating the Origins of the Cold War.* Lanham, Md.: Rowman and Littlefield, 2002.

MacDonogh, Giles. *After the Reich*. New York: Basic Books, 2007.

MacLean, Elizabeth Kimball. *Joseph E. Davies*. Westport, Conn.: Praeger, 1992.

McCullough, David G. *Truman*. New York: Simon and Schuster, 1992.

Mee, Charles L., Jr. *Meeting at Potsdam*. New York: M. Evans, 1975.

Merridale, Catherine. *Ivan's War*. London: Faber and Faber, 2005.

Miscamble, Wilson D. *From Roosevelt to Truman*. Cambridge: Cambridge University Press, 2007.

Montefiore, Simon Sebag. *Stalin*. London: Weidenfeld and Nicolson, 2003.

Moser, Charles A. *Dimitrov of Bulgaria*. Ottawa, Ill.: Caroline House, 1979.

Naimark, Norman M. *Fires of Hatred*. Cambridge, Mass.: Harvard University Press, 2001.

———. *The Russians in Germany, 1945–1949*. Cambridge, Mass.: Belknap Press of Harvard University Press, 1995.

Overmans, Rüdiger. *Deutsche militärische Verluste im Zweiten Weltkrieg*. Munich: R. Oldenbourg, 1999.

Overy, R. J. *Russia's War*. New York: TV Books, 1997.

Perrie, Maureen. *The Cult of Ivan the Terrible in Stalin's Russia*. New York: Palgrave Macmillan, 2001.

Persico, Joseph E. *Franklin and Lucy*. New York: Random House, 2008.

Petrov, Nikita V. *Pervyj Predsedatel KGB Ivan Serov*. Moscow: Materik, 2005.

Plokhy, S. M. *Yalta: The Price of Peace*. New York: Viking, 2010.

Powers, Thomas. *Heisenberg's War*. New York: Alfred A. Knopf, 1993.

Raack, R. C. *Stalin's Drive to the West, 1938–1945*. Palo Alto, Calif.: Stanford University Press, 1995.

Radzinskii, Edvard. *Stalin*. New York: Doubleday, 1996.

Rayfield, Donald. *Stalin and His Hangmen*. New York: Viking, 2004.

Rees, Laurence. *World War II Behind Closed Doors*. New York: Pantheon, 2008.

Reston, James. *Deadline*. New York: Times Books, 1992.

Reynolds, David. *From World War to Cold War*. Oxford, U.K.: Oxford University Press, 2006.

———. *In Command of History*. New York: Random House, 2005.

Rhodes, Richard. *Dark Sun*. New York: Simon and Schuster, 1995.

———. *The Making of the Atomic Bomb*. New York: Simon and Schuster, 1986.

Richards, Denis. *The Life of Marshal of the Royal Air Force, Viscount Portal of Hungerford*. London: Heinemann, 1977.

Richie, Alexandra. *Faust's Metropolis*. New York: Carroll and Graf, 1998.

Roberts, Geoffrey. *Stalin's Wars*. New Haven, Conn.: Yale University Press, 2006.

Schlesinger, Arthur M. *The Cycles of American History*. Boston: Houghton Mifflin, 1986.

Scott, Mark, and Semyon Krasilshchik, eds. *Yanks Meet Reds*. Santa Barbara, Calif.: Capra Press, 1988.

Smith, Bradley F. *Sharing Secrets with Stalin*. Lawrence: University Press of Kansas, 1996.

Smith, Jean Edward. *FDR*. New York: Random House, 2007.

Soames, Mary. *Clementine Churchill*. Boston: Houghton Mifflin, 2003.

Speer, Albert. *Inside the Third Reich*. New York: Simon and Schuster, 1997.

Spilker, Dirk. *The East German Leadership and the Division of Germany: Patriotism and Propaganda, 1945–1953*. New York: Oxford University Press, 2006.

Tessin, Georg, and Christian Zweng. *Verbände und Truppen der deutschen Wehrmacht und Waffen-SS im Zweiten Weltkrieg, 1939–1945*. Osnabrück: Biblio Verlag, 1996.

Thomas, Evan. *The Very Best Men*. New York: Simon and Schuster, 1995.

Tissier, Tony L. *Zhukov at the Oder*. London: Praeger, 1996.

Tucker, Robert C. *Stalin as Revolutionary*. New York: W. W. Norton, 1973.

Vaksberg, Arkadii, and Jan Butler. *Stalin's Prosecutor*. New York: Grove Weidenfeld, 1991.

Volkogonov, Dmitri. *Stalin*. Rocklin, Calif.: Prima, 1992.

Webster, Charles K. *British Diplomacy, 1813–1815*. London: G. Bell, 1921.

Werth, Alexander. *Russia at War*. New York: Carroll and Graf, 1984.

Zayas, Alfred M. de. *Nemesis at Potsdam*. London: Routledge and Kegan Paul, 1977.

———. *A Terrible Revenge*. New York: St. Martin's Press, 1994.

Zhukov, Georgi K. *Marshal Zhukov's Greatest Battles*. Edited by Harrison E. Salisbury. New York: Harper and Row, 1969.

Zubkova, E. I. *Russia After the War*. Armonk, N.Y.: M. E. Sharpe, 1998.

Zubok, Vladislav. *A Failed Empire*. Chapel Hill: University of North Carolina Press, 2009.

Zubok, Vladislav, and Konstantin Pleshakov. *Inside the Kremlin's Cold War*. Cambridge, Mass.: Harvard University Press, 1996.

Index

Page numbers in *italics* refer to illustrations.

A NOTE ON THE TYPE

This book was set in Monotype Dante, a typeface designed by Giovanni Mardersteig (1892–1977). Its first use was in an edition of Boccaccio's *Trattatello in laude di Dante* that appeared in 1954. Although modeled on the Aldine type used for Pietro Cardinal Bembo's treatise *De Aetna* in 1495, Dante is a thoroughly modern interpretation of the venerable face.

Typeset by Scribe, Philadelphia, Pennsylvania

Printed and bound by Berryville Graphics, Berryville, Virginia

Designed by Maggie Hinders